Hypnotic Techniques

GEORGE GAFNER, CISW
SONJA BENSON, PH.D.

W.W. Norton & Company
New York • London

For information about permission to
reproduce selections from this book, write to
Permissions, W. W. Norton & Company, Inc.,
500 Fifth Avenue, New York, NY 10110

Book design by Leeann Graham
Manufacturing by Haddon Craftsmen, Inc.

Library of Congress Cataloging-in-Publication Data
Gafner, George, 1947–
   Hypnotic Techniques: for standard psychotherapy
and formal hypnosis / George Gafner, Sonja Benson.
       p. cm.
   "A Norton professional book."
   ISBN 0-393-70399-1
   1. Hypnotism—Therapeutic use. II. Psychotherapy. I.
Benson, Sonja, 1968–. II. Title.
   RC496 .G273 2002
   618.89'162—dc21   2002033750

W. W. Norton & Company, Inc., 500 Fifth Avenue, New York, N.Y. 10110
www.wwnorton.com

W. W. Norton & Company Ltd., Castle House, 75/76 Wells St.,
London W1T 3QT

1 2 3 4 5 6 7 8 9 0

Dedications

A special thanks and appreciation to my wife, Judy, for her patience and understanding; to my children, Kenneth and David, for making us proud parents; to my mother, Christel, and my sister, Paula, for always being there; to Lynn Flance and Karen Douglas, for being *discoverers* par excellence; and to Deborah Malmud and her staff at NPB for helping us say it with clarity and precision.

G. G.

Throughout my life family has been of pivotal importance to me; the family I started with, the people that just became family over the years and a family I hope to create. This book is dedicated to all of those people.

To George. Legend, all of our hypnosis work would never have come to pass without you. I have deep gratitude and respect for you always.

To my parents: Dee Wildermuth, Rollie and Leona Benson.

To my sisters: Heidi Krig, Angela Eidenschink and Biz Coudron.

To my nieces: Sarah Krig and Hanna Becker.

All my love.

S. B.

Contents

Introduction

One day we were talking about duality in life, and how one thing invariably makes way for the other. For example, we have our work life and our personal life; our outer appearance and our inner world; our conscious mind and our unconscious mind. Sometimes it is difficult to tell where one begins and the other ends.

This book grew out of an interest in that juxtaposition, or back-and-forth flow of those things and many more. It is a natural outgrowth of our first book, *Handbook of Hypnotic Inductions* (2000), where we concentrated on the *induction phase* of hypnosis. While we were writing that book we were frustrated with the the self-imposed constraint of not being able to write more about what the therapist does once the client is in trance. So, in our minds, this book was written long before the first one. However, the real impetus for *Hypnotic Techniques* grew out of our workshops, where we were constantly faced by dualities such as: "Is it hypnosis, or not hypnosis?" or, "Where does *conscious process* end and *unconscious process* begin?"

In conventional talk therapy with individuals, couples, families, and groups, we often deliberately employ hypnotic language and other hypnotic techniques. Does that mean we use hypnosis most of the time, even though we do not always call it hypnosis? Maybe. This question will be revisited throughout the book. The main idea is that these various hypnotic techniques are compelling tools that can be used in diverse therapy contexts. *Context* is the key word, as context may help define what hypnosis is, whether we see it as a special communication between therapist and client, guided dissociation, receptivity to suggestion, or any number of other definitions. Is it hypnosis only if we call it hypnosis? Probably.

The scope of this book is intentionally broad, as we wish to demonstrate myriad and imaginative ways that hypnotic techniques can be used in therapy. In Chapter 3, we describe the use of hypnotic teaching tales whose meta-messages are mindfulness principles, such as *acceptance* and *nonjudging*. As clients listen to these stories, they frequently evince—on the outside—hypnoidal responses, behavior that we see in formal trance: eye fixation or closure, facial mask, body immobility, and similar phenomena. On the inside, they experience an absorption of attention, perhaps embarking on a highly visual journey, or becoming immersed in a private fantasy. Afterward, they may report that they experienced time distortion, dissociation, and ideosensory phenomena, such as a tingling in both hands. So, is this hypnosis? Certainly it is different from one's immersion in a movie or song, in which the *context* guides one toward a specific end. To be sure, absorption in a two-minute story is qualitatively different than a 20-minute structured session of trancework. However, objectively and subjectively, it appears to be hypnosis.

In the remaining chapters in Section I, we continue to explore the clinical application of a range of hypnotic techniques, and occasionally return to this question of "Is it hypnosis?" Our aim in these chapters is rather ambitious: to assist readers in bolstering their repertoir of psychotherapeutic techniques. However, in addition to demonstrating perhaps new or enhanced techniques, we unashamedly hope to convince readers of the value of thinking hypnotically in their work.

You may already think hypnotically if you use hypnosis in your practice, or if you regularly employ metaphor or story to influence change in your clients. You know what we are talking about when in therapy we notice subtle cues, such as a change in the rate of breathing, or, in formal hypnosis, when we detect a barely twitching finger that signals "yes," a sudden eye flutter, a flaring of one nostril, or increased vitreous fluid around the eyeballs.

You may also think—and work—hypnotically if you employ two techniques that we emphasize in this book: *utilization* and *seeding.* Both of these techniques, which come from the seminal work of Milton H. Erickson, we believe are vital and necessary if therapists are to successfully bolster their armamentarium of hypnotic techniques. So, too, you may already think and work hypnotically if you stimulate unconscious processing through the use of what we call power words, such as *wonder, story,* or *imagine,* or if you use devices such as *truisms* and *apposition of opposites* to set up a suggestion or directive.

You may see clients in your practice who have tried many treatments, but in the end their response is "the same old thing." In other words, they remain constrained by unconscious limitations, and the therapeutic job is to free them from those constraints. In fact, unconscious process, or change on the unconscious level, is what we address in both sections of this book. A person's resources for problem solving are found in the unconscious, and that is why we devote so much attention to accessing and activating unconscious process. If a carpenter could not work without a hammer and nails, we could not do therapy without embedded suggestion, and that is why we firmly believe that a required tool for every therapist's toolbox is the creative application of *embedded-meaning suggestions,* a truly potent device in unconscious work.

Some schools of yoga and meditation talk about the "third eye," a metaphor for the unconscious, or one's imagination, intuition, or some deeper level of experience. Whatever your own third eye may represent, we hope that this image will be enhanced in your work. If, for you, the third eye is just so much ocular fancy, perhaps something less exotic will fit: maybe a substitute lens, eyeglasses, or contacts, instead of a monocle; or perhaps replacing a diver's mask with nightvision goggles is more appropriate to your practice. Afterall, the goal for all of us is to see more clearly, and there are innumerable ways to get from here to there.

Seeing is one thing, and listening is quite another. That is where the "third ear" comes in. You may have read Wallas's excellent *Stories for the Third Ear* (1985). Increasing the acuity of your own third ear will stimulate your clients' third ear, which is exactly what we want to do when we address unconscious problem solving.

A common obstacle in therapy is what people call *resistance.* Sometimes resistance is nothing more than anxiety, or even a client's lack of sufficient information. If resistance is neither of these things, then it is probably *unconscious resistance.* In formal hypnosis, this is demonstrated by the client who says, "I *want* to go into trance, but I just *can't* let go." Outside of formal hypnosis, an example of unconscious resistance is the client who simply can't move forward, despite their best efforts to do so. Isn't that a common task for us as therapists: to help people in spite of themselves?

This book is about what you can *do* to overcome resistance and move therapy along in the desired direction. It's short on theory, but long on technique, and that's why it's called *Hypnotic Techniques.* Although our theoretical foundation is broad and we rely on nondirective techniques, our approach may also be seen as directive, in that we believe that the responsibility for change in therapy lies with the therapist, not the client. As such, we may be called *strategic,* as the essence of strategic therapy is that the therapist, not the client, makes things happen. In both sections of this book we strongly advocate a strategic stance.

In the chapter on chronic pain (Chapter 13), we explain various ways of transforming the symptom, and when these methods meet strong unconscious resistance, we demonstrate how *utilization* and a *two-operator induction* can bypass even the most formidable obstacles. Therapy is cooperation. Clients understand that the road to change lies in a joint venture between therapist and client, our working *with them* to bring out their best rather than doing therapy *to them* as passive recipients.

This book contains two sections: Section I addresses hypnotic techniqes without formal hypnosis; Section II deals with the application of hypnosis for a variety of clinical problems. Section II may be most useful for practitioners who are already trained in hypnosis, although these readers may find that Section I can enhance both their practice of hypnosis, as well as the application of conventional psychotherapy. As in Section I, unconscious process is woven strongly throughout Section II, while at the same time we cover some fairly straightforward techniques for the disorders most often faced by clinicians in their practices. Just as passengers and freight are the bread and butter of the airline industry, so, too, practitioners of hypnosis are likely to fill their calendars with people suffering from anxiety, depression, and pain. Our aim is to do adequate justice to each of these disorders.

If Section I has appeal, Section II will also be of interest, even if you have yet to receive formal training in hypnosis, as some of the same techniques—for example, unconscious problem solving and ego strengthening—are revisited, albeit within the structure of formal hypnosis. Can readers, with an eye to their clinical practices, borrow ideas and applications from both sections? You bet.

Let's return to this duality, the notion of one thing blending into the other, hypnosis or not hypnosis. Sections I and II are in many ways the flip side of the same coin, or a mirror image with slight alterations. The authors find meaning in such complementarity where some may find this confusing or too inexact. Maybe those readers could suspend judgment until they have read a portion of either section, keeping in mind that hypnosis is a continuing contribution to helping clients lead better lives, while at the same time making our own lives as therapists just a bit easier.

Hypnotic Techniques

Section I

Hypnotic Techniques
in Psychotherapy

1

Incorporating Hypnotic Language into Psychotherapy

Let us begin by offering three commonplace words. As you read each word, pause for a second, and see what comes to mind. The first word is *wonder*. . . . Perhaps something from the past comes to mind, or maybe nothing at all. Now, the second word is *imagine* . . . , and the third word is *story*. One or more of these words may have stimulated a memory, feeling, or association, or the recollection of your use of these words in therapy. Whichever is the case, these words, all examples of what we call "power words," will appear again and again throughout this book. The use of words like *wonder* or *explore* along with *truisms, apposition of opposites,* and the *bind of comparable alternatives* is very purposeful, as they can form the cornerstone of successful therapy.

TRUISMS

A truism is a rather self-evident term. It describes an undeniable reality, and is used to establish a yes-set in therapy so that your suggestion or directive may be accepted by the client. For example: "So far, you have picked up this book and have begun reading this chapter . . . , and now you can continue with Chapter 1. . . ."

APPOSITION OF OPPOSITES

This juxtaposition of opposite terms—up and down, light and heavy, tingling and numbness—serves to *set up* your eventual suggestion or directive. It follows naturally from a truism, and some people experience a sense of wonder when hearing this type of hypnotic language. For example: "Now, some people *start* at the *front* of the book and *finish* at the *back*, preferring the *beginning* to the *end*. . . ."

BIND OF COMPARABLE ALTERNATIVES

With a *bind of comparable alternatives*, you say essentially the same thing, but in different ways, and this can complete the *set-up*: "Maybe words like *wonder* or *imagine* stimulate something curious, possibly something interesting, or simply a sense of having fun on the inside."

SUGGESTION OR DIRECTIVE

This can be done in a number of different ways. In formal hypnosis, a suggestion can be preceded by "power words," which set up the most versatile form of suggestion, *implication*, in which the operative word is *when*: "And I *wonder*, or otherwise *imagine*, just how deeply and comfortably you can go into trance, which can be like an entrance into another state . . . and *when* your unconscious mind has selected some strength or resource from the past, you will find your head nodding every so imperceptibly . . . ." In conventional psychotherapy, we may wish to gently surround implication with a variety of power words: ". . . and beginning now, we can start to *explore* just how you have adapted to anxiety in your life, and *when* an *interesting* or *curious* perspective comes to mind during our session today, you may find that you can share it with me as it comes up, *noticing* and *appreciating* how new information can shed important light on a familiar subject."

HYPNOTIC LANGUAGE IN AN EDUCATIONAL PRESENTATION

Before resuming with therapy, let's see how hypnotic language can be used in a lecture. I (G. G.) am a member of a consultation team that trains health care professionals how to address ethical issues in staff-client relationships. We call the workshop "Boundaries."

Typically, we have an audience of fifty or sixty nurses, doctors, social workers, and other practitioners. Their attendance is usually involuntary, and sometimes they are hostile, as they are being made to take two hours from a busy day in order to listen to what is sure to be a tedious topic.

We begin by showing some slides of familiar, everyday things, such as plants and animals, sunsets, and hospital buildings, and liberally sprinkle hypnotic language into the patter:

Coming over here today *like you did,* cloudy and overcast *as it is outside, and* taking precious time *from a busy day, perhaps on the way over to this conference room you began to* wonder, *or otherwise* imagine, *will these next two hours be slow, or will they go by* fast, *when a* minute *can seem like an* hour, *or an* hour *like a* minute, *or will you simply* lose track of time, *while we show you some slides to introduce the topic. The slides will be followed by a brief videotape, and afterwards we will have some discussion of the topic.*	truisms hypnotic language apposition of opposites time distortion
Now, one person *who attended this workshop,* completed the workshop, *and for some time afterward she asked herself, "The things I learned there, will I be able to use them on the* job, *or in my* personal life, *or will I simply let them be part of my* overall experience?	metaphor age progression bind of comparable alternatives

The Tomato Story

We now show a slide of an odd-looking tomato that has an appendage sticking out of it. The story that follows contains the meta-message that people can be open to new experiences, and that they can openly discuss a difficult topic.

We debated whether to even include this slide and the story that accompanies it. We call it the 'Tomato Story.' It's relevance to the presentation today may be evident to some of you. Others may choose not to even listen to it, rather bizarre story that it is.

Prior to 1827, tomatoes had not been eaten in the United States. No one had dared to taste, much less eat, a tomato, until one day, on the steps of the court house in Salem, New Jersey, Robert Gibbon Johnson bravely took a tomato out of his pocket, raised it in the air, took a big bite of the tomato, and swallowed it down. Sure enough, Robert Gibbon Johnson did not die. And thereafter, people in this country slowly, gradually, began to add tomatoes to their diet.

We then allow a few moments for processing, and without commenting further on tomatoes, we move on to other slides, facts and figures about codes of ethics, and other information about Boundaries.

AN INITIAL STORY IN THERAPY

Juan and Elisa presented with a chronic marital problem. Like many people who feel discouraged from marital unhappiness, they were reluctant to enter therapy. It is vital in the first session to instill hope. One way to do this is to metaphorically convey what may lie ahead in future sessions. The therapist took Juan and Elisa's history, and at the end of the session told them a story.

The River-Rafting story

Let me tell you a little story about Joan, a physician I know. This story may be about courage, resolve, strength, *or* fortitude, *I'm not sure.*

bind of comparable alternatives

Joan was terrified of the water, and for years had resisted her friends' offer of a river-rafting trip. "I get a meat grinder in my stomach just thinking about it," she said.

Nevertheless, a physician colleague told her, "We have reservations in July to take a river-rafting trip through the Grand Canyon." Joan didn't say no to it, but she experienced an immediate rash on her body. "I don't think I'll be able to do it," Joan thought to herself.

Now, Joan had done a lot in her life: college, medical school, seven years of surgical residency, and she had performed hundreds of operations. She had also experienced various adversities in her life, too many to go into here.

As the day approached to embark on the trip, Joan's rash got worse. However, as they started down the river, she imme-diately noticed the contrast of the hot sun and chilling water, the slow, gentle spots in the river, and the rushing rapids, as well as the wonderful colors, the browns and reds of the canyon walls, which captured and immersed her atten-tion.

apposition of opposites

absorption of attention

As they camped the first night, the guide addressed the group. He said, "I know this is tough for some of you. Everyone's experience is different. But if you drink plenty of water, don't forget the sun-screen, and stick together, this will work out just fine. Remember, you have a guide with you who's been down this river many times before. Experience can be a great teacher, and I've had more than one person say that they learn many things about themselves on this trip."

metaphor

metaphor

As they prepared for sleep that first night, one of Joan's colleagues put her arm around Joan and said, "Joan, we've all treated a lot of patients. You know how many will do well for a while, but then they return. Medication may need to be adjusted, infections need to be treated, and sometimes, years after surgery, adhesions develop, and you have to go in again. The doctor's always there for them, for whatever may come up."

embedded meaning

metaphor

This made a lot of sense to Joan, and she learned a great deal on the rest of the trip.

A STORY AT THE END OF THERAPY

It is not uncommon for clients to backslide after the completion of successful therapy. Therapists can do many things—booster sessions, homework assignments, and other directives, to name a few—to help ensure that clients remain on track. Another, economical way to accomplish this end is by using metaphor. We often tell this story at the end of therapy; midway through therapy, after gains have been made; or even in group therapy.

The Pond Story

A man [or woman] told me a story once that began with his forty acres back in Indiana. As he started to tell his story, I wondered about its relevance and how long a story it would be, but finally I just sat back and listened to the words without trying to read any meaning into their content. It turns out that this man had always wanted a tranquil pond at the back of his house, a nice pond with plant life and fish, something he could enjoy for a long, long time.

Not caring to do the work himself, he hired a crew of workers, and soon trees were cut down and a place was cleared far back from his house. Next, they brought in a bulldozer and a large excavator. In several hours the man gazed upon a ten-foot reddish brown gash in the earth's crust. He wondered if the 50- by 125-foot hole would ever fill with water, but he knew that eventually the clay-lined hole would fill right to the top.

With the melting snows of winter and the heavy showers of spring, the pond filled up in no time. One day he noticed algae floating in the water, and soon the sound of frogs filled the air at night. In June, various insects buzzed over the water and aquatic plants appeared along the pond's edge. He knew that all this life had not materialized miraculously, but that it had been borne on the wind or carried unwittingly by the feet of waterfowl.

Eventually the pond looked like a part of the natural landscape. One morning he even spotted the tracks of deer, raccoons, and other animals along the rim. He thought about something he had read once by Henry David Thoreau, something to the effect of "no sooner will you dig your pond and nature will begin to stock it."

But nature didn't just stock his pond. Nature had seemed to strike a natural balance between predator and prey, parasite and host, each with its proper place in the larger scheme of things. As the man observed it all from his back porch one evening, he proudly contemplated what he had accomplished. "This is the way it's supposed to be," he thought. "This is something I can enjoy until the end of my days."

One month followed another and pretty soon two years had passed. The man paid less attention to his pond, just assuming that its natural balance would always remain in effect, that the pond would always take care of itself. He travelled to Europe and was gone for a couple of months. When he returned in late summer the pond appeared to be clogged with weeds. However, he thought this was only a temporary condition, and he took another trip, this time for six months. While away, he read a book about ponds. The book mentioned that as algae and weeds grow, die, and sink to the bottom, the water becomes shallower, and as more light reaches the bottom, the weeds grow more and more. Rushes and willows on the shore encroach upon the water, which steadily diminishes until the pond becomes a swamp, then just a wet spot. Finally, what was once a pond, turns into woodland, which is exactly what it was at the beginning.

He hurried home from his trip and feverishly began raking out the algae and weeds. He stocked the pond with a special kind of carp that eat weeds, and planted cattails to filter out new sediment. Pretty soon his pond was again pulsating with life. He even noticed some things that he had not seen previously, an aquatic spider, and tracks left by a fox.

Any trips he took from then on lasted only a month or less and he subscribed to a magazine called *Perpetual Pond,* though he had problems with the title.

CLINICAL COMMENTS

We adapted the "Pond Story" from "Secret World of a Pond," by Michael Pollan (*New York Times Magazine,* July 24, 1994). The "Tomato Story" appeared in Araoz's *New Hypnosis* (1985), and we alter both of these stories to fit the clinical or teaching situation. In the following chapters, we will examine many aspects of stories, including how to construct stories for your individual clients. We *never* discuss a story's meaning immediately after the telling of it, choosing instead to let the metaphor percolate in the client's unconscious mind without conscious interference. When clients return for the following session, the individual meaning derived from the metaphor may be discussed at that time, as we believe that sufficient time has transpired for unconscious processing. Now, not all therapists believe in holding off on discussing a metaphor, and we will review the pros and cons of this in subsequent chapters.

2

Metaphor and Story in Psychotherapy

A METAPHOR FOR THERAPY

Thompson (1990), who worked closely with Milton H. Erickson, was a dentist and therapist who employed a wide range of hypnotic techniques in her practice. She likened the therapist to an automobile mechanic, and clients to automobiles in need of maintenance or repair. She pointed out that a good mechanic listens closely to the car, and then fine-tunes it, not taking anything away, but working with and modifying what is there. Accepting this analogy allows therapists to embrace what clients bring to the office, and then stimulate them to achieve a greater potential—perhaps running more smoothly, or having a longer and happier life—rather than attempting to create a new and better model. The therapist may suggest a maintenance schedule, a change of route, or even other directions. However, it is the client who ultimately drives the car and determines its destination.

This idea may run counter to the view of new interns in mental health, who may be eager to try out cognitive-behavioral therapy (CBT) and other techniques they have learned in school in order to change or convert the client into a new and better model. Accordingly, Thompson's metaphor forces the therapist to slow down and notice all aspects of the client and his situation. Once this is done, the next step is to understand how every thought, word, deed, or problem is a possible resource to be *utilized* in helping the client achieve his goals. Utilization is more than a technique. In fact, it is a cornerstone of therapy, and we will revisit it in other chapters.

THE "SUBSTITUTE TEACHER" METAPHOR

The "Substitute Teacher" metaphor may help new interns see their role in brief therapy more clearly. In our own practices, we have both short-term and long-term clients. Some might attend for many weeks, while others might meet their goals, or discontinue therapy, after only a few sessions. In fact, in all settings, the average number of sessions is six or less, which means that the therapist must combine building rapport, assessment, and intervention with a short-ened time perspective. Therefore, in Tucson, Arizona, we are fond of telling this story to interns or new staff.

> *Did you ever have a substitute teacher, maybe in grade school or high school? Let's say your regular teacher was ill for a week or so, and this substitute teacher showed up at your class. These people have a real tough job, getting to know everybody, trying to follow the lesson plan, and even getting some of their own ideas across to the class. Then their job is over, and they're gone. I know in my own experience a good substitute teacher made a difference, but I can no longer remember her name.*

WHAT IS A METAPHOR?

Engineers build bridges, and so do therapists. It is useful to think of metaphor as simply that: a bridge. Metaphor is derived from two Greek words: *meta,* to transform or change, and beyond or over; and *pherein,* to carry. Metaphor, then, is that which affects us by "carrying something over." Ingram (1996) explains that the essence of metaphor is understanding, or experiencing, one kind of thing in terms of another, collapsing language and experience, thus creating a *bridge* between sensory modalities. This bridge to understanding or awareness may be used when the therapist is working with a married couple who unwittingly spend too much time together. The therapist tells them a story about two tomato plants that were planted too close together. The therapist describes the contiguous plants' competition for sun and nutrients, along with other consequences of their proximity and entanglement. Similar *bridges* were constructed by Erickson (Haley, 1973) who believed that many problems could be resolved indirectly without explicit mention of the problem. For example, in treating a couple's sexual problem, Erickson highlighted the pleasures of eating as a metaphorical way of noticing and appreciating the enjoyment of sexual intercourse and its antecedents.

Of course, therapy involves much more than creative metaphors that seem to fit a client's unique situation. In the scenario above, the therapist may tell a story or anecdote at various stages of therapy as a means of making an important point, or helping the couple work through the guilt and anxiety of a difficult situation.

Madanes (1981, 1990) recounts various ways stories told to clients can contain suggestions and solutions. Using a technique she calls "prescribing the metaphor," Madanes tells a story to a client, and then asks him to provide the ending. The case involved a twelve-year-old boy with a 150 I.Q. who was failing in school and came to therapy with his overbearing mother. The therapist told the boy a story about a special computer, the first computer ever made that could actually think like a person. But nobody knew it. The computer just sat on the store shelf with all of the ordinary computers, hoping that someone would buy him.

The next session, the boy provided various endings to the story, and Madanes even provided some herself. In the process, the boy felt understood, and his mother learned to see him within the context of how difficult it is to communicate with someone who has a special kind of intelligence.

METAPHORS IN EVERYDAY LIFE: A BRIDGE TO EXPERIENCE

One of the ways that people construct reality, according to Siegelman (1990), is by making metaphors, described as the imaginative act of comparing dissimilar things on the basis of some underlying principle that unites them. People construct their reality through perception and categories of thought. Metaphor, which is vital in this process, is an elementary structure of thought. Lakoff and Johnson (1980) have identified metaphors basic to human experience, for example, life is a journey or death is a destination. Many of these generic metaphors have become automatic and conventional in everyday speech.

We are bombarded by metaphor in everyday life—in movies, stories, conversation, and on the evening news, to name a few situations. A coworker, in criticizing his boss's apparent shortsightedness, says, "She can't see the forest for the trees." In Congress, a senator rallies support for a key vote with, "The train is about to leave the station." A politician who advocates paying down the national debt during a time of prosperity says, "Let's fix the roof while the sun is shining." A fellow legislator announces, "The president sees only the hole in the donut." Heavyweight boxer, Mike Tyson, famous for his fights both inside and out of the ring, told us he wasn't all bad when he said, "I'm not Mother Teresa, but I'm not Charles Manson either."

Because metaphor is so prevalent in all aspects of life, and clients are accustomed to experiencing and using metaphors, this technique, more than anything, lends itself to application in therapy. However, this naturally occurring tool, with its myriad applications, is greatly underutilized in all schools of therapy. In each chapter, we will explore the depth and diversity of metaphor, which, like hypnotic language, story and anecdote, are tools that can bolster the armamentarium of all therapists.

Metaphor combines the abstract and concrete in a special way, which enables people to go from the known and the sensed, to the unknown and the symbolic. Siegelman (1990) sees a paradox here, in that the abstract is arrived at through the concrete, that is, through the senses, and most often through the visual mode. Metaphor's utility for therapists lies in its capacity to *bridge* to a larger domain. In addition to utility, however, metaphor is rich and vivid, in that it connects to the world of felt and sensed experience.

LISTENING FOR A CLIENT'S METAPHORS

When we offer clients a metaphor, for example, "I can see that this problem has been a real monkey on your back for a long, long time," and the metaphor *connects* with them, clients will let us know, immediately and nonverbally, by perhaps leaning forward slightly in their chair, or showing a gleam in their eyes, or a look of surprise or acknowledgment. A verbal reaction may accompany their nonverbal response, such as, "Yes, that's it!"

We might also feel such a connection—that we *know* what they mean—when clients offer metaphors during a time of intense affect. Voth (1970) noted that during periods of emotional intensity clients may introduce metaphors that differ from their usual style. Most meaningful to us as therapists are those metaphors that clients repeat, perhaps as part of a theme. For example, "I was *crushed*" may or may not be revealing. However, a more congruent picture emerges if the client repeats that she was crunched, or flattened, or beaten down, especially if these words correspond to the affect of an overall defeated presentation.

When a client offers a metaphor early in therapy, for example, "I feel beaten to a pulp," we may ask them, "On a scale of one to ten, with ten representing the worst feeling, what number would you assign at this moment?" The therapist then has a baseline that can then be scaled later on in therapy. In addition to measurement, a client's metaphor is something that can be transformed during the course of therapy, for example, "Okay, during the past three weeks that beaten-to-a-pulp feeling has improved such that you are 'pummeled to the point of being black and blue.' Let's work on reducing that soreness even more. . . ."

Clients in distress may be prone to offering metaphors that are representaive of negative feeling states. Although these are significant, it may be more important to elicit *positive* metaphors, for example, "When the world is lifted from my shoulders," or "When I get back to being on top of the world." These positive metaphors may surface if we prompt clients by doing such things as asking for *exceptions* to the problem, or asking what life might be like in the absence of the problem.

WHEN CLIENTS DO NOT OFFER METAPHORS

When clients are not forthcoming with metaphors, it may be helpful to provide your own. For example, we are seeing an angry client with black or white cognitions, someone who is unable to recognize antecedents, or any range of feelings. She describes herself as instantly going from calm to rageful. "Oh, just like throwing gasoline on the fire?" we may query. She will likely answer, "Yes, just like that." We may then ask her to notice if early on she "sees red" or gets a "funny feeling" in her stomach, or even say, "I knew someone once and she said she noticed her breathing becoming shallow." If this connects, she may be receptive to something like, "Well, you, too, may begin to notice how these feelings in your body lead to other things, like links in a chain." During the next session, this idea of continuum may be nurtured; for example, "I don't know if in your apartment you have light switches, you know, the light is either on, or it's off. In some apartments they have rheostats, which allow a person to slowly adjust the light from dim to bright."

Long before she answers with her words, her nonverbal behavior will signal acceptance or rejection of this offering. For many people, metaphors having to do with control, or movement, or mobility, are worth probing. For example, "being in the driver's seat," or "getting back on the road," or any number of related variations, may be worth exploring.

How many times have you heard somebody mention some aspect of *eating* as a metaphor? "That was a bitter pill to swallow," or "She bit off more than she could chew," are a few examples. I (G. G.) once worked with an engineer who came to therapy with his wife, who was an attorney. He was a typical engineer—meticulous, analytical, and exacting—and he was also hypercritical. You know how it is with some couples, where the problem resides chiefly in one partner? Well, take a guess which one needed the most work. By the third session, trust had been built, and I saw him separately and asked him to try an experiment: to see if he could reduce his criticism by *exactly* 30 percent for the sake of the marriage. When they returned next session, he proudly announced that he had seen the error of his ways, and had succeeded in reducing his criticism by *100 percent*. His wife agreed: he was no longer hypercritical. The engineer, an obese man who enjoyed driving his car in the country almost as much as he enjoyed eating, had unwittingly provided me with ample metaphor material. Accordingly, I restrained him with things like, "It may be wiser to eat a bite-sized chunk instead of a whole mouthful," and "A youngster crawls before he can walk," and "I don't know if you're ready to take off the training wheels yet." After two more sessions, his criticism had crept back to 10 percent, which he rationalized as "because my wife needs a lot of guidance." I saw his wife alone and was able to convince her to tolerate 10 percent for the sake of the marriage. They got along just fine from then on.

We use certain stock metaphors. In relational problems that are characterized by diminished communication and disengagement, one or both parties may acknowledge the presence of a wall. If so, we may then ask, "It seems like a pretty sturdy wall, a brick wall perhaps?" Such a wall, to us, is a gift-wrapped metaphor, a veritable invitation to loosen the mortar here, knock out a couple of bricks over there, peep over the wall with a step-ladder, or any other number of ways to transform the symptom. I (G. G.) remember a couple I was working with in which the husband had constructed such a wall after his wife's affair. Various attempts to improve closeness, including ritual, were futile. A breakthrough happened when the husband consented to letting his wife gently touch the bricks, but only in the late evening, after the bricks had cooled. Now, he was not asked to really do anything, but to "Just imagine, in your mind, your wife's fleeting but gentle touch on those bricks. . . ."

As parenthood is common to many people, we may compare entering therapy to the labor and delivery process. The process can be long, sometimes messy, and occasionally painful, but the new life you have at the end makes it worthwhile. With athletic clients, we may note that undertaking major change is like running a marathon. Nobody starts out running the whole 26.2 miles. Instead, they may walk or run slowly for a while, then enter a five-kilometer race, and gradually work up to more distance, all the while "taking one step at a time, putting one foot in front of the other. . . ." Many disorders contain an element of fear, which is difficult for all of us to face. With these people, we may relate that fear to being in a room that is on fire. If you back into a corner to avoid the fire, eventually you will be overcome by smoke and flames. Although it may be hard to do—and you may even suffer some superficial burns—the only way out is "to walk through the fire to get to the other side."

ADVANTAGES OF METAPHOR

To our interns, we describe metaphor as shorthand for, or a shortcut to, building rapport, assessment, and intervention. One time someone in one of our workshops exclaimed, "Oh, I see, that's the *easy* way," and we answered, "Well, why make it hard if it can be easy?" Certainly, when you want to cross a river, why build the Golden Gate Bridge when a pontoon bridge will do?

We will be examining a host of advantages to employing metaphor in therapy. Some of these advantages include allowing therapists to bypass reflexive objections of clients; test clients' responses to ideas without calling attention to them; and build a careful foundation before being direct. This indirect approach encourages the client to do an active mental search in order to develop access to stored or imagined resources, or to stimulate new associative pathways. Accordingly, clients may experience a greater sense of creativity in— and responsibility for—the therapy process.

ANECDOTES AND STORIES

Two of our main tools in therapy are the anecdote and the story. Anecdotes, which are just shorter versions of stories, are extremely handy, as they can be adroitly and conveniently used several times during the therapy hour. One that we often use involves *another client*. In working with someone with complicated grief, for example, we may insert:

> *You know, just last month I was working with a man who also came to Arizona from somewhere else, and he was trying hard to get from here to there after experiencing the death of his child. After several sessions he came to experience some relief. When I asked him what it was like, he said, "It's like a hole in the ground that slowly begins to fill in. I know that it will never fill in completely, but I can feel that it's starting to fill in just a bit."*

Similar examples can be offered at various points during a session. Such anecdotes need not be complicated. They can simply, in a few sentences, point the way to improvement. For example, "I knew someone just last year who achieved a remarkable lessening of anxiety, but it took some hard work on his part." Or anecdotes can be a bit more elaborate. For the stepfather who rigidly adheres to a regimen of unreasonable discipline, we may tell him about the saguaro cactus, that tall green titan with long arms that graces the Sonoran desert. A mature saguaro may weigh several tons, and it is very slow-growing, sometimes requiring two hundred years to reach maturity.

THE SAGUARO

Let me tell you about this man I saw once. He also moved here from Nebraska, and outside his door there was a saguaro growing. It was about two feet tall, and as it didn't seem to be growing very fast, he thought it must be thirsty, so he threw some water on it. After several weeks, it still hadn't grown any, so he gave it more *water, and then even* more *water. Now, that saguaro started to lose its needles and was looking blotchy, so he figured he hadn't given it enough water, so he watered it even* more. *Soon, it looked even worse, so he decided it needed even* more *water. . . .*

The stepfather may say at that juncture, "Okay, I get the point." Or he may ask, "Well, what ever happened to the saguaro?" Whatever he says, we purposely do not continue to process the anecdote, as we believe that any anecdote, or story, is best processed, on an unconscious level, without conscious interference. If he persists, we may say, "We'll talk about it when you come back."

THE LEGACY OF MILTON H. ERICKSON

By the time he died in 1980, Erickson had transformed the field of hypnosis and psychotherapy by building on his patients' strengths, and subtly influencing behavior change with techniques that came to be known as *utilization, reframing,* and *indirection.* In the 1930s, when Sigmund Freud dominated the theory and practice of psychotherapy, the staunchly atheoretical Erickson began to influence thinkers as diverse as anthropologist Margaret Mead and philosopher Aldous Huxley. Erickson's influence continued in the second half of the last century, as he inspired the seminal work of think tanks such as the Mental Research Institute in Palo Alto, California, and the Ackerman Institute in New York. More than anyone, he is credited with the creation of strategic brief therapy and modern hypnosis.

Many of today's mental health professionals have benefited from Erickson's teachings without having read his work. One of the myths about Erickson is what Hammond (1984) termed "the tyranny of indirection." Erickson was often very direct and authoritative, but sometimes he was nondirective, adjusting fto the needs of circumstances. Let's remember, a client going in to see the famous Dr. Erickson was probably very "response attentive," and therefore receptive to direct suggestions. And let's remember that Erickson worked with formal trance only 20 percent of the time (Beahrs, 1971).

Such flexibility, the capacity to adapt technique to the problem at hand, marks Erickson as a true pioneer. According to Haley (1985), Erickson was the first strategic therapist, in that the locus of change resided in the therapist, not the client. However, Erickson was also the first *therapist*. The first *therapist*? Yes, indeed, because he was the first major clinician to concentrate on changing people. Previously clinicians had devoted themselves to understanding the human mind and exploring the nature of people. Change per se was secondary, and when change was the concern, the responsibility for change was on the client, not the therapist (Haley, 1985).

If asked about Erickson, people's thoughts may turn to Erik Erickson, not Milton. Nevertheless, virtually all present-day treatment approaches bear the stamp of Milton Erickson.

The Lost Horse

Erickson was fond of telling a story about when he was a young boy growing up in Wisconsin in the early 1900s. A lost horse had wandered into his yard, and although the horse had no identifying marks, Erickson set out to return it to its owners. He mounted the horse and patiently allowed the horse to lead the way. The horse took its time, periodically stopping to graze in a field, or to wander off the road. Finally, after a few hours, the horse arrived at its owner's yard several miles away.

"How did you know that horse came from here, and that it was our horse?" asked the surprised neighbor. Erickson said, "I didn't know—but the *horse* knew. All I did was keep him on the road."

Wellness versus Illness

The pathology model lingers ardently in mental health treatment. People take a pill to *correct* neurochemical imbalance, and therapists *root out* dysfunctional behavior for remediation. In fact, the pathology model—the model of aggressive correction of a deficit or problem—is likened to a metaphor of war by Walters and Havens (1994). Traditionally, therapists did *battle* against a rigid superego, and today they *fight* depressive cognitions, or clients *struggle* with addiction in hopes of *survival* or *recovery*. Survivors of incest may proudly proclaim *victim* status, a new and proud identity for some, while others may be held back by the negative label. With a search-and-destroy mentality, clinicians strive to identify and eliminate faulty cognitions and maladaptive behavior. In this mentality, where is happiness, joy, or productive living?

Erickson referred often to happiness. He said that people come to therapy to dissolve their unhappiness, and he sends them out to establish their happiness. He firmly believed that unhappy marriages could be turned around if the therapist helped the couple to appreciate what *is there*, instead of lamenting what *is not there*. In short, Erickson's goal was to create happiness and well-being, rather than to eradicate illness. In fact, long before wellness was a movement, and long before hardiness or self-efficacy were studied, Erickson recognized that optimism, altruism, and self-efficacy are fundamental ingredients to well-being and healing, and he was guided by these principles in his therapeutic interventions (Walters & Havens, 1994). We are guided by these proactive, indisputable, and affirmative principles of Erickson. Many times in therapy we need only use a gentle hand, along with some hypnotic techniques "to keep the horse going in the right direction." To do this, nothing helps us like the story.

THE STORY

Both an ancient tradition and a universal experience, stories were told to adults when they were children, and likely continues into the client's experience in a variety of ways. Child clients may read stories, or see them on TV, and parents and grandparents may read stories to younger family members, or experience them in songs, movies, or as part of a religious tradition. Lefort (1968) noted that the purpose of stories is not only to provide pleasure, or a useful parable, but also to connect with "a part of the individual which cannot be reached by any other convention" (62–63). In reviewing stories cross-culturally, Ornstein (1977) pointed to the storyteller as one of the most important elements in the story tradition, as the storyteller uses language to make "an end run around the verbal intellect" in order to "affect a mode of consciousness not reached by the normal verbal intellectual apparatus" (147).

In the following chapters we will delve into some of the scores of therapeutic applications of the story. Perhaps your own experience with stories has been one of didactics, when the story teaches you something, or provides an example. What about a story that provides *several* examples, and *many* possible choices? Or what about a story whose meaning, or meta-message, is vague, and different listeners of the story might draw varied meanings from it? Many times in therapy—especially when clients are stuck—we stimulate unconscious process, and a story like the following may provide sufficient instigation to help therapy proceed.

In the Freezer

It was way out in the country, in some state in the Midwest. I forget if it was Ohio, Indiana, or some place else. It was an old two-story, clapboard house, way out in the middle of nowhere, a rather ancient dwelling that had been there as long as anybody could remember.

Various families had lived in the house since the 1930s, and probably even before that. Not much had changed in that house over time, except that no doubt they had to replace the roof now and then, or at least patch up the holes. The house was set back from the road, barely visible through the trees and across the fields that perhaps had produced corn or beans in previous decades. But now the fields lay dormant, having been untilled for a long, long time.

Inside the house, on the first floor, way in back in a room that now served as a crowded laundry room, there was an old freezer, a big old appliance that was like a chest, tucked away in a corner of the room. The freezer currently shared the room with a dog dish and the washing machine and drier. From the rest of the house, you just forgot about it back there in that room, and if you were in the kitchen, you might hear the tumbling of the washer, or the hum of the drier. But the big freezer you just forgot about. Any time people moved out of the house they just left the freezer. "It goes with the house," was what a succession of owners and tenants had been told over the years.

When children fetched something from the freezer, they had to strain to lift the heavy lid, and they had to stand on a stool in order to reach way down into it, peering through the frosty fog, in search of a popsicle amidst the frozen turkeys, gallons of orange juice that had been bought on sale, containers of spaghetti sauce, and who-knows-what else in unmarked, frost-covered containers that lay down in the icy depths. Magic marker tends to wear away with the passage of time, and on other containers, the labels simply curled off and deteriorated amidst the years and years of unrelenting freeze. In there, way down in the dark, jammed under a package of hot dogs that had been there for many years, was a container of frozen strawberries. No one could remember the last time someone had defrosted the freezer, and the inside walls were thick with ice. It was a wonder that it continued to function with such remarkable efficiency.

The laundry room was rather barren except for a weathered picture of a tranquil winter scene, a page torn from some magazine and tacked to the wall. Some hardcover books with yellowed pages lay in the dust behind the drier. They may have been poems of Robert Service, or a Jack London novel. No one knew for sure, as no one had swept back there for several years. A pencil on a string hung from the wall, close to dozens of lines marked on the wall. "January 10—three feet eight inches . . . February third—three feet nine inches." The once-white linoleum melded with the sagging floor.

Over the years, someone had taken out that container of strawberries and let it thaw for a couple of hours. But they invariably put it back without consuming it. If you examined its contents, you could see evidence of the repeated partial thawing and refreezing of that block of sugary crimson. The container was always put back, deep inside, and somehow it retained its crystalized integrity, despite years of being jostled about, squashed, dented, and nicked, not to mention the thawing that occurred during summer electric storms, when power went out in the whole house.

From the window in the room, you could look out over the freezer and see the snowbanks of winter, the summer rains, and the brilliant autumn leaves. Some time back, an occupant of the house had hung a prism in the window, one of those curious little glass objects, that you could turn this way and that, and depending on how you turned it, and depending on the time of day, a person could see quite a kaleidoscope of colors.

CLINICAL COMMENTS

As we read this story in therapy, we usually give vocal emphasis to different words, or key suggestions. Such a subtle vocal shift could occur in the last sentence of the story, or maybe whenever *inside* appears in the text. It is believed that the therapist communicates with the unconscious during these times.

A story like "In the Freezer" invites sundry conscious explanations or questions. With some stories clients may comment afterward with something like, "Well, that sure was an obvious metaphor," or, "Okay, I understand: I should be like that so-and-so in the story." Some therapists might reinforce the client's "getting" of the metaphor. Michael Yapko (personal communication, December 9, 2001) argues persuasively for doing so. However, we do not, except in certain cases, such as with very concrete clients. Our response might be, "I can see you were listening very closely," but seldom more than that. Why? We believe that we reinforce critical analysis by engaging in conscious processing. Most commonly, we usually answer with a detouring response, such as, "I already know what story to tell you *next* visit," or, simply, "Remember, we don't talk about stories right afterward, and there's a good reason for that." In other words, part of our education of the client is explaining our rationale for delaying discussion of the story until later.

When we abstain from abetting conscious evaluation—and, for many of us, that is tough to do because we are so accustomed to active processing—even clients who make discounting statements may show improvement in the following weeks. Why? We believe this is because unimpeded unconscious processing allows them to incorporate key suggestions, so that they can adapt them to their own particular circumstances. Can we know that for sure? Of course not. Can we point to studies where clients were randomized to different treatment conditions, including a manualized one that was tailored to the unique needs of the individual? Of course not.

We only know that many clients—not only in our own practices, but also in the practices of other therapists who work indirectly— who have been unsuccessful with years of straight-forward therapy, suddenly show improvement from indirection and metaphor. Not that stories alone are a magic bullet. However, when their application is a part of a psychotherapy that takes into account the unique needs of the individual, meaningful change can occur. For many clients, such change must occur unconsciously before we see subjective and objective improvement.

3

Hypnotic Techniques during the First Session

When I (S. B.) see children in therapy, I structure the first session around stories in order to build rapport and defuse tension. I often ask them to "trade" stories with me, as this may be a nonthreatening way to find out key concerns from their perspective. I may begin with stories about my dogs, or neices, as icebreaker anecdotes, and then move into more pointed stories, often jumping off from the story themes provided by the child.

I (G. G.) have a much different setup in my practice, which is a family therapy training program. We cover a range of assessment and intervention strategies during the year, and many cases involve marital therapy. As some interns have had little experience in the field, we begin with fairly elementary—but also vital—concepts, such as building rapport, and raise basic questions like, "What exactly does the therapist do that first session?" This question generates much discussion, and responses range from the importance of taking a careful history, to comments such as, "I'm green at this and I'm afraid I'll look bad," to "With my limited experience, I doubt my ability to help *anyone*." Interns also typically say things like, "How can these people put their trust in a mere student?" Or, "What if they start yelling at each other?" Or even, "What if I make them worse?" One intern had been fortified years ago with this advice: "Someone told me once that it's best to just shut up and listen." These are all good questions and comments, and we reassure them that with practice they will feel better about their work, and that as their confidence grows, it will show in their work. Certainly, more than one session is usually required to gather interview essentials, and many times it may be best to "just shut up and listen," as long as they allow both partners to be heard.

Some of the cases involve children, and occasionally new therapists may feel at a loss for what to do. They have read some books on therapy with children, but the topic often is not covered in graduate school. Younger interns may not have children of their own. So, then, the prospect of having to see children may cause a bit of anxiety. We provide interns with no dearth of assessment and treatment aids, and one of these key tools is the story about Pandora's box, which also may be used with adults. To get children age six and older talking (or playing, or coloring), there may be no better story. Of course, the meta-message is that you can talk about problems without the world coming to an end. Key suggestions are underlined, and these are emphasized by the reader's slight vocal shift.

Pandora's Box

Long ago, in ancient Greece, there lived a young girl named Pandora. She went to school and helped her parents around the house, and life was really kind of boring until one day she received a big *surprise*. It was a very special gift, a heavy, jewel-encrusted box, and it came from the king of all the gods, whose name was Zeus. Zeus gave her careful instructions. He said, "Pandora, whatever you do, NEVER open this box." His voice was like thunder, and Pandora nodded meekly in agreement.

The years passed, and Pandora grew older. Each day, she looked at that box and wondered what was inside it. One day, in the late afternoon, her curiosity got the better of her. She grabbed the box, and took a sharp stone, or a knife (nobody knows for sure just what tool she used) and she *pried open the box*. The lid was *very, very heavy*. Inside, she could see that the box was lined with gold. As she lifted the lid up and up, she heard a strange noise, like many feet pounding up wooden stairs, and then she was pushed back by a WHOOSHING force coming from inside the box.

Pandora watched as *all the evils of the world* flew out of that box. Meanness, cruelty, war, and evil poured out. Poverty, homelessness, AIDS, and abandoned puppies poured out of that box. This went on for several minutes. Pandora sat back and watched. She was breathless, and her heart pounded in her chest. Finally, it was quiet, as nothing more came out of that box.

She bravely peered into the box. Her eyes soon adjusted to the inky darkness, and then she saw it. Something glimmering, way down at the bottom. And do you know what it was?

It was *hope*. *Hope* was shining, way down there at the bottom.

Stories and ancedotes are like people: dynamic and forever changing. Therapists may adapt "Pandora's Box" to their own interests, or to the particular circumstances of their clients. Of the hundreds of different stories we have used in therapy, seldom have we left one in its original form.

FRAMING THE FIRST SESSION WITH HYPNOTIC LANGUAGE

Experienced therapists realize the magnitude of the first session. Accordingly, interns are reminded, "If they don't come back, then you can't help them." To ensure that clients return for a second session, hypnotic language, reframe, and restraint can be potent allies of the therapist at the beginning of the initial session.

We started today *right at* 9:00, *this being our* first session. *I want to tell you a little about myself; but first, it's important to recognize that this isn't an* easy	truisms

door to walk through, *coming* in here *from* out there *to talk to a complete stranger about personal concerns.It's normal and natural for people to feel* nervous, *or* worried, *or to have* who-knows-what feelings *going on inside, and it probably requires some* courage *on your part to even be here today. You should know that I'll be asking some questions today to find out about you, things I need to know in order to help you. Nevertheless, it's okay to* say only what you're comfortable revealing.

We will study your case closely every week, and my supervisor here, George, says that in a first session of therapy, people may unconsciously *be thinking about cans, not a* can of corn or beans, *but a* can of worms, *in that talking about a problem can seem like a can of worms, as they say, or even worse, like a bag, where the* cat is let out of the bag.

Well, that usually doesn't happen. In fact, most often quite the opposite occurs, where people feel some relief from talking about strong feelings, and they usually leave here with the security of knowing that they have a guide as they go down this road, *along with hope that things can improve in their lives.*

metaphor
apposition of
opposites

suggestion covering
all possibilities

reframe

restraint

seeding

metaphor

metaphor

metaphor

Saying something like the above in the beginning helps accomplish several things. The therapist takes charge, but in a gentle way, structuring the session, so that the clients know what to expect. She also connects with both clients' affective states, not by being specific, but by offering a suggestion that covers all possibilities. She then encourages them to go slow with disclosure by encouraging restraint. Restraint in a highly charged first session is often very liberating for clients, who may respond with a lessening of tension, as well as expanded disclosure. As much of our intervention as possible is directed at the unconscious; *seeding* the unconscious is usually done in the first session.

Contrast the above with the therapist who simply opens the session with, "Where's a good place to start?" Certainly, we know many experienced therapists who begin with something similar, but then they slowly and adroitly elicit key affect and ask the right questions, demonstrating reflective listening and showing understanding, perhaps weaving timely metaphor and apt reframe into the session. But those therapists have had a lot of practice. New therapists, as well as clients who are unfamiliar with therapy, can benefit immensely from structure.

CONTAINING AFFECT IN THE MIDDLE OF THE SESSION

I (G. G.) will never forget one of the therapists in our mental health clinic in the 1980s. We'll call him Sam. He was an eternally patient man who tolerated frustration, ambiguity, bomb scares, fire drills, and acting-out clients better than the rest of us. For over a year, Sam saw the same client every Wednesday at 1:00 p.m. The client had a poorly controlled bipolar disorder. The client didn't talk; he would yell, in a thunderous voice nonstop for a solid hour. Presumably the man felt better when he left. However, the rest of us in the building were left shaken and disturbed by 2 p.m., as our 1 p.m. appointments or telephone calls were disturbed during this time. Even though our doors were closed, the man's angry tempest dominated the entire building. If you've ever experienced an unwanted and unabating loud noise, you know it can make you irritable and unable to concentrate on all but the most salient cues.

People told Sam to control his client somehow—get his medication increased, calm him down, see him only twice a month, anything— but nothing happened. After a year, the client left Tucson to shake the walls in Albuquerque or Denver, I don't know which. Life returned to normal. Sam later reflected on the case, and said that he had tried everything under the sun in an attempt to lower the client's volume. "Nothing worked, he was just too powerful," said Sam. Sam had trained in the 1950s, and he emulated Carl Rogers: embracing, general, permissive, and reflective to the core. Had Sam only been like *Mister* Rogers, he may have employed creative metaphor and gentle indirection to control his client. But Sam was also wise, and if he said the man was too powerful, maybe nothing would have helped.

In another case, an intern had an initial session with a warring couple, the Lockhorns, we'll call them. The videotape of the session showed the couple entering the office yelling at each other. They then took a seat as far from each other as they could. The intern first asked them to sit a bit closer to each other so the camera could capture them. He had experience as a therapist, and set the agenda, offered some stock metaphors, and strove to maintain balance and neutrality as both parties actively vied for his sympathy. The therapist was reflective and understanding, smoothly reframing strong feelings as sensitivity, but the angry shouting continued. The therapist asked them to stop and take a deep breath, but they ignored him. He finally relied on his notes and offered:

We're thirty minutes into our session, and maybe you've already noticed how easy it is to get heated up, how your heart beats faster, and your breathing. . . .	truism

The shouting then escalated even more. One of them stormed out of the room and knocked over the camera. The tape went blank. The session was a disaster.

I've had plenty of couples leave feeling worse than when they came in, and you wonder if they will make it back for another session. I am constantly reminding interns, "Don't have a funeral," but in this video, the dead appeared to have been raised. We both have had many cases like this, "martial" couples who seem to hate each other. You find yourself wondering why they even bothered to come in. But these are the clients we learn from.

The supervision group was galvinized by the video. The intern noted that he had been working his way up to the Pandora's box story, but obviously never got there. Someone told him, "Just remember the horse story, where Erickson kept the horse on the road." The comment seemed irrelevant. Others offered metaphors for the experience, things like manning the floodgates, putting your finger in the dike, or enduring a hurricane.

The intern was praised for having a plan and trying to stick to it. Then we got to the crux of the matter: What should have been done differently? One thing: Split them up early on. See one for 15 minutes, then the other, and near the end of the session, bring them back together and try to get a commitment for at least one more session. Hypnotic language, metaphor, reframing, and restraint can be aids to this end; however, first, the affect has to be contained. With this session, the best that can be said is that the camera wasn't broken and nobody was hurt.

THE HYPNOIDAL RESPONSE

In the coming weeks, the supervision group received a further glimpse of Mr. Lockhorn, as he continued in therapy after he separated from his wife. Mr. Lockhorn was unemployed, educated through the tenth grade, and was a door gunner on a helicopter in Vietnam. He served as a good example of hypnoidal behavior.

The therapist asked him to "sit back and relax as I tell you a little story. . . ." Mr. Lockhorn closed his eyes and sat immobile. He swallowed little, and showed the facial mask characteristic of trance. He was not asked about other trance indicators, such as *time distortion*, *amnesia*, or *ideosensory feelings*. Had this been done, he may have indicated that he lost track of time, forgot what the story was about, or experienced a numbness, or some other sensation, in one or both hands.

What would a non-hypnoidal response have been? Well, here we are talking about negative nonverbals that hit you square in the face: arms folded, eyes that keep darting around the room, an exhalation of exasperation, and so on.

We provide stock stories for interns, but we also encourage them to come up with their own stories. We say, "Don't try to be didactic in your story. All you want to do is absorb their attention." I was shocked and appalled by the story told to Mr. Lockhorn in the tape:

The Pillsbury Dough Boy

The Pillsbury Dough Boy died yesterday of a yeast infection and complications from repeated pokes in the belly. He was only 71. Dough Boy was buried in a lightly greased coffin. Dozens of celebrities turned out to pay their respects, including Mrs. Butterworth, Hungry Jack, the California Raisins, Betty Crocker, Hostess Twinkies, and Captain Crunch.

The grave site was piled high with "flours," as long-time friend, Aunt Jemima, delivered the eulogy, describing Dough Boy as a man who never knew how much he was "kneaded." He was not considered a very smart cookie, wasting much of his dough on half-baked schemes . . . he is survived by his wife, Play Dough, two children, John Dough and Jane Dough. . . .

The story continued. It was obviously not your average hypnotic story. "You said I needed to absorb his attention. Well, it worked, didn't it?" said the intern. I could not argue with the result. He said he got the story off the Internet. After that, I previewed his stories before he used them with clients. And Mr. Lockhorn? Well, no doubt he was *response attentive* that day, and he continued to do well until the completion of therapy.

INTRODUCING STORIES INTO YOUR WORK

We routinely see couples together and separately during every session. As this is routine, they come to expect it. So, too, with stories. Most people who are approached gradually and respectfully will be receptive to a story at the end of the session. We explain to clients at the outset that one of the things we do is tell them stories. It is framed as part of our *helping them*, which they then understand and appreciate.

Seeding can be especially helpful here. Seeding will be addressed in detail more later, but for now, simply regard it as introducing, or hinting at, an idea early in the session, and then activating the "seed" later. For example, if we intend to address *slowing down* later in the hour, we may seed the idea first, by mentioning how traffic was *slow* as we drove into work today. If we intend to tell a story later on, we may seed the word "story" into discussion at the beginning. At the end of the session, we may test the client's hypnoidal response with an anecdote or story, something like, "Let me share with you a little *story* about someone else who was here one time. . . ." We will emphasize the word *story* even though it is an anecdote we are relating, because *story* is a hypnotic word, like *wonder, explore,* or *discover.* We shift our vocal emphasis when we say it, drawing it out just a bit. This usually arrests attention, much like when the mini-blinds are yanked open, or the light switch is turned on. It is then that an unconscious search begins.

Nonverbal responses like *eye fixation* or *facial mask* may accompany this arrested attention, or *response attentiveness*. A major shift has occurred, and communication has now changed dramatically. You are speaking to their unconscious, and they are listening with their third ear. It is precisely *now* when you want to begin your story.

Choosing a Story

"The Three Lessons" (Wallas, 1985) is a good one at the beginning of therapy. It sets the stage for subsequent sessions, as its meta-message is that clients have what it takes within themselves to improve or change, and the therapist is a guide in this process. However, with many clients, especially those who show a marked hypnoidal response, we may wish to further foster the unconscious search with a less didactic story, such as "The Turtle."

The Turtle

Turtles didn't always have a shell. At one time, long, long ago, the turtle was just another soft-bodied animal that lived in a different kind of house. One day, all the animals in the animal kingdom decided to throw a feast for the gods to thank them for their good fortune. All the animals came to the feast to celebrate—all but the turtle, who chose to stay at home.

It was a grand party and there was a host of exotic and tantalizing foods at the banquet table. About an hour into the event, the gods, who were most appreciative, announced that they would grant each animal a special wish. This made all the animals very, very happy.

On the way home, one animal stopped by the turtle's house and asked him why he didn't attend the party. The turtle, who did not mince words, stated that he never attended parties, and that he simply preferred to stay at home. However, when the turtle learned that the gods had granted one special wish to all the other animals, the turtle hurried as best he could over to the banquet hall and asked the gods if he, too, could be granted one special wish.

The turtle said, "Please grant me speed because I am such a slow-moving animal." The gods then asked him why he didn't attend the party and the turtle answered, "Because I like to be at home."

The gods then gave the turtle a hard shell on his back so he could always be at home wherever he was. And that's how the turtle got his shell.

CLINICAL COMMENTS

"The Turtle" is one of our multipurpose stories, in that we have used it to promote acceptance of one's life decisions, or problems; to be "at home" with one's self, and, as used with this client, to stimulate wonderment, or *unconscious search*. This is one of many stories in which clients find their own meaning. Of course, we end the session with the story, and if clients have questions or comments about it, we say, "Let's talk about it next time." We also usually explain our purpose for not discussing it, with something like, "We really believe that this story can best help you if your unconscious mind mulls it over between now and next time, kind of like when you watch a movie alone and then go to bed without discussing it with anyone. You get to 'sleep on it,' and who knows what a person's unconscious mind can accomplish without conscious interference?"

The final moments of a first session are critical. Sometimes clients will derail us and drop a bombshell at the end, tossing out critical information or some new problem before they go out the door. This can cause the session to end feeling incomplete, or worse, on a sour note. Sometimes this is hard to avoid; however, one way to head this off is to elicit near the end of the session a hypnoidal response, and then launch into a short story. The effect on the client will be very much like a strong reframe, and they will leave feeling understood, and hopeful about the future.

Of course, these techniques are designed as a complement to cognitive-behavioral therapy (CBT) and other standard psychotherapies. We may tell the turtle story, wait a few seconds for them to absorb it, and then assign a first-session task that is general and doable, such as, "Do one thing different," or, "Don't do anything different." It is very tempting to offer a concrete directive at the end of the first session, as we may feel obligated to tell people what to do, plus, many clients may be looking for some concrete guidance. And for sure, with certain clients you *will* assign homework, such as "Complete this inventory," or "Walk around the block with your wife every evening."

A general rule of thumb is: If you encounter high reactance, go slow. Clients who are ambivalent or reluctant about therapy—and they will communicate this loudly, especially nonverbally—are communicating to us that they want to go slow. As therapists, we are trained to recognize deficits, and, being eager to help, we often rush in to fill the void. If we tell them what to do, and then they don't do it, we have a problem. Or worse, they won't come back at all. Put yourself in their place: If you went to a therapist, and she told you what to do before you trusted her, would you strive to do it? One way to respect—and embrace—this reluctance is by *not* telling them what to do too early.

We encourage interns to come up with their own resources to help them through anxious moments in therapy. One person said that as she began a story in therapy, her left eye started to twitch wildly. She slowed down her breathing, which calmed the twitching eye. Another imagined a warm bubble bath, while another said, "I think about giving my dog Bosco a dog biscuit out next to the oleanders." A relaxing breath, thinking of a calming scene—whatever it is, it can be immediately implemented without diverting attention from the client.

4

Mindfulness-Based Group Anger Treatment

THE ANGRY CLIENT

Most clients' angry feelings will disappear to some degree with appropriate treatment, or with the passage of time. Afterall, we may have very good reasons for feeling the way we do, as anger is a very natural response to unhappiness, loss, and perceived unfairness. However, people who typically attend anger groups do not present with *that* kind of anger, do they? Instead, we are likely to see clients who exhibit the slow burn of chronic depression or posttraumatic stress disorder (PTSD), the explosiveness of an unsatisfying relationship, or the simmering anger of the adjustment to illness or disability, to name a few. Some personality-disordered people have a hostility toward the world around them. Other clients may defy classification and present with a core negativity and self-loathing that has no apparent etiology. How many times has this shameful anger, a toxic and defining characteristic of the individual, sent shock waves of discouragement through us as therapists one minute into the first session of therapy?

TREATING ANGER IN GROUPS

At the Veterans Affairs Medical Center in Tucson, Arizona, we developed mindfulness-based anger treatment (MBAT) in order to treat pervasive anger. However, we did not start out treating anger that way. When I (G. G.) began my clinical practice in the early 1970s, psychodynamic therapy was giving way to behavior therapy, and this school of thought guided my thinking and practice for a number of years. In the 1980s, cognition was added to behavior therapy, and by then a host of different treatment approaches were available. I first heard of the work of Milton H. Erickson in the late 1970s, but half a decade would pass before I began to study hypnosis. It was then that Milton Erickson's work took on new meaning. Like many people, I was swept along in the tide of cognitive-behavioral, solution-focused, and brief therapies of the day. By the 1990s, managed care was a sacred watchword, and the brief therapies were emphasized even more so.

However, these approaches seemed overly pro forma and mechanistic, lacking in heart or spirit. More importantly, they were often ineffective and offered little versatility, especially with the long-term problems of difficult clients whose world was made up more of feeling than of thought. Many therapists searched for a better way, one that would both connect with the "humanness" of people and cause a fundamental change in behavior; and if not a *change* per se, an acceptance, or *reframing*, of thorny and seemingly intractable problems.

As a family therapist and practitioner of hypnosis, I came to appreciate the benefits of systemic therapy and indirect or unconsciously directed techniques, especially those begun by Erickson. These techniques eventually worked their way into our group anger treatment, buttressing traditional cognitive-behavioral techniques such as anger rehearsal, time-out, communication skills training, and the use of the anger log.

Clients learned new skills to control anger, which were reinforced unconsciously by therapeutic stories and hypnotic language. However, this blending of techniques only took them half-way down the road toward wholeness and healing. Clients—many of whom had previously experienced traditional group anger treatment—told us they appreciated this more gentle approach, but at the same time communicated that something was missing.

Shauna Shapiro introduced me to mindfulness-based psychology when she was a psychology extern in Tucson in the late 1990s. In another job, she had provided group mindfulness treatment to breast cancer survivors, and at the Veterans' Administration, she successfully applied these principles and techniques to a group of men suffering from tinnitus. We soon added mindfulness to our group anger treatment. Immediately we realized we had found the missing element that would add quality to the lives of anger clients. By adding principles such as acceptance, letting go, and nonjudging to our repertoire of cognitive-behavioral therapy and Ericksonian techniques, we realized that we had a program that could connect meaningfully and realistically with these chronically angry clients.

MINDFULNESS PSYCHOLOGY

Wellness and healing are central to the work of two prominent mindfulness advocates, Kabat-Zinn (1990), and Rosenbaum, author of *Zen and the Heart of Psychotherapy* (1999). Kabat-Zinn gained reknown with his stress clinic at the University of Massachusetts Medical Center, where patients with medical problems learned to successfully manage the stress of their illness through meditation and the application of mindfulness principles. Like Kabat-Zinn, Rosenbaum is an advocate of Zen meditation. Both are strong advocates of a mindfulness worldview that embraces such principles as happiness, acceptance, patience, and letting go.

There is evidence that mindfulness-based stress reduction is effective in treating generalized anxiety disorder and panic (Kabat-Zinn et al., 1992), and chronic pain (Kabat-Zinn, Lipworth, Burney, & Sellers, 1986). Mindfulness-based cognitive therapy has been successfully applied to clients with recurrent depression. Teasdale and colleagues (2000) found that a combination of cognitive-behavioral therapy (CBT) techniques and components of Kabat-Zinn's mindfulness stress-reduction program, helped clients disengage from ruminative, depressive processing, thus preventing the relapse of depression. Unlike conventional CBT, there is little emphasis on changing the content of thoughts. Instead, the emphasis is on changing the awareness of and relationship to depressogenic thoughts. Clients are taught a decentered, detached perspective—e.g., thoughts are not facts, or, "I am not my thoughts."

MINDFULNESS PRINCIPLES

In traditional group anger treatment, as well as in conventional psychotherapy, principles such as patience and acceptance are seldom addressed. In MBAT, we address them with open discussion, but we first present them metaphorically in a story. The process is unconsciously directed, in part, and we believe that this *indirect* approach helps clients be more receptive to mindfulness principles, as well as to CBT-type techniques, which are *direct* and consciously applied.

Such "gift wrapping" (Jeffrey Zeig, personal communication, April 5, 1999) in metaphor and the language of hypnosis has led us to think of a metaphor to describe MBAT. I (G. G.) like the metaphor of a golf ball. The hard cover is the CBT techniques; the tightly wound rubber bands underneath, which allow the ball to be driven far, represent metaphor and Erickson; and the small, liquid-filled ball at the center—the nerve center and heart—represents mindfulness.

One intern who worked with me as a cotherapist in the anger group, quickly told me that this metaphor might not be apt, since the construction of many modern golf balls is more complicated. "Golf balls are made in various ways these days," she said. "And where one part starts and the other ends is less distinct." She suggested instead the metaphor of the saguaro cactus. It has spines and a tough coat, which represent CBT. Inside are the strong wooden ribs and hard pulp, which represent mindfulness principles. Erickson and metaphor, then, would be represented by the cactus roots.

However, the roots of a saguaro are shallow, so this would not suffice for something as profound as Erickson. Alice Arrington and Chris Young, anger group cotherapists, asked why we invariably lean toward masculine metaphors, such as sports, cars, and trees. Why not a wave on the beach, or the wind, or something enduring, like love or family, something that connotes flexibility or adaptability? I just wish saguaros had deeper roots.

SEEDING

An intervention in psychotherapy is more likely to be successful if it is *seeded* ahead of time. "Seeded?" You may ask. Yes, most definitely. (We're not farmers, though one of us is a better gardener than the other.) Nevertheless, we both sow seeds with enthusiasm in our practices. There is no empirical support in the psychotherapy literature for seeding, but from experience we know that this technique, more than any other, ensures the success of a directive, suggestion, or intervention.

The origins of seeding are old, as evidenced by foreshadowing in literature, film, theater, and music. In all of these medias, a theme might be alluded to early in the piece, then developed later on. We have all seen a movie in which a dark cloud descends, or perhaps a vulture hovers nearby, and from these portentous events we sense that something serious is afoot. Dark clouds and vultures will noticeabley arouse our conscious awareness. Less obvious in a film might be a subtle shift in the soundtrack, which might pace the movement of events and heighten the viewer's mental and emotional absorption. In psychotherapy, seeding is even more subtle than a film soundtrack. By design, it is well outside the client's awareness.

Haley first mentioned "seeding ideas" in *Uncommon Therapy* (1973). Geary (1989, 1994) employed seeding in the group treatment of clients with depression, as well as in hypnosis, describing how the utilization phase of a session can be seeded ahead of time. He clarifies the distinction between suggestion and seeding, in that with seeding, there is always follow-up. *Priming* in experimental psychology is similar to seeding. In research on priming, lexical decision making, word completion, and problem solving, all improved with priming, which is defined as "the activation, or change in accessibility, of a concept by an earlier presentation of the same or a closely related concept" (Zeig, 1990 p. 223). An example from social psychology helps to illustrate this process. Groups of students were shown various word pairs prior to their selecting a brand of laundry detergent. Those who were shown "ocean–moon" more readily selected Tide.

Seeding is the clinical application of priming, in which the therapist has a target in mind, but before activating it, she offers hints about the target. For example, your client is depressed and you intend to introduce behavioral activation, such as going for a walk twice a week. Therefore, early in the session you mention the word *active*, or *activity*, in a divergent context. This seeds your target, which you will mention later on.

If you have an anxious client, and plan to tell a story about *slowing down*, or if you intend to assign a task that involves slowing down, seeding could happen in a number of ways: mentioning that the traffic coming into town today was rather *slow*; that you feel *slow* getting going today; or, nonverbally, *slowing* down your breathing, or *slowly* rising from your chair to get something from your desk.

Now, this takes a bit of planning, doesn't it? You know the therapeutic direction, and a few moments of preparation can help pave the way. Like stories, anecdotes, and hypnotic language, you will develop some stock seeds that you can adroitly sow on a regular basis. Don't overdo the seeding. The law of parsimony applies in all things hypnotic: do only enough to achieve the desired effect. In most cases, two or three seeds spaced out over time should adequately till the soil before you activate the target.

SEEDING A MINDFULNESS PRINCIPLE IN THE GROUP

Let's assume this is the third meeting of the group, and last meeting we ended the session with the "Beginner's Mind" story. (This and other stories used in the group are appended at the end of this chapter.) Participants are usually eager to discuss last week's story. They might explain the story's meaning as, "We should try to keep an open mind"; or others may liken the meta-message to permitting openness, or receptivity, to new experiences. One client usually asks what an open mind has to do with anger, and another might remind him that anger has caused him problems for many years and it is time he tried something different.

We then seed the principle that is to be "gift-wrapped" in the story at the end of the session, nearly 90 minutes away. The target in this session is "to see things differently," a capacity often lacking in the group participants. The seeding that follows is designed to set up the "Seeing Things Differently" story that we tell at the conclusion of the session.

This is our third meeting. *Each time we've begun as* close to 2:00 *as possible, and we have six meetings to go after today. You* may have begun to see *how each week we cover one or two things that are* new, *and also review a few things that are* old. *In fact, Kyle, Katharine, and I were talking just the other day, and sharing our* different views and perspectives. *Kyle said, "I* see *us going over the anger log after the break." Katharine came at it from* another point of view.

Katharine doesn't wear eyeglasses, unlike Kyle and me, so we tell her we will try to see things *through the same lens, though in reality, we have* four different lenses *on* two different sets of eyeglasses. *It might be* six distinct lenses *if Katharine wears contacts, but she's never said whether or not she uses any kind of eyewear. But first, let's review the time-out technique.*

truisms

implication

seeding

seeding

THE ANCHOR

A major tool in hypnosis, as well as in group anger treatment, is the *anchor.* We introduce this concept during the first session, and present it as "a reminder, something you have with you at all times." Discussion of the anchor shifts the responsibility for anger manage- ment to the individual, something new for some participants, who may have perceived the problem as a global external stressor, for example, "all those people out there who keep pissing me off."

We offer examples of stressors chosen by other people in previous anger groups, for example, "Some have selected a circle, gently moving their pointer finger and thumb together in the form of a circle," and emphasize that they need to generate their own anchor. A naturally occurring anchor for angry people might be a fist, which we discourage. Others might reach for a polished stone that they carry in their pocket. Some might have a coin stamped "6 months of sobriety," which they received at an Alcoholics Anonymous meeting, or, as one man did once, carry with them a beer bottle cap. Others might choose to take a deep breath, while still others might choose a thought, or a memory, such as "when I was walking along the beach. . . ." With anchors, as well as time-outs, participants help themselves with many useful suggestions.

THE TIME-OUT

In each session we review this technique, since it is perhaps the most important consciously directed tool that participants can take from the class. One woman, who had been a nurse in the army during the Vietnam War, related the successful application of time-out during the past week. She reported that she had been driving fast in her pickup truck on a desert road outside of Tucson, and a buzzard flew into her truck, damaging the windshield and a mirror. "I just pulled off the road and took a time-out," she said. The time-out she had selected was two deep breaths.

A man reported that someone gave him the finger in traffic. This immediately rivetted the attention of the group, as becoming angry in traffic is something to which the group readily relates. "What did you do?" someone asked. "Well, I *didn't* give him the finger back, and I *didn't* lay on the horn," the man answered. Instead, he used his anchor. He noted that he had yet to find an anchor to use when not in his car. However, in his car he has a bright yellow Happy Face glued to the dashboard. "I just look at that Happy Face, and that helps me," he said. Others in the group reported using similar anchors, such as a rosary hanging from the rearview mirror. A woman in the group stated, "I just shoot them," referring to a button marked "machine gun" on the dashboard of her car. We discourage ideas that hint at aggression or violence; however, over the years we have seen many who have successfully employed a fist, or something akin to the machine gun button, as an anchor. Some people, in the heat of anger, may confuse, or blend together, time-out and anchor. However, if it helps them get through a tough situation, we always support their efforts.

For many of these clients, taking a time-out successfully represents major progress. However, partners in relationships might see this as a cop-out, or an excuse to avoid problem solving. In anger involving loved ones, we instruct participants to tell the partner when they intend to return from their time-out, to avoid leaving the partner hanging. Used in this way, the time-out may be an important aid. However, many of these clients require relational therapy in addition to the anger group.

We also provide participants with a handout entitled "A Variety of Time-Outs." They are:

> *Physical time-out:* "I'm taking a time-out. I'll be back in five minutes."
>
> *Mental time-out:* Say to yourself, for example, "I'm going, in my mind, to that lake in the mountains . . . or to that walk along the beach . . .".
>
> *Self-talk time-out:* One man, while taking a series of deep breaths, thought to himself, "Time-out . . . time-out" over and over again. Another, in her mind said, "I can get through this . . . I can get through this."
>
> *Creative time-out:* "I'll wait until the next song on the radio is over before I say or do anything."
>
> *Imaginative time-out:* The type of time-out that surfaces when you least expect it.

COMPOSITION OF THE GROUPS

This group has been very popular among clients. We screen out people with pronounced hearing loss, florid substance abuse, uncontrolled psychosis, people who have been court-ordered for domestic violence, and anyone else who we think could not be a meaningful participant. We typically interview 25 potential clients, receive commitments to attend from 16, and end up with 9 to 12 who consistently attend the nine-week program.

Clients in the group are men and women from all walks of life. Some are retired and World War II veterans, while others may be in their twenties or attending college. They tend to share service in the U.S. military. They are referred from all areas of the medical center, and many are self-referred, for example, "My wife said I have to do something about my anger."

The rules are as follows:

1. They can miss one class, but must be present at the first and last meetings
2. There will be no threats
3. Confidentiality must be honored
4. We reserve the right to interrupt anyone in order to get back on course, and
5. If at any time someone feels they must leave the room, they may do so, and one of us will follow them to see if they are okay.

ANGER AS A DEFINING FEATURE

In your own practice, you may have people who seem pervasively angry, as if anger is the defining emotion to which they cling, much like a security blanket. These people, in their dysfunctional mode of operating in the world, might wear their anger like a badge. Some veterans may have had this angry persona buttressed by their military experience, and even years following their time in the service, they feel markedly different from those who did not serve in the armed forces. As such, they might feel rightfully entitled to their anger.

We remind interns of the sobering fact that veterans all learned how to kill, and many in fact have done so in wartime. When faced by a perceived threat, some may automatically revert to "combat mode," as this may have saved their life during war. This dysfunctional posture may be incomprehensible to those of us who have never experienced killing. Some say, "When someone gets in my face, I feel trapped, and I want to lash out." When faced by things that others would find innocuous or even mildly annoying, such as a slow driver in front of them, a rude clerk in a store, or a mouthy teenaged daughter, they might automatically think, "They're trying to screw me!" For some, this reactivity is life-long, and has caused them myriad problems in life. When we examine the roots of such frustration and negativity, military experience might play a role, or personality disorder might be present.

More common is shame: a core humiliation based in poverty or neglect or other unhappiness during childhood. Subsequent military service and life events might have exacerbated and compounded the lack of success. Many might have been buoyed by a good job or a nurturing spouse; however, a dominant and defining feature has remained: their anger. They may have incorporated the negative and hopeless persona of "angry person." To date, some may have mastered only one useful technique: to walk away when they begin to feel angry.

EMBRACING WHO THEY ARE

These clients have all had bosses or spouses tell them they should be different. Some have been through authoritarian anger or domestic violence classes, in which they have been plied with CBT principles that fail to connect with them as feeling people. Accordingly, a realistic way to approach such a presentation is to regard it as worthy of respect, and recognizing that it may have served a useful purpose at one time. We let them know that no one is trying to make them a different person, but that angry acting-out is something that *can* change slowly, gradually and progressively, if only they will suspend judgment for nine weeks and be open to some new ideas. Here enters metaphor. For example: the sturdy wall. We might say, "No one wants to bulldoze a hole through your wall, but during the course of this class, maybe you'll be receptive to loosening a brick here, or some mortar there. . . ."

THE "COVERT THERAPIST"

Once I (S. B.) was in the audience at a musical performance when the performers up on stage stopped playing. It was not clear if the piece was finished. There was an awkward silence, and when *one person clapped,* suddenly applause broke out and rippled through the entire audience.

In our groups, we have the equivalent of that one person who clapped. We will call him Harold. He has chronic PTSD, occasionally drinks excessively, and he is bright and articulate. Most of all, he is *one of them.* When he volunteers an example from his anger log, others pay attention, and usually follow suit with their own examples. When Harold says, "I like those stories you tell," the others seem to pay close attention the next time we tell a story.

We have done groups both with and without such a confederate, and we see many advantages to having his assistance. He is not called a therapist, he is not in on planning the day's agenda, he does not meet with us to debrief at the end of a group, and he receives no special recognition. We let him know that we appreciate his instigative skills and overall ability to communicate with others. He enjoys helping us, and he likes helping others in the group; but most of all, his regular attendance and participation helps him keep his own anger in check. At the end of the nine weeks, he receives a certificate of completion and a laminated card that contains key principles and techniques, just like the other group members. They carry this card in their wallets, and some have even used it as an anchor.

Now, the word on Harold is probably out among the other clients. Others may have noticed the number of laminated cards he has. He may even tell them he is our cotherapist, but we do not care. His role is important to him, and he is darn good at what he does. We appreciate his help.

OTHER ASPECTS OF THE GROUP

Along with hypnotic language and mindfulness principles conveyed via story, as well as the anger log and anchor, we teach them about the passive-assertive-aggressive continuum of behavior, and we employ role rehearsal with videotaped playback to teach communication and problem-solving skills. In such role-play, the cotherapist, or one of the woman interns will provoke the client, escalating his anger until he escapes through the use of his anchor, or by announcing, "I need a time-out." By the end of the class, many learn to assertively express how they feel. Some may progress only to the point of saying, "I'm going to take a time-out. I'll be back in five minutes," when faced by a demanding spouse. This is a far cry from resentfully stalking away and silently steaming without resolution, or punching the door. By the end of the class, some of these participants may have a new view of their role, as well as their partner's, in angry interactions. When we help them plan for the future during the last session, some might for the first time agree to marital therapy.

Clients complete the Trait Anger Scale (Spielberger, Jacobs, Russell, & Crane, 1983) in the first session and repeat it in the last session. On this measure, which targets attitudinal change, clients have shown improvement. The scale asks questions such as, "Am I quick-tempered?", "When I get mad, do I say nasty things?"

CLINICAL COMMENTS

In this chapter we avoided a detailed discussion of CBT techniques with domestic violence, which are covered in other books, such as Wexler's *Domestic Violence 2000* (2000). Although there is much cross-over in anger treatment and domestic violence treatment, our MBAT does not address domestic violence. People who are mandated to complete such a group are guided to other programs.

A cornerstone of mindfulness is meditation, which we do not employ. We do address deep breathing and mention the benefits of meditation, and offer suggestions of where they can go to learn the technique. As we tell our stories, some participants will go into trance, as evidenced by fixed attention, facial mask, and other indicators of trance. Hypnotic language and seeding are vital in setting up such receptivity to suggestion. In terms of seeding, some have asked us how we as therapists can "get into" seeding *slowness*, for example, in an anger group filled with a dozen resistant, highly charged individuals. I (G. G.) think of pouring molasses, or even the phrase, "slower than molasses in January," as I embed *slow* in the seeding.

That image does not work for me (S. B.), as I cannot imagine any seed sprouting in thick molasses. Instead, I think of slow-running tap water, and in recent years I have tried to incorporate bottled water into this image, although pouring water from a plastic bottle is never as *slow*, steady, or regular as the tap in my kitchen.

In mindfulness-based anger treatment we use the "Balloons" and "Three Lessons" stories, along with the "African Violets" story, which stimulates unconscious search for solutions. Its meta-message is that with assistance, there is hope, even for longstanding problems. African Violets is included with the following stories in which mindfulness principles are embedded.

Beginner's Mind

I was talking to someone once who said that what we know is the problem. I said, "What do you mean by that?" And she said, "What we *know* prevents us from seeing things as they really are. Let me give you an example."

There was this old blind man, a patient, in one of the units at the V.A. hospital. He could hardly see at all, but his hearing was good. Two days in a row he heard a young doctor talking rudely about a homeless patient. The doctor said, "Why should we bother helping that guy? He's just going to leave here and throw it all away, go back to drinking and living under the bridge. Those people are all alike."

That afternoon, before the doctor was to leave for the day, the old vet got to speak with him. He asked him, "Doctor, you see, don't you?"

"Quite obviously," answered the doctor.

"And also, you *know*, don't you, doctor?"

"Of course I know. Afterall, I am a doctor."

The old man continued, "Then you also must know that you don't see with the beginner's mind."

"You're talking in riddles, old man. I don't know what you mean by 'beginner's mind.' That's nonsense."

But as the days passed, the term "beginner's mind" kept repeating in the doctor's head. Finally, the doctor returned to the old man and asked him what he meant.

The old man told him about the homeless vet, and how there was really much more to him, much more to know. "It's like you only turned the first page of the book," said the old man.

Thereafter, the doctor thought more and more about the beginner's mind.

Making Exceptions

I saw a person one time in therapy (let's call her Sharon) and she talked about all the things in life she had come to *accept*, and as she talked, the whole idea of *acceptance* came to take on a whole new meaning.

She said she often daydreamed, just kind of drifted off, and during these times, she dreamed and drifted, drifted and dreamed, lost in thought and pleasant memories, contemplating this and that, and most of all, she thought about what her brother had told her about *acceptance*, long, long ago. She wasn't sure if she could remember his exact words, or if she could imagine them in her mind or picture them in her memory, or whether it was simply a matter of wondering about the situation way back then and just pausing . . . allowing the words to eventually come to her lips.

She had asked her brother, "Is receiving the same as *accepting*?" He answered, "You mean, like when I was in high school and was a receiver on the football team?"

"Of course not, Billy," she scolded.

"I'm Bill, not Billy. People don't call me Billy anymore," he said.

She nodded her head and just listened as he told her about when they were very young and *accepted* food on a spoon, or a drink of milk, and how people continue *accepting* things all their life.

Bill said, "Sharon, I remember your first day of school. You were afraid, but you went anyway, and eventually *accepted* it."

"But I didn't *like* it," she answered.

"Well, that's neither here nor there," he told her. "You did better in school than I did, starting with the first grade, and especially later on."

"But I didn't *like* it," she let him know.

"But you *accepted* it," her brother responded, and she had to agree with him.

Sharon suddenly had a thought, and the words came out fast. "Remember when you were just a little kid, playing in that baseball game, and you thought you scored the winning run, but the umpire called you out? Everybody *knew* you were really safe," she said.

"That was awful," said Bill. "I'll never forget it."

"But you eventually came to *accept* it," said his sister.

"I suppose so," answered Bill.

Bill went on. "I guess the main thing is that you do many things, and other people do many things, and with the passage of time, people can choose whether or not to *accept* those things."

Sharon answered, "I think I'm beginning to see what you mean. It's kind of like waking up from a dream, and when you wake up, you can't remember the dream, or only a small part of it."

"Yes, sort of like that, with only a few exceptions," said Bill.

"Well, maybe some day you'll just forget to remember all those things," said Sharon.

Bill said, "No, I won't ever forget those things." Then Sharon followed with, "Maybe then you'll remember to forget, Bill."

Bill looked confused, and after several moments said, "No, the main thing is that I see it all a bit differently, and now I just *accept* those things."

Sharon continued to show up for appointments for several weeks, and was always on time, with only one exception.

Seeing Things Differently

Someone was telling me once about how he learned to see things differently with the passage of both time and distance.

It was the Fourth of July and he found himself on a boat that was slowly going farther and farther out into the water. It was 3:00 p.m., and he watched various activities on the beach, things that he could see quite clearly, in fairly vivid detail.

There was a lifeguard perched way up on the lifeguard chair. He had one of those floppy hats on his head, and mirrored sunglasses, and that white stuff on his nose shone brightly in the sun. A volleyball game was going on, off to the right of the lifeguard chair. All around, people lay on blankets, and the sunscreen on their bodies glistened in the heat of the day. An oversized red umbrella stood out like a crimson flower blossom. Children splashed in the water, and he could hear their gleeful cries above the crash of the waves.

Everything became a bit blurry as the boat got farther from the shore; however, as a telescope was mounted on the back of the boat, he began to watch everything through the telescope, which all of a sudden brought the beach back into sharp focus. The boat continued its journey, out from the shore.

As time passed, the details of the beach through the telescope kept changing, ever so gradually. He could see that the volleyball players were still in motion, but he could no longer see the ball. People continued to splash in the water, but he could no longer hear their voices. They may have been children, but they could have just as easily been adults. The lifeguard was still perched on high, but there was no white on his nose. The oversized umbrella was now orange, or was it brown? He stepped back from the telescope, closed his eyes, and contemplated what he had seen.

Several minutes later—or maybe it was longer than several minutes—the sun had descended, and it was not quite as warm on his back as before. He put his eye to the telescope once again, and everything before him took on a most curious aspect. The lifeguard chair remained prominent, but he could not tell for sure if a person was still sitting on it. The volleyball game appeared to have stopped, just as people may have ceased lying on the sand. He saw only flickers of movement in the water where the children had been playing, and was it the umbrella that was buffeted by a gust of wind? The only sound was the boat's motor. He closed his eyes again and let his imagination drift and dream.

A while later, the sun had sunk farther down in the sky, and as he put his eye to the telescope once again, the sight before him had become only sea and shore in the distance, water and coastline, as the boat continued out.

Later on in life, he continued to experience many things, with time and distance in between, seeing them one way, and then another, and often he reflected on that journey out from the shore.

Trust and in the Moment

An old man, somebody's grandfather, told this story once, a story about Manny, who grew up on the west side of Tucson after World War II, in the 1950s and 60s. He had done many things in his life, but he said that he continued to be troubled by something that a teacher in college had told him. "I can't get it out of my mind," he said. "Do you mean you ruminate about it?" I asked him. "Yes, it's like a tape recorder that doesn't shut off, it keeps going and going," he answered.

The class in college had to do with some sort of Eastern philosophy, and they talked about such things as time, the concept of time, time being circular, like a wheel, instead of in a straight line, like one year leading to the next year. "I understood the thing about time," said Manny, but I didn't understand what they meant by being "in the moment."

"In the moment?" I asked. "You got it," said Manny. "'In the moment'. In fact, the teacher said to me, 'Manny, once you are able to trust, then you'll understand 'being in the moment.' That's what keeps going around and around in my head. I know the teacher didn't mean living *for* the moment, but *in* the moment, whatever that means."

As he talked, I thought to myself about "being in the moment." To me, it meant living moment to moment, trusting your own experience, paying attention to your mind and your body from moment to moment, rather than worrying about the past or the future.

Manny was so preoccupied by this that he was distracted, and people saw him as spacey, or at least self-absorbed. He had difficulty keeping track of time, and sometimes he was late. To remedy this, he started a collection of timepieces, everything from grandfather clocks to hourglasses, wrist watches with hands that moved slowly, and digital clocks on whose faces the seconds and minutes and hours seemed to whirr by at dizzying speed. His wife told him, "Manny, I wish I could trust you to be on time," so he bought a heavy pocket watch at the second-hand store, but lost it somewhere between the convenience store and home.

Manny worked briefly selling time deposits at Northern Trust, bought a subscription to *Time* magazine, listened nearly every waking moment to Credence Clearwater Revival tapes, counselled trustees at the state prison, contemplated the afterlife for what seemed to be an eternity (or at least a lifetime), and even grew a long beard so people could call him Father Time. However, nothing really changed until one day, while attending a men's awareness group, he stood in a circle of people, and they said, "Just fall backward, Manny, we'll catch you."

He closed his eyes, took one deep breath, and as he fell back and they caught him, he heard, in his head, the gong of his Grandfather Clock, and suddenly everything was perfectly clear.

On Patience

A man once told me a story, and most of it was a rather pleasant story, and as I listened, my mind drifted off, and fortunately I wrote down the essence of it afterward.

His name was Eddie, and he was an *inpatient* at the hospital at one time, and as he had a lot of time on his hands, he was able to imagine one thing, and then another, and on the unit the minutes just blended into hours, and he otherwise simply lost track of time. Nevertheless, Eddie constantly thought about a couple years earlier when he had a job at a floral shop.

His job at the floral shop involved a lot of hard work, which he didn't mind, as he was always in the midst of beautiful and fragrant flowers of all kinds—roses, carnations, and chrysanthemums, as well as a lot of *impatiens*, which really got on his nerves because they required special attention.

One day, Eddie lost his temper with a tray of *impatiens*, and his boss took him aside and said, "Eddie, when I was young, many years ago, I remember, in the backyard, there was a butterfly that was struggling to emerge from its cocoon. Being a curious and helpful young boy, I was about to break it open, so the butterfly could emerge faster, but my uncle said, 'Take it easy, son. Just let it emerge on its own.'"

"Now, Eddie, I hadn't thought about that butterfly all these years. It may or may not have anything to do with you; however, watching you work with that tray of *impatiens*, it really got me thinking."

Non-Judging

Someone told me once about his job as a judge at the county fair. There he was, in the cattle barn, and he easily became lost in the swirl of colors, odors, and excitement. There was a lot of pressure on the judges, as competition was stiff, and everyone thought they deserved to win the top prize.

When it came time to judge, all he would say was, "That's good" or "That's bad." The head judge angrily took him aside and said, "You can't say just good or bad! You have to follow the rating system."

"But I can't," the man answered. "Everything's either good or bad. That's how I see things."

"But there's a wide range of neutral in between," countered the head judge. "That's where the rating system comes in."

"But, then, are you telling me I can no longer be a judge?" the man asked.

"No, just think of what's neutral."

"Then I'd be a non-judge."

"No, you'd still be a judge, but you wouldn't be so judgmental," said the head judge.

Forever after, the man did his job much better. Without any conscious effort, he began to notice the wide range of neutral, both in the cattle barn, while driving his truck, and even at home.

African Violets

There was this famous doctor in Phoenix years ago, Milton Erickson, and he was asked to visit a depressed woman who would not leave her house. This Dr. Erickson was very observant as the woman showed him around her big, dark house. She talked about how she hadn't been to church for years but she liked the people there. "Nice people there," she commented.

The house was very dark except for one room in the back of the house. In that room, some light was coming through the window, and next to the window was a table with African violets—beautiful, magnificent violets thriving there on that table.

The woman perked up a bit as she talked with pride about her violets. Then she led Erickson back through the dark house. As he bid her farewell, Erickson commented, "I can just imagine . . . how some of those people in your church *might appreciate your lovely violets.*" And then he left, and he never saw her again.

Months later Erickson heard that the woman was doing much better. For some reason, she began to grow more violets. First she set some new violets by one window and opened the curtain, and then she did the same with more violets and other windows, and pretty soon every window in the house had violets. Many people at church ended up with her violets.

5

Ego-Strengthening

Before we get into ego-strengthening, we would like to relate a little story that we adapted from Rosen (1982). Milton Erickson mentioned one time that he had been accused of *manipulating* patients, to which he responded that *manipulation* is very much a part of everyday life. He noted that parents *manipulate* their children if they want them to live. They use *manipulation* in feeding and keeping their children healthy and safe. Children are subsequently *manipulated* in learning to walk and to use the potty. The first day of kindergarten, children are *manipulated* to attend.

As children learn to write, *manipulation* is applied to teach them to use a pencil. As they become adults, they go to a store and *manipulate* the clerk to do their bidding. They go on to *manipulate* their spouse to write a check for the car payment, and people even *manipulate* themselves, carrying around Life Savers, chewing gum, or cigarettes. They may even *manipulate* themselves after reading a book by Aaron Beck or Albert Ellis, as they practice thought stopping or recording their negative thoughts. Erickson emphasized the *final manipulation*, which is the really big one. Which occurs when you die and they lower your coffin into the ground. Our hope is that beginning *now*, all thoughts of manipulation will be put to rest—or at least put on hold for a few more chapters, or until you visit the chiropractor.

NOT THE FIRST "RABBIT HUNT"

During an initial session, I (S. B.) was taking a history, and when I asked about previous mental health treatment, the 50-year-old man replied, "You know, this isn't the first rabbit hunt." I was taken aback, as shooting rabbits is distasteful to me. The man delineated his years of unsuccessful psychotherapy, which included hypnosis (which he disliked); eye movement desensitization and reprocessing (EMDR); gestalt therapy and bioenergetics therapy; two courses of electrocon-vulsive therapy; and various trials of medications. It was painfully obvious why he had chosen the rabbit hunt metaphor.

Many of the people we see in our practices—with mood, anxiety, or adjustment disorders—could offer similar metaphors for failed attempts at therapy. These people are rightfully discouraged, and are understandably none too eager to begin yet another rabbit hunt with a new therapist. These people need hope that this course of therapy will offer them relief from suffering. If all we can offer them is another round of cognitive-behavioral therapy (CBT), we can under-stand why they decline the offer.

INTRODUCING EGO-STRENGTHENING

In addition to not desiring "more of the same," many clients may be reluctant to cover the same ground in therapy, especially if it means re-opening old wounds, as seen in chronic postraumatic stress disorder. Many of these clients' interests may be piqued if we tell them that our first order of business is ego-strengthening, not tradi-tional therapy.

"Ego-strengthening?" asks Mr. Rabbit Hunt. "Yes, indeed," I (S. B.) say, then go on to explain how some discouraged clients may benefit from conventional therapy if they *first* undergo a "mental strength-ening." "Mental strengthening?" he asks, suddenly incredulous. This is probably starting to sound like so much hocus-pocus. I realize that

I probably should not have used the term "mental strengthening," something we customarily say to lesser-educated clients. In his case, he has a Ph.D. in American literature, and he is widely read on a variety of topics, including hypnosis.

I go on to explain the process, with a few more details because he asks for them. The literature on ego-strengthening—ego-strengthening *within formal hypnosis*—is substantial, but largely anecdotal, and I tell him:

> It's kind of like building up a medical patient before surgery. Maybe that patient needs rest and nutrition to strengthen him prior to the surgical procedure.

Mr. Rabbit Hunt is now beginning to understand. I add:

> Here in the Arizona desert, where we have hard, alkaline soil, you wouldn't just throw tomato seeds down and expect them to grow. First, you must till that soil, adding necessary ingredients, perhaps peat moss or compost, and plenty of water. Only then have you created a proper medium for those tomato seeds to grow.

I then add that our primary means of doing this, outside of formal hypnosis, is indirect:

> We use stories. People seem to unwittingly self-reference the metaphor within the story, fitting it to their own particular needs and circumstances.

I then say a few more words about unconscious process, using metaphors like the iceberg:

> The big part of the iceberg is there, underneath the water. You don't see it, but you know it's there.

As the client has hinted about control issues and hypnosis, I add that we believe that anyone's unconscious is thought to be protective, in that the unconscious mind will not incorporate suggestions that are not acceptable to it:

> All you have to do is be open to listening to a little story at the end of each session.

He nods his assent, and I know then that we can proceed.

THE SECOND SESSION

Mr. Rabbit Hunt returns the following week. During the first part of the session, I (S. B.) elicit more information from him about his work, relationships, and past efforts to improve his mood. During this discussion I seed relaxation and *receptivity.* For example, "I see many clients every day, and during the hour, it's easy for me to just *drift off* as they tell me their stories. However, in your case, I'm impressed with the tenacity with which you've struggled with your depression." I also seed receptivity by saying things about *receiving* mail today, or *listening* with only partial awareness to a piece of music at the end of a long, *tiring* day, giving a slightly different vocal emphasis to the seeded words. Nonverbal seeding could involve allowing my body to become relaxed in immobility during our discussion, perhaps closing my eyes at intervals, as if in *deep* concentration, or absorbed in a fleeting mental image.

I remind the client that what we are about to begin today is very akin to formal hypnosis, in that while listening to a story, people often develop signs of trance. He says this is okay with him, as he's willing to try whatever he can that might help his depression. To start, I tell him that he can let his eyes move around the room, focus on a spot somewhere, or just let his eyes gently close.

We've done a fair amount of explaining, *and we're* several minutes into the session, *and now, I'd like you to know that you can* move around *in your chair,* adjust *your position, or* do whatever else you need to *in order to feel comfortable, because comfort is what we're after, here on this* excursion, *or* journey, *or* hunt *for discovery and exploration. I can remember a man, one time, sitting* there, *listening in here to our first story, and he wondered if his state of relaxation would be* mild, medium, *or* deep, *but then he remembered that I'd told him that there was absolutely* nothing at all *that he needed to* do, *or* know, *or* think about, *and that the*	truisms suggestions covering all possibilities apposition of opposites bind of comparable alternatives not knowing/not doing

words could just drift in, or drift out,
effortlessly, involuntarily, without any
conscious effort *on his part, and he*   bind of comparable
found this idea rather comforting, which   alternatives
allowed him to drift off even more . . .

   Mr. Rabbit Hunt has elected to sit in a chair, as opposed to a
recliner, which he would choose next session. He has taken me at my
word about doing *whatever* he wishes to feel comfortable, and has
crossed one leg over the other. He gazes at a framed poem, "Friend in
the Mirror" by Edward Cunningham, which I have on the wall. His
eyes focus on the poem, and every few seconds, he looks at me. I
blink my eyes twice, and then close them, as I begin the story of the
"Three Lessons" (Wallas, 1985). He closes his eyes, takes one more
deep breath, and then settles back in his chair. He becomes further
absorbed in the following ego-strengthening story.

Grizzley

   We might *wonder* about or *imagine* many things, things
in the past as well as the present. Certainly there are some
very *interesting* things in life, and then again, there are
quite a few very *boring,* monotonous things, too. Both
boring and interesting things can be purposely tuned out,
or you can be oblivious to them *without consciously
trying.* Something that is tuned out, or tuned in, is likely
to be engaging to the mind, or maybe it's just that it
catches our attention, or perhaps it's more than passingly
curious.
   It can also be very interesting to think about what's
above and what's below, whether it's upstairs and down-
stairs; the surface of the ocean and the vast life down
below; life in the earth's atmosphere and what's out in
space; or animal life on the desert floor and everything that
goes on beneath the sand.
   But despite all of those things out there, our attention
invariably returns to the earth where, high up in the air,
the great bald eagle turns lazy circles, riding a strong
thermal, then dips down to ride another. The powerful bird
has lightness in its mighty wings as he rides the current,
detached from down below, but at the same time he

studies the water down there, absorbed in what he sees. He passes over a flock of ducks, who show their respect by diving lower.

At the edge of the lake, an enormous grizzley bear stares into the bottomless middle of the dark pool of water. A few minutes earlier he had been fishing in the lake. But now as he gazes into the murky pool he seems *lost in thought*, oblivious to the swarm of gnats around his head. He doesn't hear the call of a sandhill crane.

The eagle is now back on his perch in the lodgepole pine. It is easy to see why these birds are sometimes called white-headed sea eagles—his head and tail feathers are a brilliant white. He has a dark brown body with bright yellow bill, legs and feet, and is the largest bird in North America.

The grizzley scrambles up the ridge, dislodging rocks along the way. His range is 200 square miles, most of which is here in Great Interior Park. He now lumbers along a fringe of timber above the lake. There is more work to do on his den to get it ready for winter, adding grass and branches, and the boughs of a pine tree. These days he eats 20,000 calories a day to prepare to hibernate. Maybe this is why the Blackfeet Indians tell stories about Great Bear, who goes into his den and is reborn each spring.

Not far from the bald eagle is his former nest near the top of a ponderosa pine. Generations of eagles have used this same nest, which probably weighs several hundred pounds. The nest is an immense pile of sticks shaped like a donut. One of his jobs has been to guard the nest while his mate warmed the nestlings. Of course, he also took turns keeping the baby birds warm under his feathers while his mate hunted for food. He has not been part of a breeding pair for some years now, so his main concern is simply staying safe and getting enough to eat.

Staying safe mostly means staying away from humans. Life is safer nowadays, but it wasn't always that way. These great birds were hunted in days past. There are also power poles and man-made poisons to stay away from.

Some of the same dangers could befall the grizzley bear, especially if he gets blamed for invading a human's campsite that was really the handiwork of some black bear. Five years back, this same grizzley had been stalked by the Forest Service. Although he doesn't remember anything, they shot him from a helicopter with a tranquilizer gun, and attached a radio transmitter around his neck. A plane now flying overhead brings a growl, and he retreats into dense undergrowth. He has forgotten about the radio collar, which has disappeared beneath his thick, matted fur.

The eagle leaves his perch in search of food. Strong wings bring him to the lake where he glides on top of the water, skimming the surface with his talons. But no fish is grasped this time. Again he rises into the sky. He sees his dinner in the talons of a fish hawk. He harasses the fish hawk, who drops his catch, and the eagle seizes it in mid-air. He will enjoy the meal back in the solitude of his pine tree.

The sky is steadily darkening overhead. Thunder rolls in the distance and a red squirrel chatters its objection. Grizzley paws a rusted Coleman lantern and raises his gray muzzle in the air, woofing at nothing in particular. He puts his nose to the ground and lumbers along gently and slowly, in a world of his own and smelling and hearing everything at the same time. His face looks mild and peaceful, but this quietness is contradicted by a long white scar that extends near his eye. He survived a scrape with black bears. Grizzley continues up the ridge where he comes to his day bed, a dish-shaped depression beneath a big white spruce. Here he will *drift and dream, dream and drift,* for at least a few hours.

Finally he rises from his bed. He exhales. It blares like a sounding whale. His senses are sharp as he starts out in search of food. A pair of ravens flap by and croak. He chews white bark pine nuts, then smells the perfume of blackberries. The blackberries lie near the center of the prickley undergrowth. Other animals have failed to penetrate the bush, but pain and discomfort mean little to the grizzley. What matters is moving on to another ridge, where he dines on roots and tubers beneath an Englemann spruce.

Grizzley is unaware of the eagle, who is again in the air above the lake. A dense fog rolls in. His senses are extra sharp in this semi-darkness. He continues to move, rooting out food, all the while smelling, listening, and watching. A lone coyote eyes him through a cloud of insects. To the coyote, grizzley is but a bulky form groping in the mist. But grizzley sees the coyote very clearly. The bear emits a low growl and the coyote scampers away.

Grizzley concentrates only on the here and now, eating sufficient food to get him through hibernation. Who knows if he will mate in the spring, as he has done in spring times past.

On an adjacent ridge he is especially watchful. He remembers in the deep recesses of his mind that many seasons ago he battled three black bears on this very ridge. He barely escaped with his life that time, and his wounds eventually healed. An important lesson was learned, and since then he has become extra cautious, extra vigilant. Grizzley *knows deep down that he can continue to survive and prevail,* whether it is up on a ridge or down by the lake. But for the present, every effort is directed at getting enough food before he hibernates.

THE COURSE OF THERAPY

I (S. B.) saw Mr. Rabbit Hunt six more times, with an average of two weeks between sessions. By the third session, he reported subjective improvement, along with improved sleep. He had joined a health club and he had met a woman, and the two spent a good deal of satisfying time together. He believed that the antidepresant medication prescribed him six months ago (and which he said he took on time) had "finally kicked in." I reviewed progress with him and told him that we were at an important crossroads. I reminded him of his tendency to backslide, and offered the following possibilities: formal hypnosis sessions to reinforce gains, periodic booster sessions of talk therapy combined with ego-strengthening, or group therapy. He said, "I'll think about it and get back to you." I never heard from him again.

REFLECTIONS OF MR. RABBIT HUNT

How often is it that clients disappear on us and we wonder how they are doing? We can only wonder whether the gains Mr. Rabbit Hunt made during those six sessions were the result of a supportive relationship, the talk therapy component, relaxation alone, metaphorical ego-strengthening, or a combination of all these things. Perhaps joining the health club was significant, or maybe his new relationship provided the missing link.

Our goal in metaphorical ego-strengthening is to prepare clients for subsequent therapy. But for many, ego-strengthening alone is sufficient, and many clients at that point opt to discontinue. In thinking back on the case, I believe that we could have accomplished the same thing with formal hypnosis, and in fewer sessions. Formal trance to accelerates rapport, and in a deeper state, clients appear to more readily incorporate suggestions. In formal trance, clients are more likely to demonstrate objective trance markers, such as ideosensory feelings, for example, "I felt a heaviness in both hands," along with time distortion and amnesia for all or part of the story.

In Mr. Rabbit Hunt's case, by the fourth session he reported a numbness in his feet; however, he never experienced amnesia. He turned out to be a good hypnotic subject, although I did not provide formal hypnosis, and he expressed fewer issues of control. He knew that he experienced trance, and I believe that if a future therapist offers him hypnosis, he will not object. Near the end of therapy, he and I had a discussion about what constitutes hypnosis. "Is it hypnosis if I go into trance during guided imagery or progressive muscle relaxation?" he asked. I explained that trance phenomena are common in those techniques and various others, but that experts might argue pro or con. I told him this: "If you call it hypnosis, it's hypnosis." This was acceptable to him.

Improvement, of course, may be measured in various ways. I (S. B.) rely on subjective reports, as well as objective data, such as a client's appearance and behavior. Sometimes I use a Likert scale, asking for a report on a 1 to 10 continuum at different stages of therapy. I (S. B.) always use depression and anxiety measures, as my company's protocol calls for such measures every other session. I (G. G.) am more likely to use paper-and-pencil instruments for self-efficacy, as well as for anxiety and depression.

Bandura (1997) contends that psychotherapists may bestow the greatest benefit by helping their clients build self-efficacy, not by giving them specific remedies for their problems. Bandura's emphasis is on behavior, stating that personal enablement through mastery experiences is the best way to build self-efficacy. The term self-efficacy, which we use synonymously with self-esteem, may be defined as clients' believing their behavior will lead to successful outcomes. We will delve more deeply into self-efficacy, as well as other means of ego-strengthening, in Section II.

We let people know right up front that our most effective way in working with them involves unconscious process, indirection, and metaphor. To buttress the point, we sometimes use this analogy: "If you need work inside your head, you'd go to a neurologist or neurosurgeon, or maybe a psychiatrist. You wouldn't go to a dermatologist or pediatrician, would you?"

THE STORY

We employ all of our stories in diverse ways. We have stock ego-strengthening stories that we use with and without hypnosis. In hypnosis especially, where we give suggestions that foster amnesia, clients often return the following session and say things like, "I can't remember what you told me, but I've sure felt good the past two weeks." Such amnesia occurs in conventional psychotherapy, but more rarely. For clients who return next session and wish to discuss the story, we typically talk about it for a few minutes only, as we wish to proceed with our agenda for the session. The agenda with a depressed client such as Mr. Rabbit Hunt, would usually include CBT, emphasizing behavioral activation and increasing social contacts, along with ego-strengthening.

With some clients, you may wish to devise a story for their particular needs, or you may wish to employ other story strategies, as discussed in Chapter 7. Nevertheless, the ego-strengthening stories, such as those listed at the end of chapter 18, have served us well as all-purpose stories for most adults, as well as for children ages twelve and older. If you have a busy practice, you can appreciate the economy of having a repertoire of reliable stock techniques, such as stories that can be used time and time again with minimal adaptation.

AUTHORITARIAN VERSUS PERMISSIVE APPROACHES

Not knowing/not doing is an awkward term, but it is one suggestion we always include in both hypnotic and nonhypnotic applications.

This suggestion, which facilitates unconscious responsiveness rather than conscious effort (Hammond, 1990), is both *liberating* and permissive. It is liberating in that it helps swing wide the door to responsiveness by listing all the things that you *don't* have to do:

> *There's* nothing at all *that you need to do, or know, or think about, or change . . . in fact you don't even have to listen . . . all you need to do is sit there and breathe. . . .*

The suggestion is *permissive* in that it encourages clients' responding in any way they choose, which is usually in the direction of trance. Contrast the openness and embrace of *not knowing/not doing* with authoritarian suggestions that typically use "you *will*," as in "Your left hand *will* become heavy, and you will be strong and lose weight." Permissive—and, we believe, more respectful—methods use *may* instead of *will*.

Let's look at permissiveness in *implication*, another type of permissive suggestion. In this case, it is tied to a *bind of comparable alternatives:*

> *During the story today, I wonder when you may begin to experience a lightness or heaviness, coolness or warmth, tingling or numbness, or some other interesting or curious sensation in one of those hands, or in your feet, or in some other part of your body. . . .*

With *implication*, you are implying that something is going to happen. Notice that *when* is the important word, and *if* is never employed. Using Mr. Rabbit Hunt as an example, let's say that after the story he is asked how he feels in his body and he mentions that he notices an *odd, heavy feeling* in his left hand. In the next session implication is adapted or fine-tuned to him:

> *I wonder when you will begin to notice a pleasant heaviness, or perhaps an odd, heavy feeling, out there in that left hand first, and the right hand next, or maybe in both hands at approximately the same time . . . and when you do, that pleasantness can spread out to the rest of your body, slowing down your mind, as well as your body. . . .*

The potency of hypnosis or hypnotic techniques within psycho-therapy lies in the ability to adapt to the orientations and needs of the individual. One of our colleagues, Matt Weyer, a psychologist in Phoenix, tells his audiences: "You go from the general and diffuse light of a big fluorescent bulb to a finely directed beam of an indus-trial laser. Make it fine, but not too fine."

Let's not forget, however, that permissive suggestions have only been around since Erickson began writing about them in the 1950s. Before then, direct, authoritarian methods have ruled the day, not only in hypnosis, but also in religion, medicine, and other aspects of life.We are not saying that we are never authoritarian or direct, because many times it is appropriate to be so. We are advocating *versatility* and *flexibility,* and having more tools in your toolbox than just one or two. If the direct approach is all you use, for instance, *pro forma* CBT, you will not be able to reach many clients, even if they continue in therapy with you. These include resistant clients, clients with comorbid disorders or complicated situations, and many others who may require additional measures in order to successfully engage them and influence change so that they feel better.

In managed care, notice how focused and directive psychotherapy has become in many circles. In the first of six allotted sessions, most clients are asked the "miracle question," for example, "What if you went to sleep tonight, and when you woke up, your problem was better. How would it be different? What would you be doing? And how would you be feeling?" Also to hasten therapy, exceptions to the problem are elicited, for example, "Tell me any times that the problem does not occur." Although these may be valuable techniques, their pro forma application is often insufficient to assure short-term therapy. Quality managers or the insurance company may make sure that homework tasks are documented in your progress notes. In hypnosis, many people still employ authoritarian methods, which have some advantages, and in your practice, you are likely to see clients who have experienced authoritarian hypnosis. If you begin to apply ego-strengthening to those clients, some may be wary and unreceptive, especially if they are down to earth, and put a lot of faith in authoritarian principles. These same clients in conventional psychotherapy will be of the "Just-tell-me-what's-wrong-and-then-fix-it" variety. Mechanical engineers might be apprehensive initially, as hypnotic language and metaphor might seem otherworldly to them, and not to be trusted. That is why, with all clients, we explain the rationale and give examples they can understand. If they then opt out, we have both been saved time and effort.

WHEN IT DOESN'T WORK

What about clients who do not appear to respond favorably to this approach? Let's say someone reluctantly agrees to listen to a story, but during the telling they move nervously in their chair, and their eyes keep darting around the room. Well, some of these clients will surprise you, in that *in their own way* they are responding as best they can at that time. They may be feeling anxious, doubtful, guilty, or something that is yet to be revealed. Their behavior may be lumped into the category of unconscious resistance—they *want* to let go, but just *can't*. However, it is more important to move ahead with treating the problem they came presented with, rather than dissecting the resistance. No one is dragging them in in handcuffs. If they are present and agree to participate, respect their way of responding, and reinforce what response you can. For many of these people, life has been *tearing down,* and we want them to experience *building up.*

I (G. G.) had a client once who was irascible, pessimistic, and skeptical. As I dealt with the preliminaries I asked him if I could call him by his first name, as it is rather cumbersome and impersonal to say, "There's nothing at all that you need to do, or know, *Mr. Doe. . . .*" This man said, "All my friends call me Buzzard." During our four sessions of ego-strengthening, Buzzard never appeared to show much trance depth, and during all those sessions I felt that maybe *I* was the one conveying discomfort to *him* because each time I said, "Buzzard," in my best hypnotic voice, *I* felt unsettled, as all I could think of was some big bird eating carrion on a lonely road outside Winslow, Arizona. However, the main thing is that he responded, and his depression improved. Usually clients who show more depth will demonstrate more clinical improvement. However, some of these low-hypnotizables do in fact incorporate suggestions, and show objective gains.

CLINICAL COMMENTS

When we introduce unconscious mind, many will say, "Oh, you mean the subconscious mind," and we say, "Yes, that's it," rather than dwelling on definitions. Our working definition of this construct is virtually any thought or feeling that is outside of the person's immediate awareness. With hypnotic language to set up a story, the bind of comparable alternatives is very useful. To target relaxation, or trance depth, a mild, medium, or deep state is posed, along with the apparent choice of alternatives. The inherent assumption is that some state of relaxation will occur. Unconscious process may be similarly targeted with a rather brief suggestion, such as

> *The front part of your mind may pay attention to the process, while the back part of your mind contemplates the content, the meaning, or something else of importance to the unconscious.*

Or, more elaborately, using a conscious-unconscious double bind:

> *Some people find that they listen closely and carefully with the back part of their mind, while the front part of the mind drifts and dreams. Others may discover that their unconscious mind can be distracted by some curious internal events, while the conscious mind makes note of words being said on the outside. And still others may not be certain which part is operating when, but they don't really care, because they can trust their unconscious mind to be protective as well as productive, whether or not the conscious mind is present and accounted for.*

We give the longer example for illustration purposes, to show some of the limitless possibilities of many aspects of hypnotic language. Such a long double bind may be more than is needed in most clinical situations, just as more than two or three truisms may be overkill. Remember the law of parsimony: Do only as much as necessary to achieve the desired effect.

6

Story Techniques

LOST IN THE DESERT

Bandler, in his foreward to Gordon's (1978) *Therapeutic Metaphors,*
relates a story from his own experience in college, when he studied
biology. The story had to do with a biology professor, Dr. Stewart,
who regularly led students on excursions into the desert, where they
did an intensive study of desert flora. Most of the time these study
trips were interesting, though uneventful. However, one summer day,
miles from civilization, the truck broke down. The group then set out
on foot into the fiery wilderness.

They were equipped with few provisions, and this was long before
cell phones and similar modern conveniences. They were soon dehy-
drated, exhausted, sunburned, and discouraged, hopelessly lost in the
middle of nowhere. On the morning of the third day, they reached the
summit of a great sand dune. Far off to their right they saw what
appeared to be a blue lake, surrounded by green trees. The students

leapt in the air with delight, but Dr. Stewart remained calm. He knew it was only a mirage, and he told them so. "I've been here before," he said.

But the students insisted that they saw real trees and a lake in the distance, and they wanted to go there immediately. Dr. Stewart finally gave in, but with one unyielding condition: once they arrived and confirmed it was a mirage, they were to venture no farther, sit down, and wait for help to arrive. The students agreed, and then made their way down the sand dune, aiming for the trees and lake. Dr. Stewart went off on his own, in another direction.

Three hours later, the students arrived at a plush, new resort, which had four swimming pools and six restaurants. They summoned help, and soon they were in a Land Rover with a sheriff's deputy, searching for Dr. Stewart. He was never found.

Bandler received an incomplete in biology that semester.

MAKING A DEPARTURE

Whether that story is apocrophal or true, we like it, and we use it with students to encourage taking risks in finding what works for them. We also employ it as an instigative tool in therapy. However, we place it at the beginning of this chapter to accent our position on an important aspect of story techniques.

Ever since linguists Bandler and Grinder (1975), developers of neurolinguistic programming (NLP), proclaimed the importance of representational systems, scores of writers have emphasized the need for therapists to attend to client sensory modalities (auditory, visual, kinesthetic or tactile, and sometimes gustatory). Accordingly, a therapist who hears a client say things like, "I'm in touch with . . ." and "I'm feeling my way . . . ," determines that the client's primary orientation is kinesthetic, and then matches this orientation in directives, stories, and other communications with the client. For the past 30 years, this has been a tenet for many therapists, whether or not they practice NLP, and many writers on metaphorical technique devote considerable time to sensory modality.

Although the approach is eminently respectful and thoughtful, we believe that it is largely unnecessary, and that in things like story construction, energy directed elsewhere may be more productive. We randomly selected eight therapeutic stories of varying length and format from books on the shelf, and tabulated verbs in each story that could be grouped under auditory, visual, or kinesthetic. This is what we found:

The Three Lessons (Wallas, 1985)

Auditory	Visual	Kinesthetic
1	3	1

The Green Dragon (Wallas, 1985)

Auditory	Visual	Kinesthetic
4	12	5

The Weathervane (Wallas, 1985)

Auditory	Visual	Kinesthetic
1	3	9

The Mountain Metaphor (Hunter, 1994)

Auditory	Visual	Kinesthetic
2	14	3

The Tomato Story (Rossi, 1980)

Auditory	Visual	Kinesthetic
4	5	2

Going Inside (Gafner & Benson, 2000)

Auditory	Visual	Kinesthetic
1	13	2

The Puppy Story (Mills & Crowley, 1986)

Auditory	Visual	Kinesthetic
4	13	8

Aside from "The Weathervane," in which the author purposely accented the kinesthetic, you can see that the sensory modalities are all represented, with the visual predominating. This little survey, which is in no way scientific, is used to illustrate our belief that most anecdotes, stories, inductions, or any other scripted or improvised metaphors will most likely cover the major modalities, with visual verbs occurring more frequently.

Occasionally we start out our workshops by asking the audience to think about a pleasant sensory experience that occurred in the past twenty-four hours. We then ask for a show of hands in response to, "For how many was the experience kinesthetic, etc.?" Invariably, the visual is in the majority.

Furthermore, if you examine the content in any of the above stories, you will find that most verbs, as well as other words, have nothing to do with sensory modality. The verb that occurs most often is *to be,* in one of its numerous tenses, such as "she was," or "he could have been." Other frequently occurring verbs may connote action, as in *run, explore,* or *discover,* while others may describe mental events, such as *wonder, dream, know,* and *learn.* Then, we have all the nouns and adjectives that appear in every sentence of any story. In other words, no pun intended, the biggest part of any story has nothing to do with sensory modality, and in constructing a story, we can concentrate instead on connecting with the client in other important areas, such as mood, values, theme, developmental tasks, and general orientations.

Mood

In learning about the brief mental status exam, beginning interns sometimes have difficulty distinguishing *affect* from *mood.* We tell them, "Affect is to mood, as tide is to ocean, or weather is to climate." We also tell them that often a client's mood can be described as how they make *you* feel. So, if a client's presentation is doleful, we feel sad, and the mood is depressed. We could *match* (also called pacing or modeling) this mood directly and concretely by reflection, such as, "It seems you are feeling very blue and upset. . . ." Or, we could match it with an anecdote about someone else who came in feeling sad ". . . and she really *surprised* me with her quick response to therapy." A more indirect matching metaphor could be an anecdote about a stormy day: ". . . and the sun broke through when I least expected it." If you've ever been a client yourself and in the first session the therapist failed to match your mood, you probably felt *misunderstood,* and we bet you didn't return.

Values

Next to mood, values may be the most apparent part of a client's presentation. There are a finite number of values that a person can have. Some of the common ones are strength, caring, love, duty, loyalty, closeness, and protectiveness. These and other values can be found in many stories and anecdotes, and they are easy to weave into your own therapeutic creations.

I (G. G.) was seeing a man for depression and he was not responding. I asked him to bring his wife with him one time, and all of a sudden—like yanking open the blinds so that the sun can penetrate a dark room—their overarching state or *value* became evident. It was a victim status: their horns were firmly locked in a struggle to outvictim the other person. Recognizing this value, I reached for our ally, Job, the nonpareil Old Testament sufferer. I liberally used his name, threw in some anecdotes about him, and thereby matched the value of the couple. Once they felt understood, they readily agreed to sharing victimhood every other week, an intervention that was sufficient to defuse the conflict.

Developmental Task

People who come to therapy are often stuck at some vital stage in the lifespan. Such challenges may be seen among new parents, a 5 year-old adapting to kindergarten, an 18-year-old leaving home, a person who enters retirement, or any variety of problems that arise throughout life. Whether these clients are unconsciously poised in the anticipation of change, or whether people facing developmental challenges are in some way hyper-receptive to suggestion, we don't know. Whatever the reason, these people respond superbly to metaphorical approaches, and we regard any *developmental task* as an automatic therapeutic invitation for metaphor. With a 5 year-old, it may involve hand puppets or a sand tray, and with a 95-year-old, it often involves an anecdote or story.

With older adults or their families, we often see issues of medication or compliance, such as a difficulty agreeing to go to a day program or nursing home, or some related issue. We recognize that these are not simple matters, and that problem solving them may be fraught with obstacles. At any rate, clients are stuck unconsciously and the therapist's job is to first show understanding, and second, to help them break free of their constraints, so that they can make decisions and get on with life. The following is an anecdote we often use with older adults.

Storm Clouds

Although I hadn't been born yet when people were preparing for World War II, I've read some history and know that Germany was angry about the way they were treated after World War I. In the mid-1930s Hitler was getting stronger and stronger. Under the noses of everybody, Hitler was building a war machine, but outside of Germany *nobody was aware of it*. He got stronger and stronger, and pretty soon he began to flex his muscles. First, he took over the Rhineland, offering up some lame excuse for military action. He grew stronger and stronger, but still *nobody believed it. They just hoped for the best*. They started making deals with Hitler, selling out Czechoslovakia, still *hoping for the best*. And Hitler got stronger and stronger. Then Hitler invaded Poland in 1939 and made short work of them. Still people *refused to believe what was happening*. Hitler took over Norway and Belgium and Denmark. Still, much of the world continued to *hope for the best*. He made quick work of France. About the same time, Pearl Harbor was bombed. Finally the allies wised up and *did something before it was too late*.

Dynamic or Theme

Many times clients' unique ways of behaving will be evident as they describe their relationships with others. A man with depression shows passivity in relationships. His relationship dynamic may be approach–avoid. An angry woman's conflict with her husband may be characterized by an attack–defend dynamic. Other common dynamics in relationships are control–resist, demand–refuse, discuss–avoid, criticize–defend, and accuse–deny (Shoham, Rohrbaugh, & Patterson, 1995). There are many ways we can match these kinds of behavior, along with attendant feelings. In the case of approach-avoid, I (G. G.) turned on the background sound machine that we use in hypnosis, turned it to the "ocean waves" mode, and asked the man if the sound of the waves washing up on the shore then receding reminded him of anything. After a few moments, he said, "Maybe your point is that I approach my wife up to a point, and then I retreat." That was close enough for me.

In relationships, common themes are responsibility versus irresponsibility, teacher versus student, illness versus health, closeness versus distance, and rescue versus escape (Papp, 1983). Listen to clients as they describe how they navigate through the world and you will readily glean their posture, or way of behaving with others, and a theme will develop. With practice, you will accumulate a set of stock metaphors that can be used in different situations. If one does not come readily, you can always tell the client about *someone else* who did such-and-such, and thereby match their dynamic or theme. Metaphor bypasses their critical evaluation and demonstrates that you understand, whereas direct explanation is often consciously defended. When we want to devise a story, but we are not sure which theme or dynamic is at play, we may first send out a verbal probe, for instance, ". . . it seems that the feeling that best describes you now is *seriousness*, or *sadness*, or *nervousness*, or *anger*. . . ." If we connect with one or more of these, clients' nonverbal responses will signal assent long before they answer verbally.

Further questions should confirm which theme or dynamic dominates. If not and all you are left with is the prevailing emotional tone, or mood, that's fine; go with it. We stress matching, or showing understanding, for obvious reasons: If clients do not return after the first visit, then you will not be able to use a story, anecdote, eye movement desenitization and reprocessing (EMDR), cognitive-behavioral therapy (CBT), hypnosis, narrative therapy, or anything else with them.

STORY CONSTRUCTION

We use a three-step process for story construction:

1. ABSORB attention. Hypnotic language, fluff, and meandering details do a good job absorbing attention.
2. MATCH (pace or model) the client's world. Describe a situation that generally approximates the client's situation.
3. ADD ON (lead) in the desired direction.

For example, we are working with a fourteen-year-old girl, Tanya, who is shy and has no friends. Her mother has brought her to therapy because she is worried about her "sour attitude toward life." Now, whether Tanya is depressed, has social phobia, could benefit from assertiveness training, or whether her overbearing mother is maintaining the problem—none of that matters. Right now, we simply need to connect with Tanya.

Tanya, you were three *once and now you're fourteen, and you've been in here for ten minutes, and you seem like you're not up to talking right now, so I'd like to tell you a little story that probably may take* more than five *minutes, or certainly* less than ten *minutes, but I often* lose track *of time when I tell a story, or listen to one, and that can be like* losing feeling *in one or both legs when you've sat on the floor too long. I can think now, or otherwise* imagine, *or* wonder, *how this story may not be applicable to your* special *and* unique *circumstances, because I know and you know that* not just anyone *can come in here and sit down* there *and talk to a perfect stranger about personal things.*

We had a boy in here last week—his name was Peter, and he was 16. Now, he lived *with his mother,* and she *worried all the time* about Peter, *and she was* always on to him, *and he was* never real outgoing *to start with, but he kind of* retreated *into his own world, which was kind of lonely, but at least it was his world, and no one else's.*

I had three *candles out on the table, those same candles right there, Tanya, and I said to him, "Peter,* three *is a good number, and often it takes me* three *times to get to know a person, and for them to feel comfortable talking, and I* always ask people to be sure to *hold back some, especially the real private stuff," and Peter looked at those three candles, and he said, "Fine, I'll give you* three *to do your thing."*

ABSORB ATTENTION
seeding

time distortion

ideosensory feeling

"power words"

reframe

apposition of
opposites
MATCHING

ADDING ON

activate seed

restraint

Tanya showed eye fixation and slowed breathing, and it looked like she was responding well. However, when I finished telling her about Peter, she quickly said, "I'll only give you two." When she returned I had two candles on the table instead of three. She picked them up and set them down through all seven sessions. Her mother got off her back, and Tanya made friends with another girl at school. The final session I saw her and her mom together, and I was prepared to tell them a story that matched the progress they had made together. However, Tanya beat me to the punch and told me a story about a girl who grew up and became an elementary school teacher.

A STORY WITH ALTERNATE ENDINGS

Wallas (1985) regards any story as a catalyst, something that can perturb a "stuck" situation and set in motion vital change in therapy. We often use her Three Lessons story during the first session of hypnosis, as well as in conventional therapy. The primary meta-message, or embedded suggestion, of the story is that clients have the necessary resources within themselves to solve their problems, and that the therapist is a guide in this process. In the original story, the young woman locates the wise witch in the forest, and the wise witch communicates three lessons: 1) an invitation to "come in"; 2) "I cannot teach you in words alone"; and 3) "Time is very short, so you must always give your complete attention." Other suggestions embedded in this very brief but versatile story are: 1) You know every-thing you need to know, but you don't know that you know; and 2) Now you are ready for knowing.

We sometimes rearrange these various suggestions in the three lessons. For example:

You may come in.	The door is open.
	Inside you are welcome.
Cannot teach in words alone	People learn in many ways.
	Will my voice go with you?
Time is very short.	Exploration can occur rapidly.
	Complete attention may lead to an important discovery.

| *You know everything.* | Internal resources are numerous. Who can know all that is within? |
| *Ready for knowing* | It came as a *surprise* to hear that she was ready to know. Off she went, knowing that she was ready to learn even more. |

When we tell this story at the end of a first session, and the client shows an interest or curiosity, or is otherwise absorbed, we may tell the story again, maybe a session or two later, but altering the lessons so that they lead in the direction we want to go. We omit witch and make the protagonist a wise woman, and we also make the story longer (Gafner & Benson, 2000), absorbing attention early on with suggestions for time distortion and ideosensory phenomena. For example:

> ... *and on her way to the wise woman's house, it was late November, and she could see her breath, and passing through the forest she passed by a cold, cold stream, and she knelt down and thrust one hand into the icy water. It stung at first and then became very numb. She didn't know if a minute had passed, or an hour, but eventually she arose and continued on her way. ...*

A STORY WITHOUT AN ENDING

This is a technique that we use both within and outside of formal hypnosis. In conventional psychotherapy, if a client has responded well to stories in earlier sessions, we may encourage further unconscious search by leaving a story unfinished, which is actually a doubly indirect method that may boost self-efficacy, as it results in clients' feeling a sense of empowerment, or ownership, as solutions become generated during the therapy process.

Stories without an ending do not have to be complex to create an unconscious search or a sense of wonderment. We usually employ stories about everyday, mundane, pedestrian tasks in life whose effect may be rather disarming. For example, Hanna is hosting a large and sumptuous dinner party, and in the course of the dinner, she must make decisions, or choices, in important areas, such as salads, entrees, and desserts. In the story, we may suggest any number of possibilities, and simply end the story with, " . . . and you can *imagine*, just *imagine*, what Hanna chose next," or " . . . and you *know* what Hanna selected," or, " . . . and for an extra dessert, it came as a *surprise* to her." Some regard the direct question as especially instigative. Accordingly, we may end the story with " . . . what did Hanna choose?"

We may also tell a story that leads up to resolution of a specific issue, and then ask the client to supply the ending. For example, I (S. B.) was working with a depressed client, and I told him a story about a man who was driving a truck along the beach in Mexico. He was not sure where he was headed. He was just driving along, noticing the water and shore, not paying very close attention to the road ahead. As he crept along in his truck, he gradually became aware that the sand was less solidly packed, and before he realized it, he was stuck in loose sand, unable to do much except spin his tires, which only sunk him deeper into the loose, wet sand.

At this point I stopped and asked him to tell the rest of the story. This caught him off-guard, as he certainly did not expect to be put on the spot. If he finished the story with the man remaining stuck and helpless, I would be provided with a vital perception. If he finished the story with a competent resolution, the message could have been incorporated into a resolution of his problem, *and* I would have his own words to utilize in future stories.

How many story techniques are there? We don't know, but there are many, including alternating stories, which may be more applicable within formal hypnosis. We will cover that technique in Section II.

A FEW MAGIC BULLETS

We consider stories and anecdotes, as well as other techniques, to be a vital and robust part of the therapy process, not just an end in themselves. As such, these techniques are intended to be woven into whatever therapeutic modality you employ, and are designed to instigate, provoke, and foster change in the desired direction, all on an unconscious level. Some therapists who begin to use stories in their practice tend to regard them as "magic bullets," or ends in themselves. Sometimes, for sure, we hit the mark with such a bullet, and a marvelous breakthrough occurs following the perfect story. However, those rapid successes are rare for all of us. Instead, we emphasize step-wise progress, where often we have two steps forward and one or two backward steps before moving forward again. Afterall, your clients are probably like ours, people with tough, seemingly intractable problems, people for whom this venture into therapy is not the first "rabbit hunt." Didn't someone once say that being a therapist is like being a parent, in that it is a great exercise in humility? They were right.

Other story methods may be better employed within formal hypnosis. We will cover these in Section II.

DEVELOPING STORIES AND ANECDOTES

A few years back we conducted a day-long workshop for 75 therapists, and near the end of the day we showed them a video of Gina, a 95-year-old woman. On the tape, she told her story about how as a young girl she came to the United States from Italy. Her parents were sickly and died early, and she was responsible for raising her younger siblings. She never had children of her own, and her life had been arduous. Now, in her waning days, Gina has metastatic breast cancer and looks after her husband of 60 years. Her husband constantly bombards her with verbal abuse. A sad story indeed.

After discussing story construction, we asked the audience to break into small groups and devise a story for the woman. "Remember," we explained, "whether or not you *add on* in the desired direction, the main task is to *communicate understanding*." After 15 minutes of exploration and brain storming, the following ideas emerged:

1. A young girl had a dream, and in the dream, she woke up on an island. All the other humans had died in a war, and the island was populated by many different animals. She was all alone, and realized that she had a need to take care of others, and she found comfort in caring for the animals.
2. A gardner worked very hard in her garden, growing wonderful tomatoes, lettuce, and other vegetables. She was hungry and tired, and rested in the cool shade of a big oak tree.
3. A woman found herself on a big barge that carried trash out to the middle of the ocean. Boats kept bringing new trash to the barge, and she had to decide what new trash to keep and what trash she could refuse. Some of the trash was useful, in that she could burn it for fuel.

4. A tree in Arizona was planted in rocky soil. It was the only tree around for miles. A robin's egg hatched in a nest in the tree, and robin said, "I wish there were other trees around here."
5. A woman traveller was very old and wise, and on her journey she met a man and said to him, "Let's have trust and commitment to each other."
6. A nurse, who was very old, was forced to leave her home. Then she told her story.
7. Many years ago I saw a beehive. A strong life force was pulling it apart while at the same time it was melded together.
8. An ant carried something thirty times its own weight, and eventually, deep inside the anthill, it became the queen ant.
9. A family goes to Italy and visits the leaning tower of Pisa, and they helped hold it up, even though war was going on all around.

All of these ideas, however incomplete or nonsensical some of them may seem, are excellent story or anecdote beginnings, and each holds potential for therapeutic use with the Gina. Our purpose in doing this was to demonstrate that *everyone* can generate anecdotes or stories. The number one comment we hear in our workshops is, "But I'm not creative," or "I don't know how to come up with stories."

After some discussion, we revealed to the audience Gina's main issue in therapy: she wanted to know "What makes me strong?" The general consensus was that she was born strong, and when I (G. G.) saw her a few weeks later, she was greatly relieved when I told her, "All those people believe that you were *born that way*." During that session, I reinforced this notion of innate strength with a story we developed.

The Swallows Story

There was a family of swallows that had gathered at Capistrano, over by San Diego. We know that birds can't really talk like people, but somehow these birds were able to communicate a sense of history to each other across time.

Now, in the animal world, there are many amazing stories of migration, for example, the accomplishments of the Monarch butterfly, or how very small birds that weigh only a couple of ounces can fly from Canada to South America and back in one year. The migration of these swallows in Capistrano had gone fairly smoothly for a long time, except back in the early 1900s, when there had been a terrible hurricane that really upset many things in the world.

One little swallow (we'll call her Maria) watched as her mother's right wing was broken in that hurricane, and, sadly, her mother perished. Maria had to *take charge*, *guiding* her siblings to safety. This little bird showed remarkable *strength* in the face of tremendous adversity, and certainly, whoever thought up the term "bird brain" for incompetent people, Maria's feat would have made them eat their words, just like so much bird seed scattered in the backyard.

Maria eventually took up with a male swallow, and no one knows whether she ever sat on any eggs of her own. Nevertheless, throughout her days, even with the *noise* of that hurricane stuck in her brain, and the *frightened feeling* that went along with it, she kept a vigilant, beady eye on her mate who, quite possibly, in his own way, appreciated her *strength* and *dedication* to duty.

A week later, Gina made arrangements to finally get some much-needed rest, and placed her husband in a nursing home for two weeks while she took a vacation. In this case, story was an essential part of therapy. For those who think stories are just for children, let's remember that this client was a very anxious, 95-year-old woman with two hearing aids, a life-threatening illness, and an abusive husband at home. She was starved for empathy and relief, and a story played a major role in providing her with that.

GENERATING IDEAS FOR STORIES

Many of our stories are hardly original. We often read articles in magazines, like *Smithsonian* magazine or *National Geographic,* and then develop stories from those articles, giving credit, of course, to the original source. Clients tend to self-reference both stories about *someone else* and stories of the plant and animal kingdoms. They also seem to unwittingly incorporate the experience of inanimate objects that survive adversity and go on to prosper or endure.

The ego-strengthening story, "Highway One," was adapted from a magazine article about the Pacific Coast Highway in California. This meandering road requires nearly constant repair due to landslides and other natural consequences. A client who has suffered through numerous surgeries or other illnesses may unconsciously identify with "Highway One."

We generally like articles dealing with some aspect of nature. The story in Section II, "The Playing Field," used for encouraging lateral associations, was adapted from a book on the Mojave Desert. We keep an eye out for stories that inspire, or that may be provocative or instigative in some way. A book on music that contained a biography of Beethoven moved us to compose the story that we call "Beethoven." We owned a calendar of lighthouses, which inspired the story, "Lighthouse." We read many books, both fiction and nonfiction, as well as book reviews, such as The *New York Times Book Review*. Book reviews often incapsulate key ideas, which can provide us with essential material for stories, and save us time reading the book.

Milton Erickson's story, "Going from Room to Room" (Rosen, 1982), which we expanded into what we call "Simple Rooms" (Gafner & Benson, 2000), is perhaps the best instigative story we know of for helping free people from their constraints. We use it often in therapy. We wonder, too, whether that story in turn stimulates our own unconscious search for new stories? Perhaps. We seem to spend more time driving than we want to, and I (G. G.) keep a note pad on the front seat. When I get an idea from a song on the radio, or an audiobook, I jot it down. It might only be a word, or a fragment of an idea. When we have an idea for a story, we often develop it with each other through e-mail.

My (G. G.) yard in Tucson, Arizona is comprised of desert vegetation—various varieties of cactus, bushes, and desert trees. One day I noticed a large pack-rat nest built into a rock enbankment. The rats had their nest in the ground beneath the rocks, and above the ground they had characteristically heaped a mound of desert rubbish that they had packed there to protect their nest. The mound consisted of various branches and pieces of dead cactus, but it mainly contained the long, dry seed pods of a mesquite tree. It amounted to probably a large wheel-barrowful of mesquite pods, and I immediately wondered where they had gotten all those pods, as no mesquite tree was near.

I finally realized that they had gathered pods that had fallen from a large mesquite tree a hundred feet away. What had been a thick carpet of pods beneath the tree was now bare. I immediately thought, "What industry! Now, there's a story that we can develop," as it was evident that those pack rats had labored away over the course of many nights.

Now, we know that clients readily self-reference stories about other people, animals and plants, even inanimate objects that have endured adversity and gone on to survive and prevail. But *rats*? We are still fine tuning that one. Like any kernel of an idea that is potentially useful in therapy, we find that if it is important, and if, indeed, something *appears to be there*, then it will not go away, and will keep resurfacing when least expected. Fortunately, rats are not the only thing scurrying through our unconscious.

Fairy Tales with Children

Fairy tales seem to arrest the attention of children, whose attention span may not allow for the telling of a longer story. Fairy tales hold a message that children can relate to, and which metaphorically speaks to their own inner understanding of the world and the issues they ponder on an unconscious level. I (S. B.) rely on fairy tales in working with children, but I also use them with adults. These ingeniously simple devices help people relate to critical issues such as truth ("The Emperor's New Clothes"), self-efficacy ("The Little Engine that Could"), beauty and acceptance ("The Ugly Duckling"), death ("Charlotte's Web"), and identity and the benefits of different options ("The Prince and the Pauper").

Fairy tales provide us with a facile way to work hypnotically without inducing a formal trance. Listening to a familiar story allows the listener to become absorbed in another place, and frequently we will see signs of trance whether formally induced or not. I (S. B.) often see children go from excited, hyperkinetic creatures, to quiet, enthralled little people who pay such rapt attention that they can detect if anything is left out. Afterall, they have heard the story before, and will know if a parent shortens a story to hasten bedtime!

Bettleheim (1977) called fairy tales a unique art form that not only entertains and enlightens, but also fosters personality development in children. Characters in many fairy tales are either conspicuously good or bad, industrious or lazy, which matches young children's own way of seeing the world. Barker (1985) points out that traditional fairy tales may be losing out to present-day fairy tales, such as *Star Wars*, which essentially convey the same messages.

Fairy Tales with Adults

Therapists who use fairy tales with adults realize that adults may be lulled into listening passively without analytically trying to "figure out" the embedded message. Another benefit is that fairy tales, written ostensibly for children, are seen as harmless, posing no real threat to the listener. Thus, resistance is bypassed. Hans Christian Anderson's "The Pea and Princess" is an elegantly simple fairy tale that can be told at the end of a session. In the story, a prince is looking for a *real* princess to marry. He places a pea beneath 20 mattresses and 20 quilts, and one night a woman sleeps on this pile and wakes up sore in the morning, as she felt that one pea beneath all those quilts and mattresses. The prince now knows he has found his princess. Such a fairy tale is good for generating new behavior or solutions, as it creates response attentiveness.

Hans Christian Andersen himself may provide us with a useful story. This rather sorrowful figure revolutionized children's literature by expressing the most painful and raw emotions with extraordinary aesthetic control at a time when children's stories were exclusively moral and didactic. "The Ugly Duckling" was Andersen's most obviously autobiographical story. The unloved writer was himself ugly—in fact, grotesquely so—and he was ridiculed in his youth. However, he lived to have the last laugh, and his influence remains remarkable to this day, despite the best efforts of cartoon animators, children's authors, and others who distort the meaning of his tales (Allen, 2001).

Other Stories in Literature

Many unsophisticated clients who feel like the modern world has passed them by may identify with "The Legend of John Henry" (Small, 1994), the "steel drivin' man" who challenges the new steam drill. Greek myths may connect with some people, or more modern legends and folktales may be more apt. Many Hispanics in the American Southwest appreciate the "Legend of Juan Diego," the poor Indian who in the 1500s discovered the Virgin of Guadalupe on

Tepeyac Hill outside of present-day Mexico City. Others relish the legend of La Llorona, the Mexican "Crying Lady" who is searching for her lost child (Meza, 1994), as the legend is strongly rooted in the history of Mexico. For others, La Llorona may have a negative influence, as we have found that some Hispanic children in our practices who have nightmares or night terror were previously told this story, and when they hear the wind blowing at night an image of the sad, howling woman is triggered.

SHOULD STORIES BE DISCUSSED OR EXPLAINED?

No matter what therapeutic methods you employ, clients need to be oriented to, or "trained," in how to respond within the framework you have set up. This "stimulus control" then serves to anchor you in what you are comfortable with, and clients know what to expect. So, when we tell clients any one of these stories, especially at the end of the session, and hold off discussing possible meanings or interpretations, we hope to instigate an unconscious search. We explain to clients our rationale for doing this, and it communicates to clients that story— with this mode of delivery—is a primary means of therapy.

Some therapists like us will advocate *not* discussing a story, or at least delaying discussion until the following session. Of course, our reasons have to do with allowing unconscious processing to proceed without conscious interference. Michael Yapko (personal communication, December 9, 2001) and many others will argue that stories *need* to be discussed in order to reinforce key ideas, and that even Aesop explained his fables. Brent Geary (personal communication, May 15, 1998) also leans in this direction, and explains that a metaphor might be wasted on concrete clients if no discussion follows. Like many things in this book, we encourage you to try both ways, and see what works for you and your clients.

UNCONVENTIONAL USES OF STORY

The Man Who Was Cursed

I (G. G.) was asked to see an elderly Hispanic man, who was a patient in the long-term care unit of the hospital (Gafner & Duckett, 1992). He was refusing to eat, said he wanted to die, and saw Satan standing beside his bed. This man, then in his late seventies, and severely debilitated with Parkinson's, had had a productive life, serving four years in the Army in World War II, raising a family, and working as a copper miner until he retired.

I asked him if he had ever been cursed, and indeed he had, once at age ten when two Caucasian boys "put something in my soda pop, and then hit me over the head," and later in retirement "when I fell down and my body went as rigid as stone," which corresponded with the onset of his disease.

As I routinely do, I administered the Geriatric Depression Scale, and the gentleman scored in the severe range of depression. Speaking openly about the curse helped validate and *match* his experience. I then *added on* by reading him humorous stories in Spanish about people who had been cursed. Soon he began to laugh at the stories. He then started to eat regularly, and Satan soon disappeared from the side of his bed. After a while, I switched to other stories, also in Spanish, such as Hemingway's "The Old Man and the Sea." He lived five more years, and during this time had no more episodes of "cultural delusion" or psychotic depression. Subsequent administration of the depression scale yielded no depression.

Hysterical Postpartum Paralysis

Several years ago, as part of my (G. G.) pro bono work with the Refugee Clinic at the University of Arizona, I was asked to see a 20-year-old woman, Pilar, who was from El Salvador. Two weeks previously, she had given birth to her first child. The child was normal and healthy, but Pilar was paralyzed from the waist down. An extensive diagnostic workup yielded no medical reason for the paralysis.

She lived in a modest dwelling with her husband, baby, her husband's parents, and several other relatives. Chickens scurried in the dust outside the house. I explained who I was and my reason for visiting. She had no thought disorder, and she said she was not depressed or anxious, and got along well with her family. She endorsed no previous trauma, as is sometimes seen in refugees, and prior to this, her adjustment to the United States had been good. According to her, the only problem was that she had bladder and bowel incontinence, and that she couldn't care for her baby. She showed a chilling *belle indifference* that I had last seen in a state hospital 30 years before. She spoke in an eery, flat monotone that sounded like a voice in the wilderness. She was on no medications, and her health was otherwise good.

I frankly did not know what to do; however, I asked her if I could return in a few days to chat some more, and she said fine. In the meantime, I spoke with her husband, whose information was noncontributory. Pilar had strong social and emotional support. I returned with the Three Lessons story in Spanish and asked her if she would be willing to listen *closely and carefully* to some stories, correcting them, where necessary, so that I could use these in therapy with *other people from El Salvador*. I told her listening to these stories probably would not help her paralysis, but she agreed to proceed.

I visited her six times during two months. Each visit, she listened carefully to stories that I slowly read to her. Every few lines, she would say things like, "No, say this word instead," or make some other correction. Her affect was a bit less wooden by the last visit, but functionally, she was no better. Due to scheduling difficulties, I was unable to return.

A month later, I saw her at the clinic in a wheelchair, the baby on her lap. A month after that, I saw her again at the clinic. This time she was walking with a cane. Full functioning slowly returned, and even today, she walks with a slight limp. Now, I doubt if I can take credit for her improvement. In fact, in many ways, she probably helped me a lot more than I helped her, as she taught me an entirely new way to apply stories in therapy.

Clients Who Tell Their Own Stories

In our treatment groups, where clients become accustomed to our telling stories, often they will insert, "I have a story to read for the group. Okay if I do it next time?" We encourage these efforts in groups, as we do in individual and family therapy. Also, we may as clients, especially children, to supply their own ending to a story, or to tell their own in response to one of ours.

The significance of telling one's story in the legal arena is also something that can enrich therapy. For example, in divorce mediation, parties are permitted to "tell their story," as opposed to litigated divorce, where such expression is suppressed. When I (S. B.) worked for the Veterans' Administration, I saw where the preparation of a disability claim, which sometimes required the detailed recounting of trauma, was often very therapeutic in terms of desensitization. In my (G. G.) pro bono work with immigrants, a similar process occurs, in that they must prepare an affadavit in applying for political asylum.

The testimonio, where people speak out as witnesses to horrific experiences, was seen in Argentina in the 1980s, when the mothers of disappeared children publicly told their stories in the Plaza de Mayo (Aron, 1992). Such methods can be highly therapeutic, not only as desensitization, but as going on record against injustices (Chester, 1992). Holocaust survivors and refugee clients who were tortured may post their stories online, speak in schools and participate in other public means; however, these avenues may not be appropriate for clients who were raped, or endured other abuse or injustice. With them, of course, therapists have been employing the tape recorder, the writing of letters, and other means for many years.

DIVERSITY OF STORIES

Barker (1985) tells the story of the mimosa girdler, a beetle that provides a good example of *planning ahead*. The beetle cuts a hole in the branch of a mimosa tree, lays its eggs in the cavity, and then girdles the branch, chewing a circle in the bark, so that circulation is cut off. The branch eventually dies and falls to the ground, the larvae hatch, and the life cycle starts again.

Madanes (1981) uses that story (we have shortened it here, so that maybe anecdote is more apt) as a metaphor for planning ahead. She also uses it as a metaphor for people who are stuck in a dysfunctional system, and point out to them that human beings have much more problem solving capacity than beetles.

Barker (1985) employs story to help clients decide whether or not they even want therapy. After a few sessions, if a couple cannot make up their minds whether or not to continue, he tells them about two people stumbling along a trail in the forest. They arrive at a fork in the trail, where one sign points toward "therapy," and the other sign indicates "separation." He explains that the two people on the trail are not limited to those two options, but that they could also choose to get off the trail and fight their way through the undergrowth. Barker noted that the couple he told that story to let it sink in for a few days, and then called for an appointment.

CLINICAL COMMENTS

In this chapter, we show how a story can be woven into standard psychotherapy. The right story is not a "magic bullet," but it certainly can be a catalyst. Let's imagine that you are trained in some of the popular psychotherapy methods of the day, but that you have never used a story. All of a sudden you are stuck. Your client is not moving forward, and your automatic response is to do more of the same. Instead of repeating what you have already done, try aiming for that big unconscious target the client is holding up. Afterall, that is where you are likely to break through, on an unconscious level.

Rick Gellerman, a psychologist in Arizona who worked closely with Erickson in the mid-1970s, uses stories within psychotherapy and hypnosis more than anyone we know. He said once, "It takes a lot of nerve to start telling stories" (personal communication, April 11, 2002). Gellerman was asked one time what would happen if your story missed its unconscious target. He answered that one of the first things he learned from Erickson was that the unconscious is eminently protective, and that clients will simply forget those stories that do not connect. He added that his indispensable guide in story construction is a simple question he asks himself: "What do they need to hear so they can be okay?"

7

Brief Hypnotic Techniques

In your home or office, do you have a certain drawer, or a shelf, or maybe a box over in the corner, somewhere that you put things that do not have a designated place? Maybe a valued old book is there, or a keepsake, something that you take out on the right occasion, and then put it back so that it can be there when you need it again. An elderly handyman in Minnesota once told me (S. B.), "I always remember 'the right tool for the right job.' I may not need this special wrench for another five years, but I know where it is when I do need it." Well, now you know what we have in mind for this chapter.

At the end of the chapter, we will visit some concrete hypnotic techniques, like the cups of light and saguaro ribs, hands-on metaphors that can enhance clinical practice. But first, we will cover some verbal techniques, such as discharging resistance, then examine utilization, sequencing, and finally some paradigms and associated techniques that have served us well in therapy. All of these techniques have one major goal in common: to *break up symptoms,* or *pattern interruption.* Most chronic problems in clinical practice will dissolve, or change in some significant way, when we succeed in altering one aspect of the problem (Lankton & Lankton, 1986). We will be addressing that principle from different angles in this chapter. Consider this chapter that special place over in the corner.

WHAT IS RESISTANCE?

In recent years, the word *resistance* has almost become a dirty word. With political correctness, and the kinder gentler world in which many think we live, various pejorative terms have been relabeled. For example, we no longer say "undeveloped country," but "developing country," or "emerging nation-state" instead. However, no one has yet to come up with a new label for *resistance. Oppositional* or *defiant* are usually reserved for children, and words like *uncooperative, noncompliant,* or *nonadherant* do not capture the essence of what therapists grapple with day in and day out: the help-me-but-don't-*really*-help-me posture of clients. But that is built into the job, and we have to manage it, just like a pediatrician expects to deal with nervous parents, or the plumber expects to find the blockage in the first curve of the drain pipe.

Those who eschew the word as disrespectful or incorrect labeling are not all wrong. We might call clients resistant if we do not connect with them. We might call them resistant if they do not comply with a task, but then we must make sure they understood our instructions in the first place. Sometimes what we call resistance might be anxiety, or shyness, or self-doubt, and not necessarily some negative affective or cognitive state. It also usually has nothing to do with us as therapists, even though that might be difficult to believe when we are the object of hostile or angry behavior. We view most resistance as an unconscious phenomenon, outside of the client's awareness. That is why it needs to be addressed on an unconscious level.

Checking It Out

Let's say we have a client, either in the office alone or with family members, who, with his defiant nonverbals and curt verbal responses, certainly does not look like he wants to be here. We want to make sure people with palpable *conscious resistance* have the opportunity to leave. So we ask him, "You look like you'd rather be any place else but here . . . ," or, "Did someone else tell you to come here today? Your wife? Your boss?" This might clear the air so that you can go about your work. But what if it does not clear the air? At that point, we might begin "Pandora's Box," since it is a good short story for people who refuse to talk, or who proffer abrupt, unhelpful responses. More often we will go after that big target the client is holding up, the familiar "resistance target." The black-and-white concentric circles, the bull's eye in the middle . . . Can you see it?

Discharging Resistance

IN A GROUP. Did you ever walk into a meeting or a group of people and immediately sense some unease, or negativity, or something else that you couldn't quite put your finger on? Negative nonverbals can be palpable, and a real obstacle for you if you are there to lead the meeting or to speak to the class. If you ignore that feeling and proceed, you might overcome or bypass it. But what if you don't? If that resistance—negativity, anxiety, or whatever you want to call it— is potent, it can block your way.

We use this technique now and then to discharge such resistance. You'll need a confederate here, someone in the workshop or class who will discharge the group's resistance when you give the signal. For example, let's say we are speaking to a university class, and later in the hour we intend to do a group hypnosis exercise. There is always at least one person for whom the word *hypnosis* causes anxiety. So, when we get to that point in the lecture, we announce that we are going to be doing a group exercise, ". . . and if someone doesn't want to do that, you may get up and leave and return in 15 minutes." The confederate then nervously shuffles some papers loudly at his desk, stands up quickly, and exits.

Think of a tornado sucking the air out of the room. Well, that happens here as the collective resistance of the group exits with the confederate, producing an immediate calming effect in the room. We might then reinforce it with, "Anyone else? It's okay, feel free to leave, if you want." If someone else is pondering an escape, it is no longer necessary.

We learned this serendipitously a few years ago in a university classroom, where we were giving a lecture, and all of a sudden, the professor said, "How about an experiential exercise?" The atmosphere was immediately charged with *something* unpleasant (let's call it *resistance*). We asked if anyone wanted to leave, and then a terrified-looking young woman in back loudly shuffled some papers on her desk, arose, and shot out the door. The class responded marvelously to the experiential exercise, and we had learned a valuable new technique!

I (S. B.) was at a retreat a few years ago. It had already been a long two days, and we were tired when we broke into groups for a role-play exercise. The leader of the exercise played the role of therapist, and the others in the group played the roles of employees of a colleague who had died. None of us could get into the role-play. Instead, we cracked jokes and made glib remarks, which caused us to collapse into uncontrollable, helpless laughter. The concerned and serious therapist tried to rein us in so we could proceed with the exercise, but we simply continued in the same vein. Finally, in her role as the therapist, the leader cracked a dry joke about our sheer hopelessness, which caused everyone to laugh together. Only then were we able to "get back to work." It would not have happened had the leader not joined in, making it okay for us to let go.

WITH INDIVIDUALS. Milton Erickson was the first to note that clients' resistance might be successfully discharged if they say "no" several times. Of course, we do not just ask people to say "no" several times, but ask them a series of questions to which they must answer "no." For example, "Is it still raining outside?" or, "Will the temperature break 115 degrees today?" or, "Was it easy finding a parking place today?" or, "Did they give you a questionnaire to fill out in the waiting room?" We ask these questions casually, often with a bit of conversational "filler" in between.

Is this guaranteed to transform a hostile, negative person into a pleasant and receptive one? Of course not. We have found that this works approximately 60 percent of the time. If it does not work, you will have had several minutes to size up just how formidable the person's resistance is, and you might elect to ask the client to change chairs. Gestalt therapists could teach us a lot about this and related techniques. Erickson found that resistant clients, when asked to change chairs, *leave their resistance in the first chair*. This often works if "Pandora's Box" and "no" questions have failed. You know the intuition that comes with experience? Well, with practice, you will be able to determine which clients with whom it is best to move directly into changing chairs.

I've (S. B.) found this works especially well with teenagers. One thirteen-year-old girl agreed to change chairs, and then she agreed to listen as I told a story to the girl's imaginary friend in the first chair. All resistance evaporated, and her receptivity was remarkable.

As you may have guessed, the most difficult part of this for therapists is knowing what to say when you ask them to change chairs. Of course, you have to have an office with at least three chairs. In my (G. G.) office, which can comfortably accomodate 8 people, the desk and desk chair are located in a corner, away from where I conduct sessions or meetings with students. Still, when I say, "Sit wherever you like," some people then ask, "Which is your chair?" or "Where do you like to sit?" "Sit anywhere you wish," I reiterate. If they are resistant, they usually do not select the recliner. So, if they have chosen a place on one of the small couches, I may ask something like, "This may sound like a strange question, but do you mind sitting over here instead so I can get a better perspective on your situation?" or, "This is just a hunch, but I have an idea, which may become evident later on. Anyway, would you mind sitting over in that chair instead?"

I have never had anyone say no to one of these questions. You figure that most people are going to be at least minimally cooperative. Afterall, they bothered to show up in the first place. It is more complicated if they are in a wheelchair. Many people in wheelchairs are able to get up from them and move into a conventional chair. The really resistant ones remain in the security of their wheelchairs. I might say to them, "Can you get out of that chair?" If they say yes, I ask, "Just for the heck of it, how about if you leave that wheelchair for this session only, and try out that chair with the arms? I bet you'll be able to get in and out of it quite comfortably."

In one session, after I asked the client to sit wherever he liked, he went right over to my chair in the corner, casually sat down, and put his feet up my desk. I was duly shocked, appalled, and aghast, and did my best to remain calm. I spoke with him a while, got him to answer "no" several times, and then, on his own, he nonchalantly moved over to the recliner. I thought I was really getting somewhere with this individual, until, 30 minutes into the session, he announced, "You're wasting my time. Good-bye," and off he went. I never saw him again, but I have always appreciated his providing me with a good anecdote that describes utter failure at discharging resistance!

The "Yes Set"

Let's say our client, José, has had a good part of his resistance discharged, thanks to some stock "no" questions. He is a retired police officer, and he and his wife have had to raise their 15-year-old grandson. José turns out to be quite rigid, and there is a lot of conflict and tension in the home. His wife has told him, "Get some help for your anger, or I'm leaving!" It is time to switch from "no" to "yes." Now we want to ask him several questions to which he must answer "yes." Erickson demonstrated that if people respond affirmatively to innocuous questions that require a "yes" answer, a "yes set" is established, and from then on clients will more likely answer "yes" when asked important questions. For example, "Was there a lot of traffic on the freeway this morning?" and similar questions might yield some "yes" responses. I then say, "José, I want to ask you some questions about you and your family situation so that I can help you. Is this okay?" I am looking for *any* affirmative response, and I may offer a slight head nod as a prompt. If he grunts, "Go ahead, knock yourself out," or gives me nonverbal (a head nod, more open posture, less visible tension, etc.), I will latch on to it and plunge ahead. Something else that can aid in this process is to put it into a helping frame, such as simply asking, "Will you help me . . . ?" since most people are eager to help.

UTILIZATION

Utilization, also referred to as *Ericksonian utilization*, is a cornerstone principle of the therapy of Erickson. We see examples of utilization in everyday life, in cases people turning trouble into triumph. The maxim, "If life hands you lemons, make lemonade" is an example of utilization. We knew a woman once who complained bitterly that every evening her husband watched a ballgame on TV. Finally, after steaming about it for years, she announced to him that every time he watched a game he would have to give her a foot rub. Both were happy with the new arrangement. Similarly, when a tennis player is the recipient of a challenging serve, the player *accepts* this obstacle or challenge and makes the necessary adjustments with his or her arms, legs, or feet in order to *hit the ball where it is served*.

In the 1930s, Erickson worked at a psychiatric hospital in Massachusetts, and it was there that perhaps the most famous example of utilization occurred. A chronic, paranoid schizophrenic was deemed a rather hopeless case. He resided on one of the hospital's wards, where he heard voices and exclaimed that he was Jesus Christ to anyone who would listen. Erickson built a relationship with this man, talking to him off and on over a few weeks. Then one day, he joined with the man, agreeing that he was Jesus Christ, and added, "You must be a good carpenter," a "fact" the man could not refute. Thereafter, Erickson got the man to work in the hospital's woodshop, and his progress continued, and the man eventually left the hospital for a residence in the community.

A no less dramatic and impressive example of utilization with an acutely psychotic man was provided by Edgette (1988). In the case of Screaming Bobby, the therapist was asked to approach a volatile and unpredictable young schizophrenic who was in four-point restraints in the psychiatric unit. The fearful man's eyes darted wildly about the room in search of the voices. The therapist joined with the man's behavior, *pacing* the darting of the eyes, for example, " . . . you can look quickly over here, and then back again over there . . . ," and then *leading* with suggestions for slowing down and relaxation. After a few moments, the man's disturbed behavior was completely abated.

Utilization with José

Now admittedly, our client José is not as tough a client as the schizophrenic who claimed to be Jesus Christ. In fact, José is like many clients in your practice, and his behavior can be readily utilized in the service of therapy. Listening closely to José's words, we hear things like "the world has gone soft," and "a person has to be tough to survive," and "children these days have no respect for authority," and "a man has to stand up for what's right." José, in his own way— and the only way that makes sense to him—is trying his best to have a happy household, even though you might have a hard time convincing his wife and grandson of that.

"No" and "yes" have helped me join with José. Now, I give him a reframe: "José, you're obviously a man with *high standards* who loves his family and wants the best for them, and the way this has affected you may mean that you have a heightened *sensitivity* that goes along with your *strength* of conviction." As I reel out that reframe I monitor his nonverbals. He says nothing, but he exhales deeply, which I take to mean that I might have hit the mark. It is time to proceed by *adding on*, which is really the crux of utilization.

"José, I'd like to ask you to do one thing between now and next time. I would like to put your strength of observation to use by having you notice when your grandson is being good. Just notice, nothing more. Are you willing to do that?" He nods his head. I speak further with José about what it means to "catch him being good, or even not bad or neutral." Then I ask José to go to the waiting room while I see his wife and grandson. They agree to "cut him some slack" between now and next time.

The family does very well after that. José receives an antidepressant medication two months later, and he attends the anger group. Utilization made this possible.

More on Utilization

A woman named Deb told us she had hired a landscaper to redo her yard. Deb had a limited amount of money to spend and could not provide for the removal of three large, unattractive boulders in the middle of the yard. In a nonhypnotic example of utilization, the creative landscaper *incorporated* the boulders into his plan, and by *adding* certain trees, vines, and decorative stone, he *transformed* the boulders into ornamental elements of the yard (Gafner & Benson, 2000). In therapy, utilization is defined as the "readiness of the therapist to respond strategically to any and all aspects of the patient or the environment" (Zeig, 1994). Any aspect of the psychotherapy experience can be utilized, including the patient's style, dress, mannerisms, history, family, symptoms, and resistances.

With utilization, we accept clients rather than challenging or rejecting them. Each thought, word, deed, or problem is seen as unique, a *possible resource* in the service of therapy. Utilization enhances the therapeutic relationship because the therapist expresses *interest* and *curiosity* in all aspects of the client. It presupposes that clients already possess the needed resources to live meaningful lives, and that the therapist's job is to assist in their recovery. This approach uses behaviors or beliefs that already exist, as opposed to trying to implement completely new behaviors or force the adoption of beliefs that are alien to the client. Utilization allows therapists to approach clients flexibly, permissively and respectfully. Utilization is central to the Ericksonian approach, just as interpretation is central to psychodynamic therapy, or desensitization is to behavior therapy.

Therapists who begin to employ utilization sometimes choose to utilize too much. Brent Geary (personal communication, June 6, 1999), director of training at the Erickson Foundation in Phoenix, once told us, "You can utilize virtually anything, but you don't want to utilize everything." Again, the law of parsimony. Keep it simple. We suggest that you analyze the client's overarching values, or worldview, which can provide you with ample things to utilize. You have to listen closely, and usually the client will give you what you need within the first five minutes of the session. Maybe you need to *prepare* after the first session; *write out* precisely what you intend to deliver next time, or even check it out with a colleague. In a world where we readily write prescriptions or make referrals to remedy some deficit, we do not always listen closely to a client's words, or prepare what we are going to say to them. The easy approach would have been to recommend that José attend a parenting group, and the message inherent in that is, "José, you *do not* have within you the resources needed to solve your problem."

Operationally, utilization may be seen as:

Joining + Reframing + Adding on and *Transforming*

In other words, the equation is:

Joining (accepting and embracing the symptom) plus *reframing* (respecting its purpose or function, and positively connoting it) plus *adding on* in the direction of desired change by *transforming* (giving directives designed to modify the frequency, intensity, duration, location, timing, or some other aspect of the symptom).

In José's case, his paying attention to his grandson's acceptable behavior was the catalyst that interrupted what had been a monolithic symptom. The key word here is *and*, probably the most important word in psychotherapy.

SEQUENCING

A related way to break up key components of a problem is *sequencing*, a technique that is emphasized in training at the Erickson Foundation (Geary, personal communication May 5, 2001). When clients explain their complaint, it is usually described as a static entity, whereas it is really a dynamic process. To access the dynamic process, look for sequences. Clients may view problems as discrete events, as "my bad habit," or "my depression." With anxiety, the therapist, with careful questioning, may determine a sequence such as: 1) breathing faster; 2) defocusing and becoming diffuse in perception; 3) making agitated movements; 4) perceiving others to be intimidating; 5) having anxious thoughts; and 6) having a cigarette or going for a walk to eliminate feelings of despair (Zeig, 1994).

Those precise steps could be *utilized*, or paced, in a hypnotic induction, so that the client experiences those same six steps, but they do *not* lead to a negative state. Instead, they lead to a positive state, as the therapist *adds on* in the direction of relaxation. The six steps can also be paced metaphorically, perhaps in a story about *someone else* who experiences those same six steps, but who then "slowly, ever so slowly, begins to go inside, where she notices the pleasantness and comfort of peace and relaxation."

Similarly, metaphor can be used, albeit one further step removed, by describing, for example, a train that starts out from the station, its engine revving up, all the moving parts shaking and shuddering, striving to stay on the track, etc. "Once it got out into the country, it began to *just slow down*, and out there in the country, that train, as only trains can, began to experience, in its own way, the pleasantness and sheer comfort of coasting to a stop. . . ."

O'HANLON'S LIST

O'Hanlon, who has probably elucidated the many aspects of pattern interruption better than anyone, indicates that pattern interruption is suitable for therapists who practice both directly and indirectly. In *A Brief Guide to Brief Therapy* (Cade & O'Hanlon, 1993), the authors describe the various ways therapists can accomplish this task:

1. Alter or change the rate or frequency of the symptom pattern.
2. Alter the duration.
3. Alter the time, day, week, etc.
4. Alter the location (in the body, in the world, etc.)
5. Alter the intensity.
6. Alter some other circumstance of the symptom.
7. Alter the sequence or order of events around the symptom.
8. Jump from the beginning to the end of the sequence (create a short-circuit).

9. Prevent all or part of the sequence from occurring by interrupting or derailing it.
10. Add or subtract one or more elements from the sequence.
11. Break up any previously whole element into smaller elements.
12. Perform the symptom without the symptom pattern.
13. Perform the symptom pattern minus the symptom.
14. Reverse the pattern.
15. Link the occurrence of the symptom pattern to some other ongoing pattern of behavior.

You might be able to think of even more ways of interrupting a pattern. If not, read the story, "Simple Rooms," in Chapter 19, and see if any more ways come to mind.

GETTING CLIENTS TO PARTICIPATE IN PATTERN INTERRUPTION

We sometimes tell clients a little story that delineates a pattern interruption. There are also numerous numerous direct ways, which could be another long list. You may already have some techniques in your repertoire. Hypnotic language is helpful, and setting up any directive with truisms is indispensable. Tying the directive into the goal ("better mental health," "a happier marriage") is important; however, neither of these may be enough to induce people to do something differently. Sarah Trost, a psychology intern, introduced us to "an experiment," which often arrests clients' attention. For example, "This has been a very challenging problem, and I think a little experiment may be in order so we can test out an idea. I'd like you to . . . ."

Erickson had success getting people to climb Squaw Peak, or to lie in a drainage ditch for 30 minutes. However, since we are not Erickson, we may have to bring out bigger guns to get the job done. We often use either the *study rationale,* or the *bring-under-voluntary-control rationale.* Both of these are compliance-based techniques, in that we want people to do them (at least up to a point), and people understand and agree with the rationale for doing them.

An example of the *study rationale* is:

> *José, I've given some thought to your criticizing your grandson, and I would like to understand it even better, just*

what goes on there. Accordingly, I'd like you to keep track of it [the frequency, rate, location, etc.] between now and next time. Here's a handy study card I've prepared. Would you be willing to do that?

The *bring-under-voluntary-control rationale* might be:

José, this criticizing your grandson almost seems to have a life of its own, almost as if it is involuntary on your part. Accordingly, before the next session I'd like you do it only in the morning, to limit your criticizing just to mornings. Of course, the purpose of this is to see if you can reign it in, to bring it under voluntary control. Are you willing to do that?

A related technique is to suggest that José is critizing at the behest of someone else, perhaps to pay a debt to his deceased mother. No one likes to think that someone else is controlling them. I (S. B.) often use "structured worry time." The client chooses a specific time to worry every day. My instructions to her include recording the worries and dividing them into two categories: "Can Do Something about It" and "Can't Do Something about It." Any worries that pop up outside of the designated time are dismissed with the comment, "I'll worry about *that* at my worry time." The client then implements a distractor thought. This technique often greatly diminishes worrying frequency.

RESPECT FOR DIGNITY

It is often tempting to therapists to try out some exotic technique. If you are familiar with the literature on paradoxical therapy of the 1970s and 80s, you have read those elaborate schemes that almost seem like they were written for the amusement of the therapist rather than the benefit of the client. If you schedule the symptom or prescribe an ordeal out of knee-jerk frustration, it may be perceived as disrespectful to the client. We must remember that no directive is likely to be complied with until a trusting relationship is established, and the delivery of any directive should always be done with the utmost respect. We never venture forth with technique or directive if we think the client's dignity could be compromised.

NOT JUST FOR BIRTHDAY PRESENTS

When you issue a directive to clients, you don't simply tell them what to do in a vacuum. Instead, you tie it into the presenting problem and offer a rationale for completing the task. They understand and agree to it. You're working together. This is a cooperative venture.

We do those things, but we also "gift wrap" a directive, or technique, with hypnotic language, like apposition of opposites, and "power words" (such as *discover* and *wonder*), metaphor, and story. Including these things not only fosters *conscious*-receptivity and compliance, but also enhances acceptance on an *unconscious* level. If the conscious mind is intelligent and the unconscious is even wiser, let's appeal to the most discerning part of the person. After all, if that astute and protective unconscious gives the go-ahead for a task, then we're both working on the same page.

PATTERN INTERRUPTION PARADIGM

Our clients, the Bickersons, have already been to four therapists, and their marital problem is longstanding. We've seen them for three sessions, and rapport and trust are established. We know from their history that this is the point where they bail out of therapy. To keep them in therapy, and to move the process forward, we want to think of what they do in basketball: the full-court press. In other words, let's bring our sharpest tools to bear on the problem.

We employ the following outline as a general guide:

  I. Reframe
 II. Attempts at resolution
     • To relieve anxiety?
     • To get closer?
III. DIRECTIVE: alter the sequence with one of the following:
        • splitting
        • adding
        • subtracting
        • modifying
            ■ intensity
            ■ frequency
            ■ duration
            ■ location
            ■ timing

Here is how we could deliver the directive to the Bickersons. We don't just give them the task; rather we set it up, follow it with the appropriate rationale, gain their commitment, and finish the gift wrapping with a bind.

Mr. and Mrs. Bickerson,marriage is a tough job, *and, you've shown a lot of* strength *and* staying power, *along with a good measure of loyalty and love during all these years. Now, I've been listening closely to you these past few weeks, and I can see, Mrs. Bickerson, that you* want more closeness, *and as you* reach out *to your husband, sometimes he* pulls away *because he feels ambivalent. Then, as you* try harder, *it becomes more frustrating for you. and the* angrier *you get. Mr. Bickerson, your* wife's anger and pursuit make you uncomfortable, *maybe even irritated, and you* put up a wall, *and the harder she tries, the stronger your wall becomes, and I'm sure this whole thing causes anger and frustration on your part.*

reframe
reframe

attempts at resolution

attempts at resolution

"*Now both of you seem ready to be more happy in the relationship, and it's time to make things better on your own terms, for each of you. Mrs. Bickerson, I want you to continue to provide such feedback to your husband, but* only in the living room *in the morning after breakfast and before work.*

directive: alter location
directive: alter timing

We know that people can learn from criticism *and that it definitely* has its place *in life. Mr. Bickerson, I want you to* continue to rely on your wall, *but when your wife is criticizing you in the living room in the morning, I'd like you to* not let that wall be so high, *and* lower *it just a tiny bit, maybe* loosen

rationale

directive: alter intensity

some mortar between the bricks in one area only. We recognize *the* importance *of* protecting *yourself and remaining* strong *while at the same time continuing to be* sensitive *to everything going on around you.*

rationale

Can I count *on each of you to closely follow these instructions between now and next time, for the sake of the marriage?* Okay, *let me repeat the instructions, and I can even write them out for you. . .*

commitment

You can select how you will use this when you leave here today, or discover its utility at home; or you might think of how this is useful, or simply ponder the benefits of doing it right

bind of comparable alternatives

Your conscious minds might already have some ideas of how you will use this, while your unconscious takes care of doing it correctly;

conscious/unconscious bind

or

An unconscious learning from this experience may be developed in the conscious mind as well.

conscious/unconscious bind

One couple I knew let their conscious minds select the site for using this learning, while their unconscious minds were trusted to carry it out, and another couple allowed their conscious minds to carry it out, while their unconscious minds selected the location and time;

double dissociative conscious/unconscious double bind

or

Your conscious minds can be interested in what we talked about today, while your unconscious minds can really learn from it, or perhaps your uconscious minds only allow you to develop a mild interest, as your conscious minds determine the extent of learning.

conscious/unconscious bind

THE GREEK CHORUS

For versatility, flexability, and potency, this technique has no peer. Traditionally, the Greek chorus employs a consultation group behind a one-way mirror. The group directs therapy by sending in messages to the therapist at intervals during the session. The clients never see the group. It is an invisible eye, a prophetic voice that is unapproachable, unimpeachable, and unnegotiable (Papp, 1983). The group may send in praise or encouragement to the family. More often, the group creates a therapeutic triangle, which can give important leverage to the therapist.

In Tucson we do not have a one-way mirror, but we do have a consultation group of five interns who give input on each case. This group of interns is our Greek chorus, a potent ally to the therapist. Clients experience the therapist not as working alone, but as part of a team that can provide innumerable options to the therapist. They experience the therapist as having the benefit of a panel of experts. In your own practice, you may wish to use others in your office as the Greek chorus.

The Greek chorus can be used at any time, but it is especially helpful when the therapist is stuck. For example, Karen is working with a couple, Dave and Melinda. Dave wallows in his posttraumatic stress disorder (PTSD) and chronic pain, and is quick to anger, while the younger Melinda pulls away from her husband, whose attempts at *communication* are seen by his wife as querulousness, vain anger, and manipulation.

Karen checks in with the couple and determines that there has been no change since the last session. She explains to the couple that she is pleased to present the findings of her supervision group, that has been studying their case since the beginning of therapy. First, she says something like this:

> *Dave and Melinda, I've seen you now*   truisms
> *for* five sessions, *and each time we've*
> *met at* 3:00 on Tuesday.
>
> *This list I have here before me, you*
> *don't have to listen to these helpful ideas,*   restraint
> *as I'll be giving each of you a card on*
> *which they are written out. Now, what's*
> not *on the card is the notion that these*

ideas may contain part *of the solution within the collective* whole, *while* all *of the ideas* together *may provide you with some valuable tips.*	bind of comparable alternatives
Some *of the ideas may be pertinent* now, *while* others—*or maybe just one— will be helpful* later. *You may reject all of them outright, but after hearing them,* one *may have special meaning at a* later date.	bind of comparable alternatives suggestion
One couple *we gave a similar list to, they* discovered *something profoundly useful among the ideas, but only after several days had passed.*	metaphor power word

She then produces a sheet of paper that contains the notes from of her Greek chorus.

1. Katharine notes that the couple is doing the best it can under the circumstances.
2. Charles (who is usually right about most things) says that the couple will do worse before they do better. In fact, he thinks a crisis might be just around the corner.
3. George's opinion is unclear, as he finds the case rather mystifying.
4. Both Mary and Sandy think that a surprise is forthcoming in the couple's *communication*. Mary thinks the surprise will come from Dave, but Sandy believes that both Melinda and Dave are capable of something surprising in the near future.
5. Laura (who is often wrong) thinks that the couple may be on the verge of a breakthrough.

Karen, the therapist, says she is not sure what to think. She then turns to her agenda for the rest of the session.

In subsequent sessions, the couple may expect, or want, regular opinions from the supervision group. Karen may use the technique every session, or at intervals. This technique stimulates the clients' imaginations and allows them to suspend judgment while the therapist puts forth directives in the desired direction.

RITUALS

A well-designed ritual, like an apt story, can both arrest attention and serve to transform a stuck situation. Erickson once saw a man who could only urinate through a tube. The man was rejected by the Armed Forces when he tried to enlist, so he sought Erickson's help. Erickson embraced and utilized the symptom, encouraging the man to keep peeing through the tube, albeit through a progressively shorter and shorter tube, until eventually he peed through only his curled up hand. The man was accepted into the military.

This case is a good example of ritual. Other rituals have stronger social contexts, in that they are connected to weddings, funerals, family traditions, or other occasions that carry meaning. In one of our cases at the V.A. in Tucson, Mirto Stone and Paul Sacco devised a ritual with a World War II veteran and his wife. More than 50 years after that war ended, the client, Leroy, continued to search for enemy around the perimeter of his house. He could not drive down a certain palm-tree-lined road because he could "see Japs in the palm trees," he reported. As Leroy and his wife were ill with cancer, they wanted to "help people in the future to know what veterans and their wives go through." Accordingly, the two interns helped the couple videotape their story, complete with Leroy's Army medals, family pictures, etc. Leroy and his wife are long deceased, but many continue to see the tape and learn from their experience.

In another case, Josétte had a client who couldn't make up his mind whether or not to divorce his wife from whom he had been separated for several years. Josétte was unsuccessful in helping him make up his mind until she began to work with the man's wedding ring. Part of the directive involved shifting the ring from his left hand to his right hand, and to different fingers on different days. After a few days of this, he filed for divorce.

To construct a ritual, ask clients about their traditions and listen closely as they describe their daily activities. Josétte rapidly picked up on the above client's wedding ring, how he toyed with it and frequently referred to it. Like a newspaper reporter, ask *who, what, when, where, how,* and *why.* Be a detective, dig deep, ask penetrating questions to get the information you need. Listen for the words, concepts, and values used by clients. For example, your client might say, "People wear white hats and black hats." A ritual could then be devised in which family members exchange hats, wear two at a time, or in different areas of the home, etc.

You might have used a similar technique, such as asking your client to write a letter to a deceased person, then bury or burn the letter. Or if a partner is still simmering from an affair, have him or her "put it on ice." For further reading on the subject of ritual, consult Combs and Freedman (1990), and Imber-Black (1989).

THE AMBIGUOUS FUNCTION ASSIGNMENT

You will want to use this technique when you are really stuck with clients, and when straightforward and other interventions have failed. The ambiguous function assignment (AFA) may help retrieve the essential problems faced by clients, and it may retrieve new resources for the clients to put to use. Most importantly, it can help break up the seemingly intractable chain of problematic behavior.

The chief characteristics of AFA are that it can be completed in an easy way, that it has a specific time, place, and function, and that the task has a uniqueness or unusualness that will stimulate curiosity. The difference between AFA and a regular behavior prescripion is that a behavior prescription has an expected outcome, while with AFA the outcome is unknown.

An example:

> On Tuesday and Thursday evenings—precisely at 8:35— both of you are to go into the bathroom and tie a string to the medicine cabinet. On Tuesday, you, Sharon, are to tie a red string—be sure to emphasize your left hand—and on Thursday, Clyde, you tie a blue string. Let's make sure you've got it right. . . .

Utilize the environment that is familiar to the clients. For example, Gates Pass is in one of the mountain ranges that encircles Tucson. We might say to the clients:

> Drive out to Gates Pass exactly when the sun is going down on Saturday evening. When you get there, walk on the main path that leads from the parking lot, and after you have walked 20 paces, look down at the first big rock you see, and

> *precisely at that moment,* something important will come to
> mind that will help you with your problem.

Create a positive expectation. Let them know that this is not a
worthless exercise, and that something of considerable value will
come of it. Assign a very specific task (time, place, behavior), but do
not reveal the purpose (this is the ambiguous part). Utilize some
tangible object and utilize what clients give you. Make sure the clients
are behaviorally involved in this active task. When they ask what the
purpose is say, "You'll find out . . . and you'll learn when you're there."

The AFA capitalizes on clients' capacity for discovery, allows them
to pursue personal meaning, and focuses on *new learning.* Importantly, it helps the therapist to maintain leverage. In the delivery,
imply that it is tailored to clients' special needs, for example, "I have
an assignment that you are ready for" or "that the team believes is
exactly right for you at this time." Present it with compelling
expectancy (tone, facial expression, strategic pauses) and sincerity.
When they return next session, you may not wish to accept the
meaning they have come up with: "I'd like you to go back and do this
one more time, but this time, go 30 paces. . . ." You are shooting for
the "Ah-HA!" experience.

DRUMMING

Of the various musical instruments that can be incorporated into
therapy, the drum may be the most hypnotic. A therapist in Tucson,
William Brubaker, regularly uses drumming in therapy with children.
He often begins therapy by inviting children to begin drumming, and
then he matches their rhythm with his own drumming. "All you need
is cheap drums," he says. And the noise? "Other therapists complained at first, but now they're used to it," he explains. Maurer and
colleagues (1997) found that higher hypnotizables were more likely
to report relaxed feelings and shamanic-type experiences during
drumming.

MOVIES

Have you ever had a friend tell you, "You *need* to rent this video," or,
"You *need* to read this book." Well, often these statements strike us as

overly directive, or intrusive, like someone saying, "You *should* do something about your hair." We know many therapists who routinely assign watching such-and-such a video, as its depiction, in the therapist's opinion, is a good example of surviving PTSD, or some other problem. Now, such a task is a bit more involved than reading an article, or performing some other directive, and we think that oftentimes the video may not be as meaningful to clients as it is to us. For these reasons, we recommend video viewing very judiciously.

One movie we assign is *The Mission,* as its meta-message seems to resonate with some clients who are stuck in blame, such as their partner had an affair and they are unable to forgive. *The Mission* takes place in the seventeenth century in South America. A Spaniard kills his brother and he goes to a priest and asks how he can pay a penance for his terrible sin. The priest assigns a terrible physical ordeal to the murderer. As he goes about completing his task, he asks when he will know he has paid sufficient penance, and he is told that *only he will know* when he has suffered enough.

We also use movies to warm children to therapy. I (G. G.) sometimes show a segment of the movie *Shrek* to children, and then discuss it. The big, blustery green monster, Shrek, is eminently discussable, and opens the door to processing vital feelings. What better way to join with children than to "bond" with them over a favorite movie?

CONCRETE TECHNIQUES

There is a vast array of techniques, especially for use with children, that involve dolls, play, drawing, coloring, and a sand tray. Let us review a few of our favorite techniques.

Bowls of Light

We first learned of this technique from Joyce Mills, who demonstrated bowls of light at the Erickson conference in Phoenix in 1999. The technique, also described in her book (Mills, 1999), is especially useful with children, but can also be adapted for therapy with adults. We use modeling clay as a prop. Sometimes we choose the kind that hardens as it dries, and sometimes we choose the kind that can be continually reshaped. We mold the bowls as we speak, and have clients do the same. I (S. B.) have also used it for career-day talks to high school students when they ask what a psychologist does for work. After the story, I simply tell them we are in the business of teaching people to dump out rocks. As with most stories, it can also be used effectively with adults as a simple anecdote or fable to stimulate thinking. With small children, I often alter the following story so that it is age-appropriate. It is adapted from a Mills story.

The Bowl of Light

This story comes from a long-ago Hawaiian tradition. As you may know, everyone is born with a bowl of pure light. This is the light in each of us that shines through with joy and peacefulness. We must nurture the light within each of us to allow it to continue to grow and give us each the ability to do amazing things. As we go through life, we might encounter difficulties and hardships. These are stones we pick up and place in the bowl of light. As the stones take up more and more space, the light cannot shine as well, and the bowl gets heavy. At that time, we must learn how to carefully tip the bowl over and turn out all the stones to allow the pure light to shine through once again.

The Saguaro Rib

As you may know, the saguaro is a tall cactus with mighty arms that grows in some desert regions. These green titans are supported by a rib cage composed of *strong* but *flexible* pieces of wood. In working with rigidity, either the inflexible posture of an individual client, or with stepfamilies, one person in the stepfamily may be resistant to change. To reach this person metaphorically, I (G. G.) often reach for this handy prop, the remains of a saguaro that had lived some 150 years, which I found in the desert. Holding out the rib, I ask, "What do you think this is?" Some might recognize it, while others have to be told. I then ask, "What are the properties of this saguaro rib?" Some might answer concretely: "It's wood," or "It's hard," or "It's straight." I then flex it, showing the rib's strength. Again, some might then respond, "Oh, it's strong but flexible," while others have to be told. Some clients might then say, "Oh, I see where you are going with this," or, "Okay, I get the point," at which point I often restrain them with something like, "Now don't read too much into this. Afterall, isn't it just a piece of wood from a dead cactus?"

If you do not live in the desert, is there a similar metaphor that you can employ in therapy, something in your basement or garage, or something that grows naturally nearby?

Radiator caps

Several years ago, I (S. B.) worked with a family that consisted of a father and a teenaged daughter. The father had not spent much time with his daughter during earlier years, and a crisis brought them to therapy. There were many emotions *bubbling* just below the surface, but they were kept under strict control. When asked about beginning to open up and let go of some of their feelings, their responses were of fearfulness that either the emotions would not be stopped-up again, or that severe damage would result. The following session, I gave them each a radiator cap that I had purchased from an auto-supply store. I told them:

> *When you drive a car for a long time, it gets hot. When a car is hot, you can't just open up the radiator, because you would be sprayed with scalding water. That is why they invented radiator caps that allow you to* open the radiator just enough *to let out the dangerous heat and steam. After it cools a bit, you can* take off the cap completely *and* put it back on *without fear of being burned.*

The father and his daughter smiled, and we moved on with the session. They gradually began to process a lifetime of held-back emotion. I am confident that long after they forget their therapist, or the specifics of therapy, they will remember the radiator cap.

Balloons

What is it about therapy that we spend so much time dealing with anger? I (S. B.) am seeing a client, Phil, who just does not get it. I have been over the anger log with him, and he has learned to use his anchor, albeit unsuccessfully. The doctor started him on Tegretol two months ago, but he still blows his stack, and his temper has him in constant trouble. A couple of our best stories hardly make a dent. What can I do next?

This is when balloons come in handy. "Phil, here are three balloons," I say. "Pick out whichever one you like." He selects the green one, and I instruct him to blow it up. He does so, and I ask him to hold on to it *ever so tightly* as he releases the air. It spurts out like so much irate flatulence. I continue:

> *Okay, Phil, now choose another balloon, and this time, after you blow it up so that it is good and hard, I'd like you to see if you can let the air out . . .* very, very slowly.

He does this, and seems proud of his effort. From then on, he is able to successfully apply straightforward techniques that before had not penetrated him in the least.

Raisins

Demonstrations of Zen and mindfulness have long employed raisins to arrest attention and help people *slow down* and *notice specifics*. We first saw raisins used by Shauna Shapiro during a mindfulness workshop. She passed out to each participant a small cup containing two or three raisins. She asked:

> *Pick up just one raisin and hold it in front of you, noticing the particular qualities of this raisin. Hold it up to the light. How does it appear now? Roll it between your thumb and forefinger, paying close attention to how it feels. Now, put it in your mouth and feel its texture and as you bite down on it. . . .*

In therapy, when you want people to *slow down, notice, and appreciate,* there is no better technique than the raisin. We occasionally take out the raisins for *ourselves* during a session. Let's say it is the seventh or eighth appointment of the day and your own radiator cap has blown off. At that point, asking your client to pick up the raisin can provide you with a brief respite.

Feeling cards

One year, an intern, Marianne Mora, made up some "feeling cards" on her computer, and they soon became a staple concrete technique with children, and even with some adults. The laminated cards show a variety of faces—happy, sad, angry, etc.—and corresponding cards contain the written feeling word. The therapist can employ these cards in numerous ways. Use of the card concretizes what may be difficult to discuss, thus paving the way for active verbal processing. When I (G. G.) say to two sisters, "I'd like each of you to select two cards—and only *two*—that may show how you feel," they often are eager to discuss their cards. If not, I may lapse into an anecdote, or story, that matches their anxiety or ambivalence, and such indirect permission often leads to the target discussion.

Food

We know of no better ice breaker than food. As clients reach for a piece of hard candy, they may suddenly feel "at home." Children love simple finger foods, like pretzels. Some therapists we know have cold drinks or coffee for clients. Other therapists may feel that providing food or drinks "de-professionalizes" their solemn altar of change. Maybe they simply don't like to worry about spilled drinks or picking up candy wrappers.

CLINICAL COMMENTS

Formal trance, which is covered in Section II of this book, allows the therapist much greater access, especially to the unconscious mind. However, even if you never practice formal hypnosis, there is an array of hypnotic techniques that can be incorporated into everyday talk therapy. Many of these we have drawn from the interpersonal, brief or strategic therapies, all of which have roots in the tradition of Erickson. We encourage you to read some of the writers we reference, so that you can further bolster what we hope is your burgeoning storehouse of techniques to influence behavior change. We keep mostly nonperishable goods in our storehouse. Raisins keep a long time, and a radiator cap will last forever. The history of stories is that they can last forever, too, though people tend to adapt them to changing circumstances. And your own, yet-to-be-developed metaphors will never have a shelf-life as long as you pass them on to someone else.

Section II

Hypnosis

8

An Overview of Hypnosis Applications

WHAT IS HYPNOSIS?

If you read Section I of this book, you already know the answer to the question, What is hypnosis? But if you are starting the book here, let us list a few common definitions of hypnosis: guided daydreaming; believed-in imagination, controlled dissociation; a relaxed, hypersuggestible state; a halfway point between sleep and consciousness; and a narrowing of conscious attention and facilitation of unconscious receptivity. Yapko (2001) notes that in 1993 the American Psychological Association adopted a definition of hypnosis as "a procedure wherein changes in sensations, perceptions, thoughts, feelings, or behavior are suggested."

Definitions aside, theoreticians continue to debate whether hypnosis can be explained in socio-psychological terms, or as "special

119

process"; whether it is a state or a trait; or if it is merely dissociation. Kirsch and Lynn (1995) note that within all these "warring camps" there is a complicated topography of issues, along with a continuum of positions by experts in each "camp." Others, like Yapko (1990), say it is a meaningful interaction in which the clinician and client are responsive to each other. (Who was it that said, "If you can be socialized, you can be hypnotized"?) Most important, we believe, is the idea that trance phenomena are natural and normal, something we experience every day when we lose track of time, drift off in a daydream, or become absorbed in pleasant music or a good book. In fact, we mention these naturalistic examples to clients when introducing them to trancework to show that trance is not magical, that the therapist is not a magician. In other words, the therapist is a guide who helps people elicit experiences of which we all are capable, whether it is a heaviness in one hand or the other, subjective mental and bodily relaxation, pleasant imagery, an improved sense of well-being, an overall meaningful experience, or some other therapeutic objective.

We may also reinterpret problematic behavior in terms of hypnotic phenomena (Delaney & Voit, 2001). Childhood trauma or shame may be seen as *age regression*, or a fear of failure in the future as *age progression*. Fantasies of abandonment or rejection may be viewed as *positive hallucination*, and avoidance or denial of an issue *negative hallucination*. Along the same lines, a depressed mood is equivalent to emotional *catalepsy*, or the *amnesia* of positive experiences, combined with *time distortion* (time expansion), and *anesthesia*. A person with anxiety experiences *time distortion* (time condensation) during an episode of panic, as well as *age progression* (the anticipation of future anxiety). To be sure, the most common applications for hypnosis—anxiety, pain, and depression—can all be reduced to hypnotic phenomena as component parts. Furthermore, because of this natural fit, hypnosis can be viewed as an isomorphic intervention for the most typical clinical presentations we see in practice.

WHO SHOULD PRACTICE HYPNOSIS?

Section I of this book is intended for masters-level-and-above mental health professionals licensed in psychology, social work, counseling, psychiatry, and related disciplines. Section II is intended for these same people, but with the proviso that the practice of formal hypnosis requires more than simply reading this section. We strongly encourage these clinicians to seek training with the Milton H. Erickson Foundation, which has component societies throughout the world. We have taken such training, and I (G. G.) am also a member of the American Society of Clinical Hypnosis (ASCH), as well as the International Society of Hypnosis. I (S. B.) am also a member of ASCH, and hold certification, a higher credential, with the organization.

Practitioners will want to be familiar with the many available publications centered around hypnosis. ASCH publishes the *American Journal of Clinical Hypnosis*. Other excellent, clinically oriented journals are *Contemporary Hypnosis*, published by the British Society of Clinical and Experimental Hypnosis, and the *Australian Journal of Clinical Hypnosis*. There are also *Hypnos*, published in Sweden, and the *International Journal of Clinical and Experimental Hypnosis*, though these periodicals may be of more interest to the scientist than to the clinician.

LEARN HYPNOSIS AND PSYCHOTHERAPY ONLINE

We emphasize that a practitioner of hypnosis must be a therapist first and a hypnotherapist second. As such, hypnosis ideally is one of several techniques employed by the clinician. We mention this because your clients may have previously experienced hypnosis provided by either an unlicensed professional or a licensed professional with inadequate training.

A search on the Internet yields hundreds of places where people can "learn to be a hypnotist" through a correspondence course or online or classroom training. Your clients may have undergone hypnosis with someone who has had such training. Does that mean that they did not receive adequate help? Of course not. We all know people who stopped smoking, or lost weight, by attending a two-hour, "money-back-guaranteed" seminar. However, we also know people like the schizophrenic man I (G. G.) treated who had been given several sessions of hypnosis by a counselor instead of referring him to a psychiatrist for medication.

In most states, you can't call yourself a psychologist unless you are licensed as such. Not so with hypnosis. In fact, a person with a sixth-grade education can advertise himself as a "hypnotist," and you can go to him for any imaginable problem. In the United States, there is no state license or certification in hypnosis. Instead, people are licensed, or certified, in states that do not have a licensing law, according to professional discipline, and they may practice hypnosis. The general public does not know this. Many mental health professionals may also suffer from misinformation in this area, and they too may view hypnosis through the same "magic-bullet," or negative-stereotype lens. Again, hypnosis is a loaded word, a veritable lightning rod for things positive and negative, and if you call what you do hypnosis, be prepared to explain it to clients and colleagues alike.

A woman recently phoned me (G. G.) and said she wanted to do an internship, as she had recently earned her masters degree in psychology online. She mentioned the school's name, which I had never heard of, and added, "It's fully accredited." I politely told her to look elsewhere for her training.

"Elsewhere" for practicum experiences is full to the brim. In the United States, the proliferation of masters level programs at private and public universities, along with online and correspondence education, has produced a large harvest of practitioners. Among doctoral-level psychologists alone, hundreds of interns must compete for a limited number of training sites approved by the APA. We wonder where all of these people will end up finding jobs. If we continue to psychopathologize everyday behavior, perhaps everyone will either need medication or psychotherapy, or both.

Many psychologists are interested in acquiring additional therapeutic tools, such as hypnosis. We are excited about the burgeoning interest in our favorite subject, and hope this book either sparks interest in the reader new to hypnosis, or leads to skill acquisition for the seasoned clinician. We acquired our own competence through much training and clinical practice and we regard skill acquisition as a continuing process. In the hypnosis training program that I (G. G.) conduct with Bob Hall, a medical psychologist, we train four psychology interns and five masters-level interns in psychology, social work, and counseling. They are assigned to one of two weekly experiential/didactic training groups, which are concurrent with their other mental health training experiences. They build their skills in hypnosis throughout the year, while working with their regular clients on anxiety, pain, and other problems. This is a fairly intensive process, and by the time they finish, they have a moderate level of competence in hypnosis application. We explain to them that their training in hypnosis has really only just begun, and encourage them to continue training with ASCH, the Erickson Foundation, or a similar program.

CLINICIANS VERSUS SCIENTISTS

Nadon and Laurence (1994) noted that clinicians and researchers in psychology, medicine, and related disciplines pay much less attention to each others' work than professionals in other sciences. To highlight this gap, the authors offered an example from engineering. If civil engineers are repairing bridges and they notice systematic faults in construction techniques, scientific engineers would value their findings. Similarly, if scientific engineers discovered a stronger alloy, applied engineers would welcome this development.

We respect researchers, although we do not always understand what they do and why they do it. We are clinicians, not researchers or academics, and admittedly we would rather take a leap from a rickety bridge than trade in even our Axis II clients for a professorship in which hypnotizability is conducted on undergraduates. We know what it is like to speak to academic audiences that ask us questions we cannot answer. We also know what it is like to speak on therapy techniques to professors who have not seen a real, live client for thirty years or more. We are on different planets.

We are periodically reminded that both camps can learn from each other. Busy practitioners may be quick to eschew abstract theories and statistical data that have little relevance to the complex, ideosyncratic problems of people who require individualized treatment. We clinicians may rally around the maxim, "One size does not fit all." However, Lynn (1994) cautions that "when this view is pushed to the extreme, hypnosis can be viewed as a pure art form, with no mandate to bring scientific findings into the consulting room" (81). Now, if you consider your hypnosis an art, that statement has to sting just a bit.

We will be drawing on research and case reports where applicable; however, we don't pretend to write about science. This is mostly about art, the art of psychotherapy with hypnotic techniques, and about hypnosis, through our eyes, from our experience. Some of this may be biased and opinionated, even rigid or irreverent. If you have found this to be true from reading so far, you know that instead of apologizing we would prefer to tell you a little story about hypnotizability tests.

Fulano and Mengano

It was nearly midnight in the psychology department at one of the national universities in Mexico City. Two men sat in an office, ensconced in discussion. The assistant professor, known simply as Fulano to his graduate students, was assigning a task to Mengano, one of his students.

"I want you to read every journal article and every chapter ever written on hypnotic susceptibility," commanded Fulano. "Only then will you understand the import and gravity of responsiveness and hypnotizability."

Mengano answered, "You're talking about *thousands* of articles in hypnosis and psychology journals, most of them in English. You're lucky my English is good."

"Yes, I know all that," said Fulano. "No topic is more diverse or significant than susceptibility tests. Their complete and total domination of the literature sends chills down my spine, even on a warm night like this."

Mengano braved another comment. "The clinical types outside these walls do not embrace your ideas, Fulano. They say susceptibility tests and standardized inductions are redundant, time-consuming, and produce nothing worthwhile."

Fulano was quick to respond. "Clinicians are firmly entrenched. Their self-interest is formidable as well as resilient. Forget all that, Mengano. You must begin your study at once. Time is scarce. And wear no purple ties during this endeavor."

Mengano asked, "When in the course of my reading will I discover the import and gravity I'm searching for?"

"You'll see it when you know it, and you'll know it when you see it—but only when you least expect it," answered the assistant professor.

"My dear Fulano, tell me, is this an ambiguous function assignment?" he asked.

"No strategic therapy is practiced within these walls, my friend. If you ever accuse me again of not being a scientist, I'll tell you a story that never ends," said Fulano, adjusting his tie.

MORE ON HYPNOTIZABILITY TESTS

Someone asked us once why we do not use hypnotizability tests, and our first answer was: the weather in Phoenix. We don't need to check the weather report. Close to 300 out of 365 days will be sunny, and on any of the other 65 days, we know the sun will come out eventually if we wait a while.

Most clients will respond if we are patient and give them a chance. A few will not. Clients who are "low-hypnotizable" are evident in the first session. They often exhibit little capacity for absorption, imagery, ideosensory feelings, or other phenomena. We might work hard at an induction for twenty minutes or so, while they sit stiffly, trying to "get it right." When we realert them, they say something deflating like, "Was I supposed to *feel* something?" They may be reactant, but most likely they fall into the low hypnotizable category. We would use more indirection with them the next time, perhaps employing a long, meandering embedded-meaning induction, and then, if their response is still poor, we would recommend something other than hypnotherapy.

This is the case with roughly one in twenty clients. Most clients who express interest in hypnosis will show some meaningful response and benefit from continuing sessions of trancework. For sure, those who respond with greater depth may benefit more. Many clients who show only a mild depth of response—perhaps no time distortion or amnesia, minimal ideosensory feeling or imagery, and mild dissociation—may also receive benefit. Compare this mild depth of response with a client's response who is told a story during the course of standard talk therapy. Both types may evince a quizzical or distracted look, evidence of mild absorption, and evidence that their conscious mind is occupied while their unconscious mind is mulling over a suggestion. Milton Erickson calls this the "everyday waking trance."

WHAT DO WE KNOW ABOUT HYPNOSIS?

Hypnosis is eminently effective for a wide range of disorders. Rather than review the literature here, we will cite references in the chapters that follow. Lynn (1994) summarizes the main points: "research has given me confidence that I need not be concerned about whether someone is in a 'trance' or not; that direct suggestions can be just as useful as indirect suggestions; that clients' subjective experiences during hypnosis can be powerfully affected by prehypnotic interventions and expectations; that hypnosis is an inherently safe procedure; that hypnotized subjects are cognizant, creative problem solvers who are ultimately in control of their actions; that hypnotized subjects have an array of abilities that can be exploited to therapeutic benefit; that hypnotizability can be enhanced; and that due caution must be exercized to avoid suggestive and leading therapeutic procedures that risk pseudomemory creation" (81).

PREPARING THE CLIENT FOR HYPNOSIS

When asked if they would like to experience hypnosis as part of treatment, many clients will view hypnosis as either magical or powerful, as if the therapist is somehow imbued with an other-worldly ability that can zap their problem and make it disappear. Other clients may be taken aback by the word *hypnosis*, and this negative impression will show itself nonverbally long before they say something like, "Oh, I don't know if I want to do *that*." These clients—both the magic-bullet folks and those with a negative stereotype of hypnosis—would likely *not* respond in this way if we asked them if they would like to experience progressive muscle relaxation, guided imagery, or meditation—all of which share common qualities with hypnosis.

We explain to clients that hypnosis can be indeed powerful, but that its potency comes from eliciting strengths, resources, and other natural abilities that already exist *inside*. Accordingly, the therapist is framed as a guide, hypnosis as the adjunct to overall treatment, and treatment outcome is placed in a reasonable perspective. For example, a client is told, "It wouldn't be realistic to think that we could *eliminate* your anxiety. Instead, our aim is to reduce it, to help you to better manage your anxiety." I (S. B.) like to tell clients that hypnosis is the mental and emotional equivalent of a midwife helping to deliver a baby: I help guide the process and keep them safe, but they still have to do the hard work.

There is inestimable truth in a client's nonverbals, and that is why we pay careful attention to them. Say we tell a client one of the above "therapist as guide" statements, and her posture, gestures, and facial expression communicate disappointment or reluctance, even though she *verbally* responds with, "Oh, okay. I guess I'll give it a try." With such a client it might be best to *restrain* her. We might say, "This isn't for everybody. How about if you think about it for a few days, and then give me a call?"

In the case of negative stereotypes of hypnosis, we may ask, "Have you ever seen hypnosis at a night club, or at the county fair?" Chances are they have witnessed such a demonstration. We then discuss why what they saw was indeed hypnosis, but hypnosis done for entertainment. "This kind of hypnosis is for helping people, not for entertainment," we explain.

Issues of control are closely linked to negative stereotypes, and this needs to be addressed with most clients. We might tell them they will always be in the driver's seat, and will not do anything they do not want to do. "You won't quack like a duck," we might say. Once we begin trancework, issues of control are usually neutralized if we induce trance, realert the client after a minute or two, and then ask, "How do you feel?" or, "What are you thinking about?" We process for a bit and then say, "Okay, you may close your eyes and let yourself drift off again, as I continue talking to you." People invariably achieve increased depth following this brief realerting. But more importantly, they see that they are not losing control. For anxious clients, we may induce trance and realert several times before finally continuing with the remainder of the induction, deepening, and therapy component.

CHOOSING AN INDUCTION

In *Handbook of Hypnotic Inductions*, we arbitrarily placed various stories into inductions and deepenings. This was for illustrative purposes only. Many of those individual stories could have just as easily been part of the therapy component, just as some of the deepenings could have served as an induction, and vice versa.

Many who practice hypnosis make no distinction between induction, deepening, and therapy. For illustrative purposes, we break down the process into these three categories, though in practice we may alter this process, depending on the situation.

To induce trance means to absorb the client's attention in *something*. It can be a spot on the wall, or a story. It can be an embedded-meaning or conversational induction, or a long, boring monologue that embeds power words, such as *imagine, wonder,* and *story* along with suggestions for ideosensory phenomena, time distortion, and the like. A deepening may consist of counting down from 10 to1, a period of silence, or any number of devices. The induction and deepening are designed to set the stage for the therapy component, which could be an ego-strengthening story, age progression, or any number of applications.

Now, to digress from this pro forma method, let's look at some other ways of accomplishing the same thing. We could have no recognizable divisions in the process. We could induce trance, deepen, and have a therapy component all within a story. We could absorb the client's attention in a spot on the back of his hand during *arm catalepsy*, while we tell him alternating stories. We could ask him to imagine the tingling in his right hand, and say, "once that tingling has spread throughout your body, slowing down your mind, and slowing down your body, you can take one more deep, refreshing breath. . . ." We could follow with an age progression to a time in which he can see himself with his pain diminished by 10 percent. We could absorb his attention in an ego-strengthening story, and ask him for unconscious ratification of the story, which would be communicated via ideomotor finger signals.

In other words, the routes to relaxation are innumerable, as are the therapeutic applications to use once you get there. We will cover many of these options in the remaining chapters. As you continue your practice of hypnosis, you will see the advantages in adapting your own approach to the particular needs of each client. Therein lies the art of hypnosis: knowing a variety of inductions and techniques for different problems, but being able to adapt to the situation at hand. The client does not improve because you come up with the best story for her problem. Far from it. Improvement grows out of her relationship with you. You listen closely and build upon strengths. Maybe you utilize problems, or an ongoing process. Perhaps you alternate hypnosis with talk therapy, and maybe your stories sufficiently influence her unconscious, allowing her to change, adapt, or accept. Or maybe the timing is right, and she is ready, or she has begun a medication that helps considerably. Long afterward she will remember it was a cooperative and respectful process.

MORE ON BEGINNING HYPNOSIS

Much more could be said about the various things to consider when beginning to practice hypnosis. We encourage you to explore this through further reading. The best book we can recommend is *Trance-*

work: An Introduction to the Practice of Clinical Hypnosis by Yapko (1990). Hammond's Handbook of Hypnotic Suggestions and Metaphors (1990) is a large tome, and a frequent reference for beginning to advanced clinicians. If you hear someone refer to the "red book," they are talking about the Hammond. Our own book, Handbook of Hypnotic Inductions (2000), contains much more than inductions. People have told us they appreciate its various stories, and the instruction about hypnotic concepts and principles. Haley's classic Uncommon Therapy: The Psychiatric Techniques of Milton H. Erickson, M.D. (1973) provides a good foundation for hypnotic technique and strategic therapy. Among Madanes's fine books, we often reread her Strategic Family Therapy (1981). Gilligan's Therapeutic Trances (1986) is also invaluable. More advanced, it is highly recommended for its scholarly yet practical discussion of hypnotic process and technique. The Lanktons have several fine books, and one of their best is Tales of Enchantment: Goal-Oriented Metaphors for Adults and Children in Therapy (1989).

Other excellent books are O'Hanlon's Taproots: Underlying Principles of Milton H. Erickson's Therapy and Hypnosis (1987), Rosen's My Voice Will Go with You: The Teaching Tales of Milton Erickson (1982), and The Letters of Milton H. Erickson (Zeig & Geary, 2000). Books that we return to again and again are Hypnotic Realities (Rossi, 1976), Ericksonian Psychotherapy, vol. I: Structures, and vol. II: Clinical Applications (Zeig, 1985b), and Healing Ceremonies: Creating Personal Rituals for Spiritual, Emotional, Physical and Mental Health (Hammerschlag & Silverman, 1997).

Among the many fine books that have come from our neighbors in Mexico, we recommend El Vuelo Del ave Fénix (Pérez, 1994), as well as Teresa Robles's Revisando el Pasado para Constuir el Future (1997) and Concierto para Cuatro Cerebros en Psicoterapia (1990).

GROUP HYPNOTIC TREATMENT IN THE FUTURE

Recently two interns in Tucson, Eric Jackson and Beth Darnall, conducted a hypnosis treatment group. Clients in the group carried diagnoses of posttraumatic stress disorder (PTSD) and psychotic disorders, and the therapists taught them self-hypnosis in eight sessions. Their group went remarkably smoothly, especially considering the mix of clients. A hypnotic application with more than one person, say, a couple, is inordinately more difficult than a single client. And a group of six or more clients may be exponentially more demanding, as a group application needs to be broad in scope, as opposed to tailoring your approach to an individual. Have you ever tried monitoring the nonverbals of eight clients?

Beth's and Eric's group represents the future. Why? Because in the coming years most of us—at least in the United States—stand to be doing a lot less individual hypnosis, or any other individual treatment. Duncan (2001), in discussing the future of psychotherapy, predicts that most therapists will work in "integrated health care systems," where medical and psychological services will be provided under one umbrella. There will be a seemingly inexhaustible stream of client referrals from an immense pool of medical patients who formerly identified their complaints as primarily physical. Duncan foresees various pitfalls in this system, including therapists' being in the ethically dubious position of enforcing compliance with "evidence-based" treatments and pharmacotherapy, methods with which they may not agree.

One staple of this new system will be much less individual therapy, and more therapy provided in groups. And it may not even be therapy as we currently know it. Simon (2001) recommends that we bone up on behavioral and psychological techniques of medical conditions, because we'll be conducting psychoeducational groups with hypertensives, diabetics, asthmatics, and others whose noncompliance and ill-coping with stress consumes a large portion of health care dollars.

Medical or health psychologists and other disciplines in health care settings have been doing this for years. Other clinicians who are accustomed to providing psychotherapy in office practices, may need to take some quick study courses on medical illnesses in order to be employed by the integrated health care system. In this projected world, if you are trained in hypnosis and know its applications for anxiety and pain, you may be a step ahead of your colleagues.

9

Communication in Trance

Zeig (1990) writes that early in his training he asked Milton Erickson for instruction to be able to better understand nonverbal behavior. Erickson responded with, "Do you know the definition of *zyzzyx*?" Zeig answered no, and Erickson told him to look up the word in the dictionary. He added, "First you learn the alphabet, then the words, then the grammar." Zeig learned an important lesson that day: There is no substitute for direct experience; you need to learn the basics before attempting the complex. Is nonverbal behavior really complex? Let's examine a particular case of nonverbal behavior in a client.

Nancy closes her eyes and listens to the hypnotic induction. She shifts subtly in the chair, then she blushes, but it appears there is more redness in the left cheek than the right. The therapist lets her know that when she finds herself taking one more deep, refreshing breath, this will mean she is ready to go even deeper. A moment later, one nostril flares, she takes a deep breath, and as she exhales, she settles deeper and more comfortably into her chair. Just then, Nancy's eyelids begin to twitch.

Nancy's right hand is out on the arm rest, where she was instructed to place it. In the previous session, three finger signals were established, all on her preferred or right hand. The therapist asks her unconscious mind a question, and asks her to respond to the question with either the "yes," "no," or "I-don't-know-or-I'm-not-ready-to-answer-yet" finger. A tear drips down her left cheek. The therapist waits for sixty seconds, and sees no movement in her right hand. Just then a finger on her *left hand* twitches.

After Nancy is realerted, she says, "I thought I felt my 'yes' finger move." The therapist is perplexed. All this ideomotor finger signalling may be more than he bargained for. And then there was the tear. Did that mean she felt sad?

On the other hand, we have the story of Hans the horse (Farb, 1974). In Germany in the early 1900s, a horse named Hans amazed the people of Berlin with his ability to perform mathematical calculations. When a problem was written on the blackboard in front of him, he promptly counted out the answer by tapping his front feet. He tapped with his right foot to count out the low numbers, and with his left foot he tapped out multiples of ten. A psychologist, Oskar Pfungst, who studied Hans's performances, reasoned that no trickery was involved, as Hans's owner did not charge for his performances, and Hans calculated correctly even when his owner was not present.

Pfungst was determined to figure out how Hans did it. He postulated that the explanation lay in the audience, not in Hans, as the audience was able to see the answer on the blackboard. Pfungst watched closely and noticed the *horse's observation of the audience*. As soon as the answer was written on the board, the audience bent forward almost imperceptibly to watch Hans's feet. Hans used this inclination as his cue to begin tapping. As his taps approached the correct number, the audience became tense with excitement and moved their heads ever so slightly. In other words, the *audience signalled Hans* to stop; following their cue, he proved himself a whiz at math.

EASY OR COMPLEX?

We use the zyzzyx and Hans anecdotes in our workshops to introduce the idea of nonverbal behavior and communication in trance. So, is all this easy or complex? Certainly it can be both, and it never ceases to be interesting. The important thing is that the therapist closely monitor and facilitate the myriad behavior she observes in trance. In doing so, she is communicating with clients, and as such, trancework becomes a dance, or a mutual, cooperative, ratifiable process.

With Nancy, as well as with all other clients, if they do not do what we ask, that's okay. The last thing we want to do is become engaged in a power struggle with them, or somehow communicate to them that they got it wrong. Remember, the therapist was talking to her *unconscious* mind, quite a wide territory. Maybe her "yes" finger did twitch, and the therapist did not see it. And the confounding movement in her *left* hand—was that resistance? Maybe. But more likely it meant nothing, and may not be worth attending to. And the tear? Tearing in trance is common, and usually does not mean sadness. The therapist could tell her that, if she asks about it. Otherwise, do not attend to it.

The eye flutter may be more serious. Eye flutter is thought to mean that something negative or upsetting is occurring. Something does not fit, something is not quite right. When we see eye flutter, we make a mental note of what we were saying at the time, as there could be a connection. During debriefing, we may ask, "Was there anything I said that may have been unsettling, or caused an incongruence, or is there something else I should know about?" This may provide useful data. Other times, clients may report that they felt their eyes fluttering at some point in the process, but they could not connect it to any content. It is worth looking into to some extent, but do not dwell on it.

It is better to attend to—and build on—what Nancy *did* accomplish that went in the desired direction. If we were the therapist, we would praise her for a job well done, repeat the process next time, and perhaps watch her hand more closely. With ideomotor signalling, a barely discernible twitch is thought to be a true unconscious response, and such a response is believed to occur *before* a verbal response is available. However, had Nancy deliberately raised her finger two or three inches, that would be viewed as a volitional, conscious response—*not* the desired response.

A BRIEF REVIEW OF IDEOMOTOR TECHNIQUE

David B. Cheek, a gynecologist in Santa Barbara, California who died in 1996, was to ideomotor technique as Erickson was to indirect suggestion (Ewin, 1996). Cheek believed that a person was capable of storing strong experiences *in utero*, in early childhood, and under anesthesia, and that these sensory impressions, or memories, could later be retrieved in hypnosis via ideomotor signalling. Though highly controversial, Cheek's writings are worth reading, especially his *Hypnosis: The Application of Ideomotor Techniques* (1994), and *Mind-Body Therapy: Methods of Ideodynamic Healing in Hypnosis* (1988), coauthored with Rossi.

Walsh (1997) presents an 8-step protocol for resolving repressed, suppressed, or otherwise dated affect using ideomotor questioning, a process that was developed by Leslie LeCron and Erickson in the 1930s. A strong proponent of ideomotor technique, Hammond (1997) reported that in 247 consecutive clients, 78 percent were able to develop ideomotor signals that they perceived as occurring involuntarily, and which could be seen sufficiently by the therapist to permit reliable identification. Hammond (1997) emphasizes that ideomotor signalling should not be viewed as a technique only for exploring the past. Goals, purposes, adaptive functions, and internal conflicts served by symptoms in the present can also be investigated with this procedure.

WHERE TO START

In our training groups, we stress the importance of the client's communicating in trance, right from the first session.

Most people have *a favorite place they go to in their mind, a relaxing, pleasant place where they've been before,*	implication
perhaps on the beach, *or at* home, *or* some place else, *and it can be* anywhere at all . . . *and I'd like you to let your mind go there now, and when you're there,* you will find your head nodding one time.	suggestion covering all possibilities
	suggestion

Clients soon become accustomed to hypnotic language, anecdote, and story, communicating nonverbally—and sometimes verbally—in trance, as well as debriefing at the end. In the favorite place example above, how do we know if they have achieved this image unless they tell us? Let's find out if there is a problem when it is occurring, rather than during debriefing. If we do not see a head nod, let's pace and utilize their experience:

. . . and isn't it nice to know that images, any image at all, can arise *at its own pace, in its own time, sometimes later than sooner, and other times when we least expect it, because there's* nothing	implication
consciously that a person needs to do or know or think about *when the front part of the mind can* notice, *just notice feel-*	not knowing/not doing
ings and sensations in the body, usually in the extremities. . . .	implication

If we encounter difficulty—anxiety, resistance, whatever it may be—we become even *more* indirect, general, and permissive. If they still cannot come up with an image—an easy thing for most people— we need to problem solve that before proceeding. The alternative is to just *assume*, which is never a good idea. Let's say we ask for a head nod, but do not get it after about a minute, then we see shallow breathing and eye flutter. We find out what is going on by asking for a verbal report. As people think very concretely in trance, if we say, "Tell me . . . ," they might think we want a head nod or finger signal. That is why we say instead, "Tell me *with your words* . . .":

> *. . . and movement, any kind of motion, inside or outside, and change in breathing, probably has special meaning and is worthy of exploration. Nancy, tell me now, with your words, what you are feeling and thinking. . . .*

With her eyes still closed, she says, "I don't know, I'm just struggling with this, I guess, I just don't know. . . ."
As a client's talking usually lightens trance, we might then add:

> *. . . Okay, Nancy, just let it happen, it's okay to experience whatever might be going on, and right now I'd like you to take two more deep, refreshing breaths, and let yourself sink even deeper and deeper into a nice, peaceful state of relaxation, which for many is an entrance into another state. . . .*

By doing this, many clients will successfully discharge resistance and drift off pleasantly and deeply. This session and subsequent ones will probably be smooth. However, let's say Nancy takes two deep breaths and objective distress continues. At that point we would gently realert and process. There may be a transference issue, a negative stereotype about hypnosis that we missed, or formidable unconscious resistance. Cheek believed that many times this apparent resistance is in fact the client's carrying out a posthypnotic suggestion, albeit one that was installed in a time of distress rather than formal hypnosis. For example, during a time of arousal when Nancy was a child, her mother might have screamed at her, "Don't *ever* listen to a man!" For all these years, that suggestion has remained, outside of her awareness. Perhaps it has contributed to disturbed relationships in Nancy's life. Exploring and uncovering it may be of great assistance to Nancy.

There are many ways to handle a resistance, or block, to therapy. We could explore this with standard talk therapy, or even with finger signals and verbal report within hypnosis, asking open-ended questions of the client's unconscious mind:

Nancy, someone *told me one time about* burying something, *deep in the ground, and* I forget *exactly who it was that told me that, but she knew that it was important, and* could be retrieved, *at some time in the future . . . and right now I'd like your unconscious mind to* drift and dream, *in your own way, taking as much time as you need, to any time in the past, to some time that may have to do with something important in your life being buried . . . I'll stop talking for a few minutes, and when you're there, you will know, and I will know because you'll find* that *"yes" finger twitching and developing a* life all it's own, *and moving ever so slightly up into the air. . . .*	metaphor distraction/leading away implication suggestion dissociative language

Of course, in pretrance discussion we want to inform the client that we will be doing an age regression. You never want to do that without consent. Let's suppose the above exploratory technique yields nothing. We can distract even further:

Nancy, in a moment—but not just yet—I'm going to ask your unconscious mind to drift back in time, and as it does, independently, autonomously, without any conscious effort, *I'm going to occupy your conscious mind with a little story about a shaggy dog.*

bind of comparable alternatives

Okay, let your mind now drift back in time *to any time at all where something important may be buried, taking as much time as you need, and when you're there, your "yes" finger can signal to me . . . And while that's occurring back there in your mind, I want you to pay close attention to this* little story *about a dog. . . .*

suggestion

distraction

I was once working with a client on unconscious exploration. I (G. G.) had been employing hypnosis only a few years. The client asked, "Why do I keep shooting myself in the foot?" We had established the three finger signals, and we were attempting to retrieve a feeling of mastery and competence via age regression. I had heard at a workshop that the therapist needs to allow "as much time as the client needs" to signal. With determination and resolve I peered at her hand for 45 minutes, but received no signal. Finally, she opened her eyes and broke the silence with, "Am I fighting you on this?" I let her know later than sooner that hypnosis was not her best option, and since then I usually wait for a finger movement for no longer than 5 to 10 minutes.

Age regression and unconscious exploration can be fascinating for both client and therapist. However, it can also be like mining for *unobtanium*. Are you familiar with that all too common mineral? We would recommend that you move on if nothing significant is yielded after a few sessions. If these issues are not resolved after a few sessions, we might inform Nancy that we don't think that hypnosis is for her, and that she should concentrate on talk therapy instead.

THE VERACITY OF IDEOMOTOR SIGNALS

The whole idea of ideomotor signalling is to increase the range of client responses so that trancework can be an ongoing communication process between client and therapist. But how veracious are these responses? If, during unconscous exploration, Nancy signals, then follows with a verbal report about some memory, or even a fragment, how do Nancy or the therapist know whether she *really* experienced that memory, not to mention whether her subjective experience represents fantasy, distortion, or something that actually occurred? As with all clinical data, the therapist may never know if the client's disclosures accurately reflect external of consensual reality (Diamond, 1986).

Veracity might be far less important than *utility*. As with any data gathered during the session, the clinician considers the sum total of information, and ideomotor responses represent but a portion of that total. Even if ideomotor signals are not taken at face value, they allow the therapist to assess how actively the client unconsciously or involuntarily participates (Diamond, 1986).

THE CHEVREUL PENDULUM

Some practitioners who have difficulty identifying finger movements find the Chevreul Pendulum more reliable. I (G. G.) occasionally use it in therapy, as well as for training. You can make a pendulum from something as simple as a piece of string and a metal washer. Clients are asked to hold the pendulum between their thumb and forefinger, letting it hang straight down. Montgomery and Kirsch (1996) found that allowing the elbow to be supported facilitates responding. Were this technique to be used with Nancy, it would go as follows:

> *Nancy, holding that pendulum out there like that, I'm going to ask you some questions, and I'd like you to answer with the pendulum. To answer "yes," the pendulum can swing back and forth, and your "no" answer can be the pendulum swinging from side to side. . . .*

Clients who are unaccustomed to responding with these techniques may need to be trained to do so. A good way to start is to ask easy, conscious questions, such as, "Your name is Nancy?" You can soon proceed to questioning Nancy's unconscious mind, and the pendulum swinging in a circle can represent "I don't know, or I'm not ready to answer yet."

PAULY THE PUFFER FISH

Stephen Lankton (personal communication, December 12, 2001), in his address at the Erickson Foundation's Eighth International Congress, talked about the need for therapists to concentrate on the present and the future. To underscore his point, he asked, "Are we archeologists, or are we therapists?" To be sure, sometimes we need to be archeologists, or even miners, but more often our use of ideomotor signals involves the here and now, as clients are in sore need of a greater range of responses in facing current problems.

I (S. B.) had seen Josie for five sessions, during which we worked on her catastrophizing and overgeneralization with her boss and co-workers. Our essentially consciously directed, straight-forward cognitive-behavioral therapy (CBT) sessions had yielded some results. However, it became apparent to me that a deeper issue was involved: Josie's inability to become close to others. Accordingly, the next session we switched to hypnosis. She achieved a moderate depth of trance and we established three finger signals. I then told her the following story.

Pauly the Puffer Fish

I've often wondered about the thousands of kinds of fish in the oceans and rivers and lakes and ponds of the world, and tried to imagine the sheer number of total fish in those waters. How many billions could there be? That's why the story of one single fish arrested my attention, the story of Pauly the Puffer Fish.

Now, you may know puffer fish as blowfish, those marvelous little creatures that have no ribs, which allows them to puff themselves into balloons much bigger than their usual selves. Puffer fish only inflate when they consider themselves to be in some kind of danger. They can also release poison into the water nearby. The problem with inflating is that it slows them down to half their usual speed, and then they can't maneuver so effectively in the water anymore. All these protective devices can be very limiting.

Now, Pauly was a "map" puffer—a most interesting and curious looking puffer fish, with a short nose and a body with dark lines radiating out from around his eyes. You might think that such an interesting puffer would have all kinds of friends, and that he might draw other fish to him, like pilot fish to a whale. But that wasn't the case at all. Pauly happened to be one of those rare puffers that actually released some of his poison out into the water around him when you least expected it. You see, usually puffers only emit poison when they are in extremely stressful situations, like when they are about to be eaten. One of the reasons that puffers only release poison under such dire circumstances is that, amazingly, that very same poison has fatal consequences for the puffer that released it.

Now, of course, Pauly didn't ever release so much poison that he died. But you have to wonder if those little bits of poison here and there in the water around him didn't have some sort of adverse effect on him. Certainly, it kept his friends and admirers to a minimum, which was very unfortuante, given how interesting and cool a fish Pauly truly was. All of this added up to a dilemma for Pauly. He really wanted to connect with other fish, as it's a lonely life when you drive others away. However, he didn't know how to control the poison he released. Afterall, wasn't it an instinct, or at least automatic?

Well, late one afternoon, while swimming near the moss-covered hulk of a long forgotten Spanish galleon, Pauly met a porcupine fish, a very close relative to blowfish, with sharp spines that also can inflate its body to fend off attackers. The porcupine fish's name was Harold. For whatever reason, Harold wasn't much affected by the poison Pauly slowly released into the water around them, and the two of them became friends.

Harold talked to Pauly about all the ways fish can be in danger, and feel stressed out enough to either inflate or release poison. "How do you see it?" asked Harold.

"I don't know, I just don't know," responded Pauly, taken aback and confused. But as they continued to talk, Pauly came to realize that for his whole life he had been more than a little nervous about getting too close to other puffers, even though deep down, he really wanted to connect.

Harold continued. "What if someone accidently inflates, and another gets caught in their spines?" he asked. Pauly just nodded. He was beginning to understand.

Harold knew exactly what Pauly was talking about because getting close to either puffer fish or porcupine fish always carries some risk. He helped Pauly realize that what he feared was really fear itself—the fear of getting too close and getting hurt. Harold further helped Pauly to see that loneliness and disconnection was much more hurtful than the possible pain that can go along with being close to someone.

Pauly slowly got accustomed to having Harold around. In fact, before he realized it, he began to *enjoy* Harold, and that was a very comfortable feeling. At about the same time, the slow release of poison from Pauly's body stopped, and he soon found other fish swimming closer to him. Now, Pauly, still occasionally inflated unnecessarily when he got nervous, but it happened less and less all the time.

Now, Josie, that story I just told you, it may not have anything to do *with your own situation, and many times people* make too much *of stories, which, when carefully analyzed, are merely many* letters strung *together to make words, and in turn, those many* words are thrown together to form a story. *In any event, let's turn from stories to*

restraint

restraint

restraint

restraint

*deeper things, like the unconscious mind. Just how deep is deep? I knew a man from Austria—I think it was In*sbruck—*and he worked for In*tel, *and his name was* Diep, *really a* fairly shallow individual, *but he introduced me to the various ingredients in bread, and way down in the mixing bowl all those* ingredients *mixed together quite nicely,* but two loaves *was all that resulted.*

embedded suggestion

distraction/leading away

embedded suggestion
distraction/leading away

Now, Josie, in a moment I'm going to ask a question of your unconscious mind, and you can answer with one of those fingers out there on that hand, which by now may feel rather detached *from your arm. One* woman *one time sitting right there in that same chair said I sounded like a* disembodied voice, *whatever that means.*

dissociative language
implication

metaphor
suggestion

And now, Josie, the question for your unconscious mind: That little story about the fish, is that something the back part of your mind can put to use?

Taking as much time as you need, you may answer with one of your fingers. . . .

CLINICAL COMMENTS

Josie answered affirmatively. She did quite well after this session, and her regular practice of self-hypnosis helped her to not be so hard on herself. "I can't understand why I'm getting along so well with everyone at work," she commented during a follow-up session. "You must be doing something right," I answered. No further explanation was needed.

The case of Josie demonstrates how we most often use ideomotor questioning: to gain unconscious commitment. We customarily do this with instigative and didactic stories, including ego-strengthening stories. Hammond (1990) takes this a step further, and upon real-erting, reminds clients of their unconscious commitment during debriefing. We usually don't do this, preferring instead to keep all processing on an unconscious level.

What if Josie had answered "no," or, "I don't know/not ready to answer yet"? Hammond advocates following their response with the question, "Between now and next time, is your unconscious mind willing to *consider* putting to use that little story about the puffer fish?" Many times people will answer "yes," and next session their reluctance will give way to a "yes" response when queried again with the initial question. However, if their response continues to be "no," try to understand and respect the response for what it is: unconscious resistance. If you persist and get into a power struggle with someone else's unconscious, you know who's going to lose, and what's worse, the client may end up feeling diminished.

Did Erickson's clients always communicate with him in trance in these ways? Of course not. However, some therapists, in trying to be like Erickson, naively trust this complex process without any sort of critical evaluation. We are strong advocates of communication during trancework. Nevertheless, we know of many fine therapists who employ little or no head nods, finger signals, verbal report, or any other communication in hypnosis. Does this mean that they are unable to verify ongoing process, and that their intervention, like a story, is merely some errant seed cast in the wind, hoping to find its way to fertile soil? Of course not. With practice, you will astutely glean volumes from the most subtle, minimal cues. That data, and all other subjective and objective information, along with your own unconscious, should light your path.

10

Accessing Unconscious Resources

THE UNCONSCIOUS MIND

Consider yourself for a moment. As you go about your busy day, attending to necessary tasks, what part of your waking life is truly conscious? One-half? Three-quarters? For many of us, it may be a lot less. We go from one thing to another, and most things, unless they're highly remarkable, will simply disappear, never to be retrieved again. Other things may be stored in our unconscious, and later, some aspect may be recalled. A particular odor, or a person's expression, reminds you of something, but you can't quite put your finger on it.

A vigilant, analytical, no-nonsense person would probably say that most of her waking state is conscious, while the inveterate dreamer may regard his daytime hours as a continuous volley of unconscious impulses. In both cases, the "reality" may be a constant interchange of of conscious-unconscious process, one influencing the other.

In solving a problem, we often opt to "sleep on it," as the morning may provide us with either resolution of the problem, or at least a fresh perspective on it. Other times, perhaps we concentrated hard on trying to remember something important, but despite our effort, the memory remained absent. However, once our conscious attention was occupied by something else, the memory was suddenly retrieved. These are common experiences, and we mention them to clients as illustrations of the unconscious mind's ability to help us. One of the most well-known poems in the English language, "Stopping by Woods on a Snowy Evening," surfaced in the mind of Robert Frost after he had been working all night on his long poem, "New Hampshire." He arose from his desk and went outside to look at the sun, and at that point, "Stopping by Woods" came to him. "I always thought it was the product of autointoxication coming from tiredness," he explained (Greenberg & Hepburn, 1961, p. 12).

Gilligan (1987) explains that Fredrich Kekule, the German chemist who solved the structural riddle of the benzene molecule, labored many days attempting to consciously solve the problem. Finally, in a daydream, Kekule's unconscious mind generated an analogical structure involving six snakes connected in the form of a hexagon. Upon awakening, his conscious mind recognized this metaphor as representing the elusive structure of the benzene ring.

Sidney Rosen, an intimate friend of Milton Erickson, said that when Erickson told him that most of everyone's life is unconsciously determined, he reacted with the thought that "unconsciously determined" meant "predetermined," and that the best we could hope for was to gain awareness of firmly set unconscious patterns. However, Rosen later realized that Erickson, who directed many of his interventions toward the unconscious minds of his clients, meant that the unconscious is indeed changeable, and that all of our experiences affect both our conscious as well as our unconscious mind. Rosen believes that change is accomplished most effectively and permanently when therapists focus on influencing clients' unconscious patterns, which usually includes clients' values and frames of reference (Rosen, 1982).

For years, the Freudian view of the unconscious dominated therapy. In this view, the unconscious was a negative construct, something to be avoided, or controlled as an obstacle in therapy. Erickson eschewed the idea of the unconscious as some steamy cauldron of unwanted impulses, and instead made the radical claim that the unconscious is intelligent, organized, and creative, something to be nurtured in therapy. The Ericksonian practitioner does not view the hypnotic context as one in which suggestions are "planted" into some passive recipient, but rather sees trance as a process in which the client's conscious processes are set aside so that the unconscious can generate meaningful responses (Gilligan, 1987). Isn't the task in therapy so often helping people *in spite of* themselves? If it were only so simple as telling clients what to do, our jobs would be ever so easy. That's why so much of our effort is directed at freeing people from their conscious limitations and helping them access unconscious resources.

As we tell clients about our method and rationale during the the first session, we elicit their ideas about unconscious process. To many clients, this is not a new idea, and they may mention terms like *unconscious mind*, or *subconscious mind*, to describe indirect work they have done in the past. Clients who have been unsuccessful in therapy understand what we mean when we tell them, "Here we use metaphor and story in hypnosis to get in 'underneath your radar,' and it seems like your radar is pretty strong. Is that right?" Some clients might be unfamiliar with unconscious process, or simply very linear and analytical, putting little stock in such notions. With them, it is good to mention internal process via "in" words, such as imag*in*ation, or *in*tuition. These words have the dual purpose of seeding, or setting up the target in an induction.

APPOSITION OF OPPOSITES

In everyday conversation, and even in therapy, we may employ the apposition of opposites to illustrate or make a point. If we use the device more than once or twice in these situations, it may be received as contrived, clumsy or conspicuous. However, in a hypnotic induction its "fit" seems natural as a complement to other hypnotic language. As such, it is the device we employ most often in the service of all targets in hypnosis, including unconscious process.

Breathing in relaxation and comfort,   appositions of
breathing out any tension, or nervous-   opposites
ness . . . and noticing, just noticing what
goes on on the outside, as well as the
inside. On the outside, feeling that chair   dissociative language

supporting your body, the sound of the words, and anything else that you are experiencing on the outside.

And on the inside, *a person thinks and feels many things, and* in *your body you may have begun to notice a* heaviness, *or* lightness, *or* tingling, *or* numbness, *or whatever else might be going on in* those hands out there, *or in your feet. Maybe there's a curious or interesting sensation occurring somewhere else in your body?*

appositions of opposites

dissociative language

In trance, which can be like an entrance into another state, *people experience things on the outside and the inside, just like they have a conscious mind . . . and an unconscious mind, the back part of the mind, which is deep inside, kind of like the big part of the iceberg—you don't see it, but you know it's there, beneath the water. The unconscious, where people have their imagination, intuition, memories, resources, things that can help them now. The unconscious is both wise and protective,* is it not?

pun

direct question/double negative

The conscious-unconscious apposition may be enhanced by adding a third construct, the *hidden observer*, something experienced universally in trance.

So, we have the outside *and the* inside, *the* conscious *and the* unconscious, *two things going on, but that's not all! There is also a third thing occurring, what we call the hidden observer, the part of you that's watching what's going on. . . .* One person *once noticed, in a passing way, and then wondered,*

apposition of opposites

metaphor

"How is it that I'm experiencing these things and observing everything at the same time?

Well, that was his hidden observer operating, a rather curious and natural phenomenon. One thing, two things, three things going on. Someone *named* Inskeep, *once said, "That's way too much to keep track of. I'd better just concentrate on my breathing." However, he eventually chose to not concentrate on anything in particular, and just listened with his* third ear.

         metaphor

         metaphor

PRESUPPOSING UNCONSCIOUS PROCESS

Implicit in Ericksonian hypnosis is the idea that unconscious process, as well as other trance phenomena, will occur. This is done by *implying* that these things will occur: " . . . and I can wonder, or otherwise imagine, just how easy it will be for your unconscious mind to just let go. . . ." Or: "I don't know if, with your conscious mind or your unconscious mind, you contemplated going into trance more deeply this time, or the next time you come in here. . . ." Speaking generally, but *sounding* specific, we encourage, in a permissive way, the client's accessing past trance experience: "You can recall, some time in the past, when you experienced letting go. It may have been yesterday or a long time ago, when this occurred. . . ."

POWER WORDS

Certain words, such as *learn, experience, discover, explore, wonder,* etc., are thought to facilitate unconscious processing. These words are potent allies of the therapist, and we use them liberally in discussion before and after hypnosis, as well as during actual trancework. Let's say our client, Hector, has mentioned during debriefing a memory that occurred during the session. He explains that last year, a winning move in a chess game suddenly came up during a time of complete concentration and absorption. We want to utilize this naturally occurring experience in subsequent sessions. To do so, with an authoritarian approach, would sound something like this:

> *Now, Hector, I know you can remember being immersed in that particular chess game last December, when your body and mind were totally relaxed, and your unconscious mind just drifted and dreamed, and at a certain moment, that winning move sprang to mind, all by itself. Just let that happen now . . . that experience. . . .*

Contrast such a directive approach with one that merely alludes to his experience in a general, indirect, and permissive way:

> *Hector, you may remember, some time in the past, when you were completely absorbed in something pleasant, when the back part of your mind just took over, and some* discovery *simply surfaced, all by itself, autonomously, independently. . . .*

In subsequent sessions when we allude to a *discovery* he knows what we are talking about. Furthermore, by not calling attention to specifics, Hector is encouraged to generate lateral associations that may not be possible if we limited him to a specific situation.

EXPANDING THE USE OF EMBEDDED SUGGESTIONS

Three clinicians who worked with Erickson—Lankton and Lankton (1986), and Gilligan (1987)—who have since become innovators in their own right, are among many writers who proclaim that embedded suggestions are the most simple yet powerful way of delivering indirect suggestions. We underscore this notion with a perhaps very un-Ericksonian war analogy. People in the United States who are old enough to remember will recall that during the Vietnam War, politicians, rather than generals, micromanaged the war. Many veterans returning from Vietnam complained that they were forced to "fight the war with one hand tied behind our backs."

As therapists who rely on metaphor and indirection, we can say that if we did not have embedded suggestions in our arsenals, it would be like fighting a war with *two* hands tied behind our backs. To extend this analogy a bit further, we can say that by adding *voice* to embedded suggestion, it's like having *three* hands instead of two. In other words, by employing a slight vocal shift to the delivery of embedded suggestion, we create a direct pipeline to the unconscious. For example, "Hector, I would like you now to just let it happen, all by itself, some *discovery* that can help you with this problem. . . ."

Does this vocal shift involve d-r-a-w-i-n-g out the word, saying it softly and quietly, or emphasizing it in some other way, ever so slightly altering your volume, stress, intensity, pitch, or tempo? It is very individual. We found our own hypnotic voices through trial and error, and much practice. If someone says to you, "I love you," you are likely to pay less attention to the words than to the accompanying vocal phenomena.

HYPNOTIC LANGUAGE IN ADVERTISING

When clients hear us use hypnotic language, a familiar chord might be struck on an unconscious level, or consciously they may say to themselves, "Hmmm, I've heard something like that before." Of course they have! Advertisers are highly adept at all forms of hypnotic language. A radio ad for a fitness club chain that announces, "Whether your personal fitness goal is weight loss, a more healthy appearance, increased muscle tone, more strength, or better cardio-vascular fitness, or if you simply want to be in better shape . . ." is a good example of a suggestion covering all possibilities. Many times ads exploit embedded suggestion. Often these suggestions are such that the meaning can be taken in two or more ways. An ad for a popular beverage asks, "Is it *in* you?" A magazine ad for an expensive watch shows two famous faces, both popular singers, and the caption reads, "There are *times* when it isn't silence that's golden." An ad for an insurance company asks, "Have you Met Life?" A budget motel chain assures us, "All the room you need."

These are powerful messages. Such directives, and the carefully orchestrated contexts in which they are delivered, especially in TV ads, arrest our attention and in many cases unconsciously persuade us to purchase the product. A photo of the U.S. flag in a magazine carries the caption, "These colors don't run." For some, this embedded suggestion will reinforce patriotic beliefs.

Repetition, alliteration, and rhyme are key techniques in advertising. A computer company tells us that its product is "Easy to buy, easy to use, easy to sell." A cosmetics company says, "Believe in beauty." (Can we ever forget Reese's Pieces?) Slogans are also popular with governments and politicians. In World War II, the need for natrional security was reinforced with "Loose lips sink ships," and Dwight D. Eisenhower was elected with the slogan, "I like Ike." In the Cold War, U.S. citizens were reminded, "Better dead than Red." When carelessness led to fires in the U.S. Air Force, personnel were reminded, "Learn or Burn," which was later changed to "Learn not to burn." We mention these naturally occurring examples of hypnotic language to underscore their utility in therapy, especially in hypnosis.

Rhyme and Repetition

I (S. B.) was working with a client who preferred to be called by his nickname. (Let's say his nickname was Turk.) He had a dental procedure coming up in one week, and his history in the dentist chair was very consistent: despite analgesics, muscle relaxants and even nitrous oxide, his anxiety and attendant pain rendered him "unworkable," in the words of the dentist. Turk was desperate, as he was badly in need of the dental work.

I had only two sessions with Turk before his visit to the dentist. The first session, he responded with deep trance to a *conversational induction, counting-down deepening,* and the Three Lessons story. During debriefing he mentioned that he saw himself relaxing beside a brook in a peaceful meadow. During the second visit, I employed a similar induction and deepening, along with rhyme and repetition. A portion of the session is repeated here.

> *Just sitting in that chair today, Turk, you can begin to notice that some things may be the same as they've always been. You'll continue to breathe . . . in . . . and . . . out . . . and somewhere in there that breath will begin to change. You'll continue to swallow and notice your body in that change . . . and then those experiences can begin to change, too . . .slower . . . perhaps more aware of a disconnection, such as a lightness, or maybe a heaviness, in one of those hands out there. . . and time will continue to pass, maybe speeding up . . . or slowing down . . .*

We know it can work, Turk . . . and . . . we know it can work, Turk. . .

And now, Turk, I'd like you to imagine, just imagine, yourself resting in a favorite peaceful place . . . perhaps in a meadow with a brook, or anywhere you like, getting lost in your own thoughts . . . and in those thoughts, you can imagine yourself in the future, perhaps it's as soon as a few days from now, or perhaps it's a month down the road into the future, and you can look back and see that you accomplished everything you needed to . . . even at the dentist . . . and in that future picture of looking back on the past, which is still yet the future, you have all the necessary strength and resources and information to make all that you imagine come true . . .

And one time another man told me about a dream he had that showed him the future solution to a past problem. In that dream, he seemed to be floating along . . . aware that he was connected to his body yet disconnected in a very real way as well. Only a vague sensation, of any of the usual sensations such as sound, smell, taste and touch. In that dream state, he could picture how he could watch someone touch his hand, for example, and all he was aware of feeling was just the slightest pressure . . .

We know it can work, Turk . . . and . . . we know it can work, Turk.

Turk had a successful visit to the dentist. It was with pleasure that he asked the dentist afterward, "Am I still 'unworkable'?"

Proverbs

"A rolling stone gathers no moss." How many clients have been asked their interpretation of that, or similar proverbs, to assess their abstraction abilities? Many, for sure. However, the versatile proverb is much more than a diagnostic technique. We use them all the time in therapy in a variety of ways.

When we've completed a course of hypnosis and have given the client an audiotape for continued practice, we may ask, "Do you like apples?" Whatever the client's response, it's a handy segue to the proverb, "An apple a day keeps the doctor away." To reinforce listening to the tape, we could add, "In your case, an apple three times a week may be a good thing."

When present issues invariably connect to past issues, "All roads lead to Rome" may be timely. An overly serious client may be told, "All work and no play makes Jack a dull boy." A client who has a startling insight may be offered a proverb in the form of a restraining message: "All that glitters is not gold." More than once we've told clients, "The devil is in the details," "Better the devil you know than the devil you don't," or "Give the devil his due."

One client one time, Celia, raised a panoply of important issues, and throughout the session I (S. B.) anticipated her inquiry, follow-up questions, or at least some curiosity about the things she had raised. My direct questions to her, such as, "What about that?" yielded no response. Finally, I said to her, "Remember the proverb 'Ask no questions and hear no lies'?" This immediately penetrated her resistance, and she pored forth with meaningful material. At the end of the session, Celia commented on how productive it was, and I thought I'd reinforce the process with, "Experience is the mother of wisdom." She responded with, "Sonja, did you forget all the conflict I had with my mother before she died, and how un-wise she was?" I hadn't forgotten, and I immediately regretted using the proverb. However, Celia came to the rescue by adding, "That's okay. I'll just take it as 'Experience is the father of knowledge'." I knew right then that she would continue to adapt metaphor to her own particular circumstances.

Alliteration

We often employ stories about living things around us, animals and plants, especially trees. The tree, in addition to being part of everyone's experience, is perhaps humankind's most ancient and universal symbol. It appears in myth, ritual, legend, art, poetry, and sacred literature. The branching form of the tree symbolizes shade, protection, stability, and continuity, and is a metaphor for human growth and development (Metzner, 1998).

Let's say I (G. G.) have a client, Dan, with dysthymia. Dan's behavior is marked by indecision and avoidance. Each session, we discuss how he is feeling at the beginning of the session, and most of the session is comprised of trancework. I have an idea of Dan's goal because during an age-progression exercise he described himself as an assertive, decisive individual. He is accustomed to communicating in trance with the three standard responses—"Yes," "No," and "I don't know, or don't want to answer yet"— all on his left hand, which is his preferred hand. I began a series of ego-strengthening stories three sessions ago, and this time, following induction and deepening, he is told the following story, which we call "The Forest." Alliteration is employed in the suggestion.

> *Everyone has experienced trees, maybe even the forest, ever-green trees like pine trees, and even deciduous trees, yes, that's a deciduous forest, where they drop their leaves, just deciding to, and then we experience the bare branches of winter, followed by the green leaves of spring and summer, and with all that it's easy to just forget or to decide not to think about how colorful those leaves can be on deciduous trees.*
>
> *(Yes, you can decide, Dan . . .)*
>
> *During the crisp days of autumn the leaves gradually change—the red sugar maples, rainbow colored sumacs, and purple sweet gums, make a patchwork of brilliant and fiery colors. Then it's like the leaves just decide to fall, in all the forests, millions of tons of leaves in deciduous forests all over the world, suddenly set free, some deciding to flicker and flutter down, others blowing down in a gust of wind, all those leaves, the most gigantic energy transfer on the face of the earth.*
>
> *(Yes, you can decide, Dan.)*
>
> *Where the leaves fall, the soil is deep and fertile, all those leaves that decompose within the coming year on the deciduous trees, they fall way down, to the forest's floor. But there are some exceptions, such as the leaves of the mighty oak, which pile up and sometimes take three years or more to break down, no conscious decision on their part.*
>
> *Beneath the leaves lies the humus, a deep layer of decomposed leaves and other organic matter, deep and rich, and beneath the humus is the soil, tiny pieces of rock mixed into organic matter, profoundly deep and fertile. All these soil nutrients are constantly being mixed by seeping water, freezing and thawing, thawing and freezing, and the movement of plant roots and burrowing animals. It is interesting,*

just deciding *to think of these trees as the biggest plants on the face of the earth, long winding roots that go deep in the soil* . . .

    (Yes, you can decide, Dan.)

As in previous sessions, I tell Dan the story, and then ask him, "Dan, the story I just told you, is it something your unconscious mind can put to use? Take as much time as you need, then you may answer with one of your fingers." A few seconds later, his "yes" finger twitches.

I should feel satisfied with this continued success in therapy. Afterall, it was Erickson who said something to the effect that our conscious mind is wise, but our unconscious mind is a whole lot wiser. Dan's unconscious understands and agrees, and his unconscious, unfettered by conscious interference, will continue to adapt the embedded suggestions of "The Forest" to Dan's unique needs and circumstance. Yes, I should feel satisfied . . . but wait a minute! Let's back up a bit.

NO BULLETS OR STARS

Unless we can verify progress in some objective way, we may be contributing to the hypnosis as a "magic bullet." Hammond (1990) aptly dubbed this the "When-I-wish-upon-a-star approach": you tell the client your favorite story, and then all you need to do is sit back and watch the healing happen. Hypnosis, like other methods in psychotherapy, seldom produces immediate, dramatic results. Instead, we must attend to treatment as a step-wise process that becomes increasingly fine-tuned to the individual client. In Dan's case, my stories and his unconscious agreement turned out to be a miserable failure! Why? I don't know why, but I do know that seven sessions, spaced out over three months, resulted in no corresponding *objective* improvement. Dan indicated he felt "a whole lot better," but this was not borne out on depression and self-efficacy measures. Nor was there improvement in the vital social context: he could provide no examples of being more decisive or assertive at home or work, nor were there any new friends or associations. Maybe I didn't give him enough time in therapy. In thinking back on his case, he was a very compliant young man, one who was easy to work with. Perhaps too easy.

What did I learn from Dan? I learned that I should have recognized early on that his problem might have been helped more by an assertiveness group than by hypnosis.

NON SEQUITUR

At one of our workshops a participant asked what tools in hypnosis helped us the most. We thought about it a minute and then answered, "Well, if a carpenter has a hammer, nails, and a saw, and if a baseball player relies on a bat, ball, and glove, we rely on *hypnotic language, indirection,* and the *non sequitur.*" Someone in the audience asked, "The *what?*" We answered, "You know, an out-of-context statement, the non sequitur."

When we are listening to someone, whether to a commentator on TV or in a social situation, we assume that the speaker believes what she is saying, that she knows what she is talking about, and that she believes she has something worth communicating. If, during her discourse, the speaker utters nonsense, or a non sequitur, she has violated a basic covenant between speaker and listener. The listener may recoil with, "What?" and may be wary thereafter of other things the speaker says. However, in hypnosis, the client does not evaluate a non sequitur with a critical ear.

A non sequitur in hypnosis is part of an economical and easily applied confusion technique (Gilligan, 1987) that was dubbed a "short burst" technique by Brent Geary (personal communication, May 15, 1999), training director at the Erickson Foundation in Phoenix, Arizona. With this technique, the purpose is to get "in underneath the radar" of unconscious resistance. When a client hears a non sequitur—for example, "They paved the parking lot just yesterday"—an unconscious search begins as the client seeks a way out of the confusion. We provide a way out, but in the desired direction.

In a deepening:

> *10 . . . 9 . . . 8 . . . one night I reached for the light switch, but it wasn't there . . .* You can let go . . . *7 . . . 6 . . . 5 . . . it was on the other side of the road . . .* You can let go . . . *4 . . . 3 . . . .*

In a conversational induction:

> *People may wonder how much their minds can wander, pleasantly, effortlessly . . . as they go slowly and deeply into a moderate state of relaxation, more rapidly into a mild state of relaxation, or else they may, without any conscious effort whatsoever, allow both their mind and body to go into a comfortable trance, with both the rate and depth unknown until they get there . . .* You can do it. . . .

We tell clients ahead of time that we may be saying some things to them that do not quite make sense, but that it is all in an effort to help.

CLINICAL COMMENTS

Our vast and curious world provides us with endless material for anecdotes, stories, and inductions. So do advertising and the media. We continue to be fascinated by the way they strive to influence us unconsciously. Paying close attention to the use of hypnotic language in advertising provides us with ideas we can use in therapy. If you look for embedded meaning or suggestion alone, it is evident how much they can teach us about this powerful tool.

As we will be revisiting unconscious process again and again in the remaining chapters, let us pose a question: Is the unconscious *always* wise and resourceful? An eminent therapist once said, "You might ask me to consult my inner *adviser*, but for all you know, I'll be consulting my inner *moron*."

11

Facilitating Unconscious Process in Trance

UNCONSCIOUS PROBLEM SOLVING

In her stress management group, one of our interns, Beth Darnall, used an example of unconscious problem solving from her own experience. She mentioned that when she was an undergrad she forgot the combination to her bicycle lock. For several days, as her bike remained locked and unuseable, she tried *consciously* to remember the combination, but to no avail. Finally, in desperation, she assigned the task to her *unconscious mind*. She went to sleep that night, and as she dreamed, the numbers in the combination appeared in a dream.

That same year, another intern, Heather Smith, was having difficulty with this strange notion of unconscious problem solving. In the hypnosis training group, Heather decided to tackle the problem head-on. It was her turn to be the operator, and she asked her subject in trance to work on a thorny problem that had defied resolution. She asked her subject's *unconscious mind* to work on a solution to the problem. Heather then induced amnesia for the entire discussion. The next week her subject proudly announced that he had solved his problem. Although the subject had no *conscious* awareness of what had happened, the rest of us simply smiled.

We mention these examples to demonstrate that even green interns can understand and employ what for many is a difficult phenomenon to grasp: that problem solving can occur well outside of conscious awareness.

THE ENIGMA OF THE AMYGDALA

When I (G. G.) was in graduate school at the University of Michigan in the early 1970s the unconscious was eschewed as a useless construct. The strictly behavioral professors were quick to ask questions such as, "Has anyone ever *seen* an unconscious?" Or, "Has anyone ever *measured* an unconscious?" These were sound questions to ask at that time, when academics were still striving to counter more than 70 years of Freudian thought and practice. Nowadays, however, the unconscious is studied at universities on a regular basis, usually in the realm of unconscious learning in a part of the brain called the amygdala. The mechanism studied is *unconsciously mediated emotional learning.* For example, if subjects are shown an angry face as a target visual stimulus for less than 40 milliseconds, and are then immediately shown an expressionless mask, these subjects report seeing the mask, but not the target. However, an aversively conditioned masked target elicits an emotional response from subjects without being *consciously* perceived (Morris, Ohman, & Dolan, 1998).

UNCONSCIOUS CENTIPEDE

Haley (1996) notes that the unconscious was discovered, or created, in the 1880s. It was used to explain involuntary behavior, in that people had unsavory unconscious impulses that caused them to act in different ways. Freud followed with the idea that the unconscious is the cause of all psychological and emotional problems, and that,

through therapy, people could become conscious of their unconscious motivations and be set free from their symptoms. Soon after,
Milton Erickson and others established the unconscious as a positive
force. They argued that if unconscious processing is facilitated, good
things would begin to happen. They used the example of the
centipede, which walks best if it is unconscious of how it does so.

CHOOSING THE RIGHT PINEAPPLES

Norma and Phil Barretta related a little anecdote about pineapples in
one of their workshops several years ago. A man named Fred worked
in a pineapple processing plant in Hawaii. His first day on the job,
Fred's boss took him to a conveyor belt, where thousands of pineapples passed by, one after the other. His boss said:

> *Fred, your job is very simple. When a rotten pineapple*
> *comes down the belt, you put it over there, and the good*
> *ones, you put them right here. I'll repeat that for you, Fred:*
> *Good ones here; rotten ones over there.*

This was something Fred could understand, and he worked there
at the end of that conveyor belt for many years.

The Barrettas employ that anecdote in various ways in therapy to
demonstrate one major point: that *you always get what you are
looking for.* We use the pineapples anecdote in working with the
cognitions of depressed people, and we also mention it in our workshops to underscore the importance of using the client's unconscious
as a potentially powerful resource, rather than treating it like a rotten
pineapple. However, the *real* reason we mentioned that anecdote is to
introduce a story about armadillos.

The Armadillo Family

There was a small island in the Mediterranean called
Absoluto, which was several miles off the Positivo coast.
The island was mostly a big volcano. There were no people
on Absoluto, and few had ever visited it—no anthropolo-
gists, or missionaries, or seismologists—because they all
had bigger islands to explore.

There was sparse vegetation on Absoluto, and no one
knows how armadillos got there originally, but that doesn't

really matter. In addition to armadillos, there were some lizards and a few birds, but the most dominant force on the island, besides the volcano, was the family of armadillos.

With all the inbreeding, it was hard to tell if Justin, the eldest, was the father or grandfather, or just the token leader of the family. His partner's name was Justine. They had several children, and named the first Just. Then came Just Look, followed by Just Look About. The youngest went unnamed. Because he had no name (or perhaps for some other reason) the youngest armadillo was observed more by the others, and of course, he developed a special sensitivity in addition to his various other burdens. He was especially skilled at curling himself into a ball of armor, which for most armadillos comes quite naturally when they need to protect themselves.

On their first birthday, the armadillos, just like all their forefathers, make the trek up the volcano to receive their special gift. With those little legs we know how hard it is to climb the side of a volcano, much less go inside to receive a gift, but all of them had accomplished this on their first birthday. Upon returning from the volcano, they receive their name. Just got his name, just as his parents had long ago, as did his siblings Just Look and Just Look About. Up the volcano, inside the volcano, back down with gift and name—just like that life went on, and life was not bad on Absoluto by any means.

The summer turned hot and everyone knew the youngest one's first birthday had passed three days prior and he still had not received his name. He finally got ready to make the pilgrimage up the volcano. He was irritable and worried and he complained about the toll it would take on his body as well as his mind. He didn't say so, but he worried what the gift would be, without even thinking about what name he would be given.

Finally the youngest armadillo set out on his journey. It was several days before he came back, and while he was gone his parents worried about him every minute. But there wasn't a lot of time for worrying because the armadillo family was busy with activities such as finding food, lying in the sun, and occasionally curling up into a ball of armor.

It seemed like a very long time before the young one returned. As he straggled back to his family, he was exhausted and hungry, and he had blisters on his feet. Everyone gathered around him, moving in close like armadillos do when they show their feelings, nudging each other with their noses. He bore a strangely wrapped gift, which all the others eagerly wanted to see, but the youngster had forgotten all about it. He looked up expectantly, as it was time to receive his name. The eldest armadillo presented it to him: *Just Look Inside.*

A quizzical look came on the face of *Just Look Inside,* and inside, for the first time, he really felt quite good. Forever after, he figured he got that name because he had been inside the volcano, but everyone else knew better than that. . . .

A VAGUE PRESENTING PROBLEM

Using pineapples to illustrate getting what you are looking for is a good segue into a *real* person and his problem. Guillermo, a 55-year-old man, was referred for hypnosis. "Just call me Gil," said the pleasant but intense man, who had a short and wiry build and a firm handshake. Gil had been a U.S. soldier in Vietnam in the 1960s. Small men such as he were in demand during the war as "tunnel rats," those who descended into enemy tunnel networks with a flashlight in one hand and a gun in the other. One evening, he had gone underground in pursuit of a fellow soldier who had not returned. On the surface, two men grasped ropes that were attached to Gil's ankles. The missing man was never found, and the soldiers holding the ropes were shot and killed. Gil survived, and went on to endure other stressful events in Vietnam.

Gil had no posttraumatic stress disorder (PTSD) symptoms. He had been married for 35 years, and his grown children were doing well. A successful civil engineer, he looked forward to retirement. However, he was mildly depressed, and had shown minimal response to different antidepressant medications. In trying to operationalize his problem, all I (G. G.) got from him was, "Something's just nagging at me."

"What might life be like in the absence of such nagging?" I query. "Life would be easier, more happy," he answers. He allows me to talk to his wife, but I can ferret out no other problems.

Trying to Hypnotize Gil

Gil had witnessed stage hypnosis years previously, and was quick to add, "I understand that was hypnosis for entertainment, and this is *supposed to be* clinical hypnosis." With his authoritative manner, it was *I* who felt like the patient for a few moments. He added that his preparation also included reading books by Yapko and Zeig, and that he was knowledgeable about their various techniques. As he elaborated on these specifics, I thought about how they stood out in sharp contrast to the vagueness of his presenting problem.

During the first session I tried "The Road," an embedded meaning induction (Gafner & Benson, 2000), a counting-down deepening, and "The Three Lessons" story. He was anxious the whole time, constantly moving around in his chair to get comfortable, much like a chronic pain client, though Gil had no pain in his body. He closed his eyes and scrunched them up, as though he were straining to squint at something. His forehead was creased in concentration, and periodically he scratched the middle of his forehead, rather absent-mindedly stroking the spot with the nail of his right little finger.

Debriefing yielded a subjective *increase* in tension, along with an *absence* of ideosensory feelings, time distortion, or amnesia, all common indicators of trance. "What do you think, Gil?" I asked him. "Interesting induction. A trite metaphor within a simplistic story" was his answer.

Trying not to be distracted by his comment, I asked, "What is it you want, Gil?" "I guess I want to go into trance, but I just can't," he answered. I felt like that was his most productive response so far, and maybe now I was getting somewhere.

The Second Attempt at Hypnosis

The next session, I explained how I was going to use a confusional induction to bypass his unconscious resistance. I told him what we normally tell clients: "You may hear things that don't make sense . . . this is done to help you let go . . . to get beneath your radar screen . . . , etc." "I understand the rationale. You may proceed," he answered matter-of-factly.

I employed the "Mystifying Induction" (Gafner & Benson, 2000), which is replete with confusion, distraction, and cognitive overload. It is an induction that is too detailed and elaborate for me to remember, so I always read it. Most clients we have worked with respond favorably to this rather extravagant means of helping them to let go. In other words, the taxing overload forces them to escape the confusion, and the escape route is in one direction: toward trance. "Rather curious," said Gil, when asked afterward how he felt. "But I really didn't go anywhere, and I certainly didn't go under," he added.

Ten percent of the U.S. population is considered nonhypnotizable, as measured by standard hypnotizability tests. We would venture a guess that perhaps half of that 10 percent would achieve a mild to moderate depth of trance with any variety of confusional inductions. A fraction of the remaining five percent might then go under if we used another hypnotic technique, pacing and utilizing the client's ongoing responses. I did this next with Gil. The following was recreated from therapist notes of that session.

Accessing Unconscious Processes:
Pacing and Utilizing Responses

Gil sat back in the recliner and closed his eyes, as I adjusted the volume of ocean waves on the sound machine. I offered some truisms, apposition of opposites, and general suggestions for relaxation and internal search, before beginning a confusional story.

Gil, I heard once about a police heli-coper that was up there in the sky, looking for 103 Central. Now, Central was the main east-west artery in the city,	(squirms in chair)
and South street was the main north-south street, Central east-west, and South north-south, and on any street, at any time, a person could shift around, perhaps providing a changed perspective, outside, or inside, I can't be sure, and I'm often wrong about many things.	pacing leading restraint
The streets south of Central were sequentially numbered streets . . . First	

Street, South Second Street, Second Street South, Fourth Street south of Central, Fifth Street in the same direction, you get the idea, and listening to anyone on a drum *can be boring, but also very absorbing, but most* don't care to be immersed *in anything because the devil in any details could be a hellish experience not leading to trance or anything else that's useful.*

    North of the Central-South intersection, the streets began with 30th street, North 30th Street, 31st Street, 32nd Street North, 33d, 34th, and I can—but you can't—*remember Yul Brynner in the* Flower Drum Song *and being a civil engineer you don't need a translator for that, but you can have a* trance later, *but your unconscious mind* may not permit *that now, or at any time.*

    West of the Central-South intersection, the streets were numbered sequentially one, two, three, four—First Street West, West Second Street, Third Street in the same direction, and east of that intersection, the streets began with 30, and went 29, 28, 27—East 26th Street, 25th Street East . . . and we get back to that police helicopter, way up there, looking for 103 Central, which had to be east, but I can't be real sure of anything right *now, but in* South Pacific *someone sang a song about* washing *some man out of her hair, and in Roman times, when they had all those* viaducts, *a man with* crossed eyes *could always find a job because they figured he could see in both directions at once,* and *maybe he could go deep inside, as well as* east and west,

(drums his fingers)

pacing

leading/restraint

(drums his fingers)

discharging
resistance
pacing

suggestion
restraint

(a tear drips from his right eye)

pacing

pacing

pacing
fluff

leading
suggestion

and they don't make people do the duck   fluff

walk *in basic training anymore, but*   suggestion

*basic to essential knowledge is in*trinsic

learning way down in *there. You're*

getting there, *Gil . . . .*   suggestion

That man up in the helicopter, before

he left home that day, his wife had asked

him if he knew how you could get fifteen   fluff

cents with three coins *if one of them*

wasn't a nickel, and you and I both know

that the other coin was a nickel, but   (other eye was dry)

money certainly has nothing at all to do   pacing

with numbered streets on South or   (jerks his body)

Central, east or west, up or down, . . .

masticating beef jerky *requires grinding*   pacing

back and forth, isn't that right, Gil?   (his eyes flutter)

In there, deep inside, when something

just doesn't fit, is incongruence *the*   pacing

word, or is it ambivalence? *I* get lost *in*

all that psychobabble, and often guess   restraint

wrong *anyway. But I do know for sure*

what I read in a magazine, about Roget,

the man of thesaurus fame. He was

looking through his basement window,   fluff

through a vertical venetian blind, and he

noticed that the slats of the blind broke

the passing carriage wheels into a jerky

series of still pictures, and his paper on

the topic lead to the founding of the

motion picture industry across the sea.

He came upon it serendipitously—what

a surprise *it was that day!*   suggestion

Relaxation and letting go can be most

interesting, can it not? Features flatten   (immobility/catalepsy)

on the face, and it doesn't always trans-

late into trance, an entrance into which

state?

A pause is just around the corner, Gil,

and we don't mean paws on a dog, but

simply a silence, when there're no words, and I'll be quiet now and you can allow your unconscious mind to drift and dream, and when you find yourself taking one deep comfortable refreshing breath, that will be a signal to you and me both that you are ready to proceed . . .

(deep breath after three minutes)
pacing

That's the way, *Gil, something that a person can enjoy and appreciate . . . in there. Isn't movement curious in its own right?*

(his brow furrows)

Now, creases can be an antecedent to other movement, lateral associations, Gil, and we're not talking Rotary Club here, Gil, but farmer's field, long furrows, *seed corn planted is one thing, but acorns, or mesquite seeds sprouting in those furrows* send out roots to the side, *as well as a tap root going*

pacing

suggestion

down, just how deep I've never measured with furrow responsiveness tests. A farmer one time said, "I'm in the groove," but others have said that, too, and I bet all of them have a good idea of just what they mean.

I'd like you now, Gil, to just let yourself drift and dream, or dream and drift, and let the back part of your mind work for you . . . and when something pertinent—anything at all—surfaces from the back part of your mind, you and I will both know, because you'll find yourself experiencing one more deep refreshing breath.

Very good, Gil, and now tell me with your words, what has come up?

And anything else?

(breathes deeply after one minute)
("Simple," he says)
("Light")

Like in light bulb?   ("Yes")

Okay, just let "simple" and "light" be there, as you drift and dream, . . . and I remember one time . . . Will from the power company, warm light, 100-watt bulb, 200-watt bulb, and on Las Vegas Boulevard you can read a newspaper in the middle of the night without squinting.   (both eyes tear up)

Wishing well, cracks in the side, leaking out laterally, or is it in all directions?   suggestion

The back part of your mind can continue to remember and process anything important, Gil, knowing that the next time you come in here and sit down there, just feeling that chair beneath you will be an immediate signal to let yourself go, so that this work can continue.

suggestion

posthypnotic suggestion

Right now, Gil, you may forget anything you may have intended to remember, which for some may mean forgetting to remember, and for others it's a matter of remembering to forget.

suggestions for amnesia

Wake up now, fast, as I count from one up to five, one-two-three-four-FIVE.

Gil had a disoriented, punch-drunk look about him, which is commonly seen in analytic, left-brain resistant people following their first successful venture into trance. It was almost as if the sturdy, monolithic dam had suddenly burst. Gil's inordinate response was like unforeseen flooding way downstream.

His body felt limp, and subjectively he was exhausted. He had very little conscious memory of the day's session. He was seen again in two weeks, and in the induction I made brief mention of South and Central streets, and conversationally offered suggestions for relaxation and internal process. Eye watering and brow furrowing were much less pronounced this time, but the behavior was paced and lead nonetheless. He retrieved an image of a teaching assistant in college, a woman from India who had a spot painted on her forehead. He remembered that she told him to "lighten up," and how upset he had become at the time. During debriefing, we processed this memory, and he commented that his wife and various other people had told him he needed to "lighten up." We reviewed various things he can do in this regard.

In a month I see him one more time. His mood is brighter, and he reports good results from his effort to "lighten up." Therapy is done. I tell him to call me if he needs any help in the future. I never heard from him again.

CLINICAL COMMENTS

Clients are usually amnesic for some part of trancework. To further amnesia, there are various things you can do. You can use direct suggestions, such as, "Beginning now, you can just forget. . . ." You can suggest amnesia metaphorically, as in, "I had a dream last night, and when I woke up I could remember very little of that dream." Distraction can facilitate amnesia. We often mention things that clients must answer no to, such as, "It never gets hot in Phoenix," or, "*People* magazine has no pictures in it." Clients hear statements like this, and their silent but reflexive "no" often promotes amnesia of previous content. Again, the rationale for this is so that unconscious process can proceed without conscious interference. We tell people ahead of time what we will be doing and the reason for doing it.

Amnesia can be facilitated during the session. If you have ever watched a demonstration by Stephen Gilligan, you noticed how he will offer a suggestion, say, ". . . internal resources can be accessed now. . . ." Then, he will immediately shift attention away from his suggestion by focusing on something else, like a tingling in the hand, or a book he read last month.

Pacing and utilizing a client's ongoing responses are a lot of work, and are difficult to teach. A good way to learn these techniques is to watch a live demonstration by Ernest Rossi, or one of his videotapes. He is elegant in the simplicity with which he is able to pace and lead ongoing behavior. I (S. B.) often use Rossi's induction in which you ask the client to place her hands in front of her, palms facing each other, 12 inches apart. You then offer permissive suggestions for the unconscious mind to allow the hands to close, or to open wider. No script is required. All the therapist need do is carefully observe, pace, and lead.

You may also employ one of your customary inductions, and pay close attention to the behavior the client is showing you, whether it is a gross movement, such as squirming in the chair, or a subtle cue, such as the slight reddening of one cheek. Whatever the behavior is, pace it, then lead by adding on in the desired direction. For example, "Sometimes in trance a person's left eye will twitch, and this twitching may mean that something is happening—perhaps deeper relaxation, an internal search, or something else that can lead to a more meaningful experience." To pace an eye twitch metaphorically, such as, "The leaves in the trees quivered ever so slightly," requires practice. However, with practice, you will come up with some stock metaphors. Afterall, there is a finite number of nonverbal responses that a person can evince in trance. For example, if we take just the eyes, they can open, close, twitch, flutter, tear, and not much else, can they? The same can be said for the rest of the body. If you are reading a script, it is hard to pick up all of a client's nonverbal behavior.

An unconsciously resistant client like Gil responded well to this approach. Pacing and utilizing helped him to let go. But he was only able to do this because the foundation of rapport had been laid, and he felt comfortable risking himself because it made sense to him, and he was approached respectfully.

In an induction or story, do not underestimate the importance of *fluff*. Yes, fluff—filler material that is not didactic or purposeful, but which may push the process along faster than embedded suggestion or hypnotic language. Why? Because it is *boring*, for one thing, and we all become absorbed in boredom. Or maybe because it is disarming, or because it is a pleasant contrast to something mean-ingful. Fluff may seem trite or soft; however, it can be a very solid ally.

12

Age Progression: Back to the Future

TEMPORAL MATTERS

We may remember important dates, like certain holidays, or birthdays, or other occasions, whether happy or sad. Inconsequential times past may be long forgotten, but not so with significant events seared into our memories, like what you were doing on September 11, 2001, or where you were when the Challenger exploded. Or, if you are old enough to recall the assassination of President John F. Kennedy, this may have left a lasting impression.

I (G. G.) remember the announcement President Kennedy's death over the intercom in high school. That was in 1963, yet I still contemplate it on occasion. I also remember, though more faintly, the soldier playing "Taps" at the funeral, and how he misplayed a note on his trumpet. I heard an interview with the trumpet player on National

Public Radio. They played a tape of the botched sixth note, which came out as an amateurish squawk. Interestingly, the historian and interviewer, in evaluating the event after the passage of time, interpreted the squawk as a natural "fit": the soldier had personalized the solemn occasion by erring, and in doing so had taken a naturally humble, one-down position. We can also wonder if that squawk somehow discharged a nation's collective anxiety on that day. Do you know any therapists who take similar positions and foster a discharge of anxiety or resistance?

ISSUES OF TIME IN THERAPY

How often have we heard colleagues categorize behavior in certain ways?

> *If they arrive early, they're anxious.*
> *If they show up late, they're hostile.*
> *Depression is oriented toward the past.*
> *Anxiety is oriented toward the future.*

We hear things like this repeated over and over again, and we tend to believe them. In hypnosis, the concept of *time* is consequential, and extremely interesting. Several years ago, while waiting to use the copy machine—and in those days the machine spit out one copy about every two or three seconds—I was privy to two psychiatrists' discussion of a woman's pervasive, seemingly treatment-resistant anxiety. Over a couple of decades, the woman had been treated with a plethora of medications, with no positive results. The doctors carried on a spirited and sometimes far-reaching discussion about this client, offering various diagnostic impressions, including anxiety with depression, depression with anxiety, as well as any number of personality disorders with such-and-such features. Not considering myself very strong in diagnostics, I sincerely admire and respect a depth of knowledge in this area, not to mention in pharmaceutical treatment. To be sure, I became rather absorbed in the doctors' discussion, and my unconscious must have wisely filed it away, knowing that it would be of inestimable use in the future.

Their discussion ended as I finished making my tenth copy. I remember the older, more experienced doctor saying something like this to his younger colleague: "Just remember. Both the past and the future are undesirable, and if you can get her to live in the present, you will have balanced the scales."

Many times we have been party to case discussions and presentations, equally thoughtful, wise, and respectful, in which years of clinical acumen are directed toward a client's improvement. Often the focus involves the *past*, as in helping people work through trauma or loss. Occasionally, there is a token regard for the *future*, with the asking of the miracle question, or preparing the client for adversity, as in response prevention in panic disorder treatment. But an explicit and applied *future* focus in therapy? This seldom happens, except in hypnosis.

ERICKSON'S LEGACY OF WELLNESS

One of the major contributions of Milton Erickson was his unyielding future orientation in therapy. He would seldom concentrate on the past, and instead would direct every effort toward the future. Within this orientation were the assumptions that healthy human beings are optimistic, connected to people, and convinced of their own capacity to influence life events, and that they have within themselves all the resources they need to be healthy and happy. As such, wellness and the future, not illness and the past, should be the focus of therapy (Walters & Havens, 1994).

Erickson was born in Aurum, Utah, a town that has since disappeared. In the late 1890s, when the U.S. population was migrating west, young Erickson and his family travelled east in a covered wagon, eventually settling on a farm in Wisconsin. Growing up in a farm family strongly influenced his future orientation. He often mentioned this experience to clients and students alike, noting, for example, the strength and resilience of farmers. They understand that the caprices of nature might cause the loss of a crop or livestock one year, but that hard work and a hopeful eye to the future can bring success the following year.

Erickson made abundant use of anecdotes and metaphors about plant life and nature. However, he may have made even more use of himself and his family in his examples. When Erickson's 93-year-old mother broke her hip, her determination, resolve, and future orientation aided her recovery. As a youth, Erickson was paralyzed with polio, but never gave up hope. In fact, he utilized the experience for personal growth. While immobilized, he sharpened his powers of observation, making special note of the nuances in nonverbal behavior, something that would aid him later in his practice of psychiatry.

Central to Erickson was the social context of working with clients, something we take for granted now. When Erickson introduced the idea, mental health treatment meant analyzing the single patient, who had her back to you on the couch. Also vital to Erickson are optimism, altruism, and hardiness, and a unique way of reframing problems, all of which are beyond the scope of this discussion. We encourage you to read a cogent and fascinating review of this in Walters and Havens (1994).

THE CRYSTAL BALL

A review of Erickson's work shows that he is constantly lifting a veil to the future. Whether it is a behavior prescription or a multiple embedded metaphor, the movement is forward, inexorable motion toward something that lies ahead. Erickson never looked back, unless he had a purpose in doing so, such as absorbing a client's attention in a pleasant childhood memory. The trance, then, would invariably be used for a future-oriented application.

The crystal ball was frequently employed by Erickson, often as part of what he called pseudo-orientation in time. He did not have an actual crystal ball. Instead, during therapy, he asked clients to *imagine* a crystal ball, and used this image as part of the technique. Pseudo-orientation in time is very complex, and we view it as possibly the most difficult hypnotic technique to successfully apply. It is discussed as part of unconscious problem solving in Chapter 19.

The movie, *Peewee's Big Adventure,* is a clever spoof on many things, including the crystal ball. In this comedy, the actor Peewee Herman is frantically in search of his stolen bicycle. He happens upon Madame Ruby, a classic, gypsy-style fortune-teller with her hair in a handkerchief. After taking Peewee's money, she promises to tell him his future. She theatrically waves her hand over the tool of her trade, a crystal ball, gazes deeply into it, and convinces Peewee to search for his bike in the basement of the Alamo in Texas. Of course, the Alamo has no basement, and Peewee has been duped.

We mention this movie as a good example of the crystal ball's reputation for deception and praying on people's hopes. The crystal ball may have more negative baggage attached to it than hypnosis, and rightfully so. However, the crystal ball's reputation for fraud and trickery is much more deserved. We do not use the crystal ball except when we are employing pseudo-orientation in time. Then, it seems to fit and to act as an eminently handy artifice. Other times, though, it strikes us as old-fashioned and authoritarian. For general applications of both age regression and age progression, permissive and indirect techniques are our first choice.

When Erickson employed the crystal ball in the 1930s, 40s, and 50s, crystal balls and their attendant fortune-tellers were more prominent, along with tarot cards, astrology, and similar ways of divining the future. Today, people are more likely to put their faith in electronic media, such as the fortune-teller on TV or on the Internet. Although it is an old-fashioned artifice or icon, people still understand the crystal ball's purpose, and in our practices, when we ask small children, most have heard of it.

If you like the crystal ball, we encourage you to use it. With all these techniques, if you are comfortable with certain ones, that confidence is readily transferred to the client.

AGE PROGRESSION IN THE LITERATURE

Deshazer (1978) was one of the first neo-Ericksonians to report on the use of age progression. He found the procedure useful in developing new expectations in sexual performance. Age progression soon became a brief (solution-focused) staple (Deshazer, 1982, 1985), and it is usually employed without formal hypnosis, often in the form of the miracle question. The technique is a common one in guided imagery and hypnosis, and may be referred to by many names, including time projection, pseudo-orientation in time into the future, mental rehearsal, and process imagery. In the performance enhancement arena, such as in sports, age progression may be called *goal imagery, success imagery,* or *end-result imagery* (Hammond, 1990; Kessler & Miller, 1995).

However, among some therapists and clients alike, the use of age *regression* continues to hold more appeal. Does the lure of the magic bullet account for this? Or is it the attraction of the mysterious, seemingly unfathomable past? Clients invariably say things like, "I want to find out *why* I'm the way I am," as they believe that uncovering will yield magical solutions. Therapists might buy into such a magical quest, and spend several sessions in what often turns out to be a futile search.

In the case of Dalia, we demonstrate the technique as it is most commonly used: We ask the client to imagine the way she *wishes to be* in the future. This is indeed a powerful technique, especially in deep trance. The necessity of at least a moderate depth may argue against the effectiveness of age progression without formal trance, for example, with the miracle question. Age progression can be even *more* versatile, as noted by Phillips and Frederick (1992), pioneers in ego-state therapy. They typically use the procedure to promote growth on multiple levels, to facilitate treatment goals, and to deepen the working-through process. Various writers like Stanton (1975, 1977, 1979) and Hartland (1965, 1971) employ age progression as a cornerstone of their ego-strengthening.

The Case of Dalia

I (S. B.) was completing marital therapy with an Hispanic couple, when they asked if I would see their 14-year-old daughter, Dalia, who lacked assertiveness. The parents noted that their only child's behavior had begun two months ago, when she began to avoid her friends and employed poor eye contact with people in general. She had been seen by the school psychologist, who told the parents that she would grow out of it. Dalia's grades in school were always good, but lately her schoolwork had suffered.

Dalia was a charming and articulate girl who avoided my gaze except when she discussed her schoolwork. She was proud of her good grades and the fact that she always completed assignments on time. She agreed that she had been avoiding her friends lately, but only because school demanded her full attention. Dalia admitted that she needed to feel more comfortable in social situations, and that she had difficulty "standing up to people." She did not appear depressed and she had no somatic symptoms. I immediately began to speculate on the function of her behavior, especially considering that the onset had corresponded with the diminished conflict between her parents.

The girl was interested in hypnosis, and as a way to begin, I asked her to sit back in the recliner and close her eyes, if she wished. I turned on the "rain" mode on the sound machine, as she preferred that over the other two options ("ocean waves" or "train"). I told her that we would be doing some exploration today, and that in trance, I would be asking her to see herself as she wished to be in the future. I seeded the pretrance discussion with *seeing* and *future*. I set up age progession with the following embedded meaning induction, which we call the "induction involving apposition of opposites." The apposition of opposites are not italicized in the text.

Induction Involving Apposition of Opposites

Dalia, we can think of many things in our experience, things that go fast, *and things that go* slow. *Maybe like a car, or something else,* fast *one minute, and then* slow *the next. I've never ridden on a bullet train, but they say that those trains can go well* over *100 mph before eventually slowing to a halt at the station.*

A person's breathing or heart rate can change from minute *to minute, although from* second *to second it might be difficult to tell any change; but from* one *hour to the next, changes are perfectly normal and natural, given all the things a person does and feels and thinks from* hour *to hour and* day *to day, during the course of* weeks *and* months.

One time I was at a long *and* boring *meeting whose pace* suddenly *quickened by the telling of what appeared to be a rather* curious *and* interesting *story, but which eventually became* bogged *down in* meandering *detail before* picking *up again and venturing off in another direction.*

A man with a wide bowtie standing at the podium—he spoke with a lisp—had a reputation for doing many things, some sooner *than* later. *He had a rather peculiar name, Plutard Y. Early, which was a tedious name to remember. So, he said, "Just call me Tarly," kind of a strange contraction of a name for someone who had a penchant for drawing things out, and preferring* longer *over* shorter. *Tarly was a person with* quick *hands who was* slow *on his feet, but not in his mind, which occasionally worked overtime. People still tell the story of Tarly.*

The entire story takes place as a cruise ship is heading toward an island not very far away. Tarly was on this cruise with his niece, and although I forget the name of the island, I quite vividly remember that the ship was part of Comfort

Cruise Lines. It sailed along very, very slowly, on the way to the island, "slower than molasses in January," according to Tarly. Tarly's niece was named Terry Momenti—a fleeting kind of name that, just as easily as Tarly's, could slip from the grasp of a person's mind.

Now, out on this boat, Tarly began to relate to Terry something he had been contemplating and wondering about for a long time, how one thing can go so terribly slow, *while another thing can move so* fast. *He gestured dramatically and said, "A glacier moves ever so slowly over the years, while a spinning top turns around many times in one* second. *At the same time, a jet plane,* way up in the sky, *breaks the sound barrier, and a smaller plane flies 100 miles per* hour, *while at the same time,* down *on the ground, a race car speeds around the track, and other cars glide down the freeway."*

Terry nodded leisurely as she listened, and the ship continued gently through the waves. Her gaze was fixed on her uncle and she breathed in *and* out *very gradually, swallowing only now and then. "Some* fast, *and some* slow," *she paraphrased languidly, hands like weights in her lap.*

About this time someone else sat down near them, out there on the deck. Unseen by Tarly, this other person observed them both, listening to what each person had to say, head moving back and forth woodenly, from one to the other.

Tarly continued. "Sand dunes develop over a long period of time, but space travel was accelerated *in the 1970s. On TV I saw fleet-footed racers in the Olympics, and an hour later, on that same TV, I remember someone* plodding *along in the park. In fact, driving over gently rolling hills actually goes faster than straining up Pike's Peak, if you think about it."*

"Some go fast and some take longer," said Terry, hands in her lap. She nodded leisurely as she listened, and the ship continued gently through the waves. Her gaze was fixed on her uncle, and she breathed in *and* out, *very steadily, swallowing only now and then.*

At the same time, the other person observed them both, head moving back and forth woodenly, from one to the other.

Tarly's hands moved at the same pace as his words. "The Second *coming takes longer than the* first *snowfall, and rain*

late in the season could also be the first snow of the year,"
continued Tarly, "and sleet at any time can freeze quickly. Fog
can develop overnight, but the sun can break through in the
morning before you realize it. In fact, lower down *on a*
mountain, snow can melt with the first warm day, but up *on*
top of the mountain, the snow seems to stay forever."

Terry studied her uncle, eyes unblinking, breathing in, *and*
breathing out, *seldom swallowing. Her hands stirred ever so*
slightly in her lap and she whispered, "Yes, some are fast, *and*
some are slow."

Meanwhile, the third person's head bobbed back and forth,
ever so slowly, absorbing the words and actions of both.

Tarly continued. "Chameleons change color by expanding
and contracting cells of different colors, while a traffic light
changes from yellow to red at a different pace. A shadow
appears only as suddenly as you notice it, and a tumbleweed
grows to maturity much faster than an oak tree. Terry, did
you ever think about how carrots mature down *in the soil,*
while asparagus develop fully up *on top?"*

"Yes, slowly down below, rapidly up on top," *answered*
Terry. Her eyes blinked one time, but she didn't swallow, and
her hands did not move, as her eyes watched her uncle.

At the same time, the third person's head moved slowly
back and forth, eyes watching one, then the other, listening,
contemplating, wondering.

Tarly waited a while, watching the waves, and then he
spoke again. "Sometimes, while reading, one page takes
forever, and other times, the pages seem to turn all by them-
selves. And one more thing, Terry. In some songs, the notes
are much quicker than heart beats, and I always wondered
about relative movement and velocity among the Platters,
Coasters, and Drifters."

Terry did not hear her uncle's last words, as she had sat
back and drifted off, as had the third person, who by now
was only vaguely aware of the gentle movement of the ship.
They had almost reached the island.

Dalia had now drifted off and appeared to be deep in trance,
perhaps asleep. I asked her to nod her head if she could still hear me,
and she nodded one time.

Age Progression

Dalia, we can remember things in the past, just like we can imagine things in the future. No doubt you can recall memorable occasions in the past, perhaps a birthday party, the satisfaction of a good report card, or something else that was satisfying, comfortable . . . and we know how easy it is to become pleasantly absorbed in such memories.

Now, as far as the future goes, you may have learned about the future tense in English. And in social studies, or history, you may have gleaned how important it is to look ahead. Certainly, even primitive societies had to plan ahead in order to gather food, and Phoenix or Glendale, to build a road or a new school, they have to employ the future tense, and to plan ahead.

And so, too, for you, it is easy to imagine, just imagine, something in the future. A girl can transport herself into the future in many ways, perhaps imagining herself transported on a magic carpet, or some other way. Your grandfather, he may hear one of those Big Band tunes, and he is instantly, without any conscious effort, transported back to a pleasant time in the past. But we're talking future here, are we not?

You may already be there, in the future. At any rate, I'm going to ask you now to travel to some time, any time, in the future, when you can see yourself the way you want to be. *When you are there, Dalia, taking as much time as you need, going there in your own way, and seeing yourself* the way you want to be, *there, in the future, let me know by nodding your head.* . . . [After ten seconds, she shows a slight head nod.]

Just take a few moments to notice, just notice, Dalia, and really appreciate, the Dalia you see there. . . . *You may notice if it's daytime or nighttime, if she's alone, or with others; what clothes she is wearing, and how she is* feeling. *Exactly what is the predominant* feeling *that is coming through. . . ?*

She was then realerted, and as I had let time get away from me in this session, there was no time for debriefing. We made an appointment in two weeks.

The Final Session with Dalia

When Dalia returned, I learned details of her trance experience that I would have normally elicited during debriefing in the last session. She reported an overall pleasant experience, heaviness in her hands, and the perception that only a few minutes had passed while she was "deeply asleep," as she put it, where, she actually had been in trance for nearly thirty minutes. She said, "I've been thinking about it, but I still can't remember much of what you told me." Amnesia, then, along with time distortion and ideosensory feeling—all indicators of trance—added up to moderate depth, as well as the obvious fact that she was a very good subject. I asked her what she experienced in terms of seeing herself the way she wanted to be, and she said she could not remember.

Continuing to target Dalia's presenting problem of assertiveness, we resumed. I seeded *absorption* and *control,* casually talking about my car, some new sponges I had used washing it, and how enjoyable it was to get behind the wheel after it was clean and shiny.

Symptom Alteration in Trance

That's right, Dalia, just sitting back like you are, listening to the sound of the rain, and you can remember, in your mind, in your body, or with both your body and your mind, the pleasant relaxation you experienced last time you came in here, and let yourself drift off, letting those hands become heavy, just nice and heavy, that's the way. . . .

Now, Dalia, let yourself experience being deeply asleep *one more time, just let it happen all by itself. . . . and when you feel yourself deeply* asleep, *just as deep as you want to go, taking as much time as you need, you can let me know by letting your head gently nod, because then I'll know that you are there.* [After about one minute her head nods.]

You can continue to drift and dream, or dream and drift, in your peaceful and relaxed state, while I tell you this story. As we discussed, it is not necessary for you to actively listen to this story because we can trust the back part of your mind to pick out what may be important or relevant to you. Now, if you agree with this, let me know by nodding your head. . . . [She nods.]

Now, this happened a while ago. I can't remember how many years ago, but it was in another state. This boy—his name was Sam—took pride in many things, and rightfully so. He could be counted on to be a good driver. He felt very good sitting down behind the wheel, and it felt good being in the driver's seat. *Sam drove his younger brother and sister to soccer practice, and he helped his parents around the house, which can't be said for every 16-year-old boy, am I right?* [She nods in agreement.]

Now, this boy, Sam, he was especially good at his schoolwork. He would become absorbed *in English class, and he would hold his pen—or was it his pencil?—up in the air while the teacher talked, just losing track of time, when a minute can seem like an hour, or an hour can seem like a minute, or maybe it's just a matter of not paying attention to the passage of time. At home, studying, sometimes—but not all the time—Sam would become* lost *in something he was doing. Just like at other times, he could remember when something would take forever to happen, and other times, things would seem to happen just . . . instantaneously.*

Like most people, Sam was not perfect. You would think that he would be confident in all situations, but he wasn't. Deep down, he was very shy, and it worried him. One Sunday afternoon, Sam was driving alone outside of town, and he decided to keep driving for another 50 miles, all the way to his grandmother's house. He had asked advice from his grandmother once before, and now was a good time to ask her for help with his shyness problem.

At grandmother's house, he explained everything as best he could, and his wise grandmother just sat and listened patiently with a curious smile on her face. Finally, she said, "Sam, I want you to do something that can help you with this problem. Are you willing to try it out?" Sam nodded. [Two seconds later, Dalia nods.]

"Sam, listening to you, I can tell that sometimes you are less shy than other times. For example, in geometry class, you feel a bit shy, but in history class, you feel less so; and with Tom, you feel confident, but with Maria, shyness seems to creep in again. Now, we need to test out my idea about your being in charge of this, just to see what you'll notice about shyness, and about yourself, and to see what you can learn about this curious shyness. The results may be very, very interesting.

"Accordingly, I want you to continue to feel confident in history class and when you are with Maria. And on Wednesday, only on Wednesday, I want you to pay close attention to what happens in your mind, and in your body, when you are in geometry class and with Tom. Don't actually do anything on Wednesday, just notice. How does this sound to you?" [Dalia smiles.]

Dalia was then realerted. She reported heaviness in her hands and similar trance phenomena as she had the previous session.

Dalia was seen one more time and reported improvement in shyness across all social situations. As we were finishing the session, she mentioned that she had spoken to three of her friends about the "wonders of hypnosis," and asked if I could see them for various problems. I reiterated to her that I, as the therapist, had been but a guide in her process of change. I then asked her to listen to the following story, which is adapted from Close (1998).

The Pharaoh's Wheat

Let me tell you a story that's actually a true story, or so I'm told. In the early part of the last century, an Egyptian pharaoh's tomb was discovered. They found whatever had not been plundered in previous centuries, and among the treasures was a bowl of wheatberries, unsprouted wheat, a couple of handfuls of it, as a matter of fact.

There was a time when the ancient Egyptians attributed magical powers to wheat, and the discoverers wondered if the wheat was still vital. Would it still grow?

They gave the wheat to a noted agronomist, who carefully planted and watched the wheat. In a few weeks the wheat actually sprouted!

Never before had wheat been known to maintain its viability for more than seven years. This astounded the scientific community, enhanced the agronomist's reputation, lent esteem to the unfathomable mysteries of the ancient Egyptians, and even changed the way contemporaries stored wheat. It was now recommended that it be kept only in cool, dry conditions, and strictly in the dark.

Shortly after the agronomist died, his sons published an article on the pharaoh's wheat. In the article, the sons told how they as teenagers had mixed some contemporary wheat in with the pharaoh's wheat, and they finally wished to reveal what they had done.

At the conclusion of the story, Dalia smiled and said, "I guess that will give me something to think about." She did not mention her friends again during a follow-up session. One month later, I saw her with her parents, and processed with them all the changes they had been through recently. Her parents emphasized to her that now they were doing better and that everything would be all right. I asked the parents to call me in two months, and when they called, they reported sustained improvement.

CLINICAL COMMENTS

In a case like this, there are many ways to approach the problem. Therapists who work hypnotically believe that an indirect, unconsciously directed approach may effect change more efficiently than conventional talk therapy. Dalia offered much to be utilized, such as her belief in hard work and achieving good grades. Olness and Kohen (1996) list a variety of induction techniques that are preferred for adolescents. These include favorite place or activity, arm catalepsy, videogames, driving a car, and playing or listening to music. I (G. G.) often use arm catalepsy (Gafner & Benson, 2000) for both children and adolescents, as arm catalepsy is rapid and economical. I (S. B.) prefer to absorb their attention in a story that embeds trance phenomena.

We often tag relaxation, or a target image, such as the client's seeing herself behaving confidently, to an anchor, such as a circle with the thumb and forefinger. Sometimes, too, in age progression, we will ask the client to bring a "gift" back to their present, waking state. People may select hope, strength, a memory, or something concrete, such as a pencil they used in school. This, too, can serve as an additional anchor, or reminder.

It is vital to communicate in trance so that you can be sure the person has, for example, attained the mental image you are targetting. A simple head nod works well for this. In other cases, you may need a wider range of responses, such as finger signals that communicate "yes," "no," or "I don't know," or "I'm not read to answer yet." These will be discussed in the following chapters.

With Dalia, age progression both explicated the goal and set up the intervention. I never did find out exactly what Dalia envisioned when she saw herself the way she wanted to be. But it really didn't matter.

13

The Treatment of Pain

The quest to control pain is mentioned in Egyptian papyri dating back to 4000 B.C.E., and despite advances in medical diagnostics, analgesic medications, and medical and surgical interventions, pain continues to be the most universal form of stress. Pain accounts for over 80 percent of physician visits in the United States, and costs more than $70 billion in health care costs and lost productivity (Gatchell & Turk, 1996).

PAIN AS A PRESENTING PROBLEM

Why do clients with physical pain get referred to mental health professionals? Quite simply because at this time, there exists no medical or surgical treatment available that consistently and permanently alleviates pain for all clients (Gatchell & Turk, 1996). If you have worked with these clients—and their family members—you understand their suffering and how for some, virtually every day and night can be a hopeless, demoralizing experience.

In matching any client's experience, Milton Erickson was said to have noted something like, "Place one foot in the patient's world, but be sure to keep one foot firmly planted in your own world." This may require no forethought when working with depression and anxiety, but in working with pain, we recommend that before you step, you regard your feet for a moment. Should you step with a steel-toed boot, or a soft slipper? Or, is it advisable to step with one foot, while the other foot is firmly anchored by a strong chain? We can remember the *Star of India* in San Diego, and how it was secured to the dock by a really thick rope. Or, is it best to step gingerly, as if in a minefield, or instead, regard the pitfalls of pain as a slippery slope? If so, spiked shoes are in order.

THE SITUATION IS SERIOUS

Unlike anxiety and depression, with pain clients the therapist may have a tougher time matching the experience, or somehow communicating, "I understand." Why? Because with many of these clients, their perceived suffering is so dear, and their problem seems so inordinately compelling, that, try as we may, demonstrating anything but a mere modicum of understanding may be all we can do. This situation becomes even more sober when we consider associated issues, such as secondary gain, opioid dependence, relational issues, and comorbid psychological problems. In the Veterans' Administration where I (G. G.) work, older age adds complexity, in that the therapist deals with the multiple losses and compounding problems of late life (Gafner, 1987), in addition to pain. A psychologist who works exclusively with pain told us once, "You put on your hip boots, wade out into the cold water, and you realize this is your life."

SERIOUS, BUT NOT HOPELESS

Fortunately, our own practices are diverse, so we can contemplate thick ropes instead of hip boots, and lest we paint a chill and uninviting picture, we need to say that we really appreciate these clients with pain. Why? First, we *appreciate* helping them—at least those who we succeed in helping—as that is why we got into this work in the first place. We need to keep in mind that these challenging clients were interesting and competent people *before* they became pain clients, and once we reach beyond a seemingly overwhelming symptom, we can help them build on their strengths and resources.

With tough clients, you have to take a close look at what you do and how you do it, and this is the bright side of treating pain clients: learning from them. In order to bypass formidable unconscious resistance, we have had to do a lot of experimentation with diverse inductions and indirect techniques. A benefit of this is that we can apply this knowledge to other clients for whom standard techniques do not work and we have to reach deeper into our bag of techniques to get "underneath the radar." For these reasons, we hope that clients with pain make up at least a portion of your caseload.

SOME ASSUMPTIONS

Before mental health professionals treat clients with pain, they need to be assured that clients have received appropriate diagnostic studies, that they are receiving ongoing primary medical care, and that they have been evaluated by a licensed psychologist. Just as physicians and dentists need to be cognizant of more than the biophysical aspects of pain, so, too, should mental health professionals educate themselves on at least the basics of human anatomy, along with the most common pain diagnoses, medications and side effects, and common medical and surgical treatments.

In this chapter, we do not address acute pain, such as appendicitis or a bone fracture. Barber's (1996) types of pain include: *acute*; *recurring*, such as osteoarthritis and headaches; and *chronic benign pain syndrome*, such as a lower-back pain, characterized by continued pain long after healing has occurred. A fourth type listed by Barber is *psychogenic* pain, a variant of somatoform disorder, which is rare. In this chapter we will discuss both recurring and chronic pain, but both will be referred to simply as pain.

TREATING PAIN

Clients who come to you for pain control may have already travelled a long and winding road, and now hypnosis may be yet another milepost. In our practices, people have often tried conventional treatment, such as medication, physical therapy, chiropracty, surgery, electric stimulators, and pain block. However, they may have also sought help from many varieties of massage or "energy" therapy, accupuncture, botanicals, or naturopathy, as well as meditation, and other religious or spiritual treatments, to name a few. Some people may even be ashamed to admit what they have tried in their quest for relief. Among Hispanics and Native Americans in our practices, some go to neighborhood healers, medicine people, or *curanderos*, whose treatments range from a *limpia*, or cleansing ceremony, to herbs, prayer, or the removal of a curse (Gafner & Duckett, 1992).

PSYCHOLOGICAL TREATMENT OF PAIN

People may have also tried standard psychological treatments, such as biofeedback, relaxation training, coping skills training, or multi-disciplinary treatment, all of which have proven effective in controlled studies (Jensen, 1996)

Spiegel and Bloom (1983) randomly assigned breast cancer patients to three groups: no treatment, support group, and support group with hypnosis. After one year, the hypnosis group reported the lowest levels of pain. Clinical trials involving pain related to bone marrow transplantation (Syrjala et al., 1992, 1995) demonstrated the effectiveness of hypnosis. Meditation, hypnosis, imagery, and relaxation have all demonstrated similar efficacy in providing relief for chronic pain, and various studies have shown the helpfulness of hypnosis in burn pain, migraine, and phantom limb pain (Syrjala and Abrams, 1996). Also, dating from Erickson's writings in the 1940s and continuing to the present, the literature is replete with studies and case reports touting the efficacy of hypnosis in treating acute and chronic pain in dentistry, medicine, surgery, and health psychology.

IMAGERY OR HYPNOSIS

In a meta-analysis of the efficacy of cognitive-behavioral therapy (CBT) methods for pain management, Fernandez and Turk (1989) showed that *imagery* was the most powerful component of the treatment. They reported significant effects with different types of pain across various studies. In their treatment program, Syrjala and

Abrams (1996) recognize that *imagery* and *visualization* are essentially synonymous terms, and that *hypnosis* may or may not incorporate visual imagery. At the same time, they recognize that other techniques, such as progressive muscle relaxation, meditation, deep breathing, and autogenic training, share more commonalities than differences with hypnosis. In individualizing their approach to each client, they use the term *imagery* in describing treatment to clients, and offer the term *hypnosis* only when clients ask for it. Their standard treatment also involves storytelling and metaphors and suggestions outside of the formal trance state.

All this sounds essentially like *hypnosis* as we have employed the term throughout this book. Furthermore, in our culling of the literature on pain and hypnosis, we have rarely found a hypnotic technique that does not incorporate imagery.

HYPNOSIS AND PAIN

Hypnosis has a long and successful track record in treating pain. Two highly recommended books are Barber's *Hypnosis and Suggestion in the Treatment of Pain* (1996) and Hammond's *Handbook of Hypnotic Suggestions and Metaphors* (1990). Hypnosis and pain is addressed in nearly every issue of the *American Journal of Clinical Hypnosis* and the *International Journal of Clinical and Experimental Hypnosis*, as well as other hypnosis journals, such as *Contemporary Hypnosis*, *The Australian Journal of Clinical Hypnosis*, and *Hypnos*. In addition, the topic can be found in dozens of books and journals dealing with psychological issues, dentistry, medicine, surgery, anesthesiology, and related areas.

Most writers emphasize including CBT techniques within hypnotic treatment of pain. Chaves (1994) views hypnosis within a cognitive-behavioral perspective rather than the traditional hypnotic state theory, and he cites the importance of attitudes, expectations, and beliefs in modulating the pain experience. Elmer (2000) delineates a cogent pain treatment program that includes hypnosis, cognitive coping strategies, and brief psychodynamic processing. Crasilneck (1995), a pioneer in the field, advocates the "bombardment technique" for treating intractable organic pain. His procedure includes relaxation, displacement, age regression, glove anesthesia, hypnoanesthesia, and self-hypnosis.

CHOOSING HYPNOTIC TREATMENT

Barber (1996) lists four criteria for choosing hypnosis with pain clients. They include:

1. *The client will not be harmed by the treatment.* Certain medically noncompliant or psychologically disturbed people may use hypnosis to ignore pain that signals bodily harm, and possibly injure themselves further. In general, hypnosis should not be used with clients who have a history of complications from medical procedures or more than customary side effects from medication.
2. *The client is able to tolerate the emotional intimacy often associated with hypnotic treatment.* Problems of trust could arise, which could preclude the clinician from providing adequate help.
3. *Will pain reduction facilitate loss?* If improvement may mean loss of compensation, stability in the family, or other loss, hypnosis may be contraindicated.
4. *Client will be responsible for continuing care.* Hypnosis should not be considered if clients are reluctant to initiate self-hypnosis, which is necessary for successful treatment.

Secondary gain might be at play with any disorder, but with pain, this issue might be even more relevant. Many times it takes several sessions to ferret out reasons for clients' holding on to their symptoms. With pain, if the "green poultice" (Fordyce, 1976) is elicited, efforts at improvement could be futile.

WHAT EXACTLY DOES YOUR PAIN FEEL LIKE?

Asking detailed questions about the nature and quality of a person's pain helps build rapport. It also gives the therapist raw material to be used in the application of specific techniques. Hammond (1990) customarily asks clients if any of the following words describe their pain:

Aching, beating, binding, biting, burning, caustic, cool, corroding, cramping, crushing, cutting, drilling, dull, flashing, flickering, gnawing, grinding, gripping, heavy, hot, itching, lacerating, nagging, nauseating, numb, penetrating, piercing, pinching, pounding, pulsing, rasping, searing, sharp, shooting, smarting, spasming, splitting, squeezing, stabbing, stinging, tearing, throbbing, tingling, twisting. (p. 46)

ASSESSMENT OF PAIN

Many clinics and hospitals are now required by accrediting bodies to assess pain every visit. So, clients go to their doctor for a follow-up on their hypertension, and they are asked about their pain, usually on a 1–10 scale. I (G. G.) have had more than one client who did not like the 1–10 scale. For some, a 1–100 scale might be more appropriate. The McGill Pain Questionnaire (Melzack, 1990) is but one of many instruments available for those who wish to use them.

TECHNIQUES IN TREATING PAIN

We need to remember that we are not simply applying techniques to problems, but that we are treating people. Social context drives hypnosis, and a relationship of respect, trust, and cooperation is a necessary foundation. We employ the following as standard techniques, individualizing the program to the particular client. It is presumed that we have a treatment contract, we have some knowledge of the client's particular orientations and preferences, and that we have covered negative attitudes about hypnosis. We may test response by beginning with a conversational or embedded-meaning induction, followed by the "Three Lessons" story. In subsequent sessions we would emphasize ego-strengthening, as pain clients frequently suffer from diminished self-efficacy (Hammond, 1990). By the second session we would begin to incorporate one or more of the following techniques: distraction, anesthesia and analgesia, displacement, ensory substituion, transforming the symptom, age regression and age progression, techniques of Erickson, and dissociation.

Distraction

Although this is actually a CBT technique, distraction is the most basic hypnotic method to manage pain. Clients whose attention is absorbed in any hypnotic induction, guided imagery exercise, or story automatically experience a brief vacation from their pain. A directive induction, such as the hand levitation coin drop, or arm catalepsy, is contraindicated in clients with neck or back pain, or peripheral neuropathy. Therefore, we prefer a conversational or embedded-meaning induction (Gafner & Benson, 2000), any variety of deepening, such as a counting-down deepening, followed by a story. Such an approach tests client response. As such, it is a behavioral probe, or compass, that will point us in the right direction. If during debriefing the client evinces common behavioral markers of trance, we would continue with more of the same, gradually adding on in the direction of eventual self-hypnosis and self-care. I (S. B.) make tapes of hypnosis sessions for the client to use outside of treatment to assist in self-care.

Anesthesia and Analgesia

Anesthesia means not feeling anything, while analgesia is simply not feeling pain. *Total anesthesia*, the equivalent of a negative hallucination or the perception of the complete absence of pain, can be achieved only with highly hypnotizable clients. It is indicated only in specific circumstances, such as childbirth or dental anesthesia. Total anesthesia may also be contraindicated, such as when clients need to remain aware of "signal" pain. If such pain is not attended to, further injury could result. Glove anesthesia is a popular mode of using partial anesthesia. Once the hand is numb, some therapists will prick the back of the numb hand with a paper clip to both verify anesthesia and ratify trance. The client can then transfer the numbness to her painful knee, for example.

Some of our favorite techniques for achieving numbness involve hypnotic language and indirection, either within the induction or as part of a story, in achieving the desired effect:

Someone *was telling me just the other day about numerals, yes,* numbers. *He was walking down his street and* noticed, *just noticed, the* numbers *on the mailboxes, which he could see, as opposed to the* numbers *on the curb, which were coverd with ice and snow.* His hands *were icy cold inside those heavy mittens, and he*	metaphor embedded suggestion power word metaphor

thought to himself, "I need to get those hands, and those feet inside, as that book awaits me within the Bible, the book of Numbers, *not easy reading until I warm up a bit."*

dissociative language

As we are both originally from cold climates, we may tell stories about walking on a cold winter day, picking up handfuls of snow with bare hands, packing that snow into snowballs until it is *hard to feel those hands anymore.* Alternately, we may talk about falling asleep while lying on one arm and waking up only to notice that *one hand has also gone to sleep*, with that familiar numb, almost *deadened or detached sensation*, almost as if that hand *belonged to someone else.* Or, perhaps, we simply suggest that by pulling on a pair of thick ski gloves, a person can notice how those hands begin to feel *heavier, more difficult to move.* Perhaps they are even beginning to *feel a bit numb.*

Within trance, the numbed sensation of glove anesthesia can be transferred to another part of the body, if the pain is not located in the hand. The transfer of sensation can be accomplished either imaginally, as with the displacement technique, or the client can be instructed to touch the pain location with the "gloved" hand and notice how that numbness can transfer to, or be absorbed in, the necessary location.

I (S. B.) used glove anesthesia with a pregnant woman in advance of the onset of her labor. She was instructed in both relaxation and creating glove anesthesia. Because she could reach most locations where she would likely feel pain, she was taught to gently place the gloved hand on whatever area of her body that was painful. In this way, she could press her lower back, or rest her hand on her lower abdomen, and imagine the numbness spreading out from the hand over the area of greatest pain, gradually numbing the area. Her partner or a labor coach could also be trained in helping her achieve glove anesthesia and guideing her through transferring the sensation, or placing her hand where needed, to assist in the process.

Displacement

Displacement is a process of hypnotically encouraging the client to alter the location of the pain to an area where it would be more tolerable. We sometimes seed displacement with an anecdote about this place or that place. (One therapist we know employs a New Jersey accent and mentions "dis place," and "dat place," and as New Jersey is known as the Garden State, we figure he knows more about seeding than we do.) We may also mention something about "going from here to there," or the travels of a moving van.

Hypothetically speaking, if you were to imagine, *just* imagine, sharing *that pain in your hip, I* wonder *what part of your body you would share it with? Left little finger, right big toe?* A woman *one time remarked, "Oh, maybe I would choose my belly button," strange as that might seem.*	power word suggestion power word metaphor
Sandy, let your mind drift and dream *now, and when you have selected some part of your body to share that hip pain with, you will feel your head* nodding, *and then you'll be able to* tell me *with your words . . . that's the way, take as much time as you need. . . .*	suggestion suggestion

Or, you can implement a distraction following the suggestion. The distraction serves to facilitate unconscious processing.

Sandy, you and I both know how pain can move, *going from one place to another. A famous psychologist, Dr. Joseph Barber, suggests* it can move *in a circular, outwardly spiraling direction, but that sounds like a* plain old barber pole *to me.*	implication suggestion pun/distraction

A permissive suggestion encourages any response, which is again reinforced, this time by metaphor.

Sandy, pay very close attention *now to any movement occurring, going out from that hip to somewhere else. And while you are appreciating that on the*	suggestion

inside, *on the* outside, *let me tell you about* someone else *who detected pain moving from her right shoulder to her belly button, of all places. I remarked to her, "Isn't it simply* curious *how that can occur?" It was a* wonderful *example of sharing, if you ask me. Personally, my brother* never shared *any of his Naval orange with me.*	apposition of opposities metaphor power words pun/distraction

My (S. B.) client with epidydimitis was able to displace pain in his scrotum to a thumb and a big toe, which allowed him to better tolerate—and sometimes ignore—this pain in an unfortunate location. Displacement tends to work better with people who have an ability to visualize, as they can imagine watching the pain move to the desired location.

Sensory Substitution

With this technique, therapists might be tempted to substitute a pleasant sensation for a painful one. If this is you, we would say, "Okay, go ahead, as long as you are a prodigiously gifted therapist, and your client is bestowed with remarkable hypnotic talents." Meanwhile, the rest of us in the trenches, who are being bombarded by compelling pain, will opt for a more realistic objective.

We would recommend changing a fiery, burning pain into a tingling sensation, a gnawing pain into a gentle rubbing, or a jabbing pain into an intermittent thumping or itching. As an example, we will quote Barber (1996):

> The feelings that you describe (needles stabbing into thighs) can begin to change, very slightly. Oddly enough, it may begin to seem as if the needles are becoming more and more blunt . . . broad . . . almost as if they have become tiny, massaging fingers. What an interesting sensation you can begin to have: thousands of warm buzzing fingers massaging your legs. . . . (pp. 89–90)

This more realistic approach has several advantages. The client knows the pain is still present, as with the client with cancer, who will seek proper medical attention when needed. Also, the substitute sensation is not necessarily pleasant, so it is more plausible (Barber, 1996).

Transforming the Symptom

Sometimes called direct and indirect diminution of pain, *transforming the symptom* is a close relative of sensory substitution. It offers the therapist a wide range of options within the alteration of the pain's frequency, intensity, and duration. Accomplishing this directly and rather generally, hypnotic patter can mention discomfort gradually *going away, moving farther away* from present experience, or *becoming smaller* (Barber, 1996). In using time distortion, the therapist can either suggest that the absence of pain seems to last for a long time period, or that the time during which pain is experienced seems to pass quickly. For example, ". . . and when that pain moves to that big toe, you will be amazed to discover that an hour can seem like a minute, as time on the clock." Suggestions can also be made to experience the pain for only an hour once a day rather than manifesting intermittently. When transforming the intensity, clients can use metaphors, such as radios, or use visual imagery, such as number scales, to imagine the pain decreasing on a 1–10 scale.

With indirect transformation, we can accomplish the same goal, metaphorically, without even alluding to pain.

One man, *one time, sitting in* that *chair* over there, *was able to close his eyes and see large numbers, as if on a calendar, or one of those number charts used to* teach small children *to add and subtract. And like those old-time movies where calendar pages flipping past signify time passing, and like those children learning to subtract,* you can notice *those numbers gradually decreasing, from ten down to . . . four . . . three . . . two.*	metaphor dissociative language suggestion: early learning set suggestion
In my grandparents' *home, they had one of those large, old-fashioned radios with the big knobs on the front to tune the channels and adjust the volume.*	metaphor

Well, once they had that radio adjusted to just the right frequency and location on the dial, then they would turn up the volume so loud you could feel it vibrating in your body. After some time had passed—it seemed like an hour, *but it probably was only a few* minutes—*I asked my mother to* just slowly turn that volume down, *just a bit at a time, and it was barely noticeable, but I felt, in my body, and in my mind, that everything was suddenly much more comfortable.*

time distortion

suggestion

These techniques can often produce dramatic results in only one or two sessions. My (S. B.) client, Hanna, age 50, presented with significant knee pain immediately prior to replacement surgery. She had the knee replaced previously, but now the hardware had been recalled, necessitating the follow-up surgery. Hanna was concerned about increased reliance on narcotics, whose efficacy had diminished. Hanna, who had heard that hypnosis could be helpful in pain management, agreed to one session of ego-strengthening before "getting down to business." She had in her repertoire positive naturalistic trance experiences, as well as good visualization skills. I used a dissociation induction along with an image of a rotary telephone to help her "dial down" the pain from a ten to a two. The painful knee felt stronger when she arose from her chair, and I gave her an audiotape of the session. She returned for no more sessions. When I spoke with her two months later, she noted that she continued to use the tape post-surgery, and that she required a minimum of analgesic medication.

Unintended benefits can also occur. I (S. B.) was seeing a young woman, Maria, for severe plantar fasciitis. Three sessions had produced some relief, and this time she was joined by her boyfriend, Paris. He was told that he could also go into trance, if he wished, although hypnosis would be directed at Maria's foot pain. Paris was in accord with this plan, as his own pain had prevented him from playing basketball for the past two years.

Both subjects went into a medium depth of trance, even though the stories and suggestions employed were designed solely for Maria. She was given the suggestion of stepping into a cool, soothing mud bath for her feet, as if at a fancy resort. As her feet were coated with that soothing mud, she could notice how it could harden around her foot, almost like a perfectly fitted shoe that she could step into when she needed it.

Paris requested to attend next session, but when the time came, he was not with Maria. It turned out that he was now playing basketball on a regular basis, and that day's session interfered with his game.

Age Regression and Age Progression

Jill, age 60, presented with a history of rheumatoid arthritis. A recent course of Prednisone had helped, but it also left her with swollen hands, which did not allow her to hold her art supplies. Her physician was now giving her her gold injections, which also helped to some extent. However, people may safely receive gold shots only with strictly regulated frequency. In previous years, Jill had undergone CBT and other psychological treatments; however, she had never tried hypnosis.

She had a poor ability to visualize, and distraction and symptom transormatin were unsuccessful. I employed *age regression* to a point in her life before she was limited by arthritis, and *age progression* to a time when she could imagine herself with relief from pain. Self-hypnosis at home relied heavily on time distortion, which allowed her to feel in pain with less frequency. These interventions helped *set up* imaginal gold shots, a technique that was generated in our sessions. She was given the suggestion of a hypnotic shot (a pinpoint pressure to the back of her hand). In this way, she positively hallucinated the injection and its attendant analgesia. Both she and her rheumatologist were delighted that she was able to resume her design work.

Erickson and Pain

Of course, most of these techniques originated with Erickson. It is rewarding to read Erickson in the original. Hammond (1990) distilled much of Erickson's writings on pain, and we'll look at some samples now.

DEVELOPING ANESTHESIAS. Erickson (1985) told clients about "the tremendous amount of learning you have acquired during your lifetime of experience developing anesthesias throughout your entire body . . . for example, as you sit and listen to me now, you've forgotten the shoes on your feet . . . and now you can feel them; you've forgotten the collar around your neck . . . and now you can feel it; . . . you listen to an entertaining lecture, and you forget about the hardness of the chairs" (228). He goes on to remind clients that in their lifelong learning they have acquired the automatic ability to turn sensations off and on again.

DISORIENTATION AND CONFUSION TECHNIQUE WITH PAIN. "Let us see, is that pain in your right leg, or your left leg? . . . Let us see, which is your left leg and which is your right leg?" Erickson (1983) moves on to rightness and leftness, centrality and dextrality. "I set up a body disorientation by teaching the patient to get very confused about the site of the pain, about the part of the body involved in pain, and about the direction of the pain . . . If you can move the pain to a place in the body where there is no organic cause for it, then you are in a position to produce hypnotic anesthesia for the pain at the actual site. You move the patient's subjective experience of the pain to the wrong area, bodily, because you can correct it more easily there; the patient has little resistance to accepting suggestions in the healthy area" (235).

Other Techniques

In vastness and breadth, the literature on pain and hypnosis outdistances writings on hypnosis and any other problem. In Hammond's (1990) chapter on pain, you will find a veritable banquet of creative techniques that were submitted by various practitioners. His book also covers preparation for surgery, migraines, and related areas. In general, therapists who want to educate themselves about psychological and hypnotic treatment of pain, would do well to consult Gatchel and Turk (1996), Barber (1996), as well as Hammond (1990).

In his therapy, Lehrer (1985) encourages clients to cultivate a close relationship with their unconscious mind. Such a relationship includes respecting signals from the unconscious. He described a client who had had five lumbar surgeries and intense pain from scarring. The man typically overdid physical activity and then suffered. Through therapy, he learned to receive a signal from his unconscious mind *before* his back started to hurt, and in this way successfully modulated both his activity level as well as his pain.

Dissociation

We saved the best technique for last. Those familiar with baseball may have heard the double play described as "the pitcher's best friend." Well, as a therapist, *dissociation* is your best friend in treating pain, and dissociation should also be your constant companion in all other hypnotic applications as well.

Dissociation is a naturally occurring phenomenon, as well as a cardinal feature of trance. We strive for dissocation in nearly every induction and intervention. As a general rule, the more dissociation clients experience, the more their trance is ratified, the more depth they achieve, and in many cases, the more receptive they are to suggestion. We emphasize dissociative language and images in our techniques, even with clients who dissociate problematically, such as people with posttraumatic stress disorder (PTSD) and psychotic disorders.

Dissociation often occurs spontaneously in trance. As the therapist describes a pleasant place, the client is transported to her own pleasant place. I (G. G.) once worked with a 30-year-old woman with advanced multiple sclerosis. Our target was the excruciating pain in both legs, and she achieved considerable relief as I gently and permissively invited her to journey to the colorful autumn forest she enjoyed as a youth.

We encourage you to develop your own anecdotes and stories that incorporate this strange and wonderful phenomenon. In the case example that follows, we quote from our dissociation induction, which demonstrates how you can facilitate dissociation in a story.

WHEN STANDARD METHODS DON'T WORK

Ynocencio, a 37-year-old, married, Hispanic man, five years previously had been struck in the back by the blade of a bulldozer. Two years ago the six screws and rods in his back broke loose, and he was then diagnosed with post-surgical lumbar osteomyelitis. Because infection had eaten away bone, he was not a candidate for further surgery.

Ynocencio, a pleasant and reserved man, was mildly depressed. He had no personality disorder, and his marriage was stable. He had gained only minimal relief from biofeedback and a pain management class, which emphasized CBT, abdominal breathing, and imagery. He had also responded minimally to hypnosis. His remark, "I want to let go, but I just can't," was prototypical unconscious resistance. Ynocencio was on very high narcotics, 240 mg of oxycontin, three times a day. It was decided that he would be a good candidate for a dual induction.

He arrived wearing a tortoise shell brace. He required this for protection and support. He carefully and ceremoniously removed this massive armour. Its meaning to him was obviously very dear. Initially, the medical psychologist, who had good rapport with the client, and I (G. G.) attempted our standard confusional dual induction, where one operator offers straight-forward hypnotic suggestions, while the other operator distracts and confuses. The goal of this is for the client to escape in the direction of trance. This approach did not work.

In reviewing the client's background and interests, we realized that the happiest time in his life had been when he was an overland truck driver. Clearly, this was a naturalistic trance experience. The next session, we had the client focus on a candle, and to begin counting backward slowly from 100 to 1. He understood that he could close his eyes at any time, and eye closure occurred before he reached 96. Concurrently, I offered the dissociation induction (Gafner & Benson, 2000), and at intervals, my colleage would toss in references to truck driving. Here is a re-creation of that trilateral process. Suggestions for dissociation are italicized.

Ynocencio, we have all had	100	
many experiences, some that		
were memorable, some not so,	99	
some that were pleasant and	98	
good, and others that we may		"pulling out of the
not recall. Just like dreams,		city"
everyone has had them, and		
many we forget by the time we	97	
wake up, and other times we	96	
may remember only a small		"gearing down"
part of that dream.	95	
One time I slept on my right		
arm most of the night, and	94	"faster now"
that arm was still asleep *long*	93	
after I woke up. That was	92	
similar to when my left leg fell		"The CB radio"
asleep *when I was sitting*	91	
down, and after I got up to		

walk the leg still had a strong 90
tingling sensation, or maybe it 89 "Backin' up to the
was just a numbness, *I forget.* loading dock"

   I remember back in grade 88
school a teacher said, "It's
your ears I'm speaking to," 87 "On the road again"
which seemed rather curious
at the time, how your ears 86
could be separated *from the* "the next weigh
rest of you. When the teacher station"
was speaking I would often
just drift off, maybe listening 85
to a word here or a word there,
sometimes paying attention to 84 "Country passing by"
this or that, and when she
would look at me—or maybe 83
it was the person next to me—
I would snap out of it for a 82
moment or two, and then I
would resume daydreaming.

   This went on for about 20 minutes. We lost track of his counting, and he told us later that he went from 100 to 1, and back again, two times. He responded with marked time distortion and amnesia, and most importantly, with a pain-free body. He was astounded by how he felt, and we praised him for his monumental effort at letting go. We saw him one more time for a similar session during which we recorded an audiotape for his practice at home. At this writing it has been 18 months since he was seen in Mental Health, and the record indicates he is doing fine.

CLINICAL COMMENTS

For pain clients who appear treatment resistant, we would strongly recommend working with a trusted and capable colleague if you can. When you can use two operators, exploration, problem solving, and utilization are greatly facilitated. It is like comparing the hundreds of channels of television available today to the paltry three networks that we remember from our youth. With so many channels to choose from today, the temptation may be to combine techniques into something complex and exotic, or extravagant. That's fine, if you can manage it, but the client's benefit comes first before the therapist's technique. We are again drawn back to hypnosis's law of parsimony, which dictates that you do as little as necessary to achieve the desired effect. In other words, *try* to keep it simple.

Ynocencio did not require a course of ego-strengthening. Many others would have, prior to resorting to a two-operator approach. Had Ynocencio been personality disordered or believed that he was not worthy of anything but self-punishment, then we would have opted for intense CBT, not hypnosis. For many pain clients who show strong unconscious resistance, we sometimes follow ego-strengthening with the mindfulness-based stories—all within formal hypnosis—described in chapter 3. These metaphors for acceptance, letting go, etc., are presented as the therapy component of trancework. We typically follow with unconsciously directed questions, for example, "That story you just heard, do you think your unconscious mind can put that to use? You may answer with one of your fingers. . . ."

We have also conveyed both ego-strengthening and mindfulness stories in trance, and then facilitated amnesia. Facilitating amnesia following both mindfulness and ego-strengthening stories, each with components of unconscious questioning, produces similar outcomes. With clients such as Ynocencio, where we have resorted to two-operator and other nontraditional techniques, we estimate that approximately half have responded favorably during 12 sessions or less. We think this would make a fascinating but complex research study, although those who manualize the treatment conditions may need some of Ynocencio's oxycontin for their headache.

Recently, we have been approaching some of these tough pain clients with a combination of standard techniques (sensory substitution, CBT) *and* a mindfulness story within the same session. This may send a confounding message to the client, like, "Change, but don't change." Although not intended as a paradoxical directive, a perturbation appears to result. Objectively, upon realerting, some clients show a dazed, "punch drunk" appearance, in much the same way that some respond to a confusional induction. Subjectively, clients may feel very dissociated. They acknowledge benefit and diminution or absence of pain only when asked to report. Indeed, in some cases nascent receptivity is apparent by the next session, as resistance has been bypassed. This mechanism, then, would be similar to a para-doxical directive in psychotherapy, which often takes effect within 1 to 2 weeks.

As clients become more response-attentive, and even if they do not, they may feel more vulnerable. Remember, just as we are taking risks by trying new techniques, clients are risking even more, and we need to emphasize support and respect, and also compliment them on their courage and perserverance in this process.

14

Habit Control

YOU CAN HAVE IT ALL

You've seen the ads: "Stop smoking in one session," or, "Lose all the weight you want with absolutely no effort." The promises of quick hypnotic cures and the image of the stage hypnotist suggesting seeing people in their underwear, these are the images that therapists typically have to bypass with clients new to hypnosis. Stage hypnosis is easily explained to a client, but the quick cure is another matter, as many habits are extremely tough to break, and who wouldn't want their problem solved with a virtual snap of the fingers? Wouldn't it be ideal to sit down in a chair and 30 minutes later have no urge to smoke, or to be able to resist fattening foods, or have increased motivation to exercise? We get eager, gleaming looks when people find out that we "do" hypnosis, and the first questions typically asked are about smoking and weight management. These questions are therapeutic invitations for us to begin to address readiness for change, to dispel the "magic bullet" notion, and to promote the combination of hypnosis with behavior modification and/or cognitive-behavioral therapy (CBT).

Daniel James shared this story with us.

Hope Makes the Team

I wanted to share a story that may be pertinent to your particular situation. If it is not pertinent, or pertains to the circumstances of someone else, you can feel free to tune it out completely, or if one small part of it has any meaning, or applies even in a minor way, that is the portion we would like to guide you at this time.

Now, when my brother, Damper, was growing up in Iowa, he and his friends could not wait to play ball at school. They would play before school, after school, as well as at recess, wolfing down their lunch so they could race out to the baseball field. On one of those days, my brother made a *discovery* and received a *surprise* both at the same time.

Damper and one of the older kids were captains of their respective teams, and it was their job to choose who would be on each team. The other boys lined up against the back-stop. "I like Tom," said my brother, and the other captain said, "Then I'll take Jim," as he pointed at one of the bigger boys. The selection continued with no big surprises for anyone, as they had all been through this before.

Only two kids were left to be chosen. Damper lifted up the brim of his cap and peered at the one on the left, a big ungainly girl with a huge birthmark blotting out her right cheek. "Hey, you're a girl!" he said. "Yes, my name is *Hope*," she answered politely. Her voice was thin and reedlike.

"You can't be any good," said the other captain. "Choose me and you'll find out," she answered. Her broad smile made you forget about the birthmark. As it turned out, neither captain chose Hope, who sat on the bench as the others began their game. Damper's team was soon losing by ten runs. The other team taunted Damper, who was now steaming. Someone on the other team said, "Damper, *you can always have Hope.*"

And that is how Hope got started on Damper's team. She could not run real fast, or throw very far, but she was very consistent, catching every ball that came her way. Her first time at bat the boys on the other team snickered, and the pitcher threw her a very slow pitch, a kind of mocking gesture. Hope swung hard and hit a long home run.

The next day Damper and the other captain flipped a coin to see who would choose first. Damper won and said, "*I want Hope.*" "Take her then," said the other captain. Damper knew that the odds were good that he would win the next coin toss.

THE CHANGE PROCESS

Remember who James Boswell wrote about? Samuel Johnson. Well, Boswell was to Johnson as Zeig is to Erickson, Bandura to self-efficacy, and Prochaska to change. Prochaska's oft-referred to transtheoretical model of change (Prochaska, DiClemente, & Norcross, 1992) continues to be the gold standard for explaining how people change. Using this model, *five stages of change* have been conceptualized for a variety of problem behaviors.

1. *Precontemplation,* is a stage in which there is no intent for change in the foreseeable future. People in this stage may be unaware of their problem.
2. *Contemplation* is the stage in which people are aware that a problem exists and are seriously thinking about overcoming it, but have not yet made a commitment to take action.
3. *Preparation* is a stage that combines intention and behavioral criteria. Individuals in this stage are intending to take action in the next month and have unsuccessfully taken action in the past year. Plans may include having set a date to quit smoking.
4. *Action* is the stage where change has already begun. Action involves the most overt behavioral changes and requires considerable commitment of time and energy.
5. *Maintenance* is the stage in which significant change has already occurred. People consolidate the gains attained during the *action* stage, and may be working to prevent relapse.

CLIENTS IN AN EARLY STAGE

We typically do not see clients in the precontemplation stage unless they seek therapy at the request of another. Some of these clients may attempt to seize hypnosis as an opportunity to change without any effort on their part. Unfortunately, it is not always a large step from this type of client to one in the early stages of contemplation, who is seeking "an easy way out." We like to take a fair amount of time with those in contemplation, educating them about options for changing habits, eliciting their expectations, along with what they have tried and what has worked. Of course, we do the same with preparation and action stage clients as well, but we have more material on their change processes, and a more clear indication of their readiness for change, and we can be reasonably certain that they are not in search of a "magic bullet." We also keep in mind that change within addictions typically does not travel a strict line from precontemplation to maintenance, but instead follows a cyclical pattern of change that includes regression to previous behaviors earlier in the cycle, and then, hopefully more change (Prochaska, Rossi, & Wilcox, 1991).

The processes of change are the actual activities, covert and overt, that people use to make change. Ten change processes have been identified and used with habit control issues. They are:

1. counterconditioning
2. self-reevaluation
3. helping relationships
4. contingecy management
5. consciousness raising
6. stimulus control
7. substance use
8. self-liberation
9. interpersonal control
10. corrective emotional experience

In their study assessing use of change processes within and between sessions, Prochaska and colleagues (1991) found that the most successful client used increasingly more action-related processes between sessions, and also shifted reliance from one set of change processes to a set appropriate for the next stage of change. Thus, part of what helps clients move from one stage of change to another is increasing the use of change processes tied to the next progressive stage, such as action-oriented processes, like self-liberation, as opposed to those processes directed at increasing insight, such as consciousness raising.

Knowing this, we can direct our therapeutic interventions toward increasing an action process both in talk therapy and in hypnosis. We can meet our clients where they are at hypnotically, even when they are at preliminary change stages. Hypnosis can push clients toward increased action process by influencing change at earlier stages, when there is an increasing awareness of problem areas, and when clients begin to discern mastery of their resources. We may begin seeding motivation for change, or even suggestions about change, as we ask questions about the habit, or reasons for changing the habit.

> *As you sit there thinking about losing weight through a* healthy plan, *including a* lifestyle change *of healthy eating and* increased activity, *what brings you in for assistance* now? *Clearly*, you know *and I know that* maintaining a healthy weight *brings numerous overall health benefits, and I'm wondering what* changes you are interested in making *to get to your desired goal?*

More formal hypnosis could then build upon the standard, preliminary ego-strengthening with suggestions about self-reevaluation:

> *And as you concentrate on* picturing yourself *in the future, you can notice how good it feels to be smoke-free. And as you begin to* know, really know, *that you can be a nonsmoker, you can find yourself taking two nice, clean, deep breaths.* . . .

Subsequent sessions can be geared toward stimulus control, self-liberation, or other action processes:

> *Feeling free to be a different person in your approach to the use of alcohol,* you can know *deep within your unconscious mind that you can cope productively without the use of substances, no longer having any desire to even tempt yourself with high-risk situations.* . . .

MAGIC BULLETS AND ALTERNATIVES

As we alluded to earlier in this chapter, one common misconception therapists run into when working with habit control is the notion that hypnosis will be a "magic bullet" to cure the client "miraculously." Now, while we have had some wonderful successes using hypnosis for habit control, we have also had some miserable failures. So, before jumping on the miracle-cure bandwagon, we would like to caution you against thinking this way. To be sure, at times the swiftness with which a suggestion or story takes root and effects change can *seem* almost miraculous, especially to the client who notices a dramatic difference. However, let's remember that some clients who respond so wonderfully are likely to have already been in the action stage, and many interventions, including hypnosis, may have jump-started those clients.

Remember that little story about the Rainmaker (Gafner & Benson, 2000) who is called to a village to aid in a time of severe drought? The natives build a hut for him, and the Rainmaker goes inside, and mysteriously stays ensconced for three days. The morning of the third day clouds appear, and by late afternoon glorious, life-giving showers appear. The Rainmaker emerges from his hut, and they thank him profusely for working his magic. "I didn't even do anything yet," he responds. "I was feeling sick when I got here, and I needed some rest, that was all." We sometimes tell that story to clients who have been jump-started in the action stage. Such a story can also be apt for clients in an early stage who are seeking a magic bullet.

WORKING TOGETHER

All psychotherapy should be a collaborative process. We want to be partners with our clients, and that requires the client's taking an active role in changing the habit behavior, as well as owning personal responsibility for such things as holding out against cravings, using alternate coping strategies, and/or increasing physical activity. One way I (S. B.) stack the deck in favor of a collaborative approach (versus a miracle-cure belief) is to require that habit control appointments begin with the client's dedicating time to behavior modification and/or cognitive restructuring *before* adding hypnosis to the program.

As therapists, we must be careful to recognize that habit control clients are not necessarily unmotivated to change, even when they request hypnosis right from the start. It is understandable human nature to want to avoid discomfort and failure. Let's face it, habits are hard to break—specifically because they are so strongly associated with emotional states, other entrenched behaviors, and cues from the environment. Most people have attempted to change their habitual behavior many times before visiting the office, and frequently with varying degrees of success. Brian Grodner of Albuquerque, New Mexico, pointed out in a workshop on treating habits hypnotically (personal communication, December 12, 2001) that clients' motivation may only *appear* low when there are fears about success, and the level of discomfort concomitant with the change to be implemented. When we, as therapists, are successful in conveying to clients that they can succeed over the long term, and with minimal discomfort, almost anyone would be motivated to change. Grodner suggests that one of the ways to convey this expectation of success is by working together to teach clients how to satisfy the positive intention the habit initially satisfied (e.g., decrease stress by smoking) with more ecological behaviors that do not have the high personal cost typically associated with the habit behavior. Those skills, along with connecting the changed behavior to the client's *permanent identity*, can not only increase the success rate, but can also decrease the seeming discomfort that making behavior change requires, as the changes become self-reinforcing. Within his treatment approach, Grodner recommends that habit control hypnosis include tailoring the session to the client's *envisioned* sense of a new self in the realms of seeing and behaving, emotions and results, present, past and future, and as an internal and external representation of the vision of the "new you." A hypnotic technique very useful in this regard is *age progression*.

HYPNOSIS AND WEIGHT MANAGEMENT

Obesity is an endemic problem within the United States and much of the Western world, with millions of people dieting and/or chronically concerned about their weight. Fad diets abound and tend to work minimally, at best, with poor long-term outcomes. Unfortunately, many other treatment approaches to obesity also have inconsistent results, with research literature showing a pattern of minimal long-term success. Where there have been successful cases noted, the data often come from case studies. While reliance on case study data is typically criticized in refereed journals, the complexity of obesity as a problem may suggest that such individualized reports make the most sense in determining what can work in overall weight management. Certainly within the research literature, behavioral modification programs get the highest marks. Recently, the use of hypnosis as an adjunct treatment, combined with behavioral treatment, has been lauded as increasing the long-term benefits (Barabasz & Spiegel, 1989; Bolocofsky, Spinler, & Coulthard-Morris, 1985; Levitt, 1997).

Typical hypnotic protocols for weight management involve direct suggestions, often in the direction of decreasing cravings and avoidance of "bad" foods, experiencing an aversion to certain foods by creating assocations with nausea, unpleasant odor, or tastes, or in the direction of increasing a desire to protect the body by eating more healthily (Levitt, 1997). As many overweight people have a tendency to exhibit rebelliousnes, extreme sensitivity, and interpersonal difficulty with authority figures (Cochrane, 1992), such directive treatment is not likely to be successful.

Instead, indirect hypnosis may aid in bypassing resistance and encouraging restraint so that weight loss occurs in smaller steps, consistent with a recommended loss of 1 to 2 pounds per week. Clients may come to us with such a strong desire to get moving on weight loss that anything less than 5 to 10 pounds per week seems to them like failure. Let's remember that everyone may have been influenced to some extent by the advertisements that claim, "I lost 40 pounds in two months! You can do it, too." We want to keep clients on a realistic path, emphasizing the basics in both hypnosis and behavioral management.

THE CASE OF ANTONIO

Antonio came to see me (S. B.) several years ago with a desire to get back to the fighting weight he had enjoyed as a youth. He was 60 years old, a Hispanic male with lots of white hair and a full beard (he looked a little like Santa Claus when he first arrived). As we discussed his treatment goals, he indicated that he wanted to lose at least 100 pounds. He had numerous health problems, including diabetes, high cholesterol, and arthritis. Antonio did not exercise at all and his eating habits were poor. We started with a food diary, conscious attempts to slow down when he ate, reducing portion size, and overalll awareness of nutrition—all through behavior modification methods. For two months, he made attempts here and there, and lost no weight. Finally, we started adding hypnosis to our sessions.

In his review of the literature, Cochrane (1992) reported that successful weight losers have several commonalities, including a solid grounding in nutrition and appropriate *lifestyle* diet and excercise changes, and a sense of personal empowerment, self-worth, and self-esteem. As is our custom, we began the hypnosis sessions with ego-strengthening stories, such as "The Maple Tree," and "short burst" suggestions, such as "You can do it." We like to include pieces designed to improve personal empowerment and self-esteem in virtually all of our sessions, emphasizing that the client is the one who is responsible for change. We also tailor our sessions to the client's needs and problem areas. When we use "stock" stories, we do so as a springboard for shaping the session according to the client's specific needs. One book, *The Thin Book* (Brickman, 2000), although not published when I treated Antonio, has many good basic scripts targeting a variety of covert issues within weight management, and we would recommend it as a starting point for addressing your client's individual needs.

Antonio needed to increase his activity level, change his eating habits to stay away from late-night snacking in front of the TV, and eat healthier, more balanced meals. Our colleague, Matt Weyer, wrote a wonderful story that uses a play on words to suggest eating more vegetables and using a wok. The story (Gafner & Benson, 2000) also suggests increased exercise through "woking." Antonio had a wonderful tendency to have near total amnesia for session content, and he was amazed to find himself at a flea market the following weekend, where he bought a used kitchen wok. Interestingly, he also discovered that he had begun parking farther from his destinations so that he could get more exercise.

Antonio began to lose approximately 10 pounds per month, but complained that he still felt "heavy" when he was walking. One of my (G. G.) former students, Mirto Stone, created a story that addressed this exact issue. The story about a tea taster uses embedded suggestion for *lightness*, and also suggests *slowly* savoring tastes and *slowing down* the process of eating.

The Tea Taster

There was a man not far from here whose job was to taste tea and catalogue the flavors. He would hold up his cup of tea to the *light*, swirling the tea gently in the cup, noticing the *lightness* of the taste, *slowly savoring* the tea in his mouth, and then *setting* the teacup *back on the table*. With each sip of the tea, he noticed something new, the way the *light* settled on the tea leaves or the pleasing fragrance of the blend. The tea taster thoroughly enjoyed his job, and he *became quite discerning* of all the kinds of tea, soon eschewing the lower-quality varieties in his everyday life as well, rewarding his palate with the *good quality* teas, that were flavorful and *light*.

As Antonio lost weight, his self-confidence improved, although he revealed that he had some social anxiety, as it was difficult for him to interact comfortable with others. When he was heavier, it was easier for him to isolate himself and avoid relationships. Being overweight can frequently be a cover for other, more vulnerable emotional issues, such as a history of abuse, an unconscious need to punish one's self, a fear of intimacy, a distorted sense of loyalty to family unity or expressions of love. Again, it is vitally important to the client's success that habit control treatment be highly individualized to all the overt as well as the more hidden issues related to eating. For Antonio, we needed to address letting go of anxiety and gaining connectedness to others.

Balloons

Antonio, I'd like to tell you a little story about a woman named Heidi who used to make pocket money during her school days by selling concessions at football games. Heidi was a little bit shy, although she *enjoyed interacting with others*, so she was glad to have the distance of the counter between herself and the patrons at the football games.

Well, one day Heidi was asked to participate in the show at half-time, in addition to her usual concession duties before and after the game. Her job was to *let go* of all the balloons under a net as the band announced the return of the players to the field. She used to envy the cheerleaders who seemed so comfortable with being in the limelight, working the crowd and seeming to be excited and joyful as they chatted in larger groups. This night, Heidi stood with the cheerleaders, down there on the field, as she waited for her cue to *let* the balloons *go*. She found her mind wandering as she noticed the maroon balloons and the gold ones, and she eventually realized that people were talking *to her*. Those cheerleaders, who were so easy in their social skills, were engaging her in conversation! She was *amazed to notice* that she could *interact freely* with them, even without the comfortable barrier of the concession counter. Soon, the mischievous side of Heidi came out, with the camaraderie of her new friends, as they began to *let go* first one balloon here, and another there, and soon they were *letting go* of balloons in groups of twos and threes.

Heidi *let go* of many balloons before the band began to play again, but she realized that there were many, many balloons still to *let go* when the time arrived. By the time all those balloons were *floating freely* in the sky, Heidi had made several new friends, and she'd begun to *let go* of more than just balloons.

The addition of hypnosis allowed Antonio to feel more comfortable using behavioral modification techniques. The food diaries and portion control became easier for him to maintain. As the weight came off, the lifestyle changes he'd incorporated, such as eating more vegetables and less high-fat foods, became self-reinforcing, along with increased exercise. He still had triggers for late-night snacking, particularly when he felt bored or lonely. He frequently said, "I seem to lose my willpower then." What follows is a story he was told to address his concern.

Will from the Power Plant

Antonio, let me tell you about Dee, who lived by the Tucson Electric power plant. One day in the late afternoon, Dee was out for her daily walk and she met a man who worked at the power plant. She soon learned that his name was Will—*Will* for the *power* plant. He was outside having a *light* lunch, enjoying the afternoon sun. Dee could recall quite vividly that it was a *light* lunch, though she couldn't remember exactly what it was.

Dee, being a friendly sort, struck up a conversation and soon she learned that both she and *Will* were both into meditation, as well as the *power* of the unconscious mind. Will stated emphatically that the mind is indeed powerful, and he told her a story of one of his meditative experiences. One time in trance he had an awareness of himself *breaking through some of his bad habits*. In addition, his strength, both his inner strength, or resolve, and the strength of his body, were brought into his conscious mind. After that *power*ful experience, *Will* said he felt more en*light*end and had a *new resolve* to be more holistically healthy. Dee, entranced by his story, smiled, and said little. She was glad to meet a kindred spirit. Then, she continued on her walk, happy to have *strengthened* a bond with *Will* from the *power* plant.

Happily, after 11 months of treatment, Antonio had lost the 100 pounds that had been his initial goal. He saved the belt he wore to his first session as a reminder to himself of how far he had come. He was proud of himself and liked to tell all his friends about how he had really changed his whole lifestyle. Like many of the successful weight losers, Antonio was willing to combine behavioral treatment with hypnosis, and understood that the changes he made needed to be permanent, rather than engaging in a temporary diet, or short-term but high-intensity exercise program. He continued to walk 2 to 3 times a week, and learned to allow himself small treats on occasion, and in moderation, rather than have a list of "forbidden" foods that eventually led to binges and guilt. Antonio maintained his weight loss for several years, although I recently heard that he had gone back for some refresher hypnosis to get back on track again.

"THE TUMOR-CAUSING, TEETH-STAINING, SMELLY, PUKING HABIT"

Although advertisements for smoking cessation through hypnosis often claim extraordinary success rates, the research literature is more mixed. Some studies show that inital results are good, although in the long term, clients in these studies do no better than controls (Lambe, Osier, & Franks, 1986). Other studies demonstrate no difference among hypnosis, other methods of treatment, and controls

(Frank et al., 1986; Hyman, Stanley, Burrows, & Horne, 1986). Spiegel, however, has had good success using hypnosis. In his study, 52 percent achieved complete abstinence after one week, and 23 percent maintained abstinence at a two-year follow-up (Spiegel et al., 1993). In addition, his single-session protocol has been used by many researchers with similar success (Williams & Hall, 1988). One review of the literature (Holroyd, 1980) demonstrated success rates ranging from 20 percent to 94 percent, and that hypnosis can be enhanced by increasing the length of treatment, interpersonal contact, individualized suggestions, and follow-up contact.

HYPNOSIS AND BEHAVIOR MODIFICATION

As with hypnosis for weight loss, we recommend treatment that combines highly individualized hypnosis, along with behavior modification for best results. We can take a look at a case in progress as an example of how to develop components of the hypnosis portion of treatment. Ron is a 35-year-old attorney who has been smoking for ten years. He began smoking in graduate school to cope with the stress, and he now smokes only on weekends. His heaviest use in the past was one pack per day.

He says he has a strong desire to quit, though he is never able to quit for more than a few months. In gathering his history, he indicates that the reason he wants to quit now is that he is getting older and does not feel as well after a weekend of smoking. "I'm not bouncing back as easily as I did before I was 30," he stated. In an attempt to change his motivation from a "moving away from" motivation (i.e., avoiding some result) to a "moving towards" motivation, he became stymied. However, he eventually hit upon what is likely the key reason he has not been able to permanently stop smoking: being with his friends on the weekends. Smoking with his friends on the weekends meant being carefree, and not smoking meant being settled down and having no more fun. Furthermore, among his group of friends, if a person quit smoking, the group goaded him back into the habit.

Douglas (1999) suggests that in order for therapy to be helpful to smokers who have failed to quit, it needs to emphasize the client's "memories, successes and failure patterns, . . . significant attitudes and beliefs related to smoking and to personal responsibility for recovery" (p. 219). Ron has already identified that it is his responsibility to quit, and has acknowledged that he may not be quite ready yet. "Look, I know it's killing me. If it's just a matter of wanting to quit, *why* don't I do it?" he asked. He does leave the door open, however. He indicates that he is ready to quit if he could still hang out with his friends and have fun as a nonsmoker. To initially connect with Ron and reinforce his stated idea that he knows smoking is killing him, I (S. B.) tell him the following story outside of trance.

The Boy and the Snake

One winter there was a family walking through a canyon by a small river, maybe it was even in Sedona. The boy was lagging behind and noticed a small snake trapped in the ice at the edge of the water. Hoping to revive it, he picked up the snake, put it in his pocket, and occasionally reached in to touch it. Little by little, the snake began to revive, and it moved around in his pocket. The boy brought it home and played with it. People told him it was a very poisonous snake, and that he should get rid of it. However, the boy continued to play with his snake.

One day, when he was playing with the snake, it bit him. The boy and the snake were taken to the doctor, who said, "Son, that's a very poisonous snake, and you shouldn't have been playing with it." The boy answered, "I know it's poisonous, but it's my friend, and I thought everything would be okay."

The doctor treated the boy, and gave the snake something, after which it seemed to die. The boy again took the snake, playing with it, and it again revived. The boy said to the snake, "I'm so angry with you. I took you in as my friend and you bit me."

The snake replied, "You knew all the time I was poisonous."

Ron nodded his head in comprehension and said he was ready to try something new. Hypnosis would be fine with him. He now requested that we address some other way to have fun without needing to smoke. As mentioned in Douglas (1999), one key to success is to emphasize where the client has been previously successful. Not only was Ron successful academically, he was also a good athlete and could relate to sports anecdotes. So, I employed an early learning set induction, focusing on his personal success in sports.

And Ron, you know that you've learned how to do many things, becoming quite successful even when things were difficult. *When you were a child, you learned how to write the alphabet. And when you learned those letters, in the very beginning, it took all your concentration to form those letters, didn't it? That's right. In those beginning stages, your efforts weren't as sophisticated as they have become now, and your* progress showed rather rapidly. *Sometimes a person learns things without exactly knowing how he is doing it, but he makes remarkable progress just the same.*

Now, Ron, you may be telling yourself with your conscious mind that quitting smoking is too difficult, it's a struggle, and isn't it interesting how many times difficult things for our conscious awareness can become quite easy *for our unconscious process. You certainly have had many experiences of conquering difficult situations to come out ahead, despite not knowing how you got there sometimes. Law school, although it was a struggle at times, proved to be an area of success, and passing the bar certainly required focused effort, and you succeeded there, too.*

Your unconscious mind already knows exactly what to do . . . *just allowing that unconscious mind to guide your process of letting go of unhelpful behaviors, replacing them with healthful and productive behaviors. . . .*

We can use Ron's affinity with sports as a medium for an effective metaphor for rising to the challenge ahead of him. Suggestions can be indirectly placed within the metaphor as well. For example, we used a triathalon to define an activity that required "stamina, strength, and courage," all qualities Ron had previously stated he has needed to succeed in the past, and qualities that will help him become a permanent nonsmoker as well. In telling about the swimming portion of the triathalon, we may say something along the lines of:

. . . the swimmers battled the choppy waves of the harbor, along with the pounding of the arms and legs of their peers, all moving in their own rhythm, *but subtly influencing the choices of the swimmers around them. The motivation to* separate from the pack *was palpable. Although each swimmer must have been* tired from the pressure of his

peers, and the push of the tide against him, each rose out of that harbor and got on his bike. . . .

In such a small space, we have addressed the influence of Ron's friends, as well as reinforced separating himself from the cigarettes, but not necessarily his peers.

Now, you will recall that Ron was particularly focused on finding other ways to have fun without smoking. Within another session of hypnosis, I used age regression to a time in Ron's life when he had a good time with his friends, before he was a smoker. Then, suggestions were given that he could be open to communication from his unconscious mind, giving him options for new ways to enjoy his life as a nonsmoker, giving him all that smoking gave him, but without any of the negative consequences. I then asked him to imagine himself in the future as a permanent nonsmoker, with multiple, alternate avenues for feeling carefree and having fun with his friends, and to let me know with a nod when he had that image securely in his mind. Once he had that image, a suggestion was made that he could find himself returning to that image quite vividly each time he had an urge to light up in the future.

Between sessions, Ron had been working on increasing his awareness of his urges and triggers other than times when he was with his friends. He realized that he had strong urges whenever he felt stressed, when he needed to wind down from work, and whenever he finished a portion of a tough project and needed to think about how to proceed with the next portion. Given these insights, I added suggestions linking that image of his future self with feeling calm, relaxed, and thinking clearly, as well as having fun.

Now, most smoking cessation protocols recommend addressing the client's natural desire to have a healthy body, and to protect the self from harm. Ron had already told me that he wanted to *be* healthier, as well as feel healthier. So, in addition to the following story, I also made somewhat more direct suggestions that whenever he noticed symptoms of withdrawal, he could be aware that they were a sign of toxins leaving his body, and he could tell himself, "Ah, good riddance," and reframe the symptoms as those of healing. I wanted to reinforce the positive physical aspects of quitting smoking permanently. As Ron appreciates the metaphors within stories, this was the last one I told him.

Eating Dirt

Now, Ron, let me tell you about a client I had one time who was in the habit of eating dirt. Yes, eating dirt. While this may seem extraordinary to you, this man certainly didn't think it was anything to take lightly. Now, this man, he knew that eating dirt wasn't particularly good for his body, as it could throw his digestive system out of whack, and on occasion it made him feel sick. He was embarassed about this habit, yet he felt like it was beyond his control most of the time. He tried rationalizing to himself: "It's only dirt, and all kids eat dirt at one time in their lives, so it can't be THAT bad." Or, he would say, "It's a natural substance so it can't be so bad, certainly not as bad as taking drugs."

He ate dirt by himself, then he ate dirt to amuse his friends, who, of course, thought he was quite the kidder, and they egged him on repeatedly. Then, he realized that he didn't need his friends' approval, at least not in that way, and he wasn't going to eat dirt anymore to get it. After a time, he went to the doctor who, after several tests, told him that he must be driven to eat the dirt because his body was missing some sort of mineral he wasn't getting from his diet. With that explanation, the man felt relieved, as at least there was an answer in sight that would allow him to stop eating dirt forever. When he asked the doctor what mineral he was seeking by eating dirt, the doctor told him that if he listened to his *inner voice*, he would know what good things to give himself so he wouldn't need to eat dirt anymore.

And you know, all by himself, with a bit of *introspection* and *quiet time* with himself, he realized what the dirt was providing for him, and how he could get it in healthier ways. With that knowledge, he was able to provide himself with the appropriate substitution, and to this day he has never had a need or a desire to eat dirt again.

That session was several weeks before the writing of this chapter, and so far, Ron has continued to quit. He is nearing the point of longest abstinence, and he is only a little bit worried about relapse.

However, he uses the skills he has learned in talk therapy to cope with his stress and tension, and he goes to that vivid image of his future self as a permanent nonsmoker on a daily basis. The image is growing stronger, and it seems more connected to him all the time. His friends decided to quit, too, so he has more social support for quitting than he had before. Even so, he says, he is finding that he can have fun hanging out without smoking and does not feel as compelled to "join the crowd" if his friends relapse again. He is hopeful that he will make it this time, and I think he will.

We'd like to end this chapter with ESRT. It stands for emotional self-regulation therapy, a promising treatment for smoking. It doesn't employ hypnosis per se, but incorporates suggestive techniques, along with shaping, fading, positive reinforcement, attributions, modeling, expectancies, and individualized techniques. The therapy, which relies heavily on sensory recall experiences, was developed in Spain, and appears to be a solidly grounded method for gradually reducing smoking (Bayot, Capafons, & Cardena, 1997). This cognitive-behavioral therapy is like so many that may be enhanced by the inclusion of hypnotic language, metaphor, and story.

Remember that many clients who request hypnosis for weight loss or smoking have already tried—and failed—with various other approaches. These people, in their eagerness for change, may have unrealistic expectations about hypnosis, and are hoping for a "magic bullet." Our challenge, then, is to embrace their hope, while at the same time *not* fueling unrealistic expectations. Do we need to begin therapy with a story or anecdote about *someone else* who sought a magic bullet for habit control, and came to realize that hypnosis could indeed be a valuable aid, but only as part of a more comprehensive program? We once conveyed this to a client by telling her about Élise, who after many years made the perfect spaghetti sauce. Through considerable trial and error, Élise happened on the *magic* combination of garlic, onions, and spices. "I knew it required more than tomato sauce, even though tomato sauce was the vital ingredient," Élise reported.

15

Medicine, Surgery, and Dentistry

GHOSTS AND MACHINES

We would have liked to begin this chapter with our best story without an ending; however, there is no story sufficient to introduce an unfolding and developing scenario so vast and incomplete as hypnosis's role in medicine, surgery, and dentistry. A brochure announcing an upcoming program by the American Society of Clinical Hypnosis (ASCH) features "The Psychobiology of Gene Expression and Neurogenesis: More than a Healing Metaphor." Clearly, the future frontiers of hypnosis are wide open.

It was not always this way. Medical hypnosis, after captivating clinicians in the nineteenth century, all but disappeared in the mid-twentieth century, since it was more desirable to focus on a material approach that emphasized the visible and concrete. The vast literature of medical hypnosis is now seriously challenging the belief that the mind is merely "a ghost in the machine," as mental activities are bringing about physical changes that are far beyond the capabilities of a "ghost." In the years ahead, research is likely to answer questions about what the intervening variables are between the *experience* of hypnosis and what the ghost might influence downstream in terms of the body's molecules, cells, tissues, and organs (Dossey, 1999).

THE CELTICS CALLED IT "DRUID SLEEP"

The use of hypnosis or hypnotic techniques for medical purposes is as old as the recorded history of medicine. Hypnotic "sleep" was used by ancient Egyptian physician-priests; early Celtics used "Druid sleep" to assist in treating sickness; and preColumbian Indian medicine men used hypnotic trance in their healing rituals, occasionally aided by hallucinogenic drugs (Ambrose & Newbold, 1980). As early as the mid-nineteenth century, hypnosis was being successfully employed in medical circumstances, namely in surgery. Prior to the advent of anesthesias, hypnosis was the only choice for the diminution of pain in surgery. Interestingly, hypnosis seemed to decrease the risk of infection, and increase the speed of postsurgery healing, reducing one surgeon's mortality rate from infection to only 5 percent, as compared to his colleagues' average of 25 to 50 percent at the time (Rossi & Cheek, 1988). Since then, the field of psychoneuroimmunology has given us some possible explanations for enhancing immune function when activating emotional motivation for healing.

A colleage of mine (S. B.) once spoke of a patient (in this chapter we will use *patient* instead of *client*) with a degenerative and eventually terminal illness who was seeking hypnosis for pain. Suggestions to allow the body to heal as much as possible were incorporated in the hypnotic language, along with pain-management suggestions. For some time, the patient experienced a break in degeneration, which progressed no further than when he began hypnotic treatment. Indeed, within the field of medical hypnosis seeming miracles are not wholly uncommon. It may be in this realm that hypnosis deserves its most laudatory attention.

MEDICAL REFERRALS FOR HYPNOSIS

The underutilization of hypnosis in medicine appears to be influenced by some of the same negative views held by the general public. Even though the usefulness of clinical hypnosis in the treatment of a wide variety of medical disorders has been well established (Crasilneck & Hall, 1985), whether or not hypnosis is utilized depends on a variety of factors. Elkins and Wall (1996) surveyed a large physician group in Texas, and found that 79 percent of physicians and 67 percent of medical residents had neither received training in hypnosis nor experienced hypnosis themselves. Moreover, these doctors endorsed many misconceptions about hypnosis, and had limited awareness of the appropriate applications of the modality. The authors contrasted this view of hypnosis by physicians with that of patients in the group practice, who indicated that they were willing to participate in hypnosis as part of their medical and surgical treatment.

SURGERY

Hypnosis can be used to help surgical patients in many ways. For some highly hypnotizable patients, surgery may be successful using only hypnotic anesthesia, whereas for others, hypnosis may decrease the amount of medication necessary during surgery. Interestingly, Mauer and colleagues (1999) showed that preoperative hypnosos helped a group of orthopedic hand-surgery patients make better progress in recovery, as well as experience fewer postoperative complications.

Hypnosis has been successful in maxillofacial surgery, by helping patients decrease blood pressure as well as blood loss during surgery (Enqvist, Von Kenow, & Bystedt, 1995). Research has also accumulated regarding the effect of "negative" conversation by medical personnel during surgery on patients' recovery responses. For example, although surgery patients are not conscious, they can often recall, in hypnosis after recovery, conversations between the surgeons at the time of the surgery (Jones, 1994; Rossi & Cheek, 1988). The authors postulated that careless remarks could have an anxiety-producing effect on patients, who then have difficulty with proper healing. Thus, hypnosis can be utilized to access the important information influencing patients, as well as counter negative messages that impede healing. Presurgical hypnosis can also alleviate anxiety, promote ego-strengthening, and improve patients' expectations of positive outcomes. Finally, hypnosis can also be used to lessen post-surgery pain.

CANCER

What helps cancer patients live longer lives? In Iowa, Kwekkeboom (2001) demonstrated that women undergoing surgery for gynecologic and breast cancers increased outcome expectancy through the use of guided imagery. Previous history of imagery use and perceived credibility of the imagery provider were supported as predictors of outcome expectancy. In a similar study, Cunningham and colleagues (2000) found that "psychological self-regulation" aided longer life in patients with metastatic cancer. The treatment condition consisted of relaxation, mental imaging, cognitive restructuring, and meditation. The authors showed that a significant relationship was found between degree of involvement in psychological self-regulation and survival duration. Spiegel and colleagues (1989) produced similar findings. Their study of patients with metastatic breast cancer showed that increased survival was observed in women given a weekly combination of supportive and expressive group therapy. We could find no study that involved *only* hypnosis and outcome expectancy. So, does hypnosis help cancer patients live longer? No. But it definitely helps them live *better* lives.

Quality of life of cancer patients and hypnosis is heavily documented because of hypnosis's many applications. Most commonly, hypnosis with cancer patients involves pain management (Liossi & Hatira, 1999; Lynch, 1999; Spiegel & Bloom, 1983) and anxiety and emesis control (Genuis, 1995). Cancer patients must deal with so many diverse and uncomfortable processes in the course of treatment and, sometimes, in the course of dying with the disease. I (S. B.) used hypnosis with one hospice patient, who was dying of cancer. He was extremely afraid of dying, and talk therapy was producing no good results in alleviating his anxiety. Hypnosis helped him to relax, and to visualize letting go with more peace. On the day he died, his hypnosis tape was the only thing that soothed him in the final stages until I was able to sit with him. When the tape was turned off, his breathing became labored, and his agitation greatly increased. With either the tape or the eventual in vivo hypnotic patter to promote peacefulness and calm, his facial features smoothed, his body relaxed, and his breathing became more effortless.

Hypnosis has been helpful in preserving or increasing psychological strength to cope with hair loss, body changes, locus-of-control issues, and dealing with social interactions (Harper, 1999; Jacobs,

Pelier, & Larkin, 1998). Treatment for cancer may involve invasive and painful procedures, such as chemotherapy injections, bone marrow aspirations and/or transplantation, as well as radiation treatment. Such procedures may produce extreme anxiety, anticipatory worry about the pain, or the claustrophobic conditions of the treatment, all of which can be assisted through the use of hypnotic suggesion (Steggles, 1999). Kopel and Quinn (1996) reported successful treatment of dysphagia following a cancer-precipitated total laryngectomy, and hypnotic suggestions also helped an esophageal cancer patient to swallow again postsurgery (Jones, 1994). Finally, one study (Rapkin, Straubing, & Holroyd, 1991) demonstrated that imagery-based hypnosis has prophylactic benefits for postsurgical cancer patients, as it may reduce the probability of postoperative complications, and thus the length of hospital stay.

I (G. G.) once treated a young man, John, undergoing uncomfortable chemotherapy treatments. The overall illness, as well as the injections following each treatment, made the chemotherapy an aversive circumstance. John's spirits were flagging. The following story was used for ego-strengthening, and additional suggestions and metaphor were used to assist with the nausea following each treatment. John was able to better manage his symptoms, cooling his body through self-hypnosis as becoming overheated typically led to vomiting. As this skill increased, he felt more in control and hopeful about his treatment. His cancer went into remission, and on last contact he was doing well. In the story, italicized portions indicate vocal shifts.

The Spanish Explorers

I remember someone telling me this story long ago, and I think it occurred some time in the late eighteenth century, when an expedition of Spanish explorers in the New World set out on a special mission. It had taken quite some time to receive permission to do so, as they had to go through the viceroy, who in turn had to get approval from the King of Spain. A long time they had waited, until finally, after many months of waiting, the expedition set out.

This expedition had one objective in mind: *to find Juan's Hope*, a legendary place rumored to be deep in the Zuni Mountains. It was not at all clear to the expedition what exactly they would gain when they succeeded in *finding Juan's Hope*, but they did know that it would be something *very unusual, wonderful, and possibly powerful beyond words*. "We should start out by looking near El Moro," said the sargeant. "No, Cibola and San Rafael will point the way," answered the lieutenant.

But the colonel had the final word, and he ordered them to comb the Zuni Mountains, whose rugged range contained numerous perils, whether it was in summer or in winter. "We need to be on the lookout for something *very green*, or maybe *very blue*, I'm not sure. That's where we will *locate Juan*, said the colonel.

Many months passed, searching on horseback and on foot through canyons, animal dens, grassy fields, and sheer mountain peaks. The expedition was now tiring and feeling very discouraged, as they had seen many natural things that were either very *green* or *blue*, but nothing of the intense coloration that they had expected.

"It has to be either *very* green, or *very* blue," repeated the colonel, and the rest of the soldiers nodded in agreement and muttered the words to themselves, as they were accustomed to following orders. Finally, as autumn approached, an early morning patrol came upon something. They stopped, and the sargeant grasped one of the explorers by the arm, and said to him, "Go get the colonel! Tell him we have *found Juan*." The private mounted his horse and galloped off, while the rest of the party set up camp.

They were at a rather high elevation, and a *cool and refreshing breeze* awaited the colonel when he arrived at the spot. He slowly drew his looking glass, raised it to his eye, and peered into it for what seemed the longest time. He gazed upward through the pines, past the mountain peaks, up to the powder blue sky. After only a few moments it came into focus, fuzzy at first, but then sharp and clear, a most powerful image.

For generating imagery (a peaceful, relaxing place, for example) we find it useful to allow clients to create their own imagery scene, rather than making specific suggestions. John, in the above example, needed

assistance with imagery, in addition to needing embedded suggestions for the target symptom. For many other clients, though, we do
not offer specificity or detail so as not to risk conflicting with their
own images. On the other hand, if we have spoken repeatedly with
clients about a favorite imagery scene, we may personalize the
session by using the clients' own descriptive terms to enhance the
vividness of what they are already "seeing." In such cases, using more
directly evocative terms in the client's own language, enhances rather
than conflicts with the inner vision taking place.

I (S. B.) had one cancer patient who preferred to be "started out"
in guided imagery by having her typical images repeated to her. I then
backed away from specific descriptive terms to allow her own
creativity to take hold. A tape geared toward more oneness with the
universe was especially powerful for her. I offered her a few general
descriptive statements, and then more vague, general suggestions.
Her response was, "Wow, I felt like I touched God!" This was
immensely meaningful and moving to her, and she was able to
weather a depressive period in her cancer treatment.

As you sit there in that *chair, noticing the feeling of the chair beneath you on the* outside, *you can also notice pictures as they begin to develop in your mind's eye, on the* inside.	dissociative language apposition of opposites
Walking along *that beach in San Diego,* looking over *one shoulder to see the roller coaster on Mission Beach whirl over the next big bump, you can begin to* notice *the smell of the salty air,* hearing *the sound of the sea gulls as they dip down to pick up shells, rising up again to a height sufficient to drop those shells on the rocks below. With a* slight crack, *you notice the shells begin to open, feeding those birds with nourishing meals. Up and down, those seagulls persist. Instinctively* doing just what they need to do *to take care of their survival. And relaxing in that*	suggestions directive description suggestion

favorite place, just becoming pleasantly aware *of all those sensations in and around you, allowing that mind to turn* inside, *as your awareness of the scenary* outside *sharpens. Just enjoying the time you spend in your favorite spot,* doing all the things *you love to do, enjoying life and feeling healthy and strong, connected to nature, at one.* . . .	general description

apposition of opposites

general description |

In treating patients with cancer, one additional variable must be considered. From the moment a person discovers a questionable lump, or receives the result of a biopsy, a state of negative self-hypnosis may result (Levitan, 1999). Despite much progress in the field, a cancer diagnosis is viewed by many as a sentence to death. Hopeless patients may then evince anger and sadness, as well as catastrophic thoughts and other negative thinking that might seem out-of-proportion and completely irrational to therapists. This is a critical time, and patients might drop out of therapy. At this time, clinicians might feel overwhelmed, as well as severely challenged, and they might need to reach deep into their bag of empathy and understanding. Patients during these times may greatly benefit from metaphors for communicating additional understanding.

GASTROINTESTINAL AND GENITO-URINARY PROBLEMS

Psychiatrists and other physicians readily point to certain problems as psychosomatic. These include irritable bowel syndrome, fibromyalgia, temperomandibular joint syndrome, chronic sinusitis, and chronic fatigue syndrome. As many of these disorders respond well to antidepressant medications, doctors might be quick to point this out and say, "See, it was really depression." Certainly we support any intervention that can bring relief; however, at the same time, we recognize that many of these disorders can respond well to hypnosis, with or without pharmacotherapy. These patients usually need help in managing their stress, and many can also benefit from ego-strengthening.

Many common gastrointestinal (GI) problems, for example, ulcer, Crohn's disease, and irritable bowel syndrome (IBS), are closely linked to high levels of stress, as these patients typically experience higher levels of anxiety and inner tension. Such patients might mask their emotional distress with physiological symptoms, using the symptoms as a defense mechanism (Ambrose & Newbold, 1980). It is not uncommon for these patients to have difficulty "letting go," often holding too much in, and sometimes having comorbid anxieties, phobias, or depression. For these patients, increasing their self-effi-cacy and providing a manner that helps to maintain a modicum of control over their symptoms goes a long way. Hypnotic suggestions might be aimed at relaxation, loosening up, and communicating more directly with the symptom itself.

Smith and colleagues (1999) recommend inclusion of the following techniques in a program to treat an unstable bladder: anxiety control, ego-strengthening, self-hypnosis training, and the hand-on-the-abdomen technique. These techniques, also used with irritable bowel syndrome, lead to either a reduction of symptoms or complete remission of the unstable bladder. A component of psychoeducation might enhance the techniques, as the patient learns about the physiological aspects of the disorder, as well as some of the possible emotional links and how to work through them.

For ulcer, the therapeutic focus might combine building self-effi-cacy, decreasing tension and anxiety, and modulating the pain. As mentioned in the chapter on anxiety disorders (Chapter 16), a common approach is to suggest *slowing down*. This can be accom-plished metaphorically, such as describing driving on a road and decreasing one's speed; or it can be modeled behaviorally by having the therapist slow down his speech or movements. Or, it can be done more directly with suggestions such as:

> . . . *you can notice how that breath begins to* slow down, *now, and as you slowly exhale, you begin to be aware of that mind also* slowing down, *just a bit at a time, now, that's the way. Mind . . . and body, relaxed,* slow, *and peaceful.*

Teaching stress management skills, along with hypnotic sugges-tions for decreasing stress and worry, can create a dual process of conscious and unconscious skill building.

With IBS there are no consistent physiological, biochemical, or structural abnormalities associated with the disorder. Accordingly, gastroenterologists and IBS patients are continually frustrated with often ineffective medical treatment, which usually includes antispasmodics, anti-diarrheals, and bulking agents (Galovski & Blanchard, 2002). IBS is a common referral to psychologists, with approximately 50 to 70 percent of all GI patients suffering from the disorder (Brown & Fromm, 1987). Symptoms tend to fall in either a pain-predominant category, or a diarrhea-predominant category, although a single patient can experience both symptom groups. Exacerbated by stress and anxiety, IBS sufferers might also have extreme anticipatory anxiety about episodes (i.e., fearing the onset of symptoms) which might, to some extent, condition patients to maintain their symptoms. Hypnotic techniques with IBS are varied. Glove anesthesia, as a convincer of the potency of hypnotic suggestion, has been used prior to providing direct suggestions for bowel habit control and pain relief. Hypnotic relaxation, followed by placing the patient's hand on the abdomen and generating a sense of warmth, helps to generate a sense of control over physiological responses. The patient visualizes the bowel or the gut and imagines controlling activity in the same area where the warmth was produced. (Brown & Fromm, 1987). Similarly, within hypnosis, the patient can be encouraged to give voice to the symptoms through an internal dialogue, and then give color imagery as a way to communicate with the symptoms. For example, Hornyak (1999) succeeded in having a patient visualize her intestine as a flaming red tube, which the patient then intensified while in hypnosis, noticing the sense of control. Metaphor can be used to indirectly suggest the health process, such as a river moving steadily along, as well as individual control and the calming of symptoms.

I (S. B.) have used the following story to metaphorically match IBS symptoms. The travellers' heavy packs and various aspects of weather *pace* these aspects of the disease, and *leading*, or adding on in the direction of desired change, is demonstrated by the canoeists' successful adaptation to adversity.

The Camping Trip

One time a woman talked about a camping trip she took in the Boundary Waters canoe area in northern Minnesota, right up there in the waters bordering Canada, where the water can become very cold. There was a group on this trip, and they were *heavily laden* with the *burden* of their packs, because *everything that goes in must come out* again. Canoeing in for three days through a labyrinth of lakes and rivers, on the first day going out, *storm clouds* were brewing, as the *sky darkened* and the *wind picked up*.

They set off, *watching the sky* as they paddled along. The *rains started* first, just *little drops* to catch their attention in the beginning, and then *harder, bigger drops*, until they were pelted with rain. Then came *thunder and lightning*, and of course, you'd rather be anywhere else than on a lake in an aluminum canoe in a lightning storm, as you might imagine. Paddling faster to get away from the storm, they made good time, clearing several lakes in a few hours. It's *tiring work* to *battle against natural occurrences* for too long, though, and they needed a break. *Stomachs were rumbling* with hunger as the water started to *churn and froth*, waves breaking along the sides of the canoes, and *roiling* in little eddies here and there. They realized that the *right food* could subside their hunger pangs and keep their minds busy as they kept going forward. It became something of a *rhythmic motion, paddling and moving forward* steadily through the storm. As they *let go*, they *gained control*, and soon the *storm subsided*. The churning, roiling waters became *calm once again*. The fresh, chill air on their faces helped invigorate the rest of the journey, and the rainbow on the horizon lifted their spirits. There was still some work ahead, but *each of them knew that they could make it*, as they were buoyed by the experience of *letting go and moving ahead*.

I (G. G.) once worked with Bud, a 50-year-old man with Crohn's disease. He had been refractory to various medications and one surgery, and he was essentially housebound with the disease's bloating, diarrhea, pain, constipation, and other symptoms. We began treatment with ample pre-hypnosis discussion about the generativity and resourcefulness of the unconscious mind. This concept was also seeded in conversational inductions, and finger signals were established. The third-session unconscious search yielded that he was not punishing himself, and that there were no other functional reasons for his symptoms. During the same session, I asked his unconscious mind to drift and dream until he generated a healing image. The image he came up with, a white light, was then used in two more sessions. Improvement was dramatic in that his activity level outside the home increased considerably. I audiotaped the final session, and he agreed to listen to it two times a week. That was three years ago and he is still doing fine. I expect him to call me when the tape wears out. (However, as electronic gadgets are his hobby, I suspect that he has made a copy or two of the tape.)

SKIN CONDITIONS

Several skin diseases have been successfully ameliorated or cured with hypnosis, self-hypnosis, hypnobehavioral treatment, or a combination of these methods (Brown & Fromm, 1987). Ewin (1992) notes that prepubertal children and adults with warts (*verruca fulgaris*) who do not respond to direct suggestion in hypnosis, often cure their warts when treated with hypnoanalysis. Warts also responded well to hypnosis in the study by Spanos and colleagues (1990). Pruritis and neurodermatitis both involve excessive itching and thickening of the skin. For some clients, direct suggestions that the irritation can be minimized, or that the pain can resolve upon awakening from a hypnotic trance, have proved helpful. For others, hypnosis geared at imagery or positively hallucinated treatments, such as, bathing in cool water, have greater effect in alleviating symptoms. I (S. B.) had one client with neurodermatitis who responded well to a combination of hypnotic relaxation, the alteration of symptoms to a more localized and tolerable placement, and the positive hallucination of experiencing a cooling, healing dip in a large pool. Similarly, Brown and Fromm (1987) recount the story of one woman who successfully visualized sunbathing each day to treat psoriasis without the damaging effects of the direct sunlight. Healing ointments may be positively hallucinated through trance to help soothe and relieve the discomfort of eczema, and direct hypnotic suggestion has also been helpful in reinforcing behavior geared toward the effective care of skin diseases, such as cleansing, and avoiding irritation. Having a patient imaginally apply soothing ointments or creams through hypnotic suggestion has also been used successfully with herpetic lesions and the pain of postherpetic neuralgia following herpes zoster. Nerve pain is often not circumscribed to the original area of outbreak, or the trunk of the body, and is often fund in extremities, such as in the hands and feet.

Therapists need to bear in mind patients' concrete interpretations, or trance logic. With one of my (S. B.) patients, I made an analogy, comparing his residual pain from a long-ago episode of shingles, to the phantom limb pain often experienced by amputees. This analogy, along with a dissociative suggestion that his foot could seem like it was not part of him during times of extreme pain, caused him some distress, as he thought we were going to amputate his foot!

In a similar case, I (G. G.) was working with a man who had lost both legs when he stepped on a mine. I was seeing him for headache, and near the end of a session in which I had told him a couple of stories, I offered him a restraining message, something like, "A person shouldn't read too much into *hackneyed* metaphors," and suddenly he had phantom limb pain for the first time in years. Fortunately it soon abated, and I learned to watch what I say, like *not* emphasizing breathing when you have a person on oxygen.

MOVEMENT DISORDERS

Movement disorders cover a wide variety of diagnoses that can include Parkinson's disease, Tourette's syndrome, dystonia, and Sydenham's chorea. With each of these disorders, parasympathetic nervous system responses (e.g., peacefulness, or relaxation response) help to alleviate symptoms, while sympathetic nervous system responses (e.g., stress reactions, or flight-or-fight responses) worsen the symptoms experienced. Given that hypnosis of any kind typically involves a relaxation response, it is possible that one of the ways hypnosis helps with movement disorders is simply by decreasing the adrenaline output and increasing parasympathetic response. However, Medd (1999) found that each of the above disorders showed longstanding positive effect with sustained hypnosis. One explanation posited by the author was that hypnosis decreased tremor in Parkinson's disease by inhibiting output to the brain stem, while the other three movement disorders were ameliorated by a sustained, hypnosis-induced inhibition of motor cortical activity. From a more purely psychological stand point, Medd hypothesized that the longstanding effects were initially begun by hypnosis, but maintained through conditioned response.

With these and other chronic disorders, patients may experience depression and diminished self-efficacy. Accordingly, our treatment regimen nearly always begins with a course of ego-strengthening. We have successfully employed both "short-burst" ego-strengthening, as well as metaphorical ego-strengthening, both of which are described in the ego-strengthening chapter in Section II of this book.

AUTOIMMUNE/IMMUNE SYSTEM

Hypnosis for HIV/AIDS has focused primarily on pain control, typically toward an end stage of the disease. Marcus (1999) used Ericksonian hypnosis to treat two patients on opposite ends of the illness spectrum. With one newly seroconverted HIV patient, hypnosis helped to reframe what life would look like with the new HIV status. Ego-strengthening stories and metaphor may be highly important at such a point for a newly diagnosed patient. For the end-stage AIDS patient in the Marcus study, hypnosis was used for pain control and for effectevely managing invasive procedures, such as seen in treatment for cancer. In addition, a "back-to-the-future" technique was also used to allow the patient to feel more peaceful and accepting of his impending death, as well as to decrease overall stress and anxiety about death in more general terms.

Similar to the cancer patient in the end stages, AIDS patients may appreciate a focus of "letting go" in a larger sense. It is wise for a practitioner to discuss each client's goals for the session in advance, given that some clients will want to fight against the disease to the very last breath, while others might want to work on increasing peacefulness and resolving any unfinished business. In cases where the conscious and unconscious desires of the client might be in conflict, such as choosing to work on acceptance and peace but an unconscious resistance repeatedly surfaces, ideomotore signaling can give the therapist some information about where the incongruence lies, or where unfinished business might still need attention.

Multiple sclerosis (MS), in an active phase, may create balance problems, blurred vision, pain throughout the body, poor fine and gross motor control, and loss of muscle use ranging from facial drooping, such as seen in stroke patients, to the inability to properly use arms and legs. Stress is highly implicated in the severity and onset of episodes with the recurring/remitting type of MS. Given the unpredictability of symptom onset and severity, hypnosis's alleviation of anxiety may be helpful, as well as reframing the outlook on the disease process, the perception of limitations due to symptoms, and the feeling of mastery and coping (Ambrose & Newbold, 1980).

Hypnotic pain management can also be an important treatment focus in MS to prevent increasing the number and dose of medications needed. Dane (1996) used hypnotic imagery and post-hypnotic suggestion successfully in a case study. Significant improvement in pain control, sitting balance, and diplopia (double vision) was demonstrated in follow-up at intervals of one month, one year, and eight years.

One of my (G. G.) patients, Hector, a Korean War veteran, was a retired teacher and accomplished poet, who was devastated when given a MS diagnosis at age 65. Hector immediately prepared for the worst, updating his will, and mending fences with his estranged children. After accomplishing this, he fell into a dark gloom, and was referred for therapy. He responded to hypnosis with deep trance, and over several sessions he was bombarded with ego-strengthening and mindfulness-based stories. Each session, he responded with his Yes finger to the question, "Is this story something that your unconscious mind can put to use?" Afterward, he demonstrated complete amnesia for anything told him in trance.

During one session, we did an unconscious search for " . . . something you can do, anything at all, that might help you at this time. . . ." I asked him to tell me with his own words, and he uttered, "Start writing poetry again." Upon realerting, he had no recollection of his utterance, and I did not remind him of what he said. At the next session three weeks later, he casually remarked that he was writing poetry again, and I said, "Good for you." This session was spent generating a healing image (a vague, amorphous image involving ocean and sky). This image was anchored to a circle made with his index finger and thumb, and he was realerted. This time, he was amnesic for all content, except for the healing image, which he continued to describe in vivid detail during debriefing. He was instructed to continue using his anchor during self-hypnosis, and was also given an audiotape of one of our sessions. I saw him intermittently for two years before he moved away from Arizona, and during this time his mood remained bright and the disease was stable.

HEADACHE

Headache can generally be classified within three major categories: 1) traction/inflammatory headache (caused by a tumor or subdural hematoma and bacterial infection, poisoning, and alcohol withdrawal respectively); 2) muscle-contraction headache (the prototypical "tension" or "stress" headache); and 3) vascular headache, also known as migraine or cluster (Brown & Fromm, 1987). Headache can be precipitated by numerous events and environmental factors. For example, migraine headaches are often exacerbated or initiated by the consumption of tannins from red wine, nitrates, or nitrites, aspartame found in artificial sweeteners, and monosodium glutamate. As one Phoenix migraine specialist once commented, "Go to Bank One Ballpark for a Diamondbacks' game, have a Diet Coke and a hotdog, and you'll have a dandy of a migraine by the end of the evening." Withdrawal from too much daily caffeine or alcohol can also cause headaches. Many medications, including those prescribed specifically for headache, can cause a rebound headache shortly after use, or after discontinuation of the medication. Changes in altitude, temperature, and oversensitivity to light can also precipitate headache.

Headache-prone individuals may tend to be highly stress sensitive as well, being more prone to anxiety responses. Indeed, migraine headaches are associated with low levels of serotonin, and many patients with low-level anxiety and/or depression can benefit from following a migraine diet. Individuals prone to muscle-contraction headaches tend to have a chronic overreactivity of the frontalis muscle, particularly in situations of stress, wherein the muscles along the fronal area, and sometimes the temples, stay contracted over long periods of time. Teaching a basic relaxation response, or self-hypnosis, would be highly useful for these individuals.

Vasoconstriction, particularly cranial vasoconstriction, tends to be a common problem for migraine sufferers and cluster-type headaches. Although many migrainers have a chronic vasoconstrictive response, even seen in non-headache periods, it is the subsequent vasodilation that actually creates the vascular headache. Thus, teaching self-hypnosis with a relaxation response to mediate the level of vasoconstriction during non-headache periods can help reduce the onset of headache in the first place. One hypnotic technique that might be successful is to teach the client to better control the vasomotor response through a hand-warming procedure (Brown & Fromm, 1987). Hand-warming can be accomplished by using an opposite approach to glove anesthesia, which is often introduced through indirect images of cold, numbing, and tingling. So, to heighten a patient's physical recognition of the phases of vasocon-striction and vasodilation, one might introduce the suggestion of moving from cold to warm.

I wonder *if you can* imagine, *just imagine, for a moment, the experience of* one man *who went skiing every winter. While he was out there on the slopes, he noticed the* brisk sensation *of a wintery wind on his face,* numbing *his cheeks, his ears, and his hands. The cold wind blew while he raced down the mountain, and* those *cheeks and hands first felt a little wind burned, and then they became almost pleasantly* numb, *and those fingers became* harder to flex.	power words metaphor suggestions dissociative language suggestions
The intensity of his focus sharpened to a fine point as he raced around moguls here and there, *until he finally reached the bottom. At the end of an exhilerating day, he wandered into the ski chalet, picked up a cup of* hot chocolate around which he wrapped *those* cold, *stiff hands. Sitting in front of a blazing fire, gradually that face and* those *ears* began to warm, *just a bit at a time. The cup of hot chocolate and the blazing fire both* thawed out *those hands, as they regained* more feeling *and became comfortably* warm *again.*	apposition of opposites dissociative language suggestions
Noticing the contrast *between the icy chill of the mountain, and the relaxing warmth of the fire, that man could* become aware *of his hands changing*	suggestions

from cold to warm, as the sensations
moved throughout his body . . . that's
the way. . . .

Hypnosis can also help decrease the probability of headache onset by increasing positive coping with stress and anxiety, suggesting healthier eating habits, and the alteration of habit behaviors, such as the use of caffeine and alcohol. Ego-strengthening suggestions can increase a sense of efficacy in coping, and will help prevent the common catastrophizing, or anticipatory anxiety often experienced before a full-blown headache. Such a patient's self-talk may include, "Oh, no, here comes another headache. I can't handle it." Age regression to times without headache, as well as age progression into a future of diminished headache pain, can also help the patient feel more masterful. Some therapists even view the headache in psychodynamic terms, as an expression of an unconscious conflict (Benedittis, 1998). Age regression could similarly be employed to address such issues.

DENTISTRY

In 1982, 601 dentists, or almost 15 percent of dentists in the United States, were members of ASCH. By 1995, dentist membership in the organization had dropped to 195, or more than 4 percent (Clarke, 1996). This may mean that fewer dentists currently employ hypnosis in their practice. In this section on dentistry, we wish to cover not so much how dentists can use hypnosis, but rather how mental health practitioners can employ hypnosis with patients who visit the dentist.

Many people have some trepidation about dental visits. Some have anxiety about pain, particularly if they have experienced painful dental procedures, such as extractions or root canals. Perhaps the client has hypersensitivity to even the most benign procedure, or tends to feel pain despite the use of analgesics such as novacaine. I (G. G.) had one patient who needed to use hypnosis rather than novacaine for pain during a procedure in order to test whether all the sensitive areas had been effectively treated. For 35-year-old Kristina, even teeth cleaning caused pain along the gum lines, and several teeth needed bonding to cover areas of nerve sensitivity. The bonding process involved an abrasion of the gums, followed by an acid wash and application of bonding material. Kristina responded well to the first session of hypnosis. She was then given a tape to listen to before returning to the dentist. I do not remember the story on the tape, but it had to do with a sandpiper pecking here and there. That bird is waiting for her there on the tape to help her again the next time she goes back to the dentist.

Another patient, Alex, age 45, presented with intense anxiety about a dental appointment that was one month away. One year previously, he had had a painful episode at the dentist where novacaine did not work. He now needed an extraction, and he continuously told himself, "This won't work!" We began with several sessions of general relaxation and ego-strengthening, which set up his learning to apply glove anesthesia.

And, Alex, you can now remember how that hand relaxed just enough to experience a slight numbness, and respecting the need to go slowly, now you can notice a faint tingling, or perhaps a very slight alteration in the sensation of that right hand, while you continue to breathe deeply. And while you notice, with the front part of your mind, how your breathing can begin to change, and those hands may start to feel heavy, or light, warm, or maybe a little cool, or some other sensation, and the whole time, the back part of your mind can be wondering what will come next, or maybe it's telling you that you can't not know that this isn't going to not work, can it not?

restraint

generalizable
suggestions

linking word

dissociates language
suggestion covering
all possibilities

multiple negatives

In algebra class you may have learned that two negatives make a positive. The same in hypnosis. In fact, a triple negative is thought to be received by the unconscious as a positive. You can even add one more negative, as with Alex above, and this multiple negative adds an extra confusional element. Could we keep adding negatives? Sure, and we could throw in an anecdote about being tied in knots, but then we would start to lose sight of the objective: to help Alex at the dentist. Always keep in mind the law of parsimony: Only do what is necessary to achieve the desired effect.

Alex responded with moderate depth, as evidenced by feeling "heavy in the chair," as well as some catelepsy and alteration of sensation. However, he remained doubtful that hypnosis would "work," and he feared his worry would peak again. Alex's self-talk was then targeted, and additional confusion was used to distract him from conscious analysis.

> *And, Alex, now I'd like you to realize with the deepest part of your mind, as well as the front-most part of both the front and the back parts of you mind, that you can take care of any lingering bits of wondering, as you hear my voice as if from a distance, and know that . . . you can do it . . . as any vestiges of worry dissipate like puffs of a wispy white cloud that just skim across the sky on a windy day, that's right . . . I'd like you to see in those clouds some shapes . . . any shapes that might pleasantly engage your sense of wonder . . . and when you can see this in your mind's eye, just nod your head . . . very good . . . and while you're noticing and appreciating those cloud shapes, perhaps you can begin to imagine that those clouds out there, in your mind, can turn any color you desire. Noticing that you can assign a certain color to represent the emotions you have felt in the dentist's chair up until this point, while you stay very comfortably relaxed right here.*
>
> *And watching how those clouds can move and change into new shapes with just the slightest breeze, and you can pick a new color to wash over those clouds, much as your new experiences with a relaxed body, and a relaxed mind, can wash over your previous experiences. When that new color is there, in your mind's eye, you will know, and I will know, because you will find your head nodding almost imperceptibly one more time . . . that's the way. That new color represents the calm, peaceful relaxation you will bring with you to the dentist next time. And what you can't not know when*

you hear my voice speaking to you, is that you have the ability to transform your experiences, as the breeze transforms the clouds in the sky.

The final two sessions involved both talk therapy and hypnosis to reinforce his new ability to experience the dentist's office from a different perspective, regaining the old sense of ordinariness that he used to feel when he went to the dentist. He was given an anchor to cue the body memory of relaxation and to cue a release of anxiety. As he had previously clenched his fist in nervous anticipaton, I suggested a lightly clenched fist as an anchor. He later reported that the extraction "was a breeze," and that he wasn't worried anymore about going to the dentist.

TINNITUS

At our (G. G.) mental health clinic in Tucson, we regularly receive consultation requests from audiology to treat tinnitus. These patients may be young or old, and most of them have hearing loss, in addition to tinnitus, a truly vexing problem that may be experienced as a buzzing, hissing, or any variety of other bothersome noises. One of our interns, Eric Jackson, who specialized in treating this problem, once asked a man, "How loud is it?" The patient grasped the background sound machine, put it on tropical rain mode, and turned up the volume. "It was REAL loud, as he turned it up all the way," Eric reported.

An even more graphic depiction was offered by McSpaden (1993), who noted that tinnitus is "what pain would be if you could hear it." Jacobson (1992) estimated that tinnitus may affect up to 10 percent of the U.S. population. The problem has been treated in a variety of ways, including relaxation and imagery (MacLeod-Morgan, Court, & Roberts, 1982), metaphorical techniques (O'Hanlon, 1986), client-centered hypnotherapy (Mason & Rogerson, 1995), cognitive restructuring, and traditional pain control techniques (Burte, 1993). In Tucson, we have treated these patients with the above techniques, singly and in combination. We have also included mindfulness principles, such as acceptance embedded within stories and unconscious questioning. Clearly, no single technique has stood out as more effective, and theapeutic efforts have yielded an estimated 30 to 40 percent of patients being able to sustain a modest degree of management of the symptom.

Noteworthy is the fact that many individuals with chronic and severe tinnitus do not "suffer from it." Accordingly, a program emphasizing cognitive-behavioral therapy (CBT), with hypnosis relegated to an adjunctive role, may hold the most hope for helping people with this vexing problem (Burke, 1993).

THE PSYCHOBIOLOGY OF HYPNOSIS

We would like to end this chapter with a brief glimpse at a frontier, that is likely to be the future of hypnosis. Many who see a clinical demonstration by Ernest Rossi are impressed by how deftly and economically he utilizes ongoing responses to move a client toward resolution of a problem. However, many of us are equally impressed by the difficulty and complexity of Rossi's theoretical underpinnings, as neuroscience is not easily comprehended.

In the *European Journal of Hypnosis*, Rossi, Lippincott, and Bessette (1994) demonstrate their approach with depression, smoking and stress, alcohol dependence, headache, and other problems. In this article, and in another article, "In Search of a Deep Psychobiology of Hypnosis: Visionary Hypotheses for a New Millenium" (Rossi, 2000), Rossi elucidates how psychosocial cues can modulate the mechanisms of healing at the central nervous system, autonomic, neuroendocrine, and cellular-genetic levels. If this area is of interest, you are encouraged to explore these articles, along with Rossi's *The Psychobiology of Mind-Body Healing* (1993). To be sure, we may be closer than ever to the elusive "ghost in the machine."

CLINICAL COMMENTS

In this chapter, you may have been looking for topics we did not include: functional infertility, eating disorders, needle stick phobia, emergency-room issues, or the ways dentists employ hypnosis, to name a few. We know our coverage of the vast literature on medical applications is far from complete. In treating this topic, we wanted to cover what we believe are the problems practitioners are most likely to see in an office or hospital practice. Certainly many of the hypnotic options we discussed can be generalized to a host of problems that we regrettably had to omit.

We view many of the medical issues through the same lens as we do psychological disorders. That is, hypnotic language, metaphor, story, and indirection can be a valuable adjunct to treatment, whether or not formal hypnosis is used.

16

Anxiety

THE MAP MAY NOT BE THE TERRITORY

Practitioners of hypnosis usually have in their repertoire an array of techniques for addressing anxiety disorders. Rightfully so, as any office practice contains a high percentage of clients who have diffi- culty coping with our stressful world. People may be referred for stress management, and after a few minutes we often see that the clinical picture is a bit more complex. How often is it simple, straight- forward adjustment disorder or generalized anxiety disorder (GAD)?

For many clients anxiety might be secondary to another disorder, such as major depression or a psychotic disorderor, axis II factors might need to be considered. Or, the anxiety disorder might be a significant entity in itself, such as posttraumatic stress disorder (PTSD), which has its own special treatment considerations. Further- more, cognitive factors need to be addressed in *any* presentation of anxiety, and hypnosis alone might be insufficient to treat problems that require medication or conventional talk therapy.

STRICTLY SPEAKING

Is hypnosis a recognized treatment for anxiety disorders? Not at all, if you ask the scientists. In fact, if scientists in the field were to be our lighthouse on a stormy night, many of us would have shipwrecked long ago, so much flotsam and jetsam strewn about the craggy rocks off Erickson Island. Research in recent years has focused on hypnosis as an adjunctive technique, rather than a stand-alone treatment. Schoenberger (2000) reviewed various studies of cognitive-behavioral treatments for anxiety disorders and other problems. In many of these studies, subjects who received hypnosis in addition to cognitive-behavioral therapy (CBT) showed significant improvement, as compared to those who received CBT alone. In fact, Kirsch, Montgomery, and Sapirstein (1995) emphasized in their own meta-analysis that the additon of hypnosis to CBT substantially enhanced treatment outcome, so that the average client receiving this combined treatment showed greater improvement than at least 70 percent of clients receiving non-hypnotic treatment. However, Schoenberger (2000), in her own meta-analysis of these studies discounted the value of hypnosis due to various methadological limitations in the studies. In fact, at this time *no hypnotic treatment* has met the criteria for efficacious treatment, according to the American Psychological Association (APA). The APA listed hypnosis—as an adjunct to CBT—as only *possibly efficacious*, and only for the treatment of obesity.

Does this mean we didn't crash on the rocks, or that we made land by Hammond Sound, or got through the Geary Locks, or got close to Gilligan Island? Far from it. In fact, it reminds us of the story about Milton Erickson and Jay Haley. To make a point, Erickson escorted Haley outside his house in Phoenix and asked him to look at the trees lining the street. Haley did so, was unimpressed, and said, "Yes?" "Look again," commanded Erickson. "Are they all in a straight line?" Haley looked closer this time, and sure enough, one tree was out of line. "Remember," said Erickson, "there's *always* an exception."

We would direct your attention to trees out of line on the streets of Omaha, Rotterdam, Buffalo, Johannesburg, Frankfurt, Seattle,

London, and Geneva, for starters. Are the manifold case studies useless to us? If it is not a well-designed, randomized clinical trial, should we just ignore it? Yapko (2001) reminds us of the severe limitations of research in this area. Most importantly, clients with personality disorders or multiple problems—the clients we customarily see in our practices—are usually excluded from participation in the majority of these studies.

Cochrane (1989) provides us with an articulate case report in which he employed utilization and indirect suggestions in successfully treating GAD in a 44-year-old man. So, too, Smith (1990) employed various hypnotic techniques in treating GAD and aerophobia. These techniques included age regression and directive techniques, such as the clenched-fist technique, in which the client learns to activate the therapist's suggestion to allow his tension to flow into a tightly clenched fist, before "emptying it out" as the hand is allowed to relax. In Hammond's *Handbook of Hypnotic Suggestions and Metaphors* (1990), progressive relaxation, imagery, and a panoply of other techniques are described to treat social phobia, GAD, and other anxiety disorders.

If we did not read case reports, we would not be aware of useful examples for clinical practice, such as Harris's (1991) case study involving the successful use of hypnosis in the treatment of panic disorder with agoraphobia. In this report, the author describes how hypnotic relaxation, imaginal rehearsal, and self-efficacy training allowed her client to complete a previously dreaded shopping trip to Paris. The client's newfound confidence then translated itself into her losing thirty pounds. Follow-up two years later revealed that the client was still symptom free. Indeed, an array of hypnotic applications may assist the therapist in treating problems such as panic disorder and obsessive compulsive disorder. Occasionally hypnosis alone may be sufficient to treat these disorders; however, given the resilience of symptoms, more often the treatment of choice may be hypnosis as an adjunct to CBT.

Case reports can also provide us with novel techniques. Gilbertson and Kemp (1992) reported on cases in which a combination of hypnosis and behavioral techniques were employed to successfully treat GAD. The authors instructed their clients to purchase a digital watch that beeps at hour intervals. A posthypnotic suggestion was given to focus clients' attention on anxiety symptoms whenever they heard a beep, following which they rapidly induced relaxation via self-hypnosis.

UTILIZING HYPNOTIC PHENOMENA

The cardinal feature of anxiety is a future orientation. This unwitting age progression is often accompanied by "as if" statements and predictions, which clients experience as a positive hallucination. At the very least, these symptoms constitute a *therapeutic invitation*, and even more, they might be seen as *gift-wrapped*, as you need only open the gift with a graduated age progression to open up a symptom-free future, and negate the hallucination by offering alternatives to the predictions. Paired with ongoing communication in trance, this can be potently restorative for the anxiety-ridden client.

GETTING THERE FAST WITH SLOW

The tension, urgency, and pressure caused by anxiety can be successfully counteracted metaphorically by commenting on everyday behavior. Contrasting "speeding up, and then *slowing down*" while driving a car, is an experience shared by many people. As clients tell you about themselves and their everyday behavior, have you gleaned that they sip their coffee in the morning, *wolf down* that cereal, *hurriedly peel* those two carrots while preparing their lunch, *rush around* getting their children dressed, or *absentmindedly dab* some toothpaste on the brush? By listening closely and making note of these things, you can then utilize them in trance. What can have more meaning for any of us than something so familiar as repetitive behavior that helps us organize our daily experience? For example:

> *Claudia, as your mind drifts and dreams, or dreams and drifts, you can imagine, or otherwise contemplate, in your mind, getting ready for work in the morning, and after you rapidly peel that first carrot, you grasp the second carrot, and instead of hastening to peel it, you just* slowly *draw that vegetable peeler down the full length of the carrot.*
>
> *Or perhaps, just to experience something different, you begin at the bottom of the carrot, and* slowly *peel it upward. Can you see that in your mind?*

An imaginal exercise such as this serves to *set up* an age progression to a problematic rumination, which is also a predictable, naturally occurring experience that can be altered. By attending to these behaviors and modifying them in terms of *slowness*, we can *speed up* the therapeutic process. As such, *slower* is indeed *faster*. For this, we often use a portion of "The Road" induction (Gafner & Benson, 2000), which lazily meanders over many aspects of driving.

ALTERNATING STORIES REVISITED

As we mentioned in story construction, we can also use children's stories, or alternating stories, to help reduce resistance to the embedded suggestion. Many of the anxiety disorders, such as the various phobias, or performance anxiety, have high levels of emotional perturbation associated with specific anticipated behaviors. Because the fear creates a stronger avoidance than the need to perform the behavior, resistance to suggestion for change might be higher than usual. Both the innocence of children's stories and the amnesic quality of the second story, help foster the acceptance of suggestions.

TEST ANXIETY

Sarah, a homeopathy student returning to school following a long absence, had test anxiety as well as self-defeating doubts about her own intellectual and academic abilities. She had extensive experience in meditation, skills I (S. B.) built on during hypnosis to help her achieve a deeper trance more rapidly. The following is a portion of a single session in which I incorporated the specific type of information needed for the test (plant and snake remedies), as well as ego-strengthening related to her ability to succeed in school.

> *I'd like to begin with a children's story. Perhaps you already know it. Once there was a circus train, traveling across the country loaded with animals . . . all grouped together in a logical order [grouping in a logical order was one of Sarah's study mnemonics that worked for her] . . . because those animals are* easiest to remember *when they are organized into groups.*

You know, Sarah, all those big crates together, loaded on to the train by similarity *. . . but then further grouped by unique traits, like spots versus stripes, or by color, or by temperament (temperament is a key in homeopathy) . . . and how come we don't ever hear about the snakes? Snakes are very* interesting *[internal focus] and easier to classify and remember than most people realize, if you* pay attention to the key characteristics.

Anyway, this circus train passed by all sorts of flora and fauna on its route to the big show . . . and isn't it remarkable how much sense plants make when you organize them in relation to other things? This train chugged along, moving rather slowly because it had a very big load to carry [Sarah worried about how slow she was in understanding concepts]. Chugging along, making steady progress toward the final destination . . . the big show [her final exam]. On the way, the train encountered a mountain . . .

I like to hike in the mountains. It's so relaxing *and* calming *to immerse myself in nature . . . all the plants and animals, rocks and minerals, that I can notice . . . it's a mental vacation to let my mind just* calmly catalogue *all the details, as I slowly make my way up the mountain.* And you can do it. *Did you know that Albert Einstein occasionally forgot his own phone number? And everyone knows how smart he was! And why can't you not tell yourself "I'm* plenty smart enough, too"?

Albert Einstein wasn't young when he made great discoveries in science . . . and isn't it exciting to know that age has nothing to do with anything at all, like advances, or learning new things? You can just let go into the quiet, calm realization that you are smart, wise, and logical. Putting the pieces together . . . like a jigsaw puzzle you accomplish with ease. That's the way, allowing your unconscious mind to hold a long-term conversation with yourself . . . trusting *and* believing *that part of you that knows you are* more than capable enough.

Staying calm and relaxed and focused. Adding piece by piece to your knowledge. Amazed and aware at how efficient your mind and your memory truly are. . . .

And that little engine, pulling that great big heavy load of a circus train, slowed momentarily as it faced the bottom of the mountain. It was very briefly afraid . . . and then courage and determination took over as the little engine began its ascent . . . "I think I can, I think I can," it said.

Little by little, moving itself forward up the mountain. "I think I can, I think I can." Working hard but believing in itself, that little engine hauled quite a large load up to the mountain peak, and then began the easy ride down the mountain. As the whole train burst in whoops and cheers of delight, the little engine smiled and repeated over and over, "I thought I could, I thought I could." It got the job done, delivering the train to the final destination with pride in its wonderful achievement.

EMBEDDED SUGGESTION

Embedded suggestion is an eminently useful technique in treating anxiety. With embedded suggestion, the client's conscious mind is bypassed when the therapist embeds a suggestion, for example, within a story. To encourage *slowing down*, the therapist relates a story about driving a car, in which the driver alternately speeds up and then *slows down*. To suggest an inward focus, the therapist might embed *in* words, for example, "Going *in*side can be very *in*teresting . . . *in* there where you have your imag*in*ation, fasc*in*ation, *in*tuition. . ." (Gafner & Benson, 2000).

Now, does that mean *any* word that contains *in* conveys an inward focus? Words like indiscriminate, indolent, or inviolate probably do not. Words like *in*toxicating and *in*cessant probably do, while *in*ward and *in*teresting most certainly connote the suggestion.

LETTING GO WITH BALLOONS

We commonly begin treatment of anxiety with a conversational induction and standard deepening technique, such as counting down from ten to one, or asking the client to imaginally descend a staircase one step at a time; down an elevator, one floor at a time; or down an escalator. Permissiveness allows clients to choose their own means of deepening.

I knew a client one time who simply   metaphor
allowed her trance to deepen, in her own
way, and at her own pace. I said to her,
"Marie, beginning now, I'd like you to let   metaphor
your experience deepen, and I don't know
if you'd enjoy going, in your mind, down
a staircase, *one step at a time; down an*
elevator, *starting at the top floor, and*   suggestion covering all
descending to the bottom floor; or maybe   possibilities
going down an escalator. *Or maybe*
there's something else *down which you*
can mentally and progressively descend?
And when you're there, Marie, you will   contingent
know, and I will know, because you'll
find yourself taking one more deep,   suggestion
refreshing breath."

I later asked Marie which means of
descending she had selected, and she let
me know that she appreciated that
minute or two of silence, because during
that time, she came to appreciate, deeply
appreciate, just how relaxed a person can
become. I took that to mean that silence
may lead to deeper experience than some-
thing else, but I often don't look suffi-
ciently into these things.

[The therapist stops speaking for a couple of minutes.]

We often relate the "Balloons" story (see Chapter 14) in the first or second session. The story, in which a person releases balloons into the air, strongly conveys "letting go" without consciously drawing attention to the process. The same thing can be accomplished directly once trance has been induced:

> *Beginning now, Marie, that nervousness and tension, you* *can just* let it go. . . .

Or imaginally:

> *Marie, think of a balloon, maybe a red one, or green one,*

> *I don't know which color you can see in your mind. And now, I'd like you to just* let it go. . . .

Or within a story:

> *. . . she found all those balloons there, in that big net bulging with thousands and thousands of balloons, and she opened up a corner of the net and* let one balloon go, just let it go. . . .

Or more indirectly:

> *Marie was watching a movie, and on the screen was a big net, and straining beneath the net were hundreds of thousands of balloons, and the person in the movie opened up a corner of the net, and out popped a balloon . . . she just* let it go. . . .

Or even more indirectly:

> *Marie saw, in her mind, a person watching a movie, and in the movie a person approached a net. . . .*

When would we want to be more indirect? Our general styles are pretty indirect, but we can be very direct when indicated, for example, reminding people during debriefing about the need to practice self-hypnosis, or writing down a task on a 3" x 5" card as a reminder to the client. In general, the higher the reactance, the more indirect we become.

EXAGGERATING A SYMPTOM WITH METAPHOR

By exagerating a symptom using metaphor, both anxiety and anger can be quickly and effectively diminished. This technique is often our first choice for clients who have a strong sense of self-efficacy (i.e., ego-strengthening is *not* needed), and who are nonreactant, or do not have a comorbid axis I disorder or personality disorder. This technique's potency lies in the juxtaposition of opposites, or the active imaginal experiencing of the symptom contrasted with the absence of the symptom, which is then anchored to a physical cue or reminder. The procedure is explained to the client in pretrance discussion, the dominant or preferred hand is determined, and an agreement is reached on what heretofore will be referred to as "the problem." Pretrance discussion could seed a variety of targets, such as *selecting, image,* or *circle,* followed by induction and deepening.

Now, William, I'd like you to search your mind for something that represents the problem, an image or metaphor for the problem. It can be anything you like, maybe a color, an odor, an image, or anything you like. For example, one person one time selected the sound of a shovel dragging down a sidewalk, and we know what that sounds like. Taking as much time as you like, when you've come up with an image or representation for the problem, *let me know by nodding your head . . . that's the way.*

Now, we'll leave that for a moment and turn to an image or metaphor that represents the absence of the problem, for not having the problem. *Again, it can be anything you like. For example, one person one time imagined a certain color. Now, William, taking as much time as you need, when you've come up with an image for the* absence of the problem, *let me know by nodding your head . . . that's the way . . . , very good.*

Your image that represents the problem, for having the problem, *in a moment I'm going to ask you to exaggerate that image, make it strong, intensify it, magnify it. For example, if it's the color red, I'd like you to see it in your mind in all its brilliance. And while I count to 3 I'd like you to intensify this image that represents the problem . . . now . . . one, two, three . . . and then let it go, that's the way, very good.*

Doing just fine, William. This whole idea of images or metaphors can be rather interesting, maybe even curious. Now, returning to your image for the absence of the problem, for not having the problem, *in a moment I'm going to ask you to magnify or intensify that image. But while you do so, I want you to make a small circle with the thumb and index finger of your right hand. Please slowly make that circle now . . . that's the way . . . and right now I'd like you to magnify, intensify, make strong that image for* not having the problem starting now . . . *one, two, three . . . that's the way, and then let that hand relax again.*

Following realerting, we may discuss which images they selected, and we always remind clients to practice using the circle. As this technique is both interactive and arousing for the client, people never have amnesia for the content. In fact, during the portion in which the problem is mentally exaggerated, many clients will evince shallow breathing, a tensing of muscles, and similar behavior.

PILE OF ROCKS

I (G. G.) first heard the "Pile of Rocks" technique described by Claire Frederick at an American Society for Clinical Hypnosis (ASCH) conference in the early 1990s. We do not know if she ever published this technique, or even if it orginates with her. We have written it down in different versions over the years, and we would encourage you to adapt it to your particular interests and circumstances. The basic idea is that you guide clients up a big pile of rocks, then they pick up a sledgehammer and pulverizes rocks until they are exhausted. Anxiety or anger need not even be mentioned in the exercise. Consider any limitations of your client. If they are in a wheelchair, on oxygen, or perhaps unable to wield a heavy hammer, you need to build this into the imaginal experience. Of course, in setting the agenda, clients know what they are about to experience. Any variety of targets can be seeded beforehand.

> *William, I'd like you to imagine yourself standing in front of a huge pile of rocks . . . they can be any kind of rocks you like . . . and taking as much time as you need, when you can imagine . . . just imagine . . . yourself standing there, let me know by letting your Yes finger rise . . . . That's the way . . . it can be very, very interesting . . . just let it happen . . . very good . . .*
>
> *Now, William, I want you to see yourself, in your mind, walking up that big pile of rocks . . . and I don't know if there's a path going up, a designated route, or some other way that's open to you . . . but I'd like you to go up to the top now, in your own way, taking as much time as you need, and when you're up there at the top, let me know by letting that Yes finger lift one more time.*
>
> *Up there on the top among the rocks you will find a heavy sledgehammer, one that you can pick up with ease . . . and*

also there at your feet is a pair of goggles, you know, those heavy plastic glasses for eye protection, and you can put on those goggles now . . . (pause) . . . and now I'd like you to pick up that sledgehammer and start to break those rocks, pounding hard, with all your strength . . . smashing and pulverizing those rocks until you're exhausted . . . taking as much time as you need. . . and when you're done, let me know by signalling with your Yes finger. . . .

That's the way, noticing, *just noticing how good that feels,* appreciating *what you have just accomplished . . . and I'd like you to know that from now on whenever you feel the need to break those rocks, you can imagine this experience by clenching your fist . . . and I'd like you to show me that clenched fist right now . . . that's the way. . . .*

A FAVORITE STORY

Let us share a story that I (S. B.) call "The Eagle." I use this story for a range of anxiety disorders, both within conventional therapy and with hypnosis. It can help clients focus, and can be used as an adjunct to ego-strengthening. It can also help deepen experience and reinforce unconscious resources. Following the horrible terrorist attacks in the United States on September 11, 2001, I used this story as part of a panic reduction protocol to help clients who were fearful of flying. What's more, in those disconcerting days following September 11, it has helped me focus on the task at hand, and has grounded me in the strength and comfort of a familiar and useful story. Key suggestions are highlighted, and these are given vocal emphasis.

The Eagle

One time there was a young boy, Steve, who dreamed of flying like an eagle. He would watch in awe of the *strength* clearly apparent in the bird's wings, as it could soar for what seemed forever before needing to gently flap once again.

Steve lived in Montana and was used to wide open spaces and he would lie on the grass and watch eagles for hours, as time blurred, and he became lost in his imaginings and day dreams. Eagles were easy to see in Montana, and on some occasions Steve would become absorbed in comparing different eagles he would see, noting the various strengths, or even foibles of this one, or that . . . noting that sometimes an eagle could *seem* to falter for a moment or two, and then would easily right itself and resume the usual flight pattern of gliding and dipping, circling, and watching for landing openings with those keen eyes.

Watching the eagles, those magnificent flying machines, was always a restful, calming way for Steve to pass time. He realized that he had come to associate that peaceful-ness *inside* with the hours spent contemplating just which way a certain bird would take him in his imaginings. Sometimes he would anticipate with such longing the opportunity to go *inside* into his own *inner resources*, that he would watch the eagles on the treetops, and think, "I want that bird to take off right away so I can get there . . . to that *plane of freedom*, that watching a bird in flight can give me. . . ."

It always seemed so tricky to him how those eagles could take off and land from such tight locations . . . on the edge of water, or balancing along a mountain ledge . . . and sometimes he would become afraid that the eagle would make a mistake. Of course, as his experience with eagle watching grew, he realized with certainty that eagles don't make very many mistakes, except perhaps when it came to meals, but that was another issue entirely. And with that, experience and knowledge, Steve grew more and more *secure* that the eagle would have its usual flawless flight.

As an adult, Steve often reflected on his boyhood days of eagle watching. He remembered the *peacefulness*, the inner and outer *calm* he felt, as he vicariously experienced the eagle's strength and flight. He recalled those days when his mind just took off in his own flight, he was *surprised* to *discover* many things about himself from those inner musings, an awareness of all kinds of *inner strength* that was opened to his conscious mind, and simply by being still and absorbing that eagle's flight. His shared joy in the eagle's basic love of flying and skillful execution taught him to open his own wings and discover untapped potential to navigate through his own life, and solve problems as they came up. For that boy, who grew into a man out there on the Montana expanse, the eagle became a personal symbol of *strength* and *ability*. And even today, whenever he sees an eagle, he closes his eyes, regains a sense of inner peace and reminds himself of his own strength, and says, "*I can do it, too.*"

PTSD: AGE REGRESSION, ABREACTION AND REFRAMING

Before examining other treatment options for a complex disorder, we wish to describe a rather straightforward technique that we would recommend as the hypnotic treatment of choice with clients who have suffered a single trauma. Named *age regression, abreaction*, and *reframing* (Hammond, 1990), this technique should be employed only by therapists who have experience in the treatment of trauma. Furthermore, if you have not used either age regression or abreactive techniques within trance, you may require training and supervision with this technique. We delineate this technique at the outset of this discussion, as its use early in treatment may obviate more lengthy procedures. If you have clients who have suffered various traumas over time, this technique may yield little relief. However, if they experienced a single sexual assault, motor vehicle accident, hurricane, wartime experience, or other trauma, we believe this technique may provide both affective relief and cognitive restructuring quickly and economically. Let us illustrate with the case of Bud.

Bud was in his early seventies when he was referred to me (G. G.) to learn relaxation to ease anxiety about his chronic obstructive pulmonary disease. In World War II, Bud's ship was torpedoed in the Pacific Ocean. The ship quickly sank, and he and other sailors clung to floating debris for several hours before they were rescued. During this time, several of his fellow sailors were eaten by sharks. "Does that still bother you, Bud?" I asked him. "Nope," he answered, breathing fitfully, oxygen cannula in his nose. "In fact, my main entertainment since my wife died is the big fish tank I have in my living room. I watch it for hours on end," he explained. "Does anything from the past bother you?" I queried. "Yup, one thing, and I can't get it out of my mind," he noted.

After returning from the war, he married his high school sweetheart. He and his new bride drove separately from the church to the wedding reception three miles away. He stopped to get some beer en route, and when he arrived at the reception, a policeman met him with some bad news: his new wife had just died in an auto accident. That occurred in 1946, and although he had had a successful career selling insurance, he had never remarried. Now, late in life, the incident filled his mind night and day.

Bud responded well to a conversational induction and counting-down deepening. At the second-session finger signals were established, and he was age progressed to "seeing yourself in the future . . . the way you want to feel. . . ." His verbal report emphasized being free of guilt, and immediately I knew the goal of therapy. The same session, "safe" age regressions were done, allowing him to go back in time to "eating breakfast yesterday," and "a good day selling insurance in Ohio in the 1960s."

During the third session I explained that he was to be guided with age regression to the time of the painful incident, and that we were going to "get out all those feelings bottled up in there all these years." He agreed to the plan. Following induction and deepening, he was invited to journey back, in his own way, and at his own pace, to that day in 1946, and to signal with his Yes finger when he arrived. At this point, the therapist's role then becomes highly directive:

> *Tell me, Bud, what do you see, what's going on back there . . . then?*

He recounted details, the dour expression on the policeman's face, how the news "hit me like a ton of bricks right on my chest."

> *Okay, Bud, all those feelings bottled up in there, we want to get them out now, one by one, and leave no stone unturned. If you're ready to proceed, you may signal with your Yes finger.*

He signaled, and then I told him:

> *The guilt, Bud, all those guilty feelings, tell me now about all that guilt. Tell me everything about that guilt. Taking as much time as you need, you will know, and I will know, when you've got out all that guilt, because you'll find your Yes finger lifting again.*

He spoke sadly for several minutes about how he had worn guilt like a cloak, a cloying presence, day and night.

We proceeded this way, first with guilt, which seemed to be the predominant emotion, and continued step-wise with anger, hurt, sadness, and "any other feeling that we may have missed," ratifying sufficient exposure with his Yes finger. He cried, whimpered, gasped, and stopped twice to blow his nose. All this time he remained in trance. Forty-five minutes had passed. I was feeling taxed myself.

The final step was reframing:

> *Bud, you need to know how much strength and courage it takes for a guy to do what you've done today. In fact, looking back on that incident, with the passage of time and your own perspective of maturity and life experience, you can leave the guilt and negative feelings behind you. You don't have to blame yourself. You don't have to punish yourself anymore. You can go on with life, and live that life with a newfound peace of mind. Can you accept what I've just told you? You may answer with one of your fingers. . . .*

Bud answered with his I-don't know/I'm not ready to answer yet finger. I then asked him if he would be willing to consider the same question between now and the next session, and he answered with his Yes finger, a very positive sign.

He returned two weeks later and looked much relieved, as people do when a mantle of guilt has been lifted. In trance this time, he answered Yes when the above question was repeated, and I knew our work was done. Bud lived two more years, and during that time he made no more visits to the mental health clinic.

EXPOSURE AND PTSD

According to the *Diagnostic and Statistical Manual-IV*, acute PTSD becomes chronic after only three months, and most therapists will see more chronic than acute cases. I (G. G.) once saw a World War I veteran who was still bothered by memories of dead bodies in France. He even said he could still taste the mustard gas. That was some 80 years previously! Although that man had subclinical PTSD, his experience in that war surfaced frequently in life-review therapy.

Does the case of Bud underscore the definition of PTSD as unabre-acted emotion? Some of us may point to the relaxation component, the reframing, or perhaps the overall supportive context as key vari-ables. Nevertheless, whatever psychotherapeutic method we use with PTSD, we are probably going to have to *expose* buried feelings—and reframe or restructure dysfunctional thinking—in order to see subjective and objective gains.

Hyer has edited a cogent and authoritative book on treating chronic PTSD, *Trauma Victim* (1994). Based on years of work treating combat PTSD of U.S. veterans, the book makes a clear distinction between cognition and affect, in what he calls schema therapy and symptom therapy. Cognitive therapy, along with exposure therapy, also known as systematic desensitization, flooding, prolonged expo-sure, implosive therapy, or direct therapeutic exposure, have a long and distinguised track record in the treatment of war-related (Keane, 1989) and rape-induced (Foa, Rothbaum, & Riggs, 1991) PTSD. In 1999, Foa and colleagues published their poll of clincians who treat PTSD. This consensus of experts rated cognitive therapy and expo-sure therapy as highly effective anxiety management, whereas hypnosis was rated low, along with psychodynamic therapy and eye movement desensitization and reprocessing (EMDR). Although hypnosis plays an important role in the treatment discussed in *Trauma Victim*, most often it is summarily disregarded as even an adjunct to treatment, as exposure therapies dominate research grants and the literature.

However, all may not be so happy in Exposure Land. Pitman and colleagues (1996) found that exposure techniques may exacerbate depression, panic, and alcohol consumption. Allen and Bloom (1994) found that exposure therapy was contraindicated in clients with marked psychological dysfunction, personality disorder, suicidality, impulsivity, substance abuse, or resistance. Furthermore, Litz and Blake (1990), in their study of prominent behavior therapists who treat PTSD, found that exposure techniques were used in little more than half of their cases.

All of this may be no surprise to those of you whose practices contain many of the types of clients described above. For most of them, age regression, abreaction and reframing, as was done with Bud, may be too much too fast, since they are not eager to reopen old wounds. We may be poised to lance their boil, when a warm compress is all they can tolerate.

Often it is not easy to convince people to participate in any kind of exposure-oriented individual or group therapy, which these days most often means "talking about it." Afterall, they are so accustomed to avoiding and escaping the very target we pursue. Metaphorically, it can help to explain it in terms of a splinter in the skin that periodically festers, and requires minor surgery, a thorough cleaning, and 10 days of antibiotics. Others may show understanding if we explain it in terms of a wound that requires excision and other treatment, but which leaves a small scar as a reminder of what they have endured. Still other people may respond to likening their disorder to mushrooms growing in the dark and requiring the light of day to dry up all those musty old spores.

BEWARE OF THE "GREEN POULTICE"

In the early 1990s, shortly after the Persian Gulf War, I (G. G.) saw a young former soldier, Erasmo, who had recurrent nightmares about a dessicated camel carcass that lay outside his tent in Saudi Arabia. In his dreams, the camel, whose lips were drawn back in a sneer, yelled mocking things at him through clenched teeth. The target symptom of this client was irritable bowel syndrome, which began when the first Iraqui SCUD missle sailed over his head. "It scared the shit out of me," he was quick to report. Trazodone and Zoloft helped contain his symptoms to some extent.

Erasmo declined participation in a therapy group for other Gulf War soldiers. However, he reluctantly agreed to individual therapy, and I offered him EMDR or hypnosis, both of which he rejected. We settled on the following treatment: I would videotape him talking about the worst aspects of his experience, and each time he returned to the clinic, we would view a portion of the tape and discuss it. A few sessions of this lessened his intense affect, anger, and push of speech. He then dropped out of treatment, not because this exposure was adverse, as he showed minimal distress during the sessions, but because he had filed a claim for compensation with the Veterans' Administration.

This "nervous from the service" is equivalent to the "green poultice" of secondary gain in clients with pain: they may not improve if they have a lawsuit pending, or stand to be remunerated in some other way for their symptoms. Erasmo was certainly entitled to such compensation, as he put his life on the line and suffered psychological consequences, while the rest of us watched the abbreviated war on CNN. Practitioners treating PTSD in any setting need to keep an eye out for secondary gain, and if it is there, realize that treatment may need to be supportive instead of active for the time being.

HYPNOSIS AND PTSD TREATMENT

In France in the 1880s, Pierre Janet employed hypnosis as part of a systematic, phase-oriented treatment for what we now call PTSD (Van der Hart, Brown, & Van der Kolk, 1989). Kingsbury (1988) noted that pathological symptoms of PTSD, such as dissociation, are also common phenomena in hypnosis. Because of this natural "fit," he referred to hypnosis as an isomorphic intervention for PTSD. Along the same lines, Spiegel (1997) noted that with the traumatization, clients may be accustomed to experiencing dissociation, amnesia, and emotional numbing. In therapy, these phenomena can then be utilized, linking them to *hypnotic* dissociation, amnesia, and physical numbing as a way to create a safe abreaction and to ratify trance. When in the midst of a flashback, these clients experience time distortion, whose dissociated awareness is akin to age regression. Intrusive re-experiencing of symptoms is similarly akin to attentional absorption, while stimulus sensitivity may be seen as hypnotic suggestibility. Spiegel and Cardena (1990) underscored how PTSD may cause people to have high hypnotic suggestibility, and how hypnosis is useful in restructuring traumatic memories. We often reframe this natural fit to clients by explaining to them that hypnosis might help them because it builds on their "skill," or talent, for "spacing out," or spontaneously going back in time.

At the time of this writing, there has been only one controlled, randomized study involving hypnosis as a treatment for PTSD. In their study, Brom, Kleber, and Defares (1989) showed that hypnosis was equal to anxiety management and psychodynamic therapy, but more effective than waiting-list controls. Numerous authors have described the utility of hypnosis in treating the psychological sequelae of Holocaust survivors (Somer, 1994).

AVOIDANCE OR INDIRECT TECHNIQUES

Many therapists, for example Dolan (1991) and Phillips (1993), employ indirect or metaphorical hypnotic techniques when treating survivors of sexual assault and childhood molestation. Of course, as these techniques are usually tailored to the needs of the individual, they may not lend themselves to standard research protocols. Since 1993, we (Gafner & Benson, 2001) have developed a set of indirect hypnotic techniques for a specialized PTSD population: immigrants who have experienced torture. As a result of civil war in the Central American countries of El Salvador and Guatemala, hundreds of thousands of refugees fled to the United States in the 1980s. Although our indirect techniques were developed on immigrants from Central America, in recent years there has been an influx of refugees from the Balkans and countries in Africa, and we have found these techniques also to be useful with these clients. Many of these people experienced torture and other abuse in their countries of origin, or en route to the United States. As a result, high rates of PTSD are seen in this population (Chester, 1994). I (G. G.) work as a volunteer therapist at the Refugee Clinic of the Department of Family and Community Medicine at the University of Arizona in Tucson. Like many people with PTSD, refugees may decline approach or exposure techniques, but are often amenable to avoidance or indirect strategies. We typically begin treatment with hypnotic ego-strengthening, sometimes in combination with zero balancing, a type of body work provided by a physical therapist. Following several sessions of this combined treatment (Gafner & Edmunds, in press), clients might be amenable to either more directive hypnotic techniques, or active verbal processing. We employ two types of ego-strengthening with this population, metaphorical and "short-burst" ego-strengthening, which are detailed in Chapter 5.

ASSOCIATED HYPNOTIC APPLICATIONS

Sperr and Hyer (1994) note that in their work with combat veterans, a main value of hypnosis is its ability to aid the client in finding a better perspective on some dimension of the trauma experience. In addition, the authors use hypnosis for uncovering coping resources, anxiety reduction, and related applications. Contributors to Hammond's *Handbook of Hypnotic Suggestions and Metaphors* (1990) offer a variety of techniques for victims of sexual assault, childhood sexual abuse, and related problems.

One moderately directive hypnotic technique worth noting is the "smart window" technique. This technique can be employed with any number of variations. Like some of the pain techniques, the "smart window" is used to alter some key aspect of the symptom. In trance, we ask the client to imagine a TV screen on which a traumatic memory is displayed and heard in all its vividness. We might begin by asking the client to imaginally turn down the volume. So, if there are gunshots or screams, the volume of these elements is lessened. With clients who have a good ability for imagery, we might ask them to picture a blank screen, even though they can still hear the gunshots or screams at a diminished volume.

Next, we ask the client to imagine a TV screen with the same image, and mentally to erase that screen and substitute it with a screen of what the client looks like in the present. After juxtaposing these images a few times, we then ask the client to picture a split screen, with half of it containing the target image and half of it showing the client now. The half with the target image then shrinks by one quarter, and that one quarter is filled by the client in the present. Is one half more fuzzy while the other half becomes more vivid? Do you want the client to see a full screen and experience the *content*, but without *affect*? Can *curiosity* be substituted for shock? There are numerous possibilities with this technique. It is essential to use ideomotor signalling throughout for verification, along with an anchor to cue self-hypnosis.

SOMATIC OR AFFECT BRIDGE

In your career, you might reach into your toolbox only a few times for this technique, which is useful when a client presents with a physical sensation, emotion, pain, or other symptom that is of unknown origin. In general, we use this technique sparingly, when there is no hint of secondary gain, and with people who do not have an axis II diagnosis. The technique can be a valuable aid, but it can also lead both you and your client on a fruitless fishing expedition. Watkins (1971) describes the technique, and Hammond (1990) summarizes it.

Manny, a Hispanic man in his fifties, was severely crippled with a type of muscular dystrophy. He walked with Canadian crutches, and was able to drive by using hand controls in his car. He had been divorced for many years, and lived alone in a small town near Tucson. As he said that he served uneventfully as an infantryman in the Vietnam War, I (G. G.) explored his military experience only cursorily. He was referred to the stress management program when I saw him, and he responded well after two sessions. Returning the third session, he said he had been nagged for years by a vague memory of "a little girl on a swing," that entered his mind when he least expected it. "Can we try to get to the bottom of this in hypnosis?" he queried.

Since Manny was seen in the late 1980s, hypnosis in the United States has been plagued by lawsuits and other negative publicity pertaining to "false memory syndrome" (certainly some of it justified), as therapists—often employing hypnosis and age regression techniques—were helping clients to retrieve lost memories of abuse. Many of these clients brought charges against supposed perpetrators, and even without corroborating evidence innocent people were harmed with civil and criminal penalties.

Many clients (Manny included) believe that a memory retrieved during hypnosis is factual and true, and they often are not willing to hear our explanations that such "memories" might be fantasy or distortion. With Manny, trance was induced, and he signalled Yes that he wanted to pursue exploration of the "little girl on a swing." First, he was age regressed to the time when he had recently had the thought:

THERAPIST	PROCESS	EDDIE
"Tell me the day and time where you are in your mind now, Manny."		
		"In a dream last night."
"Think hard on that picture in your mind. Magnify it . . . that's the way."	intensify	
		"She's there on the swing."
"Tell me what you see now."		
"Good, make it even stronger. That's all there is in the world, a little girl on the swing."	intensify further	
	disorient	
"Manny, listen very closely. You are beginning		

to feel very confused,
'disorientated,' everything
is blurry and fading away,
más que la chingada, and   (words typically
all you can experience is   used by
the little girl on the swing.   Erasmo)
Signal with your Yes finger
when everything else has
faded away . . . that's the
way. . . ."

He was then age regressed to the time the memory first occurred:

> *. . . going back in time . . . you're becoming younger and*
> *younger . . . , and when you've arrived at the source, at the*
> *origin of this memory, you may let your Yes finger lift one*
> *more time . . . .*

Manny then started to sob. He told about being out on a night patrol in Vietnam, when the others in his platoon were killed and he was taken prisoner. After a few days he escaped, and rejoined his unit. I was quite surprised by this sudden recollection, and I offered a reframe, which in retrospect was rather feeble. He was distraught when he left the office.

He returned two weeks later and announced that the "little girl on a swing" had disappeared from his dreams. "It's a relief to me to finally get to the bottom of it," he conceded. He was offered a referral to the PTSD team, but he declined. He said that he had "self-relax-ation down pat," and I never heard from him again.

In the intervening years, I have often thought about Manny. I wonder if his recollection was based in reality, and I still do not know what "the little girl on a swing" had to do with the traumatic memory. However, all that does not matter. Evidently, his therapeutic goal was realized.

AUTOMATIC WRITING OR DRAWING

This is another tool that is useful for unconscious exploration. A moderate-to-deep trance is preferred for this technique. To start, explain to the client what you will be doing today, then place a pen and writing pad on his or her lap. Once trance is induced, you provide step-by-step instructions, keeping in mind the concreteness of trance and the need for specificity:

> *Erasmo, with that right hand, I'd like you now to pick up that pen. . . .*

Proceed with permissive, unconsciously directed questions that allow processing. For example:

> *Erasmo, I'd like your unconscious mind to drift and dream, and as it does so, that right hand can move all by itself, independent of the rest of you, and you can write/draw* anything at all *that might have something to do with the problem. . . .*

After realerting, the material is examined and processed consciously. Two or three sessions of such exploration might yield substantive material. Or, it might result in a useless fishing expedition. If useful data does not result after a few tries, we would not recommend spending any more time on this technique, however fascinating it might be.

Matt Weyer employs a version of this technique in which he asks the client to imagine a chalk board and a piece of chalk. The piece of chalk then begins to move, all by itself, writing or drawing whatever surfaces from the client's unconscious. As there is no paper record, it is necessary to seek periodic verbal reports from the client in order to "read" what is on the chalk board.

CLINICAL COMMENTS

In this chapter, we strived to demonstrate some of the myriad possibilities for applying hypnosis to the treatment of anxiety disorders. Some times these techniques alone will be sufficient to promote affective relief and cognitive restructuring. More often, they will need to be supplemented with conventional therapy, such as CBT. With PTSD, the therapist might need to "build up" with ego-strengthening and other indirect techniques before proceeding to direct exposure.

17

Depression

THE BUGLER'S CALL

Yapko's calculating perspective on many topics, including depression, often compels us to suspend judgment and shift our thinking outside of the conventional box. Yapko (2001) reminds us that in 1999, the World Health Organization (WHO) issued a call to arms regarding depression. According to WHO, depression is the fourth most debilitating condition, ranked behind heart disease, cancer, and motor vehicle accidents. Lest we rush off to battle too quickly, Yapko asks a penetrating question: How can the rates of depression keep rising in the United States, for example, when we spend billions of dollars on antidepressant medications? Clearly, the answer is *not* more drugs.

An additional vantage point comes from the pen of Araoz in his forward to Yapko's *Treating Depression with Hypnosis: Integrating Cognitive-Behavioral and Strategic Methods* (2001). Araoz, a cogent voice in the hypnosis literature for more than 40 years, mentions that one of the recognized risk factors for depression is economic deprivation. He wonders, then, how there can be so many depressed people in an affluent nation like the United States. Along the same lines, he asks why greed, instant gratification, and materialism are not also considered risk factors.

BACKGROUND

We recognize that *depression* can mean many things, just as the word *hypnosis* connotes different possibilities, depending on its operative use and the context in which it is employed. For its use in this chapter, we refer to *depression* as meaning *major depression*, but recognize that the treatment of this disorder can also be generalized to include such clinical problems as dysthymia, adjustment disorder with depression, depressed mood secondary to PTSD, and many other disorders. Yapko (2001) summarizes what the literature currently tells us about depression: the social, economic, and physical costs of depression are astronomical; special interests such as pharmaceutical companies influence decision makers like the National Institute of Mental Health (NIMH) to increase drug therapy for the "disease of depression"; social transmission rather than genetic transmission controls the proliferation of depression; depression has many contributing factors, not one single cause; depression has numerous underlying risk factors and comorbid conditions associated with it; depression can generally be managed with medication, psychotherapy, or both; depressed people generally fare better in psychotherapy than they do in drug treatment—they feel better, have lower relapse rates, and function at a higher level; and no one antidepressant is superior to another, while some psychotherapies—of cognitive, behavioral, and interpersonal approaches—outperform others in treating depression.

Yapko (2001) also cites consensus guidelines for treating depression, which include the recommendation that treatment be an *active* process with *active* exchanges between therapist and client, psychoeducation, skill-building strategies, and homework assignments. Therapy should not only focus on problem solving, but the teaching of problem-solving *skills* as well. Therapy should be *process driven*, for example, correcting negative or erroneous interpretations, rather than *event driven*. Finally, therapy with an historical focus is of no use, as looking for the *cause* of the disorder is time poorly spent.

ART VERSUS SCIENCE REVISITED

We have striven to champion hypnosis and hypnotic techniques in this book as eminently useful *adjuncts* to other treatments for many disorders. As with anxiety disorders, hypnosis is not included among empirically supported or "evidence-based" treatments for depression. These approved methodologies are purely technique driven, and therefore ignore the vital interpersonal and contextual variables inherent in all psychological treatments. Such approved techniques imply that a set of techniques can be applied to *all* clients in *any* situation. That would be like saying that *any* embedded-meaning hypnotic induction, or *any* story about balloons, would be appropriate for *all* clients who need to experience letting go. Clearly, any rigidly structured or ritualized set of techniques needs to be adapted to the unique needs of the individual.

Let's set depression and cognitive-behavioral therapy (CBT) aside for a moment and take a wide-angle look at psychotherapy and outcome. O'Neill (2002) cited the work of psychologist Michael Lambert, who has examined outcome variance from psychotherapy: the *how* and *why* therapy works. According to Lambert, the first and largest variance in outcome, *40 percent*, can be attributed to factors *outside the therapy itself*. These contextual variables include neighborhood and family, peer, social, workplace, and spiritual supports; client variables such as intelligence, motivation, and resilience; the number and severity of symptoms; capacity to relate, etc. *Thirty percent* of outcome variance comes from the *therapeutic relationship*, which includes such things as warmth, empathy, acceptance, and encouragement. Only *15 percent* of outcome variance is attributed to *therapy techniques*.

So, maybe Yapko (2001) is right when he says that we should be studying therapists instead of techniques, as important client variables may be beyond the scope of study. Nevertheless, our current reality is that "approved" CBT techniques are the gold standard. To be sure, they should play an important role in treatment; however, other techniques need to be employed, especially when we consider clients with axis II disorders and comorbid disorders, those people who are systematically excluded from research protocols. The addition of hypnosis to a treatment regimen can have many benefits, including the addressing of anxiety reduction early in therapy, and fostering rapport, essential to all successful treatment.

STRATEGIES FOR CHANGE

We speak often to other clinicians about articles they have read or written, as well as books they may have perused. It seems that many who have read Yapko's *Hypnosis and the Treatment of Depressions: Strategies for Change* (1992), take diverse learning from the book. Some appreciate the book's breadth, in that the author draws upon social psychology, CBT, hypnosis, and other areas for the background and development of treatment. As such, Yapko seems to be both a scientist as well as an artist. Others comment on Yapko's specificity and clarity in explaining stages of treatment, and still others say that they like his ability to logically integrate key concepts and principles in ways that are useful to clinicians in their practices. We certainly agree with those opinions; however, we found Yapko's subsequent book, *Treating Depression with Hypnosis*, even richer, as it further explicates key concepts, and makes greater use of clinical vignettes.

MAKING CHOICES

We all might experience clinical depression at some point in our lives. People with depression are not sick. Instead, they are *stuck*. Rather than pathology, we see *rigidity*. Instead of fluidity and move-ment, we see *catalepsy*, that inexorable suspension of movement—psychologically, behaviorally, socially, and sometimes even physiologically *cataleptic*. Often, with so many disorders, the initial therapeutic job is to perturb *what is*. With depressed clients, we need to perturb that stasis that is represented by catalepsy early on. We counter that rigidity by encouraging *flexibility*. And a good place to begin is by talking about choices.

In his workshops, Yapko demonstrates a conversational induction, in which he begins to zero in on *frame of reference*. He builds a momentum of responsiveness, and he casually mentions naturally occurring events regarding *choice*. He demonstrates this metaphorically, for example, mentioning a quote by the actress, Lily Tomlin: "I always wanted to be someone, but now I see I should have been more specific." He might talk about a man buying a car:

> *The man innocently asks the auto salesperson, "What's the best car to buy?" And the salesperson, orienting the man toward a* frame of reference, *asks him, "Best for what?" But the man does not know how to answer. The adroit salesperson turns to the man's wife and says to her, "Madam, I had another couple in here just the other day, and they wondered what's the best car to buy, and I told them, 'You can buy a car for looks, comfort, endurance, speed, carrying capacity, resale—for many things,' and then they understood." Just then, the man comes to life and interjects, "I want one with the best blind spot. That's always been my problem: the blind spot." The salesperson answers, "We're finally getting somewhere, I have some right over here I can show you. . . ."*

You could also talk about someone else who *decided* to come to therapy, and after the first session stopped at the grocery store and *chose* certain fruits and vegetables for dinner that evening. Countless are the ways you can begin to lay the foundation. Whether subsequent sessions concern negative thoughts, behavioral activation, or any other target, *decide* and *choose* will be key words.

In a follow-up session, Yapko begins to actively explore *options* via age progression during which plausible options are identified, each option's consequences are explored, and action steps are identified. Action is associated to context and reinforced with a post-hypnotic suggestion. This approach is cognitive, behavioral, metaphorical, and above all, very hypnotic. Is it easy? Are any of our clients really *easy*? Of course not. But it is step-wise, elegant, eminently understandable, and it makes sense. We do not endorse everything Yapko advocates, but we certainly integrate a lot of his work into our everyday practices.

BEGINNING TO DANCE

In the first session, it is important for the therapist to initiate what we call "the dance," where there is a back-and-forth communication between therapist and client. The therapist offers hypnotic patter and suggestions, and the client responds with relaxation and slowing down. The therapist continues matching, or pacing, the client's response, and then leads in the desired direction. This ongoing communication is the essence of hypnosis.

I (S. B.) am seeing a very depressed 40-year-old graphic artist named Colin. He was started on Celexa but continues to have poor sleep. In addition to a retarded presentation, he is very ruminative. The first session I matched his cataleptic posture with the arm catalepsy induction, and he responded with deep trance, though he found his constant rumination a bit distracting. The second session, I followed with another arm catalepsy induction, as he responded well to it the first time, even though his eyes remained open.

> S. B.: Colin, the main thing about hypnosis is feeling comfortable, and that arm of yours that was floating in the air, and is now resting comfortably on your lap, heaviness and comfort can spread out from your arm, slowing down your mind, and slowing down you body, and as you sit back, you can let those eyes gently close if they wish . . .
>
> [Colin's eyes remain open.]
>
> S. B.: . . . or you can let those eyes stay open . . . and I see that those eyes appear to have settled on some spot out there, perhaps just the right spot that you can become absorbed in, that's the way. . . .
>
> [Colin's eyes shift from one spot to another.]
>
> Colin: I'm sorry, I just can't get into this today.
>
> S. B.: Lots of stuff on your mind?
>
> Colin: It's always racing. I'm thinking about what I have to get done later today. It just doesn't make any sense.
>
> S. B.: You're doing just fine. Just let whatever is happening continue to happen, and as those busy thoughts occur, seemingly with a life of their own, you can take two deep, refreshing breaths . . . that's the way . . . because I wonder, just wonder, how those two pleasant breaths can begin to slow down your body, while at the same time, your mind can begin to race slower than previously, perhaps slowing its pace each time you exhale, or otherwise altering its familiar rate in some other curious fashion. Colin, Dr. Hall once told me that rumination is actually a housing construct, hallways leading to rooms, and people in an active household often run from room to room, and all that running can lead

to fatigue, *or else they just become absorbed in one of those rooms, maybe the ante room, or mentally arrested by the sitting room, though some become immersed in all the hallways, or maybe the light fixtures . . . .*

[Colin's eyes close.]

S. B.: It can be very pleasant to go inside. . . .

[His leg twitches, and he moves around in his chair.]

S. B.: . . . and you can do anything you need to in order to let your experience deepen. . . .

Now, some would continue pacing and leading, as it appears that Colin is finally starting to let go. Instead, I realert him and see what's on his mind.

S. B.: Okay, Colin, I'm going to count from one to five, and when I reach five, you can tell me what you're thinking about. 1-2-3-4 and 5, please open your eyes now.

Colin: I'm just kind of blank. Not really thinking about anything.

S. B.: Very good. We like blank. You may let those eyes close one more time. I'm going to tell you a story about Escher, but first, let me say something about cats. *As an artist, no doubt you have drawn many things, animals,* cats, *and dogs perhaps, maybe drawing them very* slowly *at times, even* slowing *to a halt as that pen was poised, thinking what might come next.*

Well, Colin, in psychology we have a term for what you've been experiencing with your depression. It's called catalepsy, *where things are just* slowed *down—your body, your life, though not your mind—and I know none of that can be very pleasant. One man one time described his catalepsy this way: "My body feels so heavy and it takes a supreme effort to get anything done," he said. A woman one time told me, "Sonja, I feel like I'm stuck in quicksand and there's a thick fog all around me."*

Well, with treatment, both of them moved on to better things. His depression improved, and he ended up moving to the other side of the valley, and she got better, changing her exercise routine from running on a treadmill to walking and aerobics. Both of them noticed and appreciated, in their

minds, as well as in their bodies, how movement allowed
catalepsy to eventually fade into the background, though he
still wonders if cats sleep more than dogs.

[A pause.]

S. B.: How are you doing?

Colin: Thinking about animals.

S. B.: Good. But now I have another story. Before we
begin, I'd like you to take one more deep, refreshing breath
. . . very good. . . .

The Escher Story

Have you ever noticed how sometimes the most ordinary, mundane, or even boring things can just draw your
attention to them, absorbing you in some small detail, or
perhaps you begin to notice something else in a new way
that your eyes, or your mind, just glossed over previously?

Well, Ingrid from Duluth, Minnesota, had just such an
experience when she traveled to another city for an art
exhibit. Now Ingrid, coming from fine Scandinavian stock,
tended to be very practical and didn't spend much time
daydreaming, or wondering all the time about things like
hands, yes, hands.

"Your hands are for working," she was fond of saying.
Well, you can imagine, just imagine, how amazed Ingrid
was when she unexpectedly stumbled upon an exhibit by
the Dutch artist, M. C. Escher. The first thing she noticed
was a picture of a hand drawing another hand in kind of a
circular fashion. It wasn't clear where one hand left off,
and the other hand began. Curious, she moved closer and
looked hard at that picture. It was so interesting how the
picture showed one hand curved over the top part with just
a bit of a sleeve or cuff showing there at the wrist, and right
where you might expect an arm, there was a pencil
attached to another hand curved around the bottom part,
and at the wrist of that hand was another pencil making
that drawing.

She just looked and wondered, becoming totally
entranced in an infinite circle of movement, in those hands
out there, drawing each other. Eventually, she was able to

tear her body, if not her mind, away from that picture, as she wandered over to another drawing of stairs, yes, stairs. Ingrid was intrigued to notice how those stairs out there seemed to go both up and down at the same time. "Playing tricks on my eyes," Ingrid thought to herself, as her mind first saw the movement of the stairs in the upward direction, and then, with a blink, her mind reversed itself, seeing the movement going down.

"Well, it's just not clear to me how far those stairs would go . . . either up, or down . . . they just seem to keep going," she pondered to herself. She wondered and imagined just what those stairs got up . . . to . . . somewhere out there, past the edges of the drawing, and then she got lost in just how far down deep into somewhere else they could go.

After he was realerted, Colin reported that his left hand felt detached from his arm. He responded very favorably during five sessions of hypnosis and CBT. His mood brightened considerably and he was much less ruminative. "Maybe the medication is starting to work," he reported. Perhaps it was. Concerning the hypnotic part of his treatment, building on his successful arm catalepsy was pivotal, as was realerting him at a critical juncture, since this both deepened and ratified his trance, and allowed me to verify absorption and diminished rumination.

BACK AT THE DANCE

Contrast this "dance" with a standardized induction (the kind that is read to a client for a hypnotizability test), or with another type of induction that is read to the client. Reading the latter type induction, which hopefully is general and permissive in suggesting many ways of responding, the client will often show a good response. However, reading something causes you to miss vital, ongoing responses. So, what is to be done?

We recommend *reading* an induction, or a story, when you begin to practice hypnosis, and encourage you to "take the training wheels off the bicycle" once you can ad lib your hypnotic patter. Afterall, prepared inductions, like the ones in our earlier book (Gafner & Benson, 2000) or similar guides, contain the recipe's most crucial ingredients: hypnotic language and suggestions that lead to trance. We wrote *Handbook of Hypnotic Inductions* to provide a place from which *to start*, and to show some of the myriad possibilities to induce trance.

The same with the deepening. Like the induction, it is merely an artifice. For teaching purposes, we construe a session of hypnosis to have three fairly distinct parts: induction, deepening, and therapy component. For many therapists, these components are either nonexistent or unidentifiable, blurred, or somehow blended together. What you eventually want to get to is the ongoing communication between you and the client. What did John Travolta do in those movies? He *danced*. What did Fred Astaire and Ginger Rogers do together? They danced marvelously together.

That said, we have one caveat. We continue to read confusional inductions or elaborate stories, as we want to be sure we get them right.

REFRAMING

A phase-oriented treatment, especially in the treatment of depression, may be hastened through ample use of reframing. We all have read elegant uses of this technique, whether by Haley (1973), Watzlawick, Weakland, and Fisch (1974), or by other faculty from the early days of Palo Alto's Mental Research Institute. Many of us, early in our education and training, learned the value of putting a positive connotation on problematic behavior. Reframing and its mechanism still seems almost magical, as client's see things differently following such a reconceptualization. This new perspective, often incorporated by clients outside of their awareness, can have a sudden and dramatic effect on the therapy process.

The anthropologist Gregory Bateson was the first to use the term "frame." After Bateson's use of the term in 1955, therapists soon put it to practice. Robbins and colleagues (1996), in their study of therapist effect on family roles, showed that positive responses were most likely to be elicited from delinquent adolescents following a reframe. Shoham-Salomon and colleagues (1989), in their study of paradoxical directives, claimed that reframing may be the most healing technique in psychotherapy. But most reframes in therapy do not occur within a paradoxical paradigm. Therapists might employ them at the beginning, or end, of a session, when they "frame" ambivalence about therapy as courage. Indeed, virtually any problem can be successfully reframed. A daughter's *acting out* can be reframed as *scared* or *frightened*, just as her *stubborn* behavior can be reframed as *determined* (Eckstein, 1997).

The raw material we need for reframes will often be supplied by the client within the first few minutes of the initial session. We listen closely to a client's words, as these words reveal *values*, such as *strength, honesty, sensitivity, caring, commitment, loyalty, duty, courage,* and *protectiveness*. An effective reframe not only connects with the client, and shows understanding, but it may also neutralize negativity, as well as inject needed hope into a seemingly hopeless situation. We believe that an effective reframe to a person in distress is a true unconscious communication, and is every bit as potent as a deftly delivered suggestion in deep trance.

We are meeting for the first time with a client who has retarded depression. We match his catalepsy in the ways discussed above, and we try to end on a strong note, with an apt reframe. We tell him it takes *courage* to walk through that door, that, by *committing* himself to a course of change, he must *care* a lot about himself and his family. He perks up a bit, and then we deliver the coup de grace reframe: "You must have an extreme *sensitivity* to the world around you." And he replies, "You're just blowing smoke up my ass." I (G. G.) have had that happen more than once, and I am always crushed, but I keep working on my reframes. Seven or eight out of ten usually hit the mark, and that is a pretty good batting average.

John Wax (personal communication, April 23, 1979) demonstrated the versatility of reframing in diverse situations. For example, a depressed woman and her cheerful husband come to therapy. They show little distress or insight into a dysfunctional relationship, which they term a *communication problem*. The therapist then reframes their experience as a *matter of survival*, or the *life or death of the relationship*. Such a reframe might perturb the process, thereby giving the therapist more emotional content to work with. Conversely, a couple who sees their problem as a *dire dillema* may have their perspective reframed *down* the affective ladder, by labeling the problem as a matter of *semantics, priorities,* or even *communication deficit*. Of course, reframing takes practice, and sometimes we err. When we do, clients let us know immediately through their nonverbals. However, an effective reframe will "fit" and be appreciated, even by people who are accustomed to politicians and others who "put a positive spin" on a problem.

Many depression cases will have a strong relational component, and indeed, with any disorder, we need to emphasize the social context. Much discussion of reframing occurs in the family therapy literature, which typically examines the technique in relation to marital interaction. A couple who claims, "We haven't had sex in months, and all we do is fight," may have their view reframed as, "Your constant arguing may in fact be a misguided effort to get close. Have you ever thought of that?" Such a reframe, especially when reinforced with a follow-up question, makes a *suggestion* in the absence of an explicit directive, as it *encourages* the couple to perceive, identify, and label critical events differently (Coyne, 1985).

NEGATIVE REFRAME

A *negative* reframe, when used judiciously, can serve to motivate. Let's say we are seeing another depressed man, the husband of a substance abuser. As this man seems to revel in his *patient* response, he might experience his *patience* perturbed when it is reframed as *enabling*. Similarly, some clients might become motivated if their *lack of involvement*, or *passivity*, is reframed as *weakness*, or *not caring*.

If we are working with a couple and one partner maintains an angry posture, we might say, "Velma, just remember: You can't hug a porcupine." For an unassertive person who has difficulty setting limits, we might say, "Phillip, Mussolini made the trains run on time." For a person who resists attempts to reign in her self-defeating rumi-nations, we might say, "Priscilla, have you ever heard of sexual compulsion? Well, what you're doing is very reminiscent of mental masturbation." Such negative reframes are often employed after other measures have failed. Of course, they should always be used carefully and respectfully.

REFRAMING WITH DEPRESSED CLIENTS

We have all had clients who come in wearing a satisfied grin and say, "The doctor told me I have a chemical balance. That's why I'm depressed!" A useful reframe in this situation is to talk about the social versus the genetic transmission of the disorder, and how economic factors and stress can precipitate and maintain depression.

Some reframes are more effective than others. A few years back, I (G. G.) worked with Charmaine, whose career in the Air Force had been interrupted when she was sexually assaulted. Although she had largely worked through this trauma in previous therapy, recent stressors brought her back to treatment. Charmaine constantly told herself, "I'm no good." After six sessions, which included metaphorical ego-strengthening in trance and CBT out of trance, she remained very depressed. Let's look at some possible reframes of "I'm no good."

Weak reframe:	At least you're giving yourself *some* feedback. That's more than most people do.
Strong reframe:	Such internal dialogue demonstrates *movement*, although its direction remains uncertain at this point.
Stronger reframe:	You show a definite *consistency* in your *self*-talk, and such *consistency* can lead to responsible *self*-care.

COUNTERING NEGATIVE SELF-TALK

In hypnosis, we mentioned the importance of *repetition*: If it's important, repeat it. Well, the same thing happens, in the wrong direction when people silently tell themselves negative things, over and over, all day long. This negative self-hypnosis is vigorous and influential, and must be countered with something potent. Teaching clients self-hypnosis, which is positive, and getting them to practice it, puts clients in charge of changing the problem. An analogy I (S. B.) use involves driving on snowy and icy roads. The car gets stuck and the wheels spin. You open up the trunk and reach in for that handy box of gravel or salt, which enables you to get back on the road. But once on the road, *you still have to drive the car because it won't steer itself.*

Sometimes we might be at a loss for a reframe. The client's dysphoria and overall unfortunate circumstances makes us feel overwhelmed. A psychologist we know once said that the therapist's job of having to receive negative affect all day long makes him feel like the waste hole in a recreation vehicle park.

However, you can never be wrong if you reframe the client's presumed *intent* behind the behavior. In other words, behind Charmaine's stuckness is an obvious intent and willingness to get better, and that's what we aim for:

> *Charmaine, with all the sadness and loss you've faced in recent months, as well as earlier in life, I admire the* strength *and* drive *you continue to show in order to feel better.*

A corollary to many clients' negative self-talk is the core belief that they cannot change. One thing that I noticed from the first session was her frequent use of the word *care*, which I utilized whenever possible. She often mentioned *caring deeply* about her husband, her dog, Buster, and her parents, whom she lost three months ago in a traffic accident. After examining Charmaine's log that she kept for two weeks, we turned to the trancework portion, and in it she was offered two little stories in succession.

Making Change I

Now, Charmaine, I don't know if you've had much experience *caring* for babies of the human variety, and there's no doubt that taking care of puppies can be hard work, but it's *inter*esting to note how much effort is involved in caring for a small child as she *changes* and grows. Let me tell you about little Mary Grace, a very happy baby whose eyes draw you into their very depths. Now, they say eyes are the windows to the soul, and sometimes they are transparent, filmy fabric covering, and sometimes black-out drapes , but that's neither here nor there. Now, even happy babies like Mary Grace have to be *changed* regularly in an average day of caring for them. There are the many diapers and bibs, and let's not forget the number of outfits they can go through. An unhappy baby may require even greater challenges and creativity in the area of caregiving. For example, you may need to *alter the environment* in some way, like going to a different room, or rotating through new toys.

If you *care* to, you can also make *modifications preventively*, so the emotional upset doesn't actually arise, like going for a walk, or speaking in a soothing voice when the first glimpses of unhappiness peek through. *Caregivers* often *modulate* their voices to connect in a different way, with emotion and interest, as much of the communication occurs on a nonverbal basis with babies. Your voice gives messages of love and care on so many levels, internally and on the outside as well. And, at the end of the day, all the caring doesn't go unrewarded, as the day *shifts* into night, you can feel very satisfied with the efforts put forth, helping that little person grow and move toward becoming the very best she can be.

Making Change II

This story took place in Venice, Florida, a little island town with drawbridges and wild parrots nesting in the tall trees. Down below, on a quiet street, two children had a lemonade stand. They were Penny Devereaux and Nick El Dorado, and they talked about quarter horses and sand dollars as they waited for their next customer. Nick yawned, as he was tired from the cold medicine his mother had given him. He couldn't remember if it was Dimetap, or some other brand, but that really didn't matter. He yawned again, listening to the chatter of crows in the distance.

A man approached. "Gimme three glasses of that cold stuff, small change," he demanded, as he handed Nick El Dorado a twenty-dollar bill. Nick struggled with the bills and coins, and finally Penny stepped in to help. The man drank two glasses and left with one.

"I just can't make change," complained Nick. "I bet you can," answered Penny. "It just takes practice," she added. "Why can't we just swipe a credit card like every place else, and be done with it quick?" "You mean steal a card?" asked Penny. "No, like slide it through a machine," said Nick. "Well, we're not set up for that. We're just a small-time operation," said Penny.

All day long, and into the next, Penny and Nick practiced. They set out all the coins in rows, and paper money in stacks, and right before noon of the second day, they had something to show for their concentration and effort.

Charmaine continued to make slow progress. During a trancework portion of a subsequent session, synonyms for *change* were interspersed following *caring* in an induction that involved travel (Gafner & Benson, 2001).

Travel Induction

One day I was flying on American Airlines, and I don't know if it was a matter of becoming fascinated by or *absorbed in* what was going on during the descent of that airplane. At any rate, I'll never forget that day (*caring: altering or varying?*).

As that airliner began its descent into Dallas-Fort Worth, I thought about being down on the ground, and during those moments time can seem to *speed up* or *slow down*, or maybe you just lose track of time altogether, I don't know. They had just announced that it was time to put on your seatbelt and put up the tray table, but I kept my tray table down anyway, even though the person next to me promptly raised his tray table and put away the book he was reading (She thought, "*Caring deeply,* can it be *moderated* or *modulated?*")

I continued studying a road map, *out there* on the tray table, examining details of my final destination *down there* on the ground. I thought briefly of putting on my seatbelt, but I didn't do that until much later, long after everyone else had done so. It was very interesting to notice just then that my hand had fallen asleep *out there*, off to the side, on the armrest. The numbness had already spread up my arm, but I soon turned my attention to other things (She wondered, " With *caring:* where can there be a *shift?*")

We were now below 30,000 feet and as I looked *out there* from *inside*, things down there became clearer the lower we got. I adjusted the map with my one useful hand, as the other one was so numb, and then the flight attendant—her voice seemed to drift in and then drift out—began to announce connecting gate information: "Abilene, gate 36; Albuquerque, gate 41; Amarillo, gate 37 . . ." and I thought, "I'm going to Sacramento, so I've got lots of time before she gets to the S's." At that point I just tuned her out as she continued with Austin and Bakersfield and all the other city names in alphabetical order (She contemplated, "Can *caring* contain *transformation?*")

The passenger in the next seat saw what I was doing and he said, "Don't worry. *There's nothing to know and you don't have to do anything either,*" and I still wonder what he meant by that, but at that moment I just drifted off a bit more, into the map in front of me, as the plane continued its descent.

Looking at any map it can be difficult at first to orient yourself among the tangle of colored lines going in every direction. The rivers are blue lines, and the state roads are one thing, and the interstate highways are something else. The broken lines show the county lines, and there appeared to be all solid lines between the states, but on any map it's all too easy to *rapidly drift from one state to another*. A person gets a different point of view, descending in a plane, or studying a map, just being *detached* from it all, kind of like children—and they all do this sooner or later—who bend over and look at the world from between their legs. I would get light-headed if I did that now, and I still remember being in that classroom years before, holding my hand in the air *for the longest time*, but I can't recall if that was my numb hand or the other one.

I turned back to the voice overhead and she had only gotten to the C's: Carlsbad, gate 35; Colorado Springs, gate 40 . . . and the man next to me—the voice was in a tunnel far away—said, "*You don't even have to listen,*" and I immediately returned to my map. Turkey Hollow was a strange name, but no more unusual than Deep Hollow. Both places you'd probably miss if you blinked or just closed your eyes going by. *In*spiration Point reminded me of breathing, or maybe imagi*na*tion, I don't know, but *Explore*rs' Post just seemed like something remote. Wilderness *Re*treat *lacks* something as far as names go, and *In*skeep Corners just sounded like something very remote, perhaps a good place to spend some time. *Slow*poke Ridge probably overlooked a small canyon or ravine down there, and just then the voice overhead announced San Jose, gate 29. I finally put up my tray table and buckled the seat belt with the one hand available to me. Things on the ground were rapidly coming into focus, and the man in the next seat was sitting back, eyes closed. I knew it was time to begin counting silently to myself, down from ten to one. I felt very, very comfortable as the descent continued (And she imagined, "*caring* can involve turning over")

Charmaine continued to make progress, then took a couple of steps backward. Heretofore she had denied a relational problem with her husband. However, one session she noted, "My husband is getting impatient with my depression." I asked her to bring him along next time. Her husband of 20 years seemed generally supportive, though a bit avoidant. When pressed about their sex life, both admitted that they feared initiating sex. "Everything would at least be tolerable if we could enjoy each other in bed on occasion," he said.

By the time he returned with her next time, I had a story that I asked them to listen to. This story, called "Omelettes," was provided by Jim Gilchrist, an intern who was a student of Milton Erickon's stories.

Omelettes

I once had a friend named Bob, who had lived in many parts of the United States. He was a man of considerable *depth*, perhaps due to his *diversity* of experience, having lived in Texas, Maine, California, and two different times in the *deep* South. Bob considered himself to be a very good cook, and one of the things he specialized in was *omelettes*. His wife, Eleanore, had a fond appreciation for Bob's omelettes, and she liked them just the way he made them. "Don't change a thing," she told her husband. "Variation is good in some things, but not when it comes to your *omelettes*."

Bob took special care to ensure that the outcome would be just right. He would go into the kitchen and choose a bowl that was precisely the proper size, and he had a pan he used exclusively for *omelettes*. He knew the ingredients his wife liked best, but sometimes Eleanor would become playful and adventurous, saying, "Let's *experiment* this time." Bob felt like saying, "But you said I shouldn't change a thing." However, he kept this thought to himself, smiling inwardly, but perhaps outwardly, too, as he had a hard time hiding things from his wife.

He got out the cheese, sometimes three different varieties of cheese, and carefully cut it into tiny cubes. Bob always purchased a particular brand of aged cheddar and Monterey Jack from the delicatessen. He wouldn't even consider one of those flavorless processed cheeses. As he got out the ham, Eleanor would gently nudge him away from the cutting board, and slice the ham a bit differently. "A most interesting variation," Bob would comment. "I thought you'd be intrigued by those delicate little slivers," she responded.

Next, Bob selected a tomato of just the right texture and color. "Red, but not too red," he instructed his wife. "Firm, but not too firm," she instructed in return, a mock professorial seriousness through pouted lips. They continued this way, with the green peppers, mushrooms, and especially the eggs.

Each time they prepared *omelettes*, but *not* when they prepared other dishes, they judiciously selected a place to dine. Sometimes in the living room, either on the couch or carpet, and sometimes even in the bedroom, though if they did it in the dining room they were closer to the kitchen. When they first married, they had *omelettes* any time of the day or night. Of course, when they were at work, they were forced to be sustained by the *mere thought* of *omelettes*, at least until the end of the day. One time, they even met during the lunch hour and prepared an *omelette*. Bob was able to buy only one kind of cheese that time, but Eleanor had no complaints.

It was much different on weekends, especially before children arrived, and before Bob's ample extended family moved to town. "The sky was the limit back then," recalled Eleanor. As they were together longer, *omelettes* continued to take on a totally new meaning, something both Bob and Eleanor could become absorbed in one time, fulfilled by other times, or simply amused by their individual appreciation, depending on how the tomatoes were sliced.

I had expected a reexperiencing of symptoms related to the sexual assault, but this never happened. Two weeks after they listened to the "Omelettes" story, the couple experienced a new-found intimacy. I saw them for two more sessions together, and then they did well. Charmaine's mood remained bright, and although she wanted to discontinue her antidepressant medication, I encouraged her to stay on it for at least six months as her doctor had recommended.

CLINICAL COMMENTS

When working with depressed clients, we may need to be much more flexible—and patient—than when treating people with other problems. Therapists must have a solid grounding in the CBT of Aaron Beck, Albert Ellis, or other authors. However, these techniques alone will leave you little room to maneuver when faced with multifaceted or complex issues that can be present in a person with depression. To bolster your arsenal, we recommend the books of Yapko and other writers, and we also believe that a foundation in hypnosis can be your trustworthy companion. So many clinical problems have a formidable unconscious component, and these can often be addressed through indirection and metaphor.

Before you become overwhelmed by any complex or chronic problem, stop, and think of Ma Kate. Ma Kate was Erickson's landlady in the 1940s. She was 70 years old and illiterate. For 20 years she had tried to learn to read and write. Erickson learned that each time she had been taught as small children were taught, and this obviously had not worked. Some teachers occupied that rooming house, and Erickson announced to them that he would teach Ma Kate to read and write within three weeks. The teachers simply jeered at him. In three weeks, Ma Kate was reading the *Reader's Digest*. How did Erickson do it? Through utilization.

Erickson started with recognizing what Ma Kate already knew how to do. She could draw horizontal lines, slanted lines, vertical lines, and circles, and Erickson instructed her, "Go ahead, fill up the whole page with those circles and lines. You're learning how to read and write." He then guided her in making an E and other letters, putting them together into words, and pronouncing the words. "I taught her to enjoy the satisfactions she already possessed," said Erickson (Haley, 1985, vol I, pp. 244–245).

18

Ego-Strengthening

TAILORING THERAPY TO THE INDIVIDUAL

In every chapter of this book we have emphasized some aspect of *indirection*, which is thought to be a main route to the unconscious. At the same time, we hope we have adequately demonstrated ways that therapy can be directed to the particular requirements of the individual client. We have often read Erickson's reknown statement about how psychotherapy should be formulated to meet the uniqueness of the individual's needs, rather than try to tailor the person to fit the Procrustean bed of a hypothetical theory of human behavior. However, is this always possible?

ERNIE PAYS A VISIT

You might wonder where we come up with the clients we describe to you. Of course, we are required to protect privacy, and that is why details are substantially changed and composites are used in the vignettes. Nevertheless, the examples are based on real events that happened with these interesting folks, who may not be much different from some of the people you see in your practice.

Let's contemplate *unconscious mind* for a moment as we take a glimpse at Ernie. As a young child, he saw his father kill his mother. He grew up in an orphanage and several foster homes before joining the army. He committed atrocities in Vietnam, and was kicked out of the service for heroin addiction. He was just released from prison, where he had survived a stabbing.

Now, just imagine for a moment that Ernie has come in for his first appointment with you. There he is, sitting opposite you, sleeveless shirt, arms full of tatoos. He removes his mirrored sunglasses and says, "The last shrink told me that I'm antisocial. Is that a *good thing* to be?"

Maybe we can appreciate the challenge of utilizing Ernie's varied problematic behavior. Can we also presume that Ernie's unconscious mind is benign and resourceful, a vast storehouse of information to be accessed by a therapist who doesn't sleep on a Procrustean bed?

BILLY VISITS THE NEXT DAY

Another client was Billy. His family "gave him away" to a circus when he was one year old. He grew up in the circus, which became his family. When he turned 18 he enlisted in the navy, and the Navy was his family for many years, although "nothing beat the circus," he said. While Ernie had no workable presenting problem, Billy said he wanted to be happier, which was a good place to start. He had no substance abuse, and had never been in prison. However, he was passive, dependent, avoidant, and very, very bland.

Billy responded well to hypnotic ego-strengthening, and not just with passive overcompliance. He demonstrated good hypnotic talents, time distortion, and amnesia. Ernie did not request hypnosis or any kind of psychotherapy. He was given a prescription for medication and sent back to his halfway house.

But suppose Ernie *had* requested hypnosis? Would we be untrue to our method, and write him off as treatment resistant, or unconsciously unworkable? All those personality-disordered folks you see in your practice—what is reasonable to expect in terms of unconscious change?

THE PRISTINE MYTH

What was the New World like when Columbus first stepped ashore? Why, everyone knows that the Americas, from Canada down through South America, was an undisturbed, undefiled wilderness, nearly empty of people, with multitudes of game in the virgin forests. The streams virtually boiled with fish, and the Indians were exemplary stewards of the land—at least until Europeans set about rearranging nature.

Recently, new light was shed on this pristine myth. Evidence uncovered by geographic scholars reveals that the Americas contained many more people than was previously thought. Many of them died from epidemic disease introduced by Europeans. In Peru, for example, the population was 9 million in 1520, but fell to little over .5 million by 1620. In most of the Americas population fell by 90 percent, though in 1492, before this precipitous decline, the indigenous population in the Americas is estimated to have been between *40 and 80 million people.*

What about vegetation? Were the forests of North America silent, vast, and impenetrable? Hardly so. Regular and widespread burning and clearing by Indians was confirmed by sedimentary charcoal accumulations from the subarctic to the Sonoran Desert. Furthermore, researchers found that in Central and South America, even when accounting for natural fire, human ignitions were frequent and unrestrained. In fact, the prairies of Wisconsin, Illinois, Kansas, and Nebraska would have long since disappeared, turning again into forests, had it not been for annual burning over the last 5,000 years. Forty percent of the tropical forest of Latin America is secondary, as a result of human clearing. In Panama, there are no virgin tropical forests today, and none were present in 1492.

Europeans in the sixteenth century found extensive preexisting agriculture in the Americas, ranging from sweet potato mounds to corn crib pilings to great fields of beans and squash. In northern Florida in 1539, Hernando de Soto's army passed through fields of maize that stretched "as far as the eye could see." Millions of extant agricultural features continue to be studied today. They include terraces, irrigation works, raised and sunken fields, dams, reservoirs, drainage ditches, diversion walls, and field borders. Soil erosion was extensive. Mounds of different shapes and sizes were constructed for temples and burials, as were various types of earthworks. Many causeways, roads, and pathways cut through forests, connecting the numerous settlements. However, despite compelling and credible evidence to the contrary, the pristine myth of the pristine may continue to linger (Denevan, 1992).

Perhaps the pristine myth is an inexact metaphor for the unconscious mind. Clients like Ernie and Billy and all the borderlines who grace our practices, surprise us. Our point here is that we should try and give them the benefit of the doubt. If they have some distress and *say* that they want help, most will respond positively. With many of them, ego-strengthening is the place to start.

EGO-STRENGTHENING

Hartland (1971), an early promoter of ego-strengthening within hypnosis, advocated directive suggestions, such as you *will* lose weight, or you *will* be strong. Less directive is the approach of Stanton (1993), who used ego-strengthening as a cornerstone of his therapy. These writers, along with Hammond (1990), advocate ego-strengthening early in therapy, recognizing that many clients may not let go of their symptoms until they feel strong enough to do so. We sometimes provide clients with a medical analogy, telling them that just as physicians need patients to be as healthy and strong as possible before an operation, in our work we try to build up or strengthen the ego before moving on to deeper work. Clients with chronic psychological disorders have often experienced years of dissatisfaction, and seem to readily understand our rationale of "mental strengthening."

SELF-EFFICACY

Improved self-efficacy can be defined as clients' believing that their behavior will lead to successful outcomes. Bandura (1997), a long-time proponent of building self-efficacy, believes that the greatest benefits bestowed by psychological interventions are not specific remedies for particular problems, but rather helping clients acquire the sociocognitive tools necessary to deal with diverse life situations. Ironically, this approach of the eminent sociocognitve academician is very similar to the approach of the staunchly atheoretical Milton Erickson, who similarly strove to strengthen each individual client by accessing unconscious resources and amplifying those strengths for improved psychological functioning.

Bandura (1999) contends that among the mechanisms of human agency none is more central or pervasive than beliefs of personal efficacy. He believes that personal enablement through mastery experiences is the most powerful way to instill a strong and resilient sense of personal efficacy. Bandura does not address unconscious process as such, but does note that vicarious experience is less likely to produce strong and generalized efficacy beliefs than guided enactive mastery. He adds that people generalize personal efficacy across different activities, especially for tasks for which they already possess requisite competencies, and that modeling with cognitive rehearsal builds stronger self-efficacy than modeling alone.

This is pertinent to indirect hypnotic ego-strengthening in that clients who self-reference metaphors—for example, a story about survival and strength—often gain more control over their symptoms. This foundation, then, sets the stage for further therapy, which for us typically includes a combination of hypnosis and conventional psychotherapy. Hypnosis that is interactive, such as employing verification through finger signals of imagined mastery in age progression, approximates an in vivo mastery experience, and sets the stage for actual behavioral change. The authors have also discussed hypnotic ego-strengthening in the treatment of posttraumatic stress disorder (PTSD) in immigrants from Central America (Gafner & Benson, 2001).

TWO TYPES OF HYPNOTIC EGO-STRENGTHENING

We employ two general ego-strengthening techniques in hypnosis. One involves a story, which we call metaphorical ego-strengthening, while the other was dubbed "short burst" ego-strengthening by Brent Geary (personal communication, June 6, 1997). Both are typically implemented following any variety of inductions and deepenings, and may be incorporated into inductions, deepenings, or stories.

In metaphorical ego-strengthening, the story might *be* the therapy portion of hypnosis, or additional suggestions might follow the story. We usually ask for unconscious acceptance of the metaphor and use finger signals to verify the acceptance, rejection, or I-don't-know response. We might tailor stories to a client's particular needs, but we also have many standard stories, such as the story we call "The Greenhouse," which is adapted from Wallas's (1985) story entitled "The Seedling."

The Greenhouse

Once upon a time, in another state, there was this magnificent greenhouse. A boy [or girl] walked by it every day on his way to school. He always wondered what it might be like to have a job inside that marvelous greenhouse. School would soon be done for the summer, and one day the boy stopped at the greenhouse and asked if he could have a job there. The boy sat on a sack of peat moss as he waited for the boss to interview him. He waited only a few moments, but it seemed like a very, very long time, and then the boss arrived. She was a large woman with very strong arms. "You can have the job," she said, "but only if you work very hard and do a good job. You must pay close attention and not let your mind drift off in here," she instructed.

The boy was delighted to get the job. When he reported to work the next morning it was immediately evident what the boss had meant, as there was a lot inside the greenhouse to notice and appreciate besides the job. The greenhouse was an immense structure, its windows shining in the sun on the outside, and once inside, the boy noticed the rays of the sun slanting through the thousands of panes of glass. Inside there it was warm and humid, and you could find all varieties of plants, hanging from up above, down below on shelves, and down farther yet on the floor, all kinds of plants, in various sizes of pots. Stepping from one aisle to another he was enveloped by many smells. Some were familiar to him, but most were unrecognizable odors that blended together into one extraordinary humid scent, something that arrested his attention in a most pleasing way. Time simply stood still inside there in that marvelous reverie, and he forgot about the outside world.

There were long rows of flowers of one color, then other colors. In whatever direction he looked there was a magnificent profusion of color. In whichever direction he turned he could see, smell, and almost feel the growth of those remarkable plants, losing track of time while he breathed in his surroundings, absorbed in the greenhouse, inwardly amused that his attention could be engaged while the time on his pocket watch, which hung from his belt, could be suspended.

As you can imagine, it takes several people to keep a big greenouse going, but only one person was in charge of the operation. She was serious and "all-business," but worked right alongside the others, carefully tending to all the plants. His second day on the job, the boy realized that going to work every day was like walking into a magical, sunny kingdom. One morning he was working with several dozen seedlings, putting them in small pots, and then lining them up so he could observe and take care of them while they grew.

Little did the boy know that on his work bench, weeks or months before, someone else had also been transplanting seedlings, and lining them up in order to care for them and watch them grow. One day, way back then, a little seedling at the back of the row had fallen over and rolled off, tumbling to the floor in back where it was dark and no one could see it. And there it lay for the longest time, lost and forgotten, defeated, lifeless, shrivelled, and brown on top, and down below the surface, it was dry, compact, and hard, down inside the shallow pot.

One day, while sweeping behind the bench, the boy found this little pot. "What is this?" he asked himself. "This little plant doesn't look like any others. What could it be?" He held it up to the light and figured right then that the seedling was dead. But as he examined it more closely he saw a speck of green near the top of the root ball. His imagination took over as he thought to himself, "Hmm, I wonder what I could do with this. . . ."

He went to the boss and said, "Look what I found. Is it okay if I keep this?" The woman replied, "That's no good, just throw it away. I'll get you a better one. Don't waste your time on dead plants." But the boy persisted and got his way. At the end of the day, the boy looked more carefully at the little seedling. As he broke open the cracked pot he found that down below, deep inside, the plant was very much alive. In fact, it had continued to grow in the dryness and dark, and had formed a strong, compact *root system*. And those roots had continued to grow despite the lack of light and water, and eventually the root ball had become too big for the pot, which cracked from the life force within it. He examined the very *strong root system* that had developed. Sure enough, down below, it was very much alive.

He planted the seedling in rich soil where it had enough water and room to grow, away from the other plants. After a few weeks it began putting out leaves and branches with more leaves, as its *powerful roots* absorbed the moisture and nutrients from down below and delivered them upward. Yes, the little seedling was definitely growing. The boy continued caring for the little seedling, which soon grew bigger and bigger and soon needed a larger pot.

The boy left his job at the end of the summer, and years later he thought back on his experience in the greenhouse. He thought about that little seedling that was now no doubt a big sturdy tree in somebody's yard. He especially thought about how that little seedling had survived, endured, and eventually prospered—all because of its *strong root system*.

While metaphorical ego-strengthening usually does not involve confusion, short-burst ego-strengthening relies exclusively on a confusion technique. This technique employs a short confusional statement, or non sequitur, followed by a suggestion, such as "You can overcome this." For example, a non sequitur such as, "Why do shopping carts often stick together?" followed by a suggestion, "You *can* be in control."

Gilligan (1987) noted that when clients hear an out-of-context statement such as a non sequitur, an unconscious search begins, as clients seek a way out of the confusion. We provide a way out by way of a suggestion in the desired direction. We prefer bland and neutral non sequiturs that are devoid of meaning or negativity. At the same time, we do not want the non sequitur to be purposeful or didactic. So, for example, we would use, "Each blade of grass appeared to be a different shade of green," instead of, "Will there ever be peace in the

Middle East?" Or, we would use "He could hear a silence between the leaves" as opposed to "She saw spider webs in the garden, which was overgrown with weeds." Usually three or four short bursts are sufficent. The technique is demonstrated as part of the following induction, which was adapted from "Taking the Measure of Time" (Ola & D'Aulaire, 1999).

Timepiece Induction

One time we heard about a client who had successfully experienced various aspects of trance, but she had yet to experience *time distortion*, that phenomenon where a person simply loses track of time.

Her name was Mary, Mary Ourless, and she often got kidded about her name, people saying things like, "Mary, less ours than theirs," things like that, but in fact she did trace her descendents back to the Minutemen of the Revolutionary War, something that people could remember for a long time. She actually went through life being called Ourless, a name that a person can easily disregard, not take seriously, or otherwise forget.

(She stood in an evening gown beside the busy freeway at night.[short burst] . . . You can begin to slow down.[suggestion])

Now, Ourless had achieved, in trance, with no conscious effort on her part, dissociation, where, for example, a hand or a foot feels detached from the rest of the body, and she had also experienced various feelings in her body, just involuntarily, tingling in one or both hands one time, heaviness or lightness another, as well as numbness in one foot, and warmth, and even coolness, in different parts. "I feel it, out there in my body," she was prone to remark.

But time distortion eluded her. "No," said Ourless, "I have yet to experience what many have described, when a minute seems like an hour, an hour like a minute, or when you just forget about it and let go, allowing yourself to not remember about the passage of time, or even the curious phenomenon of not really paying attention to time at all, or even disregarding it to the extent that time, as we know it, doesn't really matter."

(He had four sisters living in Minnesota.[short burst] . . . *You* can *begin to slow down.* [suggestion]*)*

Listening to her cover all the bases like that actually got the interviewer looking at his watch, wondering just how long she would go on talking about time, but finally she was done with the sentence, and they told her, "Ourless, let's conduct a little experiment. I'm going to read you a story about the development of clocks, the history of keeping time, and as I read you this story about very early timepieces, all the way up to the present, where they keep time with satellites and the Global Positioning System, I'd like you to adjust yourself in that chair, doing whatever you need to do for maximum comfort. And while I read you this story, I'd like you to keep *very careful* track of the passing seconds, or minutes, in your head, in your own way, so that we can check at the conclusion of today's experience to see just how close you are to the actual time as we know it." She nodded in the affirmative, smiling inwardly.

They then asked her, "Ourless, the time is now right for you to begin to let yourself sink into a light, medium, or deep state of relaxation," and she just closed her eyes, and as she settled back in the chair, she touched her wristwatch every so gently with the fingers of her hand on the other side.

There is a museum in Greenwich, England, where the main attraction is an imaginary line that circles the globe, north to south, marking zero degrees longitude. This is where east meets west, where time begins. There, you can see the observatory's digital clock, where the milliseconds flash by with lightning speed. At the time, it was December 31, 1999, and the clock counted down to midnight, and people watched that clock and felt the overwhelming sensation of time slipping away, as they were propelled toward the year 2000.

Nearby was a vending machine. If you inserted a Britsh pound, in no time at all the machine delivered an official certificate that noted the exact moment, to the one-hundredth of a second, proof that you had visited the historic spot.

Inside the observatory, which was designed by Christopher Wren in 1675, you will find 1,500 timepieces, including the crown jewel called H4, the most famous clock in the world. The H stands for John Harrison who, in 1759, constructed the first timepiece that allowed sailors to keep precise time at sea. With this invention sailors could measure longitude accurately when out of sight of land, an accomplishement that changed the course of history.

Going way back near the beginning, as we understand it to have been, way back then, time was first measured by cavemen, who were only able to keep track of big chunks of time, a far cry from milliseconds measured on a digital clock. Scientists once discovered a 30,000-year-old bone in France that contained etched grooves, evidence of early attempts to measure the moon's travels over a period of several months.

Now, much time passed before people measured time in smaller chunks—days, hours, minutes, and seconds—until today, when time can be measured in picoseconds, or trillionths of a second. If you were to measure light, which travels at 186,000 miles per second, the measure of one one-hundredth of an inch was simply more than lightning speed.

Now, Ourless was simply drifting and dreaming, and they told her, "Ourless, if you could imagine, or just wonder, about this for a moment, at that speed light takes only 1.2 seconds to travel from the earth to the moon, and measuring only one hundredth of an inch of that, which is faster than lightning speed, that is one picosecond."

When they checked later, Ourless said that the notion of a picosecond certainly gave her pause, not just when she heard it, but it also occupied her mind in a most curious way thereafter.

(He was a dog [short burst] *named Buster, and he dug underneath the fence . . . You* can *slow down.* [suggestion]*)*

Some of the earliest time-measuring devices were sundials, as people noticed that the shadow cast by a post changed in direction and length as the position of the sun moved throughout the day. By 3500 B.C.E., the Egyptians had constructed obelisks, whose moving shadows divided the day into morning and afternoon. Of course, the sundial didn't work at night or on cloudy days, and the length of the day, as measured by sundials in different locations, varied considerably.

Next in line in this progression of time, which was certainly linear rather than circular or some other direction, was the water clock. Egyptians etched a series of lines on the inside of a bowl, and they kept time by measuring water as it dripped from a hole in the bottom of the bowl. Naturally, time stood still during freezing weather, which maybe provided the Egyptians with a convenient time-out from time-keeping, something that was probably welcomed by more than a fraction of the population.

Moving forward rather rapidly in time, to 8th-century Europe, the hourglass, or sandglass, was the standard timepiece for quite a number of years. Sandglasses were small, and allowed for the measurement of short intervals, such as sermons or lectures, and even determined the speed of a ship, believe it or not. Knots on a rope, combined with the sandglass, measured the velocity of a vessel at sea, and notwithstanding the ship in the bottle phenomenon, the knot, as a unit of speed in the water, continues to be used to this day, although this story is not as much about ships as it is about time.

Now, some time-keeping devices have definitely stood the test of time, but for an interval in history timepieces appear to have stood still in time, or to have become lost among the years before 1300 c.e., when someone, somewhere, invented the first mechanical clock.

Those early clocks had no faces, and no hour or minute hands, but they did tell time by striking a bell every hour. Those clocks rang out across Europe, from towers and cathedrals, and one person described the beautiful sound of a bell floating across the meadow, almost as if the sound of it, or the image of the sound, in the mind's eye, was somehow frozen in time across the centuries.

Mechanical clocks were soon fitted with pivoting levers, weights, springs, gears, and wheels, all of which put the *tick-tock* into the clock, something that can still be heard in certain timepieces to this day, although the quietness of night may be more conducive to hearing it.

Clocks soon began to have fancy face pieces and dials, hour hands at first, and then soon they saw that nothing was lost, and in fact time efficiency was gained, by adding minute hands.

Ourless wondered why nobody mentioned second hands, as both hands were always very functional, and she, especially, was able to express feeling through gestures with them, as opposed to feet.

Today, atomic clocks lose only one second in 1.4 million years; however, an improvement on that is in the works, as new clocks will soon be operational ones that use super-cooled atoms, and those clocks will lose only one second every 313 million years.

Time and time again, with any discussion of clocks, the whole concept can appear elusive and mysterious. "What is time?" asked Augustine of Hippo some 1,500 years ago, and answered his own question when he said, "I know if no one asks me, but if I want to explain it, I don't know how."

With both techniques, we explain to clients beforehand what we are doing: "We may be saying some things that don't quite make sense, and all this is done to help you feel better, to help you be stronger." Clients appreciate these efforts. Not explaining what will occur may be viewed by some clients as disrespect.

We usually use metaphorical ego-strengthening first, and build in short-burst if there is resistance. However, metaphor in any form often bypasses resistance. Even clients who say things like "That was a dumb story" can't help but self-reference the metameaning. To them, *consciously* it was a dumb story, but unconsciously they might self-reference the metaphor and show benefit objectively in self-efficacy, or in demonstrating new behavior.

After two or more sessions of ego-strengthening we usually move on to other means of building self-efficacy, such as encouraging skill acquisition and expanded social contacts. In this regard, we employ role rehearsal and similar traditional methods. These methods can be buttressed with various hypnotic techniques. An important technique is *interspersal*.

INTERSPERSAL

After embedded meaning and hypnotic language, interspersal ranks next in potency in the arsenal of the practitioner. Probably the most famous example of interspersal occurred when Milton Erickson employed the technique with a terminally ill cancer patient named Joe. As Joe's pain and poor sleep were not responding to narcotics and barbiturates, Erickson was called in on the case as a last resort. Erickson had learned that Joe was a successful florist, and that success and hard work had governed his life. Now, Joe lay there in the hospital, unable to talk due to a tracheostomy, his feelings of frustration and failure fueled by intractable pain.

Cognizant of the these things, Erickson approached Joe and introduced himself. Joe wrote on a piece of paper, "What do you want?" Erickson then began a monologue about growing tomatoes. Early on, he inserted in his patter about tomatoes, "You don't want this," which communicated to Joe that he understood his helpless state. Erickson then resumed his monologue, and every so often he would obliquely insert words such as "comfort," "rest," and "sleep." Joe responded magnificently to these interspersed suggestions, and he gained immediate comfort, reduced pain, weight gain, and improved sleep.

Joe recovered sufficiently enough to return home. The following month Erickson visited him there. Once again the doctor offered Joe a monologue interspersed with suggestions, this time expanding it to include subjects other than tomato plants, such as the paintings on the wall of Joe's home. Joe responded well once again to this interspersal of suggestions. Two months later, Erickson was on a lecture tour and he received a letter that indicated that Joe had died recently. The family was profoundly grateful to Erickson for his help in their time of need.

Our psychologist colleage, Matt Weyer, keeps his handy statistics textbook prominently on his desk. At first glance, you might think that Matt reads statistics like he does *Sports Illustrated*. In fact, he loathes statistics, but he loves his text book, which he often puts to use in hypnosis. To most clients, it sounds like mumbo-jumbo, a hard-to-follow distraction that occupies the conscious mind. As the client tries to make sense of what she hears, Matt, with a subtle vocal shift, intersperses suggestions. He also uses it in a two-operator induction, where one therapist, the confuser, reads from the text-book. At intervals, the therapist stops reading, and the second therapist offers suggestions for trance. The back-and-forth process has the effect of overloading clients so that they invariably escape in the desired direction—into trance. We employ the poetry of E. E. Cummings for this purpose, but virtually any esoteric material will do.

The main thing to think about with interspersal is your *target*. If your aim is *comfort, slowing down, going deep, letting go*, etc., toss it in several times, and be sure to give a slight vocal shift to the suggestion.

CONSIDERING VARIOUS TECHNIQUES

Let's remember that it is not necessary to resort to confusion techniques unless it is indicated. A general rule of thumb is the higher the reactance, the more we use indirection, and if the client is very reactant, confusion might be necessary. So, for example, the goal is to *let go*. If the client has responded well in trance by achieving ideosensory phenomena, for example, tingling in her hands, time distortion, and a minimum of conscious critical evaluation, then we may proceed with one or more of the following over the next several sessions:

- Ego-strengthening story, set up finger signals, anchor, (e.g., circle with thumb and first finger).
- The "Balloons" story, whose embedded suggestion is "let go," along with ratification of unconscious acceptance of the metaphor via finger signals.
- Pre-trancework, seeding of letting go followed by a story that features letting go (e.g., some other client who flew a kite and let it go, or had tenants in his apartment and let them go). Ratification of unconscious acceptance.
- Age regression to previous time when he let go (retrieving past mastery or competence).
- Permissive age progression to time in future when he sees himself letting go.
- Guided age progression to imagined stressful situation, employing anchor to let go.
- Amplifying the metaphor technique, contrast not letting go with letting go.
- Assign in post-trancework discussion any one of several tasks, or directives, whose objective is to practice letting go.

You will recognize a reactant client by the time you have tried one or two of the above, and you will then know that less straightforward techniques are indicated. These could include:

- Interspersal of suggestions in a story, or monologue, whose content is relevant to the client's orientations or interests.
- Interspersal of suggestions in alternating stories, story within a story, or in a story without an ending.
- Assign in post-trancework discussion any one of several tasks, or directives, whose objective is to practice *not* letting go. (This would require the appropriate accompanying rationale, such as the need to study and keep track of this curious symptom, or the need to attempt to bring this vexing symptom under voluntary control.)

So, you have tried one or two of these techniques, and the client is hanging on to "not letting go" more than ever. He *wants* to let go, but just can't. In other words, he has unconscious resistance, so you have to go to your armory for some bigger guns, and train those guns in one direction: at his unconscious. Therapy should include frank discussion about how you are using some additional techniques to help him let go, saying, for example, ". . . Although some of these things may not make conscious sense to you, these are designed to get in underneath the radar, so that I can help you." Without such a discussion, the implicit power struggle might be amplified in the client's mind, and he may feel discouraged or defeated, or that he is "not getting it." Accordingly, these additional techniques might include:

- Confusional induction, such as the mystifying induction (Gafner & Benson, 2000), with interspersal of paradoxical directive, such as "Don't let go."
- Candle flame induction (Gafner & Benson, 2000) that employs client's absorption in a candle flame, while he counts aloud from 100 to one. At the same time, the therapist offers conversational induction, and alternates induction with an embedded-meaning story. The story lends itself well to interspersal.
- Sometimes these clients will respond to techniques designed to facilitate amnesia. (See Chapter 19 on unconscious problem solving.)

- Two-operator induction (Gafner & Benson, 2000), whose purpose is to overload and distract with confusion so that the client escapes into trance. (See Chapter 13 on pain for an example of this.)
- Or, suggestions interspersed amidst something that is hard to track, like the following induction, adapted from Hofstadter (1979).

Mi Mii Miii MU. There may be an invalid step in this alleged derivation with unintended complication and rati-fication. It is the step from the second to the third line, on alternating pages, 4, 6, 10, and 2 from Mii to Miii. There is no rule of inference in the MIU-system which permits such a typographical step, especially not with a metaphorical footfall, indirect footdrop, or essential overbite intended. Correspondingly— and this is most crucial—there is no arithmetical rule of inference which carries you from 311 to 3111. This is perhaps a trivial observation in light of our discussion in Chapter 10, yet it is at the heart of the Gödel isomorphism. What we do in any formal system has its parallel in arithmetical computations. (Letting go can be very pleasant.)   suggestion
Computations being computations, X + Z, N – 347.2, fourth line down from two, zero capacity, Bach, Vivaldi, and Mesmer had no responsiveness tests or other exams, nor did Zeig on Cypress Street, 5, 7, 9, 845.3.

In any case, the values m+31311311130, n+30 certainly do not form a MIU-proof pair. (Comfortable   suggestion
letting go.) *This in itself does not imply that 30 is not a MIU-number. There*

could be another value of m which forms a MIU-proof pair with 30. Actually, we know by earlier reasoning that MU is not a MIU-theorem, and therefore no number at all can form a MIU proof pair with 30. (Letting go.)   suggestion

CLINICAL COMMENTS

Have you ever seen the Italian movie, *Cinema Paradiso*? In it, an old man, Alfredo, weaves in various stories, like the one about a young man who performed a self-imposed ordeal. He announced that he would prove his devotion to a woman by standing outside her house for 100 consecutive days. He endured rain, cold, bee stings, and other adversity, becoming chaulky white and near dessicated in the process. On the 98th day, he abruptly leaves, mysteriously abandoning his vigil. Alfredo's listener asks, "Why? What happened?" Alfredo responds, "I don't know. You figure it out."

The movie is rich in age regression, age progression, and a variety of story techniques. Now, some therapists attempt to be just as artful. One therapist we know, who had tried several techniques, announced that the next session he was going to employ *multiple* embedded suggestions within *three* alternating stories, and also use *two* operators along with *multiple* interspersal targets. Is that overkill? We think so. Keep it simple. If it seems like it might be too extravagant, it probably is.

Some people new to ego-strengthening tell us that it is difficult at first to *hold back* from beginning active intervention and stay with what seems like passive treatment for a few sessions. However, you will soon find that ego-strengthening is anything but passive. Carefully building the foundation of anything can pay off over the long run. And going slowly can really get you there a lot faster.

We will end our discussion of ego-strengthening and interspersal and leave you with a selection of our stock stories, which are appended at the end of this chapter. "The Greenhouse" and "Grizzley" were mentioned in previous chapters. "Pills," the last story, can be used to encourage problem solving; however, there is no bigger boost to self-efficacy than freeing up people to exercise a greater range of behavior in this important realm.

STOCK STORIES FOR EGO-STRENGTHENING

<u>Lighthouse</u>

A story was told to me one time by a man [or woman] who was old, very old. He had had a long life of adventures, and he had many stories to tell, as he had enjoyed various travels around the world. As I listened to him, I reflected upon my own experiences, although my own were pretty bland by comparison.

Now, this man—I had listened to him for some time—and you know how some people tend to digress and go from here to there, and back again, and how, in your own mind, you can drift off, and all the time you try to listen closely for the salient details of seemingly mundane events, or maybe you try to grasp the important meaning as a whole, and sometimes you even try to put the whole thing together in some meaningful way. And other times, it's easy, and even effortless, to simply not pay attention at all.

Well, this man told about various life events, people and places, excursions in fact, and journeys in his mind, travels that he had intended but never really undertaken, back and forth, from one place to another, meandering this way, and eventually wandering back again. *Listening*, just *listening*, I found it rather easy to just let the words drift in, and drift out.

I learned long ago that it is probably more important to just listen rather than ask questions, or try to attach special meaning to this or that. Just then—it rather came as a *surprise*—the man began a story, and although I can't remember all of it, I can't help but think he may have been trying to tell me something, but only if I read between the lines with the back part of my mind, while at the same time allowing the sound of the words to just flow in and out of my conscious awareness.

One summer, this man had visited several lighthouses on the Atlantic coast of the United States. He learned that sailors journeying in total darkness may feel like a black liquid is swirling about them, and the dizzying disorientation can make it difficult to tell up from down, or right from left, or east from west. Sailors came to *deeply appre-*

ciate these light stations that were still in operation after many, many years of service. He remembered speaking with ships' pilots who continued to rely on these familiar fixtures, even though they also had radar and satellites for modern guidance. "I like something I can see with my own eyes," said one pilot, who could close his eyes and still experience a lighthouse's powerful white flashes that blazed every ten seconds, and were visible from as far away as 20 miles.

One such lighthouse, located at Discovery Point, on a rocky island, two miles off the coast, had a 70-foot tower made of massive granite blocks that dovetailed in such a way that the walls grew *even stronger* when pounded by the waves. The Discovery Point lighthouse had seen more than 200 years of duty, and countless ships, alone in dark or fog, came to *appreciate* the special way Discovery warned sailors of notorious sea hazards.

In 1760, Discovery began as a mere lantern on a pole, which gave way to a whale oil lantern and reflector, once the granite tower was built. Several years later, no one knew precisely when, someone put in a 2,000-pound fog bell that was rung by a mechanical device powered by the waves. Years later—the exact date is in question, but it had to be in the early 1800s—a first-order Fresnel lens was imported from France. This lens was replaced briefly in the 1920s by an electric fog horn, but in the 1930s, a second-order Erickson lens was inserted, which continues in operation to this day.

Now, Discovery encountered a good deal of adversity and change over the years. On four occasions in 1778, it was fired on by a British frigate. The cannonballs bounced off the rocks down below, and one found its mark half-way up the tower, but Discovery *survived* this direct hit. Three similar blows were endured during the Civil War, but the damage was quickly repaired, and the lighthouse continued on, doing its job year after year, *vigilant, strong,* and *reliable*.

Originally, a lighthouse keeper lived in Discovery, but soon they realized that this wasn't necessary, as way up on top, way up the tight spiral staircase, the durable lens required only minor maintenance every month or so. Those responsible for Discovery soon came to rely on the second-order Erickson lens as a remarkably resilient device.

There were other things that happened with the passage of time. For a period, the county didn't have enough money in its budget, and the lighthouse suffered some neglect, which was soon remedied by the repair of mortar between the granite blocks. Vandalism in the early 1940s turned out to be minor, just a one-time occurrence.

However, the greatest adversity faced by Discovery was the relentless pounding of the waves, year after year, strong and continuous one season, less so the next year, but persistent and severe nonetheless. Repair from erosion was necessary every once in a while due to the fierce weather, the biting seas, the battering waves, the surging water, and the tenacious cold foam and swirling green.

The man remembered scaling the staircase of Discovery late one afternoon, which soon had him gasping for breath. He realized, after going from ground level to up at the top, that the structure felt really *solid* beneath his feet. If someone could have seen him up there, gazing out, they would have observed the twilight flooding the sea, and when the coast dropped behind the horizon, only the lighthouse remained.

Highway One

When people go out for a drive, going from here to there, they can see many things, in nature, as well as buildings, roads, bridges, and anything else created by people.

With driving in mind, someone was telling me once that he had been on many, many roads in his life, in the day and during the night, and even in fog so dense that he couldn't tell if afternoon had given way to evening. His name was Spoad Trilling, and Spoad told me about California's Highway One, when he was a construction worker on that road. "Every day was different," said Spoad, who then added that even back then he looked forward to the time he could look back, all of which he could see quite clearly in his memory now.

"'PCH' is what they call it in California," he said, meaning the Pacific Coast Highway. "But we'll call it Highway One for you so you don't forget it, and so we're both on the same page," said Spoad, even though he was one who seldom picked up a book. As he began to tell his story, it reminded me of stories I'd heard about the big fish that got away, and even though Spoad was ostensibly telling me about a famous road, I could tell the real purpose was to tell about himself and his work. But Highway One was what I really tuned in to, at least with my third ear, or however I was paying attention at the time.

He described how the sheer strength of Highway One exerts a powerful pull on motorists and everyone else. It goes for more than 600 miles, from Dana Point in southern California, to north of San Francisco. Listening to Spoad, that road takes on a life of its own, and even though he was talking about construction workers, I heard him put the road in the first person, so that for a while it was Highway One telling its own story, while Spoad and everything faded into the background.

It was named one of the first All-American Roads, as well as the first scenic highway in California, and it resides with seashores and forests, ecological preserves, parks, and beaches, and all manner of towns and cities and people along the way.

"Now, keeping that road open is a neverending and expensive repair job," said Spoad, and he told about its traversing unstable wetlands and high cliffs, and crossing slow-moving landslides. "It goes where no road was meant to go," declared Spoad. He and his companions worked for years, coming up with ways to keep the road open: burying sensors that detect the movement of unstable ground, and building a variety of walls, supports, and nets that hold back the earth, as it continually reaches for the sea. "We patch the blacktop where the road sinks or buckles, and we clean up landslides. I could clear fallen rock in my sleep," he added. "It goes where no road was meant to go," he threw in as an appendage, no doubt unaware that he was repeating himself.

In the south, it passes through fashionable towns with palm trees and beaches, and then climbs to the Malibu bluffs over Santa Monica Bay. Spoad said, "We think up and we think down, high and low." A landslide is what happens above the road, and a slipout is what happens below the road. The state straddles two slowly moving tectonic plates that are constantly grinding and pulling apart. "And we're not talking about dinner plates," said Spoad, "but the Pacific Plate and the North American Plate." He told me more about the inexorable geologic movement and I thought about when I was a working as a G.I., and I recalled the blue plate special long ago, as a stomach grumbling can mean it's time for lunch.

"The hills keep reaching for the ocean, and that means that bulldozers and backhoes are kept busy year-round," he said. Any weather change can cause rocks from above to pelt the road below, along hundreds of miles of the highway. At Point Mugu, the rocks above are covered with a net of woven steel, joined together with metal rings, and secured in the ground with steel anchors. "Strong earth and rock; stronger steel," commented Spoad. I quickly threw in some words about the road going where it wasn't supposed to, and Spoad just winked conspiratorily.

He vividly recalls working on a bridge high over Highway One, "way up there," said Spoad, and that same day working down below the bridge, 40 feet down in a hole where they were to pour a concrete piling. "I found a little frog way down there, and I brought it up, in my pocket. I got shivers from that cold ground, or maybe from watching that little frog scamper away, I can't remember," he said. Not far away, at a place called Plain Rocks, two 80-ton drill rigs would grind away at a rock cliff, for the steel beam uprights that support concrete crossbeams to hold back the sliding earth. "We called that piece of work Soldier Pile," as veteran workers had put heart and soul into the job. "It's one tough road," announced Spoad, but it's had some help along the way.

Down south on the Pacific Coast Highway is one thing, almost the same as way up north, by the redwood forest. A storm surge from the Russian River closes Strong Road by Fort Ross, but in no time it is open. On up the coast, or down the coast, waves slowly chew at the base of the cliff, and the road continues on.

Beethoven

Many people have similar experiences, going through one thing or another in some way that is familiar to one as well as the other, and still, other people may share in common a similar activity or experience, one that was pleasant or absorbing, or one that led to a curious absorption, or maybe even an interesting detachment.

Not too long ago there was a man [or woman], and he had two weeks to do whatever he wanted, and he chose to travel to Europe, where he saw many things, experiencing the sites of Italy and France during long days that seemed to pass in no time at all. During this trip he spent several hours riding lazily in cars or trains, and during his wandering from here to there, he constantly thought about the ebb and flow of things, the way castles were razed, and then rose again; much like the way the tide, or a storm, erodes the shoreline, only to eventually be built up again. Or how with natural disasters, things eventually are built up again.

Finally, on the last day of his trip, he found himself in Bonn, Germany, at the Beethoven museum. He gazed at the enormous bronze bust of the famous composer, absorbed in both the totality of the statue as well as the minute details of the artist's rendering. He didn't even hear the hustle and bustle of the other tourists, lost in the time-less moments of his experience.

He sensed someone at his side, and turned to the friendly docent, who handed him a Walkman. He absent-mindedly put on the headset, and it was as if his hand belonged to someone else as he pushed the button that began the self-guided tour.

Beethoven had been born on a cold December day in Bonn in 1770, and was the first of six children that would survive infancy. The Rhineland city of 10,000 people was of Roman origin and streets were paved in black lava.

("The streets were paved in black lava," he thought, and his mind further wandered, wondering and knowing that he could do it.)

Many in the city were very poor, and the nearby Rhone River often overflowed its banks in bad weather, spreading dirt and debris through the narrow streets that were in disrepair. Beethoven's family lived in extreme poverty, up on the second floor of the apartment building. And even though there was illness and not enough to eat, people noticed early on that the young Beethoven had a strong, natural curiosity about many things.

(". . . a strong, natural curiosity about many things," he thought, and his mind further wandered, wondering and knowing that he could do it.)

Beethoven's family was able to obtain some music lessons for the youth, and when he was not at school, his father gave him lessons on the violin and the clavier. Beethoven's father was very strict. He offered the boy little praise for a job well done, and instead criticized the boy severely. In fact, his father even threatened to box his ears if he didn't play correctly. By the age of 10, Beethoven wanted to play his own way, but his father said no.

Beethoven was a shy and quiet boy, and he often became lost in his dream world. One day, he was looking out the window, his head in his hands, and his mother called out to him, but he did not answer. She then scolded the boy for his impoliteness, and he apologized, saying, "Forgive me, mother. I was so taken up with profound and beautiful thoughts that I could not bear to be disturbed."

("In a dream world with profound and beautiful thoughts," and his mind further wandered, wondering and knowing that he could do it.)

Beethoven continued to progress, and at age eleven he worked for the Court Organist, and by age 12, he published his first music, and soon he was providing music lessons for wealthy people in Bonn. Soon afterwards, he travelled to Vienna, where he played for Mozart, who later remarked, "Keep your eyes on him; some day he will give the world something to talk about."

Beethoven's mother was ill and his father also had health problems and drank excessively. With all this, Beethoven grew up to be lonely and an outsider. At age 22, he moved to Vienna, a city 20 times the size of Bonn. At this time, Beethoven was described as short, thin, and with a large forehead and pockmarked face, an intense, dark-eyed, and brooding young musician. Throughout his life, Beethoven proposed marriage to many women, but he was always rejected.

The political map of Europe showed relative calm only at the beginning and end of the musician's life. During his middle years, revolutionary upheaval dominated the landscape, and this was reflected in his music, which expressed great individuality and freedom.

(". . . expressed great individuality and freedom," he thought, and he wondered while his mind wandered.)

By now his father had passed away and he was the sole support for his mother, brothers, and sisters. Nevertheless, his fame and accomplishment continued. After dedicating a popular set of variations on Russian dance to a countess, she gave Beethoven a handsome riding horse, which he soon forgot about, as he preferred to spend his free time alone with his books and newspapers.

But his health began to fade in his early thirties. He had stomach, breathing, and heart problms, and his joints were in constant pain. He complained that his ears buzzed and hummed day and night. Doctors treated him with an infusion of almond oil, which only made the problem worse. In despair, he thought he didn't have much longer to live, and he wrote a will to his brothers.

This proved to be a turning point in his life, as he suddenly gained no strength and hope. He played brilliant concerts from memory alone, and his fame spread. Ideas came to him during his long, daily walks. One day, a student was waiting at his house for an afternoon lesson. However, Beethoven did not return from his walk until 8:00 in the evening. When he arrived, he remarked, "As I was walking, a theme for the last movement of the sonata occurred to me. Give me a few moments while I write it down."

(". . . it just occurred to him," he thought, and his mind wandered while he wondered. The words, "Certainly he can do it" resonated in his head.)

By now the composer was experiencing irrational and kaleidoscopic shifts of mood. His two-room apartment in Vienna was messy and dirty. He left an unemptied chamber pot beneath the piano, which was covered with dust. Inflation caused financial strain. He was constantly in a sour and cantankerous mood. He flew into a rage when people didn't understand him, as he was now very deaf. His piano was out of tune, but he didn't notice. While conducting an orchestra, he would wave his baton back and forth with violent motions, and he didn't hear a note. His final concerts were conducted by both him and another conductor who stood behind him. The orchestra ignored him and followed the lead of the other conductor.

He was finally finished with the tour of the museum. His mind wandered as he left, and for a long time he wondered about his experience, and the words "can" and "do it" appeared in his mind when he least expected it.

Maple Tree

I've often thought about how many different kinds of trees there are, but it really doesn't matter at all if we wonder or imagine about their number, because we go on experiencing many things without knowing the specifics. There are many trees in different parts of the country, short, stubby trees in the desert, or trees in the forest, evergreen trees like pine trees, or trees that drop their leaves and show their bare branches in winter. Those bare branches are soon covered by the green leaves of spring and summer, and during the crisp days of autumn those leaves gradually change—the red sugar maples, rainbow-colored sumacs and purple sweet gums, a patchwork of brilliant and fiery colors. Then the leaves begin to fall, in all the forests, millions of tons of leaves all over the world, suddenly set free, some flickering and fluttering down, and others blowing down in a gust of wind, all those leaves, perhaps the most gigantic energy transer on the face of the earth.

Where the leaves fall, the soil is deep and fertile, all those leaves that decompose within the coming year on the floor of the forest. But there are some exceptions like the leaves from the mighty oak, which pile up and sometimes take three years or more to break down.

Beneath the leaves lies the humus, a deep layer of leaves and other organic matter, deep and rich, and beneath the humus is the soil, tiny pieces of rock mixed into organic matter, profoundly deep and fertile. All these soil nutrients are constantly being mixed by seeping water, freezing and thawing, thawing and freezing, and the movement of plant roots and insects and burrowing of animals, and while all this goes on time might seem to stand still, which fits with what someone once said when he thought that trees were oblivious to the passage of time. It can be interesting, maybe even curious to think of these trees as the biggest and strongest plants on the face of the earth, long winding roots that go deep in the soil.

Not so long ago, in another state, it was a blustery autumn in the forest, in a grove of ordinary maple trees, where the crows cawed up above and lower down squirrels jumped from tree to tree, and way down below leaves were blowing on the ground.

Seeds were blowing down from the maple trees, and like most seeds, the vast majority of them didn't sprout or take root but got eaten, or just decomposed on the floor of the forest. But one seed landed on an old log and just lingered there, and eventually it became covered by the snows of winter, and there it stayed, unnoticed by deer and rabbits, nestled deep in a crack in the decaying log, snug and protected. Deep inside, it didn't matter to the seed that outside there were below-zero temperatures, howling winds and great drifts of snow.

In the spring, the seed was still there. It swelled with moisture and sprouted, and a tiny root crept down into the damp, rich, rotting wood of the old log. And slowly it grew a seedling with scrawny branches and little green leaves that stretched up toward the sun, while down below a strong root system started to develop and spread out. And it continued to grow, and soon it was a good-sized tree, and the years passed, and the rich and fertile soil allowed it to survive drought, and somehow the animals never ate it, and two times during a forest fire rain blew in and saved it at the last minute.

In the fall this mature tree's green leaves turned a yellow- orange and then a burning red. In the winter, the maple tree sleeps, just like all the other trees, and just like insects in the logs and chipmunks underground, dormant, resting for the winter. Birds sat up high in the tall branches. One day, the unbearable weight of the snow caused a huge branch to break off. The sharp sound cracked through he forest. But then spring came and green leaves grew out again and sap flowed through the tree. Bees and insects and birds lived in and around the tree, and animals ran down below. One summer day a bolt of lightning crashed into the tree and split it up near the top, and although the lightning caused considerable damage, the tree survived and kept growing. The seasons continued on, roots deep in the soil, roots intermingled with other roots deep below the ground.

We thank Swain (1983) for providing us with material for the following story.

Beside the Tracks

St. Louis, Missouri, is many things, such as the Gateway to the West. It also brings to mind Lewis and Clark, Charles Lindbergh, and the Cardinals baseball team. It has a famous botanical garden, and also one that is not so famous, a botanical garden beside the railroad tracks. This botanical garden beside the tracks differs from the famous one in many ways. It occupies more land, admission is free, you can walk on the grass, and you can even pick the wildflowers.

This garden, that goes by the name of Feral Flora, is located beside the tracks of St. Louis' freight and switching yards. Most people in St. Louis don't even know it's there. Now, many of the plants in Feral Flora look like weeds. That's because they are weeds, there at the end of the sidings, in the gravel and in the sand and cinders. But it would be a serious mistake to dismiss them as mere weeds, because they are beautiful and resilient, most unique in their very own way.

If the famous botanical garden in St. Louis were a general in the army, Feral Flora would be the foot soldier, ever-ready, and vigilant, a strong and reliable international regiment of soldiers. A multitude of plants grow there, some strange and rare: the Japanese honesuckle from Asia, the creeping bellflower from Europe, the castor bean from Africa, and special verbena from South America. You will also find garlic, sesame, coriander and dill, flourishing in what at first glance is a common, pedestrian, or otherwise everyday switching yard.

Asparagus, beans, corn, cucumbers, melons, and squashes are also present, though you have to look harder to find them. In these sparse and rugged conditions you will also find fruit trees, though of the dwarf variety: peach trees, apple, apricot, and pear, growing amidst larkspurs, roses of sharon, and even petunias. How can it be that this rich and varied garden grows there, yet few know of its existence?

What is so remarkable is that Feral Flora was not planted. No, neither human hand nor divine guidance caused it to happen. In St. Louis's famous botanical garden, plants are carefully introduced and professionally cultivated, and records are kept, and people pay admission to see the unnatural beauty. But not here, not in Feral Flora beside the tracks.

How, then, you may ask, did all these plants get there? It turns out that railroads are especially good at dispersing seeds. This was noted as far back as 1825 in England, where the first railroad with steam traction was inaugurated. Someone noticed, and appreciated, way back then, that wherever tracks are laid, unfamiliar plants begin to appear. Many of the seeds travel on freight trains. Shipments of grain often contain smaller seeds that shift to the bottom of the cars, and fall out as the cars bump together in the switching yard, or go around a curve.

Packing material, such as hay or straw, may contain seeds that escape the confines of the cars. The seeds, in the runners of the sliding doors, or on cattle, or even in the pant cuffs of workers, find their way to the side of the tracks. Apple cores cast aside, garden cuttings borne by the wind, or by birds . . . many are the routes.

Even more extraordinary is the plants' resistance to eradication. The railroads spend a great deal of time and money trying to rid the tracks of Feral Flora, but it continues on, relentlessly, falling and rising again. Even with chemical spills and gravel replacement, it continues to grow, flourishing there beside the tracks.

Bird Migration

He [or she] was out in the yard at night, and it was a clear, cool night in autumn. He had set up his telescope so it pointed at the full moon. He *breathed in* the nice, cool air, and then he began his task for the evening.

He gazed into the telescope and waited, *watching* and *waiting, observing*, and biding his time, eventually crossing one leg over the other on the chair, and no matter how he moved, both legs eventually would experience some semblance of sleep, tingling and then *numbing*, all by themselves, so that eventually they would be there, but not really part of him. At the same time the rest of his body, and especially his mind, remains keenly alert. He loses track of time as he becomes more and more *absorbed* in the telescope. Had he not swallowed in a long time?

At some point in the evening a flutter of birds shone by the light of the moon. He *looked closer*, and there they were, a flock of migrating birds, and he watched them intently, as they flew by, and they seemed both close and far away, sometimes going fast, and other times slow. Were they barn swallows? They certainly could be.

He thought of his own travels, as well as the migration of the birds themselves. As he became more *absorbed* in his thoughts and *watching* the birds—it was an incredible *numb*er of birds—he experienced a rather strange disorientation, like he was watching from outside of himself, or from somewhere else, and maybe during that time a hand, or arm, fell *asleep*, he couldn't remember later. Or maybe his mind became sort of *numb* to everything, but thinking back later, it really didn't matter, because the only important thing at the time was *gazing into* the telescope.

He could recall accounts of ship pilots on the high seas, or pilots of low-flying airplanes, describing how in total darkness it was difficult to distinguish up from down, and he continued *watching* those barn swallows fly across the moon, and then he began to *wonder*, to just *imagine*, whether the season was spring or fall. But if it was spring they would be flying south to north, and in the fall it was reversed. Certainly the coolness on his skin could develop in either spring or fall, depending on the month, and the time of day. Just then he knew for sure because he could feel the dried leaves crinkling beneath his feet, but he couldn't really see them down there in the darkness.

He thought of years ago when he had seen a flock of birds flying across the sky, but then it was day time and he could see the entire flock, but now his focus was restricted to the dark forms flitting across the yellow of the moon. As he became more *absorbed in* his observation, he lost track of time. It was night for sure, but it could just as easily have been day time. He could imagine standing up rather than sitting down, and the more he observed and imagined, the more he felt curiously detached as if removed, out there, in a peculiar way, while at the same time going *deeper* and *deeper inside*.

Drifting and *dreaming* on the *inside* did not diminish acute observation on the outside. Certainly they *had* to be barn swallows. The barn swallow, a feathered flying machine that weighs only half an ounce, but migrates 3 to 5,000 miles twice each year. He pressed his eye to the telescope as the birds continued to fly across the moon. He didn't know if they continued for a few minutes or longer, and he began to dream, dreaming of his own travels and at the same time dreaming of migrating barn swallows, and one journey simply blended into another, a dream within a dream as he continued to *observe, imagine,* and *wonder.*

He had studied barn swallows a long time ago. He couldn't remember all the details, but he thought they had some sort of internal timing mechanism and directional orientation. Did they set their course by the sun, moon, or stars? He wondered about his own inclinations, certain feelings in the spring as opposed to the fall of the year, and how some things were easier to do at certain times of the day, or evening. Wouldn't it be wonderful to possess celestial navigation as an unearthly means of getting from *here* to *there*?

Sometimes a flock is dispersed by danger, perhaps by a hawk, but the flock quickly reassembles and adjusts its flight pattern, and continues on its way, wary of other things, such as a plane, that might impede progress forward. The barn swallow's vision is considerable and far-reaching, as the eyes of birds are enormous relative to the rest of the head. Is it true that they actually *see* a plane, or do they *feel* the vibrations? He thought about his own journeys, and saw himself, on the inside, pushing himself from *here* to *there*, sometimes pulled along by outside forces, knowing most of the time where he was going. He couldn't see himself as part of a flock.

If he were up there flying he could also extract information about a distant goal from the sky or landscape, but he would be in a plane. Barn swallows seem to know natural signposts, proceeding along coastlines, or river valleys, or parallel to mountain ranges. Did some birds really fly from Alaska to the Amazon and back every year?

If he were walking from here to there, or driving, his body, or his car, and certainly his mind, did not have to think about the mechanics of movement. The aerodynamics of bird flight was more intricate than that of airplanes, and more impressive except for speed. Going fast, and then slowing down, in his mind, he thought of wheels on a car, or his own legs. The whole shape of a bird's wing changes throughout the cycle of its wing beats, and at each stage, every feather is working effectively, through lifts, propulsion, turns, takeoffs, and landings.

Pills

One day I saw Eloise, a client who was referred by her doctor for a rather interesting problem. The doctor had prescribed a particular medication—maybe they were antibiotics, I forget—and for several weeks Eloise had taken the pills exactly as prescribed, one three times a day with food. Eloise religiously took one pill with milk and crackers at 8:00, 12:00, and 4:00. But the desired effect had not been achieved, and the doctor indicated that Eloise would need to find a different way to make the pills work.

As you probably know, often when people are referred to a therapist they have already tried many things. Sometimes therapy is a last resort. They have attempted every possible solution, but they still have not gotten *from here to there*. In Eloise's case, she and the doctor had tried taking half a pill at 8:00, another half at 10:00, and another half at 12:00, 2:00, 4:00, 6:00, and 8:00. They had tried taking a half at 9:00, 11:00, 1:00, 3:00, 5:00, and 7:00, and they also tried taking a half pill on the half hour six times a day, and even one quarter of a pill 12 times a day on both the hour and the half hour. They even attempted an eighth of a pill every hour during the day and night, even though Eloise protested having to awaken every hour at night to take her medication. "Milk and crackers every hour is a bit much," complained Eloise. The doctor also had concerns about absorption and therapeutic effect.

After reading all the reports and discussing this with Eloise, we began to examine *other ways of getting from here to there*. As we discussed and noticed some new possibilities, both she and I came to appreciate the *infinite number* of things that could be tried. We agreed that the pills would still need to be cut into fractions, but that Eloise could use a different knife and a different cutting board. She had fifteen other knives at home and two alternate cutting boards, but then she realized that a variety of other flat surfaces in her apartment might also serve the purpose. The pharmaceutical company had conveniently imprinted its name and the number 23 on the pill. Eloise could cut one pill on the 3 and another on the 2, and then a host of other cutting possibilites became evident.

She could also cut those pills during different times of the day, or she could have her mother cut every other pill. She could take one dose in the bathroom and one in the living room and another while driving to work. Instead of milk and crackers, she could take juice and half a cookie one time and soda and one-third can of tuna another time. She could have friends present while she cut or took her dose, or she could have the TV on, or if she played music, she could have a classical music compact disk or a rock and roll tape, or maybe even one of her father's old vinyl records.

"I could even think different thoughts each time," Eloise joked. The whole thing seemed comical, but it was also serious, and I don't have to tell you that a solution was forthcoming.

19

Unconscious Problem Solving

RECOGNIZING HYPNOTIC PHENOMENA

Warning: This is not a test. Various hypnotic phenomena will be cited in the right-hand column in the following story. We would like you to guess which phenomenon may be most salient in unconscious problem solving. (Please note that time *distortion* is a general term for this temporal phenomenon, and time *expansion*, or time *condensation*, are simply more specific variants of time distortion.)

Dulce and Alma

Two women from New Mexico asked to be seen together. An appointment was made, and when they came in, the two women turned out to be niece and aunt, Dulce Agonía and Alma Perdida, respectively (rather provocative names). They turned out to be highly interesting people, in what they did, and how they did it, though much of their account was lost, available to neither present memory nor past recollection. Fortunately, we kept some notes of the session.

They told us their story, and Dulce spoke first, and Alma picked up where Dulce left off, and they continued on, one after the other, one more animated, and one less so, certainly a rather curious way to relate their experience. Our heads were spinning by the end of *however long* we were with them that morning.

time distortion

Several years back, they were living on a ranch in the Mexican state of Sonora, and late one afternoon they found themselves gazing into a pond, a half mile or so in back of the ranch house. A flood of memories and emotions came to them as they peered into the pond, which to any objective observer appeared dark, stagnant, sluggish, and unmoving.

"How fascinating, the *colors* and all," remarked Alma. "Shimmering *greens*, a compelling turquoise *blue* woven through that wonderful *terra cotta*. See how the sunlight catches the jagged lid of that rusty *soup can* down there? Remind me to tell you what you did with that Campbell's soup can when you were two," she said, as she stopped in mid-sentence, *mouth agape* and *finger pointing* frozenly.

positive hallucination

catalepsy

"How absolutely boring and tedious this pond is," retorted Dulce. "I look at it and I see nothing but torpid muck, and your voice is a gauzey whisper, a million miles away. How long must we stay in this barren place? No doubt an *hour* has passed already.

time expansion

"*Mere seconds have passed*," answered Alma, a rueful expression through dry lips. "However, the sun continues to go down, so maybe it's later than I think. This arm of mine pointing out there is like *somebody else's* limb, and it seems to have a mind of its own," continued Alma. She kneels down at the edge of the pond, *arm* still woodenly extended. The hand on her other arm begins to scribble absent-mindedly in the sand. "I see something in the sand here," she says. "It's the face of your mother, my sister. It seems like *only yesterday*," she says."I'm *back there* now," she adds.

time condensation

dissociation

catalepsy

automatic drawing

hyperamnesia
age regression

"It's just a blurry mess to me," answers Dulce, who then adds, I can see us in several days, back across the border, away from this excretory blotch of water," she pondered aloud.

age progression

"It's been a while since you complained about that hot, prickly sweater you're wearing. It no longer feels like a horse blanket?" asked Dulce.

"*I forgot all about it*, how did you know?" asked Alma.

anesthesia

"I can remember when you bought it, many years ago at Olvidado's Mercantile," noted Dulce. I can *see us there now*, by the old pickle barrel, sawdust on the floor."

age regression

Alma closes her eyes and draws some *letters in the sand* with her index finger.

automatic writing

Dulce cries out, "What *is* that?!"

Alma doesn't answer, but chortles to herself.

Dulce asks, "Tia Alma, what did I do
with that Campbell's soup can when I
was two?"

Alma answers, "I *have no idea* what   amnesia
you're talking about."

AMNESIA

When Milton Erickson was developing his techniques in the 1930s
and 40s, the psychoanalysis of Sigmund Freud ruled the day. In the
Freudian view, people are influenced by events forgotten, and the
repression of past conflicts leads to psychopathology. Accordingly,
amnesia is regarded as something negative.

Erickson, who relentlessly pursued the positive, showed that
amnesia cannot only be applied constructively, but can be used in
therapy in myriad ways. As such, the Ericksonian tradition is one of
appreciating the flowers rather than speculating about the seeds
(Zeig, 1985b).

Amnesia as a Fact of Life

Zeig (1985b) notes that therapists often see amnesia in their clients.
For example, clients return the next session and report a scintillating
new insight they had recently, which, in fact, was something that the
therapist had mentioned in passing during the previous appointment. The clients had forgotten that new insight until now, something for which they remain amnestic. Similarly, unconscious
plagiarism can occur among writers, who report a "new" idea
without realizing that it was something they read in another
company's memorable titles on hypnosis, something the authors of
this book either forget to remember, or simply remember to forget,
as many of that company's titles are unindexed, unlike this book,
which also has ample references, which just proves that we claim no
totally new ideas.

Why Use Amnesia?

Erickson used amnesia chiefly in two ways: in therapy, with clients,
and in "therapy" with his students, to demonstrate how they could be
influenced hypnotically. More than one former student of Erickson's
has mentioned that they had a session with Erickson, and afterward,
when they listened to the audiotape of the session, they realized how

much they had forgotten. In therapy, Erickson used amnesia with indirect suggestion so that the suggestion was not recognized by the conscious mind, which could negate it.

This process of carefully placing suggestions where they can be protected and "settle in" is much like gardeners who sow seed and then cover it with straw or black plastic so it can germinate. In our experience, small birds sometimes find seeds amidst the straw, and big, aggressive birds may peck holes through the plastic. So, we surround the mulch with wire mesh. We have learned that rabbits can lean into, or jump over, a short screen fence, gobbling up the helpless little plants once they sprout. Accordingly, we have learned to build a fence that's at least 12 inches high, and bury it a couple inches in the soil to prevent rabbits, or countless other critters, from digging under it.

Experimental and Clinical Amnesia

Many of you may have seen amnesia used experimentally. You are in a hypnosis training group, and in trance, the desigated subject is told that when he hears *"one sharp tap* of this pencil on my spiral notepad, you will cough, and you will forget all about it until you hear that *one sharp tap* of my pencil." During post-trancework discussion, the operator taps two times with her pencil, and a few moments later, taps three times. Each time, the former subject shifts almost imperceptibly in his chair. More questions, answers, and further discussion follow, and then the operator taps her pencil *one time sharply* on her notepad. Immediately, the former subject ejaculates a reflexive cough, and then wonders why everyone is looking at him. All observers are duly impressed, they remember the experience, and talk about it every opportunity they get.

Experimental amnesia, much like in the above scenario, has to do with inducing such hypnotic forgetting, which is then reversed on cue with partial or full awareness. In clinical amnesia, there is no reversal. Clients forget, and you don't want them to remember they forgot. The only thing important is that they implement the suggestion.

Ways to Foster Amnesia

DIRECT SUGGESTIONS

As direct suggestions for amnesia are most often used experimentally, many practitioners feel comfortable expanding on this referent in the clinical setting. Direct suggestions may vary in an number of ways, for example:

> *Beginning now, I'd like you to just forget anything you may have intended to remember.*

Or metaphorically:

> *I told a client once, "your trance experience today—just forget about it."*

Also metaphorical, but still in a direct vein:

> *I knew a woman once who fell asleep, and as she slept, she dreamed; but when she awoke, she could only remmember a small portion of her dream.*

The words *forget* and *remember* can be toyed with, for example:

> *Can you remember to forget, or will you forget to remember?*

Or:

> *Olivia said it's a matter of remembering to forget, and Marianne argued persuasively that it's a matter of forgetting to remember, and I still get confused by both of those.*

Zeig (1985b) used the eminently economical: "You can't possibly remember everything in your conscious mind" (p. 329).

INDIRECT SUGGESTIONS

There is obviously a blurry line between the direct and the indirect, just as there is between the indirect and the confusional. If we have used direct suggestions for amnesia, we are oriented to the elimination, or blotting out, of memory. However, suggestions for *altering* an experience may be more effective than *deleting* it. Why? Perhaps because subtle techniques are more likely to penetrate defenses. You might suggest, "Pay close attention only to my voice, and everything else can fade into the background." If you draw the client's attention to the *foreground*, for example, "Everything that you need to remember is in the chair supporting your body," then the implication is that all things in the *background* can be forgotten (Zeig, 1985b). We especially like the delicateness and elegance of this type of suggestion. Contrast that with a more elaborate suggestion that involves dissociation and double bind: "Between now and next time your conscious mind may work at resolving the problem while your unconscious mind wonders about the implications, or your unconscious mind may generate some answers while your conscious mind ponders the implications." The target in this suggestion is problem solving, but it often effects amnesia as well.

DISTRACTION

Erickson was known to facilitate amnesia by quickly realerting a client, and then perhaps hurrying him to the waiting room. Such an interruption, or distraction, promotes amnesia. He would also realert and begin a shaggy dog story, causing the same effect. We like to realert by omitting a number in the counting up, for example, "I'm going to count from five up to one, and when I reach one, you can reawaken, alert and refreshed, 5, 4, 3, and *one*." Attention drawn to the missing digit often causes people to forget preceding content. Erickson was also known to realert and innocently ask, "And what is your name?" This had the effect of orienting attention to when they first met Erickson, thus leaving a blank for everything since then (Zeig, 1985b).

"AS IF"

Once the trancework portion of the session has ended, you can act like trance has not yet occurred. For example, the client is realerted and then asked, "Is now a good time to begin hypnosis?" We recommend using this only with clients who have a strong sense of self-efficacy, as it can have a very disorienting effect. One man one time (Bru was his name) was realerted and offered the "as if" question. He gave a very bewildering look and I (S. B.) asked him how he felt. "Discombobulated," was his reply.

STRUCTURED

Miguel de Unamuno, a Spanish writer around the turn of the nineteenth century, was arrested and spent some years in prison. When he returned to his lectern at the University of Salamanca, he began with, "Como decia . . ." ("as I was saying . . ."). This could have effected hyperamnesia among his students, but a more likely result may have been amnesia. According to Zeig (1985b), Erickson commonly answered the telephone when it rang during a session. As he picked up the receiver, he stopped in midsentence his discussion with his client. Then, after hanging up the phone, he would resume talking precisely where he left off. The client would often be amnesic for preceding content.

If you begin your induction with a particular phrase, such as, "Lateral associations may have nothing to do with climbing up a ladder, or *down*," and then you repeat this pharase before relaerting, the effect can be amnesia for all content in between.

Many other therapists refused to shake hands with Erickson because he was so adept at inducing trance via this everday behavior. He would begin the handshake, elicit catalepsy verbally or nonverbally, leave the hand floating in the air, and after some brief trance-work, grasp the hand again to complete the handshake. (It's no wonder that a *Time* magazine article in 1973 called him the Svengali of Arizona.)

THE CASE OF HUMBERTO

Humberto was a man who came to see me (G. G.) from a small town in a nearby state. He had been a paratrooper in World War II, and had endured much fighting and gore in Europe. After the war, he was a heavy drinker and barroom brawler, but when he came to therapy, he had been sober for 20 years. He had no posttraumatic stress disorder (PTSD) symptoms, but he had considerable pain from a parachute accident. However, the presenting problem was something else.

A few months back, he had been arrested for child molestation, something which had turned out to be a case of mistaken identity. The local newspaper printed a retraction, and offered him a prolific public apology; nevertheless, the damage had been done. "Everybody in town stares at me. I can't get it out of my mind," he reported.

Humberto had been started on Lorazepam, which provided some relief. His wife was supportive, but very frustrated by his fussing and ruminations. As he came from nearly 300 miles away, three sessions of psychotherapy were spread out over two months.

The client had a very long beard, something that had been growing for many years. He also wore rather shabby clothes. He had a mildly dysphoric presentation. He was also an eager therapy participant. The three sessions of therapy, which included discussion and reframing, his recording antecedents, behavior, and consequences, and even paradoxical scheduling of his ruminations had no effect. The fourth session we began hypnosis. He responded with deep trance and complete amnesia for content. However, he resisted instituting his anchor, one deep breath, at the onset of ruminations. This suggested unconscious resistance, and the idea that unconscious problem solving was indicated.

Now, in talking to Humberto, I had gathered some very useful information about his daily activities, especially about his daily drive, and the country roads he typically travelled on. In the fifth session, he was told:

> *On your daily drive, when you cross Mormon Road by the railroad tracks,* something *will come to you that will help you with this problem. However, you will forget that I even mentioned this to you.*

When he returned in two weeks, there was a dramatic change in his appearance. He had shaved his beard, and he was neatly dressed. "I'm not bothered anymore by those thoughts," he reported. "Doing anything differently?" I inquired. "Yes, I'm using that anchor." "Oh, good, keep up that anchor," I told him, and then added. "You don't need to come back anymore."

That was 12 years ago, and he has not returned to the clinic. Now, what happened? In the absence of any other intervening event, I can only conclude that Humberto was able to solve his problem unconsciously. He does not know that, but that does not matter.

OTHER WAYS TO PROBLEM SOLVE UNCONSCIOUSLY

A tool for unconscious problem solving that we often reach for first is an elegant little story, which we call "Simple Rooms." This story about "getting from here to there" is of course based on a similar story called "Going from Room to Room" (Rosen, 1982) that Erickson told his students as part of his fabled teaching tales. We typically employ it for clients who may be "stuck" in any variety of ways.

Going from Room to Room

One day a client—let's call her Sarah—came *inside* from out in the cold, and she said her problem was that she was having trouble *getting from here to there*. So, I asked her, "Sarah, *in* your house, how would you get from one room to another?" She then recounted all the possible ways she could think of for getting from *one room to another*. She said first she would walk in, or crawl in on her knees; she could sommersault in; she could go in backwards; she could enter slowly or quickly; crawl in on her belly; scoot in on her back; or move in with her back against the door jamb; or she could go in with big steps, medium steps, or on tip toes; and she could even go around the house and climb in the back window. Finally, after several minutes, she thought she had exhausted all the possible ways to *get from here to there*. But then, as we discussed it further, it came to light that there were many other possible ways to *get from one room to another*. She could go in on the hour or half hour; she could go in after drinking a quarter glass of diet soda, or a half glass of whole milk; she could go in while listening to the radio; she could enter that other room while thinking of something important one time, followed by having her mind blank another time; or she could have a friend present while she went into that other room. Or, if she crawled in wearing shorts one time, she could wear jeans another time. She could even walk around the block one and one-half times first, or she could take a taxi to the airport and fly from Tucson to Phoenix to Chicago and back again, and then *go from one room to another*. We were still coming up with a long, long list of possibilities when we ran out of time. At any rate, it was evident to Sarah that there was an *infinite number of ways to get from one room to another*.

You can offer a suggestion and tag it to a behavior that is likely to occur, as in the case of Humberto. But often that is not necessary. You can simply tell the client the story, and then ask an unconsciously directed question, for example, "Humberto, that story I just told you about that woman named Julie. Is that something that your unconscious mind can put to use? Taking as much time as you need, you may answer with one of your fingers. . . ." If Humberto answers with his No finger, or I-don't-know/I'm-not-ready-to-answer-yet finger, you can follow up immediately with, "Between now and next time, is your unconscious mind willing to contemplate that question further? You may answer with one of your fingers. . . ." Clients frequently answer yes, and next session, when the first question is repeated, people usually respond with their Yes finger. To verify that change has indeed occurred, in the next few weeks you will want to see objective behavioral change, or a subjective report that verifies improvement.

THE CASE OF NIGEL

His given name was Roy, and he was from Kansas. However, after his tour in the U.S. Air Force, he married a woman from England and settled in London. He not only lived in London, but took on the behavior of a Londoner, even adopting the accent and changing his name to Nigel. In the early 1990s, Nigel and his wife moved to Arizona, and one day he and his wife became clients in the mental health clinic at the Tucson Veterans' Administration.

After several sessions of communication training, behavior exchange, and similar straightforward techniques, it became clear that Nigel, not his wife, was impeding resolution of their problem. He was then seen individually, and hypnosis was directed at Nigel's block at pleasing his wife. Early on, the client experienced an intense visual experience when listening to the "Balloons" story. Whenever one of these vivid visuals occurred, he muttered, "Well, bugger me, mate!" I (G. G.) was rather taken aback by this odd statement, and instead of trying to metaphorically pace his words with a rejoinder about insects, I chose to just say, "That's the way. . . ."

One session the following agenda was set. I told him that I would be telling him a series of what we call instigative anecdotes, something designed to stimulate lateral associations, with the target being "what I need to do to please my wife."

Mental Pictures

Nigel, a mental picture may be worth much more than a thousand words. We can think of a TV screen, or a computer monitor. A visual image on them is comprised of many small pieces, or pixels, divided into horizontal and vertical lines. Each pixel is a colored dot that the human eye can't distinguish individually, but blended together, they make a smooth visual image. A mix of various colors on 500-plus lines makes 275,000 pixels. Higher definition TVs have over 1,000 lines and 1.25 million pixels at any one time, and you know how often the screen changes.

We can only wonder how the mind, drifting and dreaming, deep inside, comprises a mental picture, and beginning now, I'd like you to let that unconscious mind drift and dream, and taking as much time as you need, when something arises that may help you with the problem, let me know with your words. . . ."

After a few seconds, he loosed the familiar, "Well, bugger me, mate!" And that was all. Throughout that session, and continuing into the next, we continued in the same way. Following each of these anecdotes, he responded with the same statement. The only exception occurred when he said with even more enthusiasm, "Well, bugger me mate, again!"

Robert Frost

One of the more famous poems of the English language, "Stopping by Woods on a Snowy Evening," surfaced in the mind of Robert Frost after he had been working all night on another poem. He got up from his desk and went outside to look at the sun, and as he gazed in the distance, "Stopping By Woods" suddenly *came to him*. "I always thought it was the product of autointoxication coming from tiredness," he explained.

Rings in a Dream

Fredrich Kekule, the German chemist who solved the structural riddle of the benzene molecule, labored many days attempting to consciously solve the problem. Then, in a daydream, his unconscious mind generated a structure involving six snakes connected in the form of a hexagon. Upon arousing, his conscious mind recognized this metaphor as representing the elusive structure of the benzene ring.

The Shipworm

In the early nineteenth century in France, Marc Brunel had a lot of time on his hands in a debtor's prison. He found himself studying a common shipworm as it tunnelled through a piece of wood. He noticed that as the shipworm gnawed its way into the wood, it secreted a liquid that hardened, and this firm base allowed it to keep pushing forward.

This inspired Brunel's invention, the cast iron tunnelling shield, that enabled him to build twin tunnels under the Thames River in London. The project was an instant success, as more than a million people used the tunnel in the first four months alone.

News from BOW

All week long, Dee watched as people lined up with their telescopes beside the road to Samish Island. She watched them, and periodically one of them would look up to watch her. Dee may have been mysterious, but it was a veritable mystery what they were looking for. One day she asked one of them and they told her they were trying to catch a glimpse of a rare biped duck, that they thought had disappeared from there long ago.

Painting Landscapes

Vincent Van Gogh journeyed to southern France so he could see nature under a brighter sky. "One feels that the colors of the prism are veiled in the mist of the North," he wrote in a letter. When he arrived, he threw himself into one of the most productive periods of his life, painting haystacks, landscapes, flowering trees, and anything that caught his eye. "I have a terrible lucidity at moments, when nature is so glorious that I am hardly conscious of myself and the picture comes to me as in a dream," he recounted. (Harriss, 2001, 54).

Disappearing Art

Some artists have little regard for permanence. Shamanic Indian sand paintings are done with great care and precision, and then they are allowed to disappear within hours or days after serving their purpose in a healing ritual.

By now, therapy with Nigel was beginning to pall. I decided to try something different. He was told the following story, which was adapted from *Desert: The Mojave and Death Valley* (Dykinga & Bowers, 1999).

Playing Field

This is a story about Nestor Nalga, who was seated on a big rock in the Mojave Desert. The rock overlooked what is commonly known as Racetrack Playa, or the playing field, the place where stones as heavy as 300 pounds were known to *move mysteriously* along the perfectly flat surface, leaving long, shiny tracks in the cobbletone silt.

Now, Nestor had done much study and practice in hypnosis and other deep mental states, plumbing the depths of the deep, that ineffable downward movement, or internal shift, that has to do with the deepest part of his unconscious self. To date, Nestor had *nearly* achieved what he was looking for, and at the same time he had experienced strange and wonderous sensations in his body, stimulating and provocative feelings in his extremities and elsewhere, that ranged from a glowing warmth in a portion of one hand, to a prickly tingling in the other, to an interesting and indescribable electric feeling back in the first hand. The shimmering sensation in the other hand reminded him of the northern lights, and the leaden, weighty feeling in the hand on the other side led to thoughts of a scale and balance, but this had nothing to do with the curious feelings in both feet, which had yet to emerge, out there. Also, uncertain sensations had yet to show themselves in one other part of his body.

Thoughts of depth caused him to think of up and down, like those heavy old windows at his grandmother's house. They were either up or down, open or closed, all of the way, or part of the way, unequivocal, however you looked at it, whether or not there was a screen or storm window on the outside. So, too, he thought about going inside from out there, the outside influencing the inside. He still did not know for sure if a person who breathed deeply into a balloon, and watched it grow big and round, if that person poked his finger inside, was that finger then inside the balloon, or outside? At one time, Japan was totally isolated from the rest of the world. Contact with the outside, as a result of traders and missionaries, changed the inside, even though the religious influences from outside spawned apologetics and various polemics in more than one region inside the country.

Nestor had spent a lot of time finding the precise location of the Playing Field. He finally got a park ranger to tell him the exact location, but the ranger also warned him, "Under no circumstances should you stay overnight in that valley. Nestor came armed with a back issue of the *U.S. Geological Society Monograph* with its article, "Sliding Stones: The Playing Field in the Mojave Desert," with its accompanying sepia toned photographs of big rocks and the long tracks trailing behind them. Now, Nestor knew that over the years many scientists had studied the Playing Field phenomenon, and still, none had ever witnessed the rocks moving, laterally, east to west, or west to east, or even north to south or vice versa, which may be up or down, depending on your perspective. But it was all lateral movement to Nestor.

Early scientists, in an attempt to actually *see* lateral motion, had driven steel spikes into the earth to mark different rocks' positions, and they had also attached ribbons to the rocks—bright red ribbons—in hopes that they might see the ribbons flutter when the wind was blowing, but to no avail. The wind either occurred at night, or the scientists were too distracted by the searing heat and pesty desert insects. Scientists had even given names to the rocks they were studying, names like, Flank, Wing, Border, Skip, Side-Step, Alongside, Sideways, Beside, Aside, *Nigel*, *Spoad*, *Dee*, and *Buster*, but still, success eluded them, and they felt as if they were grasping at mere straws blowing in a warm wind on a moonlesss night. Later, geologists with

modern instrumentation were able to track lateral movement, but never did they actually observe it.

Nestor looked closely at the stones and their tracks, laid
out before him in the valley. He could see that smooth
stones were like boats without keels, that cannot steer a
straight course. Their tracks were smooth, while the tracks
left by rough rocks were straight. The sliding stones
pushed mud ahead of them, and a little levee was formed
on either side. Some went straight for long stretches and
then swerved, probably because of the wind.

Maybe the story loosened up my own lateral associations, as I then
said something that maybe I should have said the first session:

*Nigel, taking as much time as you need, I'd like your
unconscious mind to generate something pertinent to the
problem at hand. It's okay to think "bugger me, mate," but I'd
like your words to reflect a less penetrating lateral solution to
your problem. Taking as much time as you need. . . .*

"I need to do what she wants," he uttered. "Anything else?" I asked.
"No, simple as that. I see it clearly now," I reported.

Nigel was done with therapy. He and his wife did fine after that.
Since then, I seem to use the Playing Field even more than instigative
anecdotes to encourage lateral associations.

ALTERNATING STORIES

Think back to Chapter 16, on anxiety disorders, in which the client
with test anxiety was told the story, "The Little Engine that Could,"
which was alternated with another story. This is one of my (S. B.)
favorite techniques, which is attributed to Erickson and improved on
by Stephen and Carol Lankton. To employ this technique, prepare
two stories. The second story contains key suggestions directed at
your target. You begin the first story, leave it at a critical juncture,
and immediately launch into the second story. You complete the story
and return to the first story, and continue it to the end. We don't use
any kind of segue into the second story, or go back into the first. As a
result, we get a response similar to when Erickson took phone calls
in midsentence.

People seem to forget the second story, which is what you want. We position the more delicate, or harder to change, target in the second story. Sometimes, though, they are amnesic for both stories. Whichever is the case, the goal is behavioral or attitudinal change, which should show up within two weeks if the client's unconscious mind has incorporated the suggestion.

CLINICAL COMMENTS

The search for solutions, unconsciously speaking, can take many routes, and our tendency may be to first look deep. Sometimes that's a good place to look; however, you usually don't need a backhoe when a garden trowel will do. Oftentimes thinking and looking *laterally*—instead of *down*—may be more fruitful. Deep, sideways, these are all rather speculative constructs anyway, and maybe all unconsciously directed routes lead to Rome.

Pieces of the puzzle, or building blocks that we help the client generate in step-wise fashion, *may* be things that they have thought of (consciously) previously, or something that their grandmother told them long ago, or something that they alluded to in therapy, or even something that you suggested in therapy. Where it came from does not really matter. The main thing is that you helped them loosen their unconscious constraints.

Remember that some degree of amnesia usually occurs *naturally* in trance, like it does in everyday waking experience. Just think of how many things you've forgotten in your life, and how little you can remember. Can these techniques be used in unison? You bet. Can you go overboard with these techniques? Of course. Two rules of thumb for newcomers to amnesia and unconscious problem solving: be s-u-b-t-l-e, and remember when you were in your kitchen, preparing to make a salad, and that bunch of cilantro was there on the counter. Look again. It's not cilantro, it's *parsley*, as in the law of *parsimony*. In hypnosis, less is always more.

And the most important thing to remember about doing hypnosis is the Wildermuth principle: Don't forget to breathe.

20

Training in Hypnosis

In our regular contacts with various mental health professionals, and when we give workshops, we conduct informal polls asking practitioners if they have had formal training in hypnosis, and if so, if they use hypnosis in their practice. We have found that many people might attend a one-hour talk on hypnosis, a day-long workshop, a four-day congress or convention on the topic, or even formal hands-on training by a recognized organization, such as the American Society of Clinical Hypnosis (ASCH) or the Milton H. Erickson Foundation. Some practitioners will then incorporate hypnosis into their practices. Many others will not for a variety of reasons, including a lack of appropriate clients, an unsuitable office setting, or an unreceptive attitude from the company or agency for whom they work. Consequently, many simply give up on hypnosis.

NEGATIVE ATTITUDES ABOUT HYPNOSIS

Now, some of those people may have relented too easily to roadblocks, such as a boss who is hostile to hypnosis. Let us share some ways to get around these obstacles, methods fellow practitioners have passed on to us throughout the years. Certainly, we are accustomed to the negative baggage attached to the word hypnosis. To some, hypnosis might connote regression to a past life, or mind control. In these cases, more neutral terms, like *relaxation training*, *guided imagery*, or *stress management*, can be used. One counselor was very adept at hypnosis applications. She had attended training in California by Michael Yapko, including two Erickson Congresses, as well as our own training at the Veterans' Administration. She graduated with a masters degree in counseling and began work in a program for sexually abused girls in New Mexico. She was eager to begin applying hypnosis, but her supervisor vetoed its use because she was not "certified" in hypnosis. She then opted to play down the word hypnosis, and eventually employed group guided imagery, in which she interspersed ego-strengthening stories, and called it "relaxation" instead of hypnosis.

DO WE CALL IT *HYPNOSIS*?

Another person in one of our workshops had had similar training, and the school system for which he worked, as well as his clientele (parents and children in rural Arizona) regarded hypnosis as satanic because of their fundamentalist religious views. This social worker ended up telling stories to his clients, and by using hypnotic language and embedded suggestion he was able to achieve relaxation, ego-strengthening, and similar goals. Clearly, in some settings, the practitioner might need to exercise some creativity and relabeling in order to apply hypnosis.

People invariably ask, "Aren't you being dishonest if you purposely misrepresent hypnosis?" We answer that in our practice we always call it hypnosis, *and*, at the same time, we liken hypnosis to guided imagery and similar techniques. Also, in explaining hypnosis early on in therapy, we emphasize "naturalistic" trance states: for example, "Tell me when you naturally drift off, or become absorbed in something pleasant, like driving a car, or listening to music." Almost all clients can relate to this, and it then "fits" when we tell them that hypnosis in therapy is very much like when they become pleasantly absorbed in reading a good book. We may say, "It's just like when you become lost in reading, except that here you will have a guide, which can allow you to go deeper, and to achieve your goals" (such as relaxation or lessening pain).

Such a discussion early on, along with disspelling negative stereotypes for someone who has witnessed stage hypnosis, usually adequately prepares clients for subsequent hypnosis as part of therapy. We believe that it is absolutely essential to cover these things—even with clients who have previously had hypnosis—in order for hypnosis in therapy to successfully move forward. Other resistances can be expected as you proceed. Let's get the big ones—trust and control—out of the way at the outset.

What about the practitioner who calls it "guided imagery"? We tell her it is her obligation to disclose, if asked, that her group relaxation and guided imagery is very much like hypnosis, and that some would call it hypnosis. However, at the same time, many mental health professionals—those who have had no formal training in hypnosis—call what they do "relaxation training," or "stress management." If asked if what they do is hypnosis, they may provide a qualified response, such as the one above. However, we believe that most of these people would say that it is *not* hypnosis, period. End of discussion.

In other words, a general rule of thumb is this: If you call it hypnosis, it's hypnosis. You can see how the whole issue can become controversial. In Tucson, we train people in hypnosis. We practice hypnosis, and we tell that to our clients. If we have patients who say, "I want progressive muscle relation (PMR), not hypnosis," our choices then would include: 1) giving them PMR alone, or 2) processing negative stereotypes with them, etc. In our view, an option would *not* be lapsing into a hypnotic story laden with embedded suggestion, as this would be dishonest. With many such clients, the wise choice would be simply to do PMR, achieve a good response, link that response to hypnosis as you debrief, and then keep trying to get consent to do formal hypnosis.

One of the worst outcomes of psychotherapy is a power struggle between client and practitioner. Who needs it? Someone once attributed to Bill O'Hanlon the following statement: "Ride the horse in the direction that it's already going." If clients insist on PMR, and can't be gently persuaded into hypnosis, we must respect this and try to understand where they are coming from. We combine PMR with conventional talk therapy, just as we allow for processing, or discussion of other issues, within a hypnosis session. In doing hypnosis, every so many sessions we take stock of the client's progress with verbal processing alone, and put hypnosis on hold for that session.

ONE TRAINING PROGRAM

At the V.A. in Tucson, I (G. G.) conduct two hypnosis training groups with Bob Hall, one of the staff psychologists. This is something we have done since 1986. Each year ten interns leave the program with a good foundation in hypnosis principles and practice. Ours is not a formal program, such as that provided by the ASCH or the Erickson Foundation (see the list of hypnosis training organizations provided in the appendices). Instead, it is designed to complement the interns' overall skill acquisition during the year, so that when they finish, hypnosis is one more tool in their repertoire.

Typically, we have four or five doctoral-level psychology interns, along with five masters-level interns in social work, counseling, and psychology. These people are assigned to one of our two hour-long Friday hypnosis training groups, and throughout the year they function closely within their group, practicing inductions and hypnotic techniques on each other. Hall and I colead each of these groups. The emphasis is on learning by doing, so that most of the hour is practicing and experiencing hypnosis, with less time spent on discussion or didactics, although during the hour interns may receive supervision regarding their ongoing hypnosis cases.

We stress to the interns that the purpose of our experiential work is training, not therapy, although at times the line might blur. For example, interns might be experiencing anxiety, or procrastination, about their dissertation, and we will do some work on one of those issues. Other times, they might be grappling with a client's problem in their ongoing clinical practice and wish to work on that. In those cases, one of the group will "become" the client in question, and one or more of the group will act as the operators. Accordingly, the intern in question can experience the situation in different ways—as subject, operator, or observer.

Most interns have had little or no experience with hypnosis, and it is common for them to begin by reading inductions, deepenings, and stories. Our expectation is that by the end of the year, they will be able to do two conversational or embedded-meaning inductions, and two directive inductions, along with appropriate deepenings, without reliance on a script. By the end of the year, it is also expected that interns will have a working knowledge of seeding, utilization, and other concepts and principles discussed in this book.

Each intern receives a training manual containing our policy, procedures, and sample inductions, deepenings, and stories. In the majority of cases, interns function within the scope of our Stress Management Program, in which clients are taught self-hypnosis in a maximum of six sessions. Some of these clients carry diagnoses of adjustment disorder secondary to medical illness. Others might be depressed or have an anxiety disorder as their primary diagnosis. However, the majority of clients treated in this program have a psychotic disorder, most commonly chronic paranoid schizophrenia (Gafner & Young, 1998). These clients are stable on medication, but have difficulty coping with anxiety. As one client once told me, "Wouldn't you be nervous too if you had to go through life like this?"

The referring psychiatrist's endorsement of hypnosis goes a long way toward dispelling any negative beliefs about hypnotic treatment. During the first session, some clients express marked issues of control and they are then excluded. The majority, however, participate much like nonpsychotic clients, and we then proceed in a step-wise process, which includes conversational inductions and deepenings, ego-strengthening and other stories with unconscious ratification via finger signalling, imaginal rehearsal, during which they employ an anchor (such as a deep breath or a circle with their thumb and forefinger) to trigger self-hypnosis at home. The sixth-session clients are provided with an individualized audiotape, and they commit to listening to the tape at least three times a week. Any roadblocks that impede progress, such as cognitive distortions, negative beliefs, or resistance, are dealt with directly in a session or two of talk therapy. Clients who complete the six sessions consistently show a significant reduction in symptoms on pre- and post-administration of the Beck Anxiety Inventory.

FINDING YOUR HYPNOTIC VOICE

One issue interns grapple with is finding their hypnotic voice. Some interns feel that in order to be effective they must imitate the voice of an experienced practitioner—either Hall's voice or mine (G. G.), or perhaps someone they once witnessed in a training tape or workshop somewhere. Some even try and imitate the throaty whisper of Erickson, as they may have heard his famous "Tha-a-a-t's right . . ." on a training tape. We quickly point out to them that all of us have our conversational voice (rather casual), our therapy voice (measured, confident), and our hypnosis voice (low, carefully modulated), which may start out as a louder therapy voice, and then gradually shift to one that is low and slow, and eventually geared toward a whisper.

This is difficult for interns who have paid little attention to their voice. Some even say things like, "But I don't *like* the sound of my voice." One woman intern had a rather squeaky voice that sounded like Marilyn Monroe's. Through much practice on her own with the help of a tape recorder, this woman attained a very professional-sounding hypnotic voice.

We emphasize that everyone is able to find their own voice, that is effortless, that they are comfortable with, and that is truly their own. In fact, we even have a story we tell interns.

Finding Your Own Voice

Samuel Edgar loved life. He especially loved going to work every day as an announcer at KVZX Radio. He was very comfortable at work, and confident that he did an excellent job.

At KVZX, Samuel played music and interviewed people on the air. It was called "Hour with Edgar," although it lasted an hour and a half. Every day there was a different topic that listeners called in about: foreign policy, teen pregracy, the next solar eclipse—something different every day. Samuel talked and people listened. They listened in cars, at work, and while jogging. "Hour with Edgar" enjoyed the highest rating in the city. Samuel Edgar was famous, a celebrity. Everybody knew his voice, although virtually no one knew his face. In the supermarket one day a woman recognized his voice as he spoke to the cashier. "It's amazing! You sound just like you do on the radio," she exclaimed. One time he was even offered his own TV show, but he turned it down. He couldn't be happier doing just what he was doing, his "Hour with Edgar" on the radio.

Samuel's voice was strong, resonant, and commanding. He was keenly aware that he didn't look the way he sounded, but it didn't matter that Samuel was skinny, pale-faced with acne scars, had a pronounced overbite, and was stoop-shouldered. Ever since he had fine-tuned his voice back in radio school he had come to notice every aspect of his voice. He revelled in his ability to find just the right inflection, or how he could draw out a vowel, the precision matching the call-in situation. "It's a gift," said his boss. "It's intuition and timing," said the production assistant. "No, it's just practice," answered Samuel modestly. At any rate, he had a deep appreciation for his voice. And privately Samuel actually found the sound of his own voice quite stimulating, nearly intoxicating, in fact. Sometimes he would begin to speak to himself and just drift off. . . .

One day at work Samuel's throat became very dry. He drank a quart of water and a bottle of juice, but his throat remained dry as a bone. After the show he said, "I don't think it went very well today." The technician just smiled politely. When he awoke the next morning Samuel's throat was drier than ever, and scratchy. His customary singing in the shower yielded only a painful croak. "I sound like a sick frog," he thought. After breakfast he essentially had no voice. Just a squawky whisper. At work, a substitute filled in. "Come back when you're ready," said his boss.

Samuel consulted a specialist who told him, "We need to do some tests." A week later the doctor said, "We still don't know. We have to do some more tests." Samuel was devastated. He fingered his throat where his voice used to be and tears welled up in his eyes. KVXZ told listeners that Samuel Edgar was "out sick" and "Hour with Edgar" was replaced by music and news. The doctor sent for more x-rays and blood tests, and more specialists were called in. His case was even presented at the university.

"What do I have, Doc?" he pleaded. "We still don't know. I'm very sorry," replied the doctor. Then one day the doctor called him. "Come in today at 2:00. We have some very good news." In the office, the doctor regarded him seriously. With a wan smile she said, "You have *essential voice loss*." "But what's that? What's the treatment?" he pleaded.

Samuel never understood the diagnosis or the treatment, which began immediately. He was given pills and throat sprays and speech therapy for two hours every day. After three weeks he was no better and he was more aggravated than ever. The doctor tried to be reassuring: "Samuel, these treatments will help. The body eventually heals itself, you'll see." She even told Samuel a story about a little boy who skinned his knee. "A scab formed and as the skin healed, the scab fell off, and today you can barely see the scar," she told him. But the story just infuriated Samuel. "I don't want stories, I don't want hackneyed metaphors. I just want my voice back!" he yelled in a loud whisper.

Three more weeks passed with no improvement. Samuel complained. He wrote angry letters to the doctor and left croaky messages with her answering service. "I want a second opinion!" he demanded. "We've already had fifteen second opinions," answered the doctor patiently. At the next visit, the doctor grasped his shoulder, gazed into his sad eyes, and said seriously, "You've got to relax, calm down. This will take time. You've got to cool off, let your body heal. This is absolutely essential. Afterall, you have *essential voice loss*."

Samuel redoubled his efforts to follow what they had taught him about relaxing his mind and his body. Every once in awhile his fingers would wander up to his throat. Maybe it was starting to feel different in there. One day the speech therapist praised him for responding so well. "It's coming back," she said. "Yes!" said Samuel. For the first time in months he was encouraged.

One day the speech therapist announced, "Okay, we're there. It's time for you to select your voice." "What do you mean?" asked Samuel. "Your voice has essentially improved as much as it can on its own. It is now time to select a voice implant. There are a lot to choose from, but the decision is up to you." Samuel was perplexed. The therapist added, *"You'll discover this in your own way.* One client one time said that in selecting her voice she learned a lot about herself, things she might not have discovered in any other way."

Samuel was given a packet of compact discs to listen to at home. On each disc were 57 essential voices, each with dozens of variations, with names like Effortless Voice and

Calm Voice. He soon realized that all the potential combinations afforded him an *infinite number of voices*. Samuel could sound exactly like he did before, with the ability to modify or modulate his voice according to the situation. Or he could have a completely different voice, one that would be totally unrecognizable to the radio audience. The flexibility and versatility of it all was nearly overwhelming. After narrowing down the possibilities, he said, "I'll sleep on it."

The next day Samuel met with the doctor and speech therapist and he still had not made a selection. "I've decided to keep listening and noticing, just to see what comes up," reported Samuel. "That's fine," they told him. "We know that, when you're ready, you will make a choice."

CLINICAL COMMENTS

After using this story in our hypnosis training groups, we soon learned that it is also useful in encouraging clients to acquire new behaviors. An intern in one of our groups in the early 1990s listened to this story in trance. We cannot remember whether the operator followed the story with finger signals ratifying unconscious acceptance of the message, whether or not amnesia was encouraged, or whether the story was followed with a restraining message. At any rate, the intern soon found her own voice, and shortly thereafter she resumed work on her dissertation, something she had not done for several months.

With clients, this story can be used with or without formal hypnosis. As a device for freeing people from conscious limitations, that is, encouraging unconsious problem solving, it can be as effective as the "Simple Rooms" story.

Appendices

Glossary

abreaction Trauma clients may experience intense emotions, such as panic or fear, which may be accompanied by a flashback or intrusive thought. This expression of emotions might occur during direct treatment of the trauma, but also occur during simple relaxation. In hypnotherapy, one of several techniques for treating trauma involves age regression to the time the trauma occurred, a facilitated abreaction, and reframing. This process often provides the client considerable relief and a new understanding of the traumatic experience. This should be attempted only by experienced therapists. Incomplete abreaction of underlying feelings may be a cause of therapeutic failure.

absorption of attention Necessary for successful trance, the client's attention is focused on, for example, a spot on the wall, a story, a bodily sensation, or anything else. Eye fixation, eye closure, facial mask, diminished movement, lack of swallowing, and other signs might indicate an absorption of attention.

age progression Essentially the opposite of age regression, clients are asked to imagine themselves in the future, feeling or behaving confident, strong, or in control. The technique is also called time projection, among other names.

age regression A technique useful in hypnotherapy for accessing resources during problem solving and other applications, age regression is experienced naturally whenever someone has a memory or reminiscence. As part of trancework, age regression may be structured and guided, for example, "I want you to ride a magic carpet back through time to age 15," or general and permissive, for example, "I want you, starting now, to go back in your own way, taking as much time as you need, back to any time in the past that might be important to the problem at hand, and when you get there, let me know by nodding your head. . . ." The therapist should try not to impede clients, as they invariably go back in time much faster than we can guide them.

amnesia Some practitioners believe that inducing amnesia is necessary for later problem resolution, as amnesia allows unconscious processing to go on without conscious interference. Amnesia can be encouraged with suggestions such as "Will you forget to remember, or simply remember to forget?" or "When you go to sleep you dream, and when you wake up you cannot remember that dream." Many clients will have amnesia for some portion of the trance experience even if it is not facilitated.

and A very important word in psychotherapy, *and* leads and links. Following a pacing statement, for example, "You feel the comfort of that one deep breath," the word then leads, "*and* you can use that one deep breath to let yourself sink deeper and deeper. . . ." It might also link a truism to a directive or suggestion, for example, "You have experienced the comfort of trance here for the past 30 minutes or so, *and* you can now begin to use this experience at work when you need it the most. . . ."

apposition of opposites An example of hypnotic language, this technique juxtaposes polarities or opposites, for example, "As that right hand develops a *lightness*, your body can sink even deeper into *heaviness* and relaxation." The therapist can experiment with warm–cold, up–down, light–heavy, right–left, or any number of opposites.

arm catalepsy Catalepsy means a "suspension of movement." In this book, a cataleptic or rigid arm is part of the arm catalepsy induction—an effective, rapid, and highly directive means for inducing trance.

bind of comparable alternatives A potent ally of the therapist, this appears to offer the client a choice between two or more alternatives, offering the illusion of choice, for example, "Today would you like to go into a light trance, a medium trance, or a deep trance?" or, "What you learned today might be useful in your personal life, or maybe you can use it at work, or perhaps you can simply incorporate it into your overall experience."

commitment Social psychology ascertains that if people commit to doing something, they are more likely to comply. A vital concept in hypnotherapy, commitment is a potent therapeutic tool for increasing the effectiveness of suggestions, for example, "Taking one deep breath can help you in a stressful situation. If this is something you're willing to practice at least once a day, your yes finger will rise." (See also **unconscious commitment**)

confusion Employed to counter unconscious resistance, this is a broad category of techniques that interrupt, overload or distract the conscious mind. In this book, the non sequitur is used, for example, "I wonder why shopping carts always seem to stick together," and as the client tries to make sense of the confusing statement, she is receptive to a suggestion, for example, "You can go deep," an avenue of escape provided by the therapist. Confusion is generally more effective in short bursts, and should always be used judiciously and respectfully.

conscious-unconscious bind A bind limits choice, channeling behavior in the desired direction. This type of suggestion helps bypass conscious, learned limitations by accessing the unconscious mind, for example, "An unconscious learning from this experience today may be developed in your conscious mind as well," or, "When your conscious mind is ready to provide some useful information about this problem, you will experience a peculiar sensation in your right hand. If such information comes from your unconscious mind, the sensation will be in your left hand."

contingent suggestion Also known as *chaining*, this type of suggestion connects the suggestion to an ongoing or inevitable behavior, for example, "And as you become aware of that peculiar sensation in your right hand, you can begin to float back in time"; or as a posthypnotic suggestion, "When you return here and sit there in that chair, you can resume that deep and pleasant sense of relaxation." It is believed that it is more difficult to reject two or more suggestions when they are linked together in this way.

conversational induction This type of induction *sounds* like the therapist is having a one-way conversation with clients, when in fact they are weaving into the induction suggestions for ideosensory feeling, dissociation, time distortion, and other hypnotic phenomena.

counting-down deepening Some clinicians prefer a formal deepening following the induction phase of hypnosis. By saying, for example, "As I count down from ten to one, you can let your experience deepen. Ten, nine. . . ." Such a deepening can occur in any variety of ways, such as with a period of silence.

displacement As used for pain management, the locus of pain is displaced to another area of the body, or to an area outside of the body. The client may continue to experience the sensation, but in a less painful or vulnerable way.

dissociative language Dissociation is a hallmark of trance and an excellent convincer of trance. The more clients experience it, for example, their hand separated from their body, the more their hypnotic experience is ratified. Whenever possible, the therapist should say *that* hand instead of your hand, and employ similar language, especially during induction and deepening. Encouraging dissociation deepens trance.

double dissociative conscious-unconscious double bind Confusional suggestions such as this are complex and interesting. However, they are probably the least important type of suggestion to become skillful in using. Example: "Between now and next time your conscious mind may work at resolving the problem while your unconscious mind wonders about the implications; or your unconscious mind may come up with answers while your unconscious mind ponders the implications."

double negative An example of hypnotic language, it is believed that a double negative may lead some clients to accept the suggestion more than a simple positive suggestion alone. For example, "You can't not pay attention to the warmth developing in the soles of your feet." The two negatives negate each other to form a positive suggestion, and the hint of confusion enhances acceptance. (See also **triple negative**.)

embedded suggestion The client's conscious mind is bypassed when the therapist embeds a suggestion. To encourage an inward focus, the therapist may embed *in* words, for example, "Going *in*side can be very *in*teresting . . . *in* there where you have your imagi*n*ation, fasci*n*ation, *in*tuition. . . ." Also, the therapist might suggest *security*, for example, by embedding it in a story that emphasizes *security* provided at a large outdoor concert.

eye closure Some therapists feel uncomfortable if clients do not readily close their eyes. We can suggest that their eyes will blink, and their eyelids might feel heavy, and that their eyes can gently close whenever they wish. Clients can experience deep trance through eye fixation alone, and open eyes permit the therapist an observation of ongoing process.

eye fixation For clients who fear loss of control, it is helpful to let them focus their gaze on a spot of their choice, for example, somewhere on the wall, the ceiling, or the back of their hand. They may eventually feel comfortable enough to close their eyes.

facial mask An indicator of trance, the client's facial musculature shows a flattening, or immobility. This is often accompanied by a lack of swallowing.

fluff This refers to meaningless filler that the therapist includes either in the conversational patter in an induction, or in a story. Purposeless, meandering detail is thought to bore the client and deepen absorption. A therapist we work with once said, "It took many years for me to learn to be boring." Too often we may believe that things we say to the client must be purposeful or didactic; however, a few well-placed suggestions inserted amidst a flurry of fluff might be much more effective.

hidden observer A normal occurrence in trance is for clients to experience a part of them that observes the process. The therapist may call attention to this phenomenon in the induction: "It is common in trance to have three things occurring, sometimes simultaneously. Part of you listens consciously and responds, while another part of you listens unconsciously, and responds without any conscious effort. At the same time, it is natural to have an active hidden observer, the part of you that observes the process."

hypnotic language Certain words such as story, imagine, wonder, curious, explore, and interesting are thought to activate a sense of wonderment, which may enhance the trance process.

ideosensory feelings An indicator of trance, as well as a strong ratifier of a client's experience, the therapist suggests that *something* is likely to occur: "You may begin to notice feelings or sensations beginning to develop, usually in your extremities. One time I said to a woman sitting right there in that chair, 'I wonder if you'll experience a heaviness or lightness, a coolness or warmth, or a tingling or numbness. Or, in your case, maybe you'll detect some other interesting or curious sensation somewhere in your body.'"

implication An important method of indirect suggestion, the therapist stimulates trance experience by conveying positive expectancy. "When you are aware of warmth beginning to spread out, you may nod your head." The therapist does not ask, *"Does* one of your hands feel *light?"* but *"Which* one of your hands is *lighter?"* In implication, *when* is often the operative word, not the authoritarian *will,* which does not imply or suggest, but commands or directs. In accessing unconscious resources, the therapist might say, "Taking as much time as you need, *when* your unconscious mind has selected some strength or resource from the past, your Yes finger can move all by itself."

indirection Indirection encompasses a hypnotic modus operandi that includes implication, metaphor, story, and similar techniques whose purpose is to bypass critical evaluation and influence unconscious processing.

interspersal The therapist's hypnotic patter is interspersed with words, phrases, metaphors, or anecdotes to indirectly influence the client. For example, while therapists count backward from ten to one during deepening, they might insert a brief anecdote about another client who experienced a peculiar heaviness in her hand. Words such as heavy, light, or deep might be inserted randomly, or a phrase such as "Just let go." Attention is drawn to an interspersed suggestion that is set apart from hypnotic patter by a pause, and thus it becomes more potent.

issues of control and trust Clients need to be reassured that they will not lose control during the session. Building rapport and trust neutralizes this fear, as does concrete reassurance, for example, "You are always in the driver's seat," or perhaps humorously, "Don't worry, I'll tell you if you quack like a duck." Trust is also maintained by discussing the agenda for the session. For example, we would not want to do age regression without permission.

law of parsimony This "law" holds that the therapist should say or do as little as is necessary to achieve the desired response. A long or elaborate induction is not necessary if the client can go into trance by simply recalling a pleasant scene. With a client experienced in trance-work, this less-is-more approach is manifested by a minimalist induction such as "Just sit back now, close your eyes, and let yourself go into trance."

metaphor A broad class of indirect techniques, the use of metaphor allows the therapist to bypass the conscious mind and tap into unconscious processes, which tend to be represented and comprehended metaphorically. A client's situation or ideosyncratic speech such as "I feel like there is a wall around me" provides the therapist with imagery to be utilized. Stories or symbols stimulate self-referencing at an unconscious level.

naturalistic trance states Pre-hypnosis discussion should elicit situations when the client naturally drifts off or becomes absorbed in something pleasant, such as a favorite activity. This establishes trance as a naturally occurring behavior within the client's control. Examples include "highway hypnosis" while driving, immersion in a book, or movie, etc.

negative hallucination Milton Erickson employed *positive* hallucination when he had children imagine a furry animal next to them. Even more useful—and easier to induce—is negative hallucination, for example, "You will notice the sound of the air conditioner, people talking in the hallway, and my voice speaking to you, and all these sounds may simply drift in and out of your ears, or you may not hear them at all."

negative reframe To be used judiciously, a negative reframe is useful for redirecting the client's attention or perturbing monolithic behavior. A man's reluctance to carry out an assignment can be reframed as passivity or weakness. A woman's interpersonal conflict can be reframed as uncaring or unprotective.

non sequitor Used for distraction or interruption, a statement that is totally out of context can depotentiate conscious mental sets. One of a wide variety of confusion techniques such as statements or stories, a non sequitur can overload or distract the conscious mind. As the conscious mind seeks to escape from this incongruence or dissonance, the client may be receptive to suggestion, for example, an ego-strengthening suggestion, "You can do it." Non sequiturs can be virtually any phrase or question, for example, "And the rain fell silently in the forest," or "Do you like dogs?"

not knowing/not doing Actually a suggestion for restraint, this elegant device is very liberating in that it facilitates unconscious responsiveness rather than conscious effort. The therapeutic process may be facilitated if, early in the induction, the therapist says something like, "There's absolutely nothing to do or to know, or to think about, or to change; in fact, isn't it nice to know that by just sitting there and breathing, you can go into trance, and you don't even have to listen to the words." It may also help clients discharge resistance or anxiety.

permissive suggestion It is believed that many clients respond well when given a wide range of choice, for example, "You may begin to notice sensations, feelings, or experiences beginning to develop in those hands, or will it be in your feet?"

positive expectancy Clients are more likely to be responsive when the therapist conveys confidence and certainty that improvement can be expected. The therapist may express confidence or hopefulness about a successful problem resolution, or during an induction when the therapist suggests hand levitation, both his verbal and nonverbal behavior convey overt positive expectancy.

posthypnotic suggestion This is a suggestion, given in trance, for behavior to occur outside of trance. For example, "When you return here next time and sit down there, the feeling of that chair will be a signal for you to resume the pleasantness and relaxation of trance," or, "At work or at home you will be able to begin to relax when you take one big, deep satisfying breath," or "During the next two weeks when you're going to work on the bus and you cross 22nd street you will notice something that can help you with this problem. . . ." The last posthypnotic suggestion—notice something—is tagged to a naturally occurring behavior.

pun A play on words, this can cause a sense of wonderment. An embedded suggestion in a pun is a useful indirect technique, for example, "Your experience in trance today is like an *entrance* into another state."

question A direct question will focus attention, stimulate associations, and facilitate responsiveness. A question such as "And the tingling down there in that foot, do you notice it yet?" bypasses the conscious mind and is useful as a probe when the therapist is discovering the client's hypnotic talents, or when resistance is present.

reactance Highly reactant individuals are thought to be guarded about perceived threats to loss of freedom. In therapy, reactance shows itself as resistance to being told what to do. These clients may best be restrained from change.

reframe A new understanding or appreciation comes about because of new information provided by the therapist. By relabeling or wrapping a positive connotation around problem behavior, the client is given hope, along with seeing the problem in a new light. Virtually anything the client brings to therapy can be reframed. The session itself ,might be reframed as an effort to make things better. When there is little to reframe, therapists may reframe the presumed motivation *behind* the distress or problem in the same way that they might reframe the therapy session itself as an *effort*, or *intention*, to make things better. A reframe also sets the stage for a suggestion or directive, so that it is more likely to be accepted. Reframe is a vital element in all methods of psychotherapy, as virtually any behavior can be reframed as strength, protectiveness, caring, or any other value dear to the client. (See also **negative reframe**.)

repetition Suggestions that are important should be repeated. The therapist might repeat "breathing in comfort and relaxation" several times in an induction. It is also useful to repeat a suggestion in a different way, for example, "feeling a particular heaviness in those feet" may be followed later by the same suggestion that is metaphorical: "another person felt like he had heavy boots on his feet, and he could barely move them."

resistance A client who says, "I don't want to go into trance" displays conscious resistance. A client who says, "I want to go into trance, but I just can't" is showing unconscious resistance. Many clients are keenly aware of their resistance, which might be anxiety, negativity, or feared loss of control. Resistance might be discharged in various ways including general and permissive suggestions, suggestions covering all possibilities, not knowing/not doing, metaphor, story, confusion techniques, having the client switch chairs (so he leaves his resistance in the first chair), and asking the client questions to which he must answer no, for example, "In the winter the temperature in Phoenix is the same as Minneapolis." Many times clients' resistance will abate as rapport builds, and as they feel more comfortable in therapy.

response-attentive The state or condition when a client is believed to be receptive to suggestion. In trance such receptivity may exist when a client shows facial mask, body rigidity, lack of swallowing, and similar indicators of deeper trance. In standard psychotherapy, it may exist when a client shows a hypnoidal response, or blankness, indicating an unconscious openess, or the occurrence of an unconscious search.

restraint Resistant clients might become more resistant if we encourage change or adaptation too rapidly. These clients' resistance can be lessened if we restrain or hold them back from moving ahead, for example, "Go slow . . . change presents uncertainty . . . you might not be ready yet . . . it could be dangerous to move ahead too fast." Early in trancework, inducing trance, bringing clients out of trance, and then resuming hypnosis, holds back something pleasant, builds responsiveness, and enhances client control.

seeding A suggestion mightbe more successful when it has been seeded beforehand. A target suggestion is mentioned, or seeded, and later, mentioning the suggestion again, the target is activated. In prehypnosis, the therapist might mention breathing, slowing down, or deep relaxation, as these suggestions will follow in trancework. If therapists know that they will be offering suggestions to slow down eating, they can cue this idea by appreciably slowing down their rhythm in advance.

sequencing   This technique involves feeding back to the client the specific chain of experiences (thoughts, emotions, sensations, images, or behaviors) of a problematic behavior, or component steps, of a problematic behavior. Then, through deletion, disruption, distortion, or substituioon of one or more of the steps, the sequence is turned in a desired direction. For example, in anxiety, a client might typically experience accelerated breathing, feelings of tension, diffuse perception, and other thoughts, emotions and behaviors. This characteristically leads to something undesirbable, such as having a cigarette, avoidance, or embarassment. The therapist feeds back these steps in the sequence, matching the client's experience. The direction of the sequence is altered, however, to something more productive. Focusing on breathing and how it can slow down, and noticing feelings of tension as they gradually drift away, and really enjoying the changes in perception that come with relaxation and trance, can allow the client to "go inside and consider the resources you are learning and using to help yourself." The steps match, but the outcome (going into hypnosis, exploring options, feeling calmer) is more desirable. Sequencing can be done in standard psychotherpay or within hypnosis. Clients readily learn that the problem is not global, such as "my nervousness, or "my bad habit," but is instead a series of discrete events that can be altered. The problem becomes a process rather than a thing. A process affords multiple opportunities for intervention.

speaking the client's langauge   By incorporating the client's own language, and literally using the words of the client, the therapist's suggestions may conform more to the client's thinking, and be more effective.

suggestion covering all possiblities   This can be especially useful when combined with metaphor, for example, describing someone else's experience in trance: "As a person goes deeper into trance she can begin to notice various sensations starting to develop in her hands. It might be a tingling in one hand; maybe a numbness in the other; perhaps a warm feeling, or a cold one, or some other interesting feeling. One woman one time sitting right there in that chair wondered privately, 'How is it that one time coming in here I can sense a slight coldness up here in my right ear lobe, and another time I feel a tingling down there in my right big toe?'" (See also **bind of comparable alternatives** and **permissive suggestion**.)

time distortion This is a common trance phenomenon, as well as a ratifier of client experience. Clients might perceive time as speeding up (time expansion), or slowing down (time contraction). Time distortion may be facilitated by suggestions such as, "In trance, which can be like an entrance into another state, time may seem to speed up or slow down, and sometimes a person is simply unaware of the passage of time."

triple negative It is believed that a triple negative is received positively by the unconscious mind. A statement such as "Your unconscious mind *never can't not* process this problem between now and next session" might facilitate processing, or it might best serve to give the client a mild confusion or pleasant sense of wonderment.

truism This is an undeniable statement of fact, for example, "Everyone has felt the warm sun on their skin." A series of truisms leads to a yes-set that builds commitment and acceptance of ideas, for example, "Coming in here today on a hot day, sitting for a while out there in the waiting room, walking down the hall, coming in here, and sitting down there, I know that you can begin to let yourself go. . . ." (See also **yes-set**.)

unconscious commitment Therapists may consult the unconscious mind through nonverbal signalling, for example, "And when your unconscious mind has identified a time in the past when you felt confident, you may signal with your Yes finger." Unconscious committment is obtained by a direct question, for example, "I want to direct a question to your unconscious mind: After exploring this problem and understanding it as you do, are you now willing to let go of the problem? Taking as much time as you need, you may signal with one of your fingers." (See also **commitment**.)

unconscious mind Many therapists refer to this construct as meaning virtually any thought or feeling that is outside of the client's immediate awareness. With some clients, it might be helpful to refer to this as either "the subsconscious mind" or "the back part of the mind."

unconscious search In response to the therapist's suggestion, the client in trance responds to a search for unconscious information. For example, "Beginning now, I'd like your unconscious mind to drift and dream, and search for something—anything at all—that might be helpful for your problem. You may take as much time as you need, and when the back part of your mind has discovered *something*, your Yes finger will twitch and move up into the air."

utilization Tailoring therapy, or hypnosis, to the individual takes into account the client's unique motivations, interests, preferences, and use of language. The client's behavior, however problematic, is accepted and suggestions are attached to it, for example, the client yawns and the therapist notes, "Have you ever noticed how even a simple yawn can lead to even deeper relaxation?" The therapist conveys the importance of utterly accepting whatever occurs with the client and then seeks to use and transform it. The therapist follows and then guides the ongoing behavior of the client.

yes-set An ally of the therapist in any modality, this involves mentioning truisms, or aspects of undeniable reality, to create a yes-set acceptance, thus allowing the client to be more receptive to a suggestion that follows. For example, "You've done very well coming in here for five sessions now, working hard each time, *and* I know that today you can make even more progress toward your goal."

Hypnosis Organizations

The American Society of Clinical Hypnosis (ASCH)
140 N. Bloomingdale Road
Bloomingdale, Illinois 60108-1017, United States
Website: http://www.asch.net

ASCH is the largest U.S. organization for health and mental health care professionals using clinical hypnosis. Several times a year ASCH provides regional workshops in the United States on clinical hypnosis. Members receive *The American Journal of Clinical Hypnosis*. ASCH Press has various publications available. In addition to membership, ASCH provides a certification in clinical hypnosis and an approved consultant certification.

The Milton H. Erickson Foundation
3606 N. 24th Street
Phoenix, Arizona 85016 United States
Website: http://www.erickson-foundation.org

The Erickson Foundation provides a variety of training in the U.S. and in other countries. Members receive the *Newsletter of the Milton H. Erickson Foundation*. The Erickson Foundation has many component organizations in the United States and throughout the world.

The Society for Clinical and Experimental Hypnosis (SCEH)
2201 Haeder Road
Pullman, WA 99163 United States
Website: http://sunsite.utk.edu/IJCEH/scehframe.htm

SCEH provides training opportunities along with other services and publishes the *International Journal of Clinical and Experimental Hypnosis*.

International Society of Hypnosis (ISH)
ISH Central Office
Austin & Repatriation Medical Centre
Repatriation Campus, Locked Bag 1
West Heidelberg, VIC 3081, Australia
Website: http://www.ish.unimelb.edu.au

ISH is an organization of professional hypnotherapists from various disciplines, is dedicated to improving clinical practice and research in hypnosis. ISH's website describes its activities, publications and conferences.

References

Allen, B. (2001). The uses of enchantment. Review of J. Wullschlager's Hans Christian Andersen: *The life of a storyteller. New York Times Book Review,* May 20, 12–13.

Allen, S. N., & Bloom, S. L. (1994). Group and family treatment of posttraumatic stress disorder. *Psychiatric Clinics of North America, 17,* 426–30.

Ambrose, G., & Newbold, G. (1980). *A handbook of medical hypnosis* (4th ed.). London: Bailliere Tindall.

American Psychiatric Association (2000). *Diagnostic and statistical manual of mental disorders: Fourth edition, Text Revision* (DSM-IV-TR). Washington, DC: American Psychiatric Association Press.

Araoz, D. (1985). *The new hypnosis.* New York: Brunner/Mazel.

Aron, A (1992). *Testimonio*: A bridge between psychotherapy and sociotherapy. In Cole, E., Espin, O., & Rothblum, E. (Eds.), *Refugee women and their mental health* (pp. 173–89). New York: The Hawthorne Press.

Bandler, R., & Grinder, J. (1975). *Patterns of the hypnotic techniques of Milton H. Erickson, M. D.* (Vol. 1). Cupertino, CA: Meta.

Bandura, A. (1997). *Self-efficacy: The exercise of control.* New York: Freeman.

Bandura, A., Pastorelli, C., Barbaranelli, C., & Carara, G. V. (1999). Self-efficacy pathways to childhood depression. *Journal of Personality and Social Psychology, 76* (2), 258–69.

Barabasz, M., & Spiegel, D. (1989). Hypnotizability and weight loss in obese subjects. *International Journal of Eating Disorders, 8* (3), 335–41.

Barber, J. (1996). *Hypnosis and suggestion in the treatment of pain.* New York: Norton.

Barker, P. (1985). *Using metaphors in psychotherapy.* New York: Brunner/Mazel.

Bayot, A., Capafons, A., & Cardena, E. (1997). Emotional self-regulation therapy: A new and efficacious treatment for smoking. *American Journal of Clinical Hypnosis, 40* (2), 146–56.

Beahrs, J. O. (1971). The hypnotic psychotherapy of Milton H. Erickson. *The American Journal of Clinical Hypnosis, 14* (2), 73–90.

Benedittis, G. (1998). The poisoned gift: The use of hypnosis treatment for severe chronic headache (a long-term follow-up case report). *American Journal of Clinical Hypnosis, 41* (2), 118–29.

Bettelheim, B. (1977). *The uses of enchantment.* New York: Vintage.

Bolocofsky, D., Spinler, D., & Coulthard-Morris, L. (1985). Effectiveness of hypnosis as an adjunct to behavioral weight management. *Journal of Clinical Psychology, 41* (1), 35–41.

Brickman, H. (2000). *The thin book: Hypnotherapy trance scripts for weight management.* Phoenix, AZ: Zeig, Tucker, & Theisen.

Brom, D., Kleber, R. J., & Defares, P. B. (1989). Brief psychotherapy for posttraumatic stress disorders. *Journal of Consulting and Clinical Psychology, 57,* 607–12.

Brown, D., & Fromm, E. (1987). *Hypnosis and behavioral medicine.* Hillsdale, NJ: Erlbaum.

Burte, J. M. (1993). The role of hypnosis in the treatment of tinnitus. *The Australian Journal of Clinical Hypnosis, 14* (2), 41–52.

Cade, B., & O'Hanlon, B. (1993). *A brief guide to brief therapy.* New York: Norton

Chaves, J. F. (1994). Recent advances in the application of hypnosis to pain management. *American Journal of Clinical Hypnosis, 37* (2), 117–29.

Cheek, D. (1994). *Hypnosis: The application of ideomotor techniques.* Boston: Allyn & Bacon.

Chester, B. (1994). That which does not destroy me. In M. B. Williams & J. F. Somer, Jr. (Eds.), *Handbook of posttraumatic therapy* (pp. 93–107). Westport, CT: Greenwood.

Chester, B., & Holtan, N. (1992). Working with refugee survivors of torture, *The Western Journal of Medicine, 157* (3), 48–53.

Clarke, J. H. (1996). Teaching clinical hypnosis in U. S. and Canadian Dental Schools. *American Journal of Clinical Hypnosis, 39* (2), 89–92.

Close, H. T. (1998). *Metaphor in psychotherapy.* San Luis Obispo, CA: Impact.

Cochrane, G. (1989). The use of indirect hypnotic suggestions for insomnia arising from generalized anxiety: A case report. *American Journal of Clinical Hypnosis, 31* (3), 199–203.

Cochrane, G. (1992). Hypnosis and weight reduction: Which is the car and which is the horse? *American Journal of Clinical Hypnosis, 35* (2), 109–18.

Combs, G., & Freedman, J. (1990). *Symbol, story and ceremony: Using metaphor in individual and family therapy.* New York: Norton.

Coyne, J. C. (1985). Toward a theory of frames and reframing: The social nature of frames. *Journal of Marital and Family Therapy, 11* (4), 337–44.

Crasilneck, H. B. (1995). The use of the Crasilneck bombardment technique in problems of intractable organic pain. *American Journal of Clinical Hypnosis, 37* (4), 255–66.

Crasilneck, H. B., & Hall, J. A. (1985). *Clinical hypnosis: Principles and applications.* Orlando, FL: Grune & Stratton.

Cunningham, A. J., Phillips, C., Lockwood, G. A., Hedley, D. W., & Edmonds, C. V. (2000). Association of involvement in psychological self-regulation with longer survival in patients with metastatic cancer: An exploratory study. *Advances in Mind-Body Medicine, 16* (4), 276–87.

Dane, J. (1996). Hypnosis for pain and neuromuscular rehabilitation with multiple sclerosis: Case summary, literature review and analysis of outcomes. *International Journal of Clinical & Experimental Hypnosis, 44* (3), 208–31.

Delaney, M., & Voit, R. (2001). *Fusion and flow: Integrating hypnosis into your clinical practice.* Unpublished manuscript.

Denevan, W. M. (1992). The pristine myth: The landscape of the Americas in 1492. *Annals of the American Association of Geographers, 82* (3), 369–85.

Deshazer, S. (1978). Brief hypnotherapy of two sexual dysfunctions: The crystal ball technique. *American Journal of Clinical Hypnosis, 20* (3), 203–08.

Deshazer, S. (1982). *Patterns of brief family therapy.* New York: Guilford.

Deshazer, S. (1985). *Keys to solutions in brief therapy.* New York: Norton.

Diamond, M. J. (1986). The veracity of ideomotor signals. In B. Zilberseld, M. G. Edelstien, & D. L. Araoz (Eds.), *Hypnosis: Questions and answers* (pp. 47–49). New York: Brunner/Mazel.

Dolan, Y. (1991). *Resolving sexual abuse.* New York: Norton.

Dossey, L. (1999). Foreword. In R. Temes (Ed.), *Medical hypnosis* (pp. vii–viii). New York: Churchill Livingstone.

Douglas, D. (1999). Stopping smoking: A study on the nature of resistance and the use of hypnosis. In D. Seidman & L. Covey, (Eds.), *Helping the hardcore smoker: A clinician's guide* (pp. 213–23). Hillsdale, NJ: Erlbaum.

Duncan, B. (2001). The future of psychotherapy. *Psychotherapy Networker, 25* (4), 24–33.

Dyas, R. (2001). Augmenting intravenous sedation with hypnosis: A controlled retrospective study. *Contemporary Hypnosis, 39* (3), 145–54.

Dye, E., & Roth, S. (1991). Psychotherapy with Vietnam veterans and rape and incest survivors. *Psychotherapy, 28,* 103–20.

Dykinga, J., & Bowers, J. E. (1999). *Desert: The Mojave and Death Valley.* New York: Abrams.

Eckstein, D. (1997). Reframing as a specific interpretive counseling technique. *Individual Psychology, 53* (4), 418–28.

Edgette, J. H. (1988). "Dangerous to self and others": The management of acute psychosis using Ericksonian techniques of hypnosis and hypnotherapy. In S. Lankton & J. Zeig (Eds.), *Ericksonian Monographs: No. 3. Treatment of Special Populations with Ericksonian Approaches* (pp 96–103). New York: Brunner/Mazel.

Elkins, G. R., & Wall, V. J. (1996). Medical referrals for hypnotherapy: Opinions of physicians, residents, family practice outpatients, and psychiatry outpatients. *American Journal of Clinical Hypnosis, 38* (4), 254–62.

Elmer, B. N. (2000). Clinical applications of hypnosis for brief and efficient pain management psychotherapy. *American Journal of Clinical Hypnosis, 43* (1), 17–40.

Enqvist, B., Von Konow, L., & Bystedt, H. (1995). Pre- and perioperative suggestion in maxillofacial surgery: Effects on blood loss and recovery. *International Journal of Clinical and Experimental Hypnosis, 43* (3), 284–394.

Erickson, M. H. (1983). *Healing in hypnosis: The seminars, workshops & lectures of Milton H. Erickson* (Vol. 1) (E. L. Rossi, M. O. Ryan, & F. A. Sharp, Eds.). New York: Irvington.

Erickson, M. H. (1985). *Life reframing in hypnosis: The seminars, workshops & lectures of Milton H. Erickson* (Vol. 2) (E. L. Rossi & M. O. Ryan, Eds.). New York: Irvington.

Erickson, M. H., Rossi, E. L., & Rossi, S. I. (1976). *Hypnotic realities*. New York: Irvington.

Ewin, D. M. (1992). Hypnotherapy for warts. *American Journal of Clinical Hypnosis, 35* (1), 1–10.

Ewin, D. (1996). In memoriam: David B. Cheek, M. D. *American Journal of Clinical Hypnosis, 39* (1), 1.

Ewin, D. (1999). Hypnosis in the emergency room. In R. Temes (Ed.), *Medical Hypnosis* (pp. 59–64). New York: Churchill-Livingstone.

Farb, P. (1974). *Word play*. New York: Knopf.

Fernandez, E., & Turk, D. C. (1989). The utility of cognitive coping strategies for altering pain perception: A meta-analysis. *Pain, 38,* 123–35.

Flack, A. (1986). Art and soul. New York: Dutton.

Foa, E. B., Rothbaum, B. O., Riggs, K. D. (1991). Treatment of posttraumatic stress disorder in rape victims: A comparison between cognitive-behavioral procedures and counseling. *Journal of Consulting and Clinical Psychology, 59,* 715–23.

Foa, E. B., Davidson, G., & Frances, A. (1999). Treatment of posttraumatic stress disorder: The Expert consensus guideline series. *Journal of Clinical Psychiatry, 60,* 1–76.

Fordyce, W. E. (1976). *Behavioral methods for chronic pain and illness.* St. Louis: Mosby.

Frank, R., Umlauf, R., Wonderlich, S., & Ashkanazi, G. (1986). Hypnosis and behavioral treatment in a worksite smoking cessation program. *Addictive Behaviors, 11,* 59–62.

Gafner, G. (1987). Engaging the elderly couple in marital therapy. *The American Journal of Family Therapy, 15* (4), 305–15.

Gafner, G., & Benson, S. (2000). *Handbook of hypnotic inductions.* New York: Norton.

Gafner, G., & Duckett, S. (1992). Treating the sequelae of a curse in elderly Mexican-Americans/ In T. L. Brink (Ed.), *Hispanic aged mental health* (pp. 45–53). New York: Haworth.

Gafner, G., & Young, C. (1998). Hypnosis as an adjuvant in the treatment of chronic paranoid schizophrenia. *Contemporary Hypnosis, 15* (4), 223–26.

Gafner, G., & Edmunds, D. (In press). Touching trauma: Combining hypnotic ego-strengthening and Zero Balancing. *Torture.*

Galovski, T. E., & Blanchard, E. B. (2002). Hypnotherapy and refractory irritable bowel syndrome: A single case study. *American Journal of Clinical Hypnosis, 45* (1), 31–38.

Gatchel, R. J., & Turk, D. C. (Eds.) (1996). *Psychological approaches to pain management.* New York: Guilford.

Geary, B. (1989). Integrating Ericksonian strategies into structured groups for depression. In M. Yapko (Ed.), *Brief therapy approaches to treating anxiety and depression* (pp. 184–204). New York: Brunner/Mazel.

Geary, B. (1994). Seeding responsiveness to hypnotic processes. In J. Zeig (Ed.), *Ericksonian methods: The essence of the story* (pp. 315–32). New York: Brunner/Mazel.

Genuis, M. L. (1995). The use of hypnosis in helping cancer patients control anxiety, pain, and emesis: A review of recent empirical studies. *American Journal of Clinical Hypnosis, 37* (4), 316–25.

Gilbertson, A. D., & Kemp, K. (1992). Uses of hypnosis in treating anxiety states. *Psychiatric Medicine, 10* (4), 13–20.

Gilligan, S. G. (1987). *Therapeutic trances: The cooperative principle in Erickson's therapy.* New York: Brunner/Mazel.

Gordon, D. (1978). *Therapeutic metaphors.* Cupertino, CA: Meta.

Greenberg, R. A., & Hepburn, J. G. (1961). *Robert Frost: An introduction.* New York: Holt, Rhinehart, and Winston.

Haley, J. (1973). *Uncommon therapy: The psychiatric techniques of Milton H. Erickson, M. D.* New York: Norton

Haley, J. (1985). *Conversations with Milton H. Erickson: Vol. 1. Changing individuals.* New York: Triangle Press.

Haley, J. (1996). *Learning and teaching therapy.* New York: Guilford.

Hammerschlag, C., & Silverman, H. (1997). *Healing ceremonies: Creating personal rituals for spiritual, emotional, physical and mental health.* New York: Perigee.

Hammond, D. C. (1984). Myths about Erickson and Ericksonian hypnosis. *American Journal of Clinical Hypnosis, 26* (4), 236–45.

Hammond, D. C. (1990). *Handbook of hypnotic suggestions and metaphors.* New York: Norton.

Hammond, D. C. (1997). Advantages and safeguards in using the ideomotor signaling technique: A commentary of Walsh and clinical practice. *American Journal of Clinical Hypnosis, 40* (1), 360–67.

Harper, G., (1999). A developmentally sensitive approach to clinical hypnosis for chronically and terminally ill adolescents. *American Journal of Clinical Hypnosis, 42* (1), 50–60.

Harris, G. M. (1991). Hypnotherapy for agoraphobia: A case study. *International Journal of Psychosomatics, 38* (4), 92–94.

Harriss, J. (2001). Strange bedfellows. *Smithsonian, 32* (9), 50–58.

Hartland, J. (1965). The value of ego-strengthening procedures prior to direct symptom removal under hypnosis. *American Journal of Clinical Hypnosis, 8,* 89–93.

Hartland, J. (1971). Further observations on the use of ego-strengthening techniques. *American Journal of Clinical Hypnosis, 14,* 1–8.

Hofstadter, D. R. (1979). *Gödel, Escher, Bach: An eternal golden braid.* New York: Basic Books.

Holroyd, J. (1980). Hypnosis treatment for smoking: An evaluation review. *The International Journal of Clinical & Experimental Hypnosis, 28,* 341–57.

Hornyak, L. (1999). Empowerment through giving symptoms voice. *American Jouranl of Clinical Hypnosis, 42* (2), 132–39.

Hunter, M. (1994). *Creative scripts for hypnotherapy.* New York: Brunner/Mazel.

Hyer, L. (Ed.) (1994). *Trauma victim.* Muncie, IN: Accelerated Development.

Hyman, G., Stanley, R., Burrows, G., & Horne, D. (1986). Treatment effectiveness of hypnosis and behaviour therapy in smoking cessation: A methodological refinement. *Addictive Behaviors, 11,* 355–65.

Imber-Black, E. (1989). *Rituals in family therapy.* New York: Brunner/Mazel.

Ingram, D. H. (1996). The vigor of metaphor in clinical practice. *The American Journal of Psychoanalysis, 56* (1), 17–34.

Jacobs, E., Pelier, E., & Larkin, D. (1998). Ericksonian hypnosis and approaches with pediatric hematology oncology patients. *American Journal of Clinical Hypnosis, 41* (2), 139–54.

Jacobson, G. (1992). Some comments about tinnitus. *Tinnitus Today, 17* (3), 4–6.

Jensen, M. P. (1996). Enhancing motivation to change in pain treatment. In R. J. Gatchel & D. C. Turk (Eds.), *Psychological approaches to pain management* (pp. 78–111). New York: Guilford.

Jones, M. (1994). Apnea in postsurgical hypnotherapy of an esophageal cancer patient: A brief communication. *International Journal of Clinical & Experimental Hypnosis, 42* (3), 179–83.

Kabat-Zinn, J. (1990). *Full catastrophe living: The program of the Stress Reduction Clinic at the University of Massachusetts Medical Center.* New York: Delta

Kabat-Zinn, J., Lipworth, L. Burney, R., & Sellers, W. (1986). Four-year follow-up of a meditation-based program for the self-regulation of chronic pain: Treatment outcomes and compliance. *Clinical Journal of Pain, 2,* 159–73.

Kabat-Zinn, J., Massion, A. O., Kristeller, J., Peterson, L. G., Fletcher, K. E., Pbert, L., Lenderking, W. R., & Santorelli, S. F. (1992). Effectiveness of a meditation-based stress reduction program in the treatment of anxiety disorders. *American Journal of Psychiatry, 149,* 936–43.

Keane, T. M. (1989). Implosive (flooding) therapy that reduces symptoms of PTSD in Vietnam combat veterans. *Behaviour Therapy, 20,* 245–60.

Kessler, R. S., & Miller, S. D. (1995). The use of a future time frame in psychotherapy with and without hypnosis. *American Journal of Clinical Hypnosis, 38* (1), 39–46.

Kingsbury, S. (1988). Interacting with trauma. *American Journal of Clinical Hypnosis, 36,* 241–47.

Kirsch, I., & Lynn, S. J. (1995). The altered state of hypnosis. *American Psychologist, 50* (10), 846–858.

Kirsch, I., Montgomery, G., & Sapirstein, S. (1995). Hypnosis as an adjunct to cognitive-behavioral psychotherapy: A meta-analysis. *Journal of Consulting and Clinical Psychology, 63* (2), 214–20.

Kopel, K., & Quinn, M. (1996). Hypnotherapy treatment of dysphagia. *International Journal of Clinical and Experimental Hypnosis, 44* (2), 101–05

Kwekkeboom, K. L. (2001). Outcome expectancy and success with cognitive-behavioral interventions: the case of guided imagery. *Oncology Nursing Forum, 18* (7), 1125–32.

Lakoff, G., & Johnson, M. (1980). *Metaphors we live by.* Chicago: University of Chicago Press.

Lambe, R., Osier, C., & Franks, P. (1986). A randomized controlled trial of hypnotherapy for smoking cessation. *The Journal of Family Practice, 22* (1), 61–65.

Lankton, S. & Lankton, C. (1983). *The answer within: A clinical framework for Ericksonian hypnotherapy.* New York: Brunner/Mazel.

Lankton, S., & Lankton, C. (1986). *Enchantment and Intervention in Family Therapy.* New York: Brunner/Mazel.

Lankton, S., & Lankton, C. (1989). *Tales of enchantment: Goal-oriented metaphors for adults and children in therapy.* New York: Brunner-Routledge.

Lefort, R. (1968). *The teachers of Gurdjieff.* London: Gollancz.

Lehrer, M. (1985). Hypnotic identification: Metaphors for personal change. In J. K. Zeig (Ed.), *Ericksonian psychotherapy: Vol. 1. Structures* (pp. 359–69). New York: Brunner/Mazel.

Levitan, A. A. (1999). Oncology. In R. Temes (Ed.), *Medical hypnosis* (pp. 107–14). New York: Churchill Livingstone.

Levitt, E. (1997). Hypnosis in the treatment of obesity. In J. Rhue, S. Lynn, & I. Kirsch (Eds.), *Handbook of clinical hypnosis* (pp. 533–54). Washington, DC: American Psychological Association.

Liossi, C., & Hatira, P. (1999). Clinical hypnosis versus cognitive-behavioral training for pain management with pediatric cancer patients undergoing bone marrow aspirations. *International Journal of Clinical & Experimental Hypnosis, 47* (2), 104–16.

Litz, B. T., & Blake, D. D. (1990). Decision-making guidelines for the use of direct therapeutic exposure in the treatment of posttraumatic stress disorder. *Behaviour Therapy, 17,* 91–93.

Lynch, D. (1999). Empowering the patient: Hypnosis in the management of cancer, surgical disease and chronic pain. *American Journal of Clinical Hypnosis, 42* (2), 122–30.

Lynn, S. J. (1994). The interface of research and clinical practice. *American Journal of Clinical Hypnosis, 37* (2), 81–83.

MacLeod-Morgan, C, Court, J & Roberts, R. (1982). Cognitive restructuring: A technique for the relief of chronic tinnitus. *Australian Journal of Clinical Hypnosis, 10* (1), 27–33.

Madanes, C. (1981). *Strategic family therapy.* San Francisco: Jossey-Bass.

Madanes, C. (1990). *Sex, love, and violence: Strategies for transformation.* New York: Norton

Marcus, J. D., (1999). Hypnosis and HIV/AIDS spectrum illnesses: An Ericksonian method of utilization. *Contemporary Hypnosis, 16* (2), 103–12.

Mason, J., & Rogerson, D. (1995). Client-centered hypnotherapy for tinnitus: Who is likely to benefit? *American Journal of Clinical Hypnosis, 37* (4), 294–99.

Mauer, M., Burnett, Kl, Ouellete, E., Ironson, G., & Dandes, H. (1999). Medical hypnosis and orthopedic hand surgery. *International Journal of Clinical & Experimental Hypnosis, 47* (2), 144–61.

Maurer, R. L., Kumar, V. K., Woodside, L., & Pekala, R. J. (1997). Phenomenological experience in response to monotonous drumming and hypnotizability. *American Journal of Clinical Hypnosis, 40* (2), 130–45.

McSpaden, J. B. (1993). Tinnitus Aurium. *Tinnitus Today, 18* (2), 15–17.

Medd, D. (1999). Hypnosis with selected movement disorders. *Contemporary Hypnosis, 16* (2), 81–86.

Melzack, R. (1990). The tragedy of needless pain. *Scientific American, 262,* 27–33.

Metzner, R. (1998). *The unfolding self.* Novato, CA: Origin Press.

Meza, O. (1994). *Legends: Leyendas prehispanicas mexicanas.* Mexico City: Panorama Editorial.

Millar, H. (1999). Ups and downs of Highway One. *Smithsonian Magazine, 30* (3), 48–58.

Mills, J. C. (1999). *Reconnecting to the magic of life*. Kaua'i, HI: Imaginal Press.

Mills, J. C., & Crowley, R. J. (1986). *Therapeutic metaphors for children and the child within*. New York: Brunner/Mazel.

Montgomery, G., & Kirsch, I. (1996). The effects of subject arm position and initial experience on Chevreul pendulum responses. *American Journal of Clinical Hypnosis, 38* (3), 185–90.

Morris, J. S., Ohman, A., & Dolan, R. J. (1998). Conscious and unconscious emotional learning in the human amygdala. *Nature, 393*, 467–70.

Nadon, R., & Laurence, J. R. (1994). Ideographic approaches to hypnosis research (or how therapeutic practice can inform science). *American Journal of Clinical Hypnosis, 37* (2), 85–94.

O'Hanlon, B. (1986). The use of metaphor for treating somatic complaints in psychotherapy. In J. C. Hansen (Ed.), *Family therapy: Indirect approaches in therapy* (pp. 19–24). Rockville, CO: Aspen.

Ola, P., & D'Aulaire, E. (1999). Taking the measure of time. *Smithsonian Magazine, 30* (9), 52–65.

Olness, K., & Kohen, D. P. (1996). *Hypnosis and hypnotherapy with children*. New York: Guilford.

O'Neill, J. V. (2002). Therapy technique may not matter much. *NASW News*, March, 3.

Ornstein, R. E. (1977). *The psychology of consciousness*. New York: Harcourt Brace Jovanovich.

Papp, P. (1983). *The process of change*. New York: Norton.

Perez, R. (1994). *El vuelo del ave fénex*. Mexico City: Editorial Pax México.

Phillips, M., & Frederick, C. (1992). The use of hypnotic age progressions as prognostic, ego-strengthening, and integrating techniques. *American Journal of Clinical Hypnosis, 35* (2), 99–108.

Phillips, M. (1993). Turning symptoms into allies: Utilization approaches with posttraumatic symptoms. *American Journal of Clinical Hypnosis, 35*, 179–89.

Pitman, R. K., Orr, S. P., Altman, B., Longpre, R. E., Poire, R. E., Macklin, M. L., Michaels, M. J., & Steketee, G. S. (1996). Emotional processing and outcome of imaginal flooding therapy in Vietnam veterans with chronic posttraumatic stress disorder. *Comprehensive Psychiatry, 37* (6), 409–18.

Pollan, M. (1994). Secret world of a pond. *New York Times Magazine*, July 24, 35–37.

Prochaska, J. O., DiClemente, C. C., & Norcross, J. C. (1992). In search of how people change. *American Psychologist, 47,* 1102–14.

Prochaska, J. O., Rossi, J., & Wilcox, N. (1991). Change processes and psychotherapy outcome in integrative case research. *Journal of Psychotherapy Integration, 1* (2), 103–20.

Prochaska, J. O., Velicer, W. F., Rossi, J. S., Goldstein, M. G, Marcus, B. H., Rakowski, W., Fiore, C., Harlow, L. L., Redding, C. A., Rosenbloom, D., & Rossi, S. R. (1994). Stages of change and decisional balance for twelve problem behaviors. *Health Psychology, 13,* 39–46.

Rapkin, D., Straubing, M., & Holroyd, J. C. (1991). Guided imagery, hypnosis and recovery from head and neck cancer surgery: An exploratory study. *International Journal of Clinical & Experimental Hypnosis, 39* (4), 215–26.

Robbins, M. S., Alexander, J. F., Newell, R. M., & Turner, C. W. (1996). The immediate effect of reframing on client attitude in family therapy. *Journal of Family Psychology, 10* (1), 28–34.

Robles, T. (1990). *Concierto para cuatro cerebros en psicoterapia.* Mexico City: Institutio Milton H. Erickson.

Robles, T. (1997) *Revisando el pasado para construir el future.* Mexico City: Institutio Milton H. Erickson.

Rosen, S. (1982). *My voice will go with you: The teaching tales of Milton H. Erickson, M. D.* New York: Norton.

Rosenbaum, R. (1999). *Zen and the heart of psychotherapy.* New York: Brunner/Mazel.

Rossi, E. L. (1993). *The psychobiology of mind-body healing.* New York: Norton.

Rossi, E. L. (2000). In search of a deep psychobiology of hypnosis: Visionary hypothesis for a new millenium. *American Journal of Clinical Hypnosis, 42,* 178–207.

Rossi, E. L. (Ed.) (1980). *Collected Papers of Milton H. Erickson* (Vols. 1–4). New York: Irvington.

Rossi, E. L., & Cheek, D. (1988). *Mind-body therapy: Ideodynamic healing in hypnosis.* New York: Norton.

Rossi, E. L., Lippincott, B., & Bessette, A. (1994). The chronobiology of mind-body healing: Ultradian dynamics in hypnotherapy. *European Journal of Clinical Hypnosis, 2* (1/2), 2–20.

Schoenberger, N. E., (2000). Research on hypnosis as an adjunct to cognitive-behavioral therapy. *The International Journal of Clinical and Experimental Hypnosis, 48* (2), 154–69.

Shoham, V., Rohrbaugh, M., & Patterson, J. (1995). Problem and solution-focused couple therapies: The MRI and Milwaukee Models. In A. S. Gurman & N. S. Jacobson (Eds.), *Clinical handbook of couple therapy* (pp. 142–63). New York: Guilford.

Shoham-Salomon, V., Avner, R., & Neeman, R. (1989). You are changed if you do and changed if you don't: Mechanisms underlying paradoxical interventions. *Journal of Consulting and Clinical Psychology, 57,* 590–98.

Siegelman, E. Y. (1990). *Metaphor and meaning in psychotherapy.* New York: Guilford.

Simon, R. (2001). Psychotherapy's soothsayer. *Psychotherapy Networker, 25* (4), 34–39.

Small, T. (1994). *The legend of John Henry.* New York: Delacorte.

Smith, N., D'Hooghe, V., Duffin, S., Fitzsimmons, D., Rippin, C., & Wilde, G. (1999). Hypnotherapy for the unstable bladder. *Contemporary Hypnosis, 16* (2), 87–94.

Smith, W. H. (1990). Hypnosis in the treatment of anxiety. *Bulletin of the Menninger Clinic, 54,* 209–16.

Somer, E. (1991). Hypnotherapy in the treatment of the chronic nocturnal use of a dental splint prescribed for bruxism. *International Journal of Clinical & Experimental Hypnosis, 39* (3), 145–54.

Somer, E. (1994). Hypnotherapy and regulated uncovering in the treatment of older survivors of Nazi persecution. *Clinical Gerontologist, 14,* 47–65.

Spanos, N. P., Williams, V., & Gwynn, M. I. (1990). Effects of hypnotic, placebo, and salicylic acid treatments on wart regression. *Psychosomatic Medicine, 52* (1), 109–14.

Sperr, E., & Hyer, L. (1994). Stress management in the care of PTSD. In L. Hyer (Ed.), *Trauma Victim* (pp. 587–632). Muncie, IN: Accelerated Development.

Spiegel, D., & Bloom, J. R. (1983). Group therapy and hypnosis reduce metastatic breast carcinoma pain. *Psychosomatic Medicine, 45* (4), 333–39.

Spiegel, D. (1997). Hypnosis in the treatment of posttraumatic stress disorders. In J. W. Rhue, S. J. Lynn, & I. Kirsch (Eds), *Handbook of clinical hypnosis* (pp. 493–508). Washington, DC: American Psychological Association.

Spiegel, D., Bloom, J. R., Kraemer, H. C., & Gottheil, E. (1989). Effect of psychosocial treatment on survival of patients with metastatic breast cancer. *Lancet, 2* (8668), 888–91.

Spiegel, D., & Cardena, E. (1990). New uses of hypnosis in the treatment of posttraumatic stress disorder. *Journal of Clinical Psychiatry, 51,* 39–42.

Spiegel, D., Frischholz, E., Fleiss, J., & Spiegel, H. (1993). Predictors of smoking abstinence following a single-session restructuring intervention with self-hypnosis. *American Journal of Psychiatry, 150,* 1090–97.

Spielberger, C. D., Jacobs, G., Russell, S., & Crane, R. S. (1983). Assessment of anger: The state-trait anger scale. In J. N. Butcher & C. D. Spielberger (Eds.), *Advances in personality assessment* (Vol. 2) (pp. 159–89). Hillsdale, NJ: Erlbaum.

Stanton, H. E. (1975). Ego enhancement through positive suggestions. *Australian Journal of Clinical Hypnosis, 3,* 32–36.

Stanton, H. E. (1977). The utilization of suggestions derived from rational-emotive therapy. *International Journal of Clinical and Experimental Hypnosis, 25,* 18–26.

Stanton, H. E. (1979). Increasing internal control through hypnotic ego enhancement. *Australian Journal of Clinical and Experimental Hypnosis, 7,* 219–23.

Stanton, H. E. (1993). Ego-enhancement for positive change. *Australian Journal of Clinical and Experimental Hypnosis, 21,* 59–64.

Steggles, S. (1999). The use of cognitive-behavioral treatment including hypnosis for claustrophobia in cancer patients. *American Journal of Clinical Hypnosis, 41* (4), 319–26.

Swain, R. (1983). Trackside. *Field Days: Journal of an Itinerant Biologist* (pp. 117–22). New York: Penguin.

Syrjala, K. L., & Abrams, J. R. (1996). Hypnosis and imagery in the treatment of pain. In R. J. Gatchel & D. C. Turk (Eds.), *Psychological approaches to pain management* (pp. 231–58). New York: Guilford.

Syrjala, K. L., Danis, B., Abrams, J. R., & Keenan, R. (1992). *Coping skills for bone marrow transplantation.* Seattle, WA: Fred Hutchinson Cancer Research Center.

Syrjala, K. L., Donaldson, G. W., Davis, M. W., Kippes, M. E., & Carr, J. E. (1995). Relaxation and imagery and cognitive-behavioral training reduce cancer pain during cancer treatment: A controlled clinical trial. *Pain, 63* (2), 189–98.

Teasdale, J. D., Segal, Z. V., Williams, J. M. G., Ridgeway, V. A., Soulsby, J. M., & Lau, M. A. (2000). Prevention of relapse/recurrence in major depression by mindfulness-based cognitive therapy. *Journal of Consulting and Clinical Psychology, 68* (4), 615–23.

Thompson, K. (1985). Almost 1984. In J. K. Zeig (Ed.), *Ericksonian psychotherapy: Vol. I. Structures* (pp. 89–99). New York: Brunner/Mazel.

Thompson, K. (1990). Metaphor: A myth with a method. In J. Zeig & S. Gilligan (Eds.), *Brief therapy: Myths, methods and metaphors* (pp. 247–57). New York: Brunner/Mazel.

Torem, M. J. (1990). Ego-strenthening. In D. C. Hammond (Ed.), *Handbook of hypnotic suggestions and metaphors* (pp. 110–112). New York: Norton.

Van der Hart, O., Brown, P., & Van der Kolk, B. A. (1989). Pierre Janet's treatment of posttraumatic stress. *Journal of Traumatic Stress, 2,* 379–95.

Voth, H. (1970). The analysis of metaphor. *Journal of the American Psychoanalytic Association, 18,* 599–621.

Wallas, L. (1985). *Stories for the third ear.* New York: Norton.

Walsh, B. J. (1997). Goldfinger: A framework for resolving affect using ideomotor questions. *American Journal of Clinical Hypnosis, 40* (1), 349–359.

Walters, C., & Havens, R. A. (1994). Good news for a change: Optimism, altruism and hardiness as the bases for Erickson's approach. In J. Zeig (Ed.), *Ericksonian methods: The essence of the story* (pp. 163–81). New York: Brunner/Mazel.

Watkins, J. G. (1971). The affect bridge: A hypnoanalytic technique. *International Journal of Clinical & Experimental Hypnosis, 19,* 21–27.

Watzlawick, P., Weakland, J. H., & Fisch, R. (1974). *Change: Principles of problem formation and problem resolution.* New York: Norton.

Wexler, D. (2000). *Domestic violence 2000.* New York: Norton, 2000.

Williams, J., & Hall, D. (1988). Use of single session-hypnosis for smoking cessation. *Addictive Behaviors, 3,* 205–08.

Wood, G. J., & Zadeh, H. H. (1999) Potential adjunctive applications of hypnosis in the management of periodontal diseases. *American Journal of Clinical Hypnosis, 41* (3), 212–25.

Yapko, M. (1990). *Trancework.* New York: Brunner/Mazel.

Yapko, M. (1992). *Hypnosis and the treatment of depressions: Strategies for change.* New York: Brunner/Mazel.

Yapko, M. (2001). *Treating depression with hypnosis: Integrating cognitive-behavioral and strategic approaches.* New York: Brunner/Routledge.

Zeig, J. K. (1985a). *Experiencing Erickson.* New York: Brunner/Mazel.

Zeig, J. K. (1985b). The clinical use of amnesia: Ericksonian methods. In J. K. Zeig (Ed.), *Ericksonian psychotherapy: Vol. 1. Structures* (pp. 317–37). New York: Brunner/Mazel.

Zeig, J. K. (1990) Seeding. In J. K. Zeig & S. J. Gilligan (Eds.), *Brief therapy: Myths and metaphors* (pp. 221–246). New York: Brunner/Mazel.

Zeig, J. K. (1994). Advanced techniques of utilization: An intervention metamodel and the use of sequences, symptom words, and figures of speech. In J. K. Zeig (Ed.), *Ericksonian methods: The essence of the story* (pp. 295–314). New York: Brunner/Mazel, 295–314.

Zeig, J. K. (Ed.) (1985). *Ericksonian psychotherapy: Vol. 2. Clinical applications.* New York: Brunner/Mazel.

Zeig, J. K., & Geary, B. B. (Eds.) (2000). *The letters of Milton H. Erickson.* Phoenix, AZ: Zeig, Tucker & Theisen.

Index